France at Bay
1870–1871

France at Bay 1870–1871

The Struggle for Paris

Douglas Fermer

Pen & Sword

MILITARY

First published in Great Britain in 2011 by
PEN & SWORD MILITARY
An imprint of
Pen & Sword Books Ltd
47 Church Street
Barnsley
South Yorkshire
S70 2AS

ISBN 978-1-84884-325-7

A CIP catalogue record for this book is
available from the British Library.

Typeset by Concept, Huddersfield, West Yorkshire
Printed and bound in Great Britain by CPI Antony Rowe, Chippenham, Wiltshire

Pen & Sword Books Ltd incorporates the Imprints of Pen & Sword Aviation,
Pen & Sword Maritime, Pen & Sword Military, Wharncliffe Local History,
Pen & Sword Select, Pen & Sword Military Classics, Leo Cooper, Remember When,
Seaforth Publishing and Frontline Publishing.

For a complete list of Pen & Sword titles please contact
PEN & SWORD BOOKS LIMITED
47 Church Street, Barnsley, South Yorkshire, S70 2AS, England
E-mail: enquiries@pen-and-sword.co.uk
Website: www.pen-and-sword.co.uk

Contents

List of Maps

List of Plates

Plate sources: *Cassell's Illustrated History of the Franco-German War*, London, 1899, Nos. 1, 4, 10; Jules Claretie, *Histoire de la Révolution de 1870–71*, Paris, 1872, Nos. 2, 26; Lorédan Larchey, *Mémorial illustré des deux sièges de Paris, 1870–1871*, Paris, 1872, No. 11; J.F. Maurice, ed., *The Franco-German War 1870–71, by Generals And Other Officers Who Took Part In The Campaign*, London, 1900, Nos. 3, 12, 19, 28, 30; Amédée Le Faure, *Histoire de la Guerre Franco-Allemande 1870–71*, 2 vols., Paris, 1875, Nos, 6, 20; L. Rousset, *Histoire Générale de la Guerre Franco-Allemande (1870–1871)*, illustrated edition, 2 vols., Paris, 1910–12, Nos. 5, 7, 13, 14, 15, 16, 17, 21, 24, 25; Jules Richard, *En Campagne: Tableaux et Dessins de A. de Neuville*, Paris [n.d.], Nos. 9, 18, 22, 23, 27; Jules Richard, *En Campagne (deuxième série)*, Paris [n.d.], Nos. 8, 29. Photography by Tony Weller.

Preface

The news that spread around Paris on the evening of Saturday 3 September 1870 seemed incredible. Crowds besieged the news kiosks and read the papers by the light of gas-lamps in the street. After days of uncertainty and rumours the truth had emerged. The Emperor Napoleon III had been captured after the Battle of Sedan on 1 September, together with most of the Army of Châlons. The war which France had declared on Prussia so confidently only six weeks earlier had brought nothing but humiliating defeats, culminating in this astounding catastrophe. Within three weeks of the start of hostilities the half of the French army commanded by Marshal Bazaine had been bottled up in the eastern fortress of Metz. Now, a fortnight later, the other half which had marched eastward to try to rescue it had been encircled and forced to capitulate by overwhelmingly superior German forces. France had few regular forces left and the Germans expected it to concede defeat shortly.

Yet the Franco-German War begun in July 1870 did not end in September. It took a course neither side had foreseen, and continued for a further five months. Ostensibly triggered by a dynastic dispute, the war had become a contest of national wills. The French national will to resist, which was particularly strong in the major cities, dictated a continuation of the war until the enemy was expelled from French soil. German national feeling was equally determined that the French should be defeated and punished by the loss of their eastern provinces. Yet if Alsace and Lorraine had become the stake for which the war was being fought, military operations resolved themselves into a contest for Paris: for while Paris held out, France was undefeated.

The struggle for Paris had many facets. The French defenders sought not only to keep the besieging Germans at bay, but made two desperate attempts to break out. Simultaneously, French armies hastily levied in the provinces attempted to relieve the siege. Their courageous though ultimately forlorn efforts merit as much attention as the sufferings of the besieged capital.

For their part, the Germans strove to force the war to a conclusion by tightening their grip on Paris, while defending their flanks and communications from the threats posed by rescue attempts from the outside and by guerrilla warfare waged by *francs-tireurs*. While General Helmuth von Moltke, Chief of the German General Staff, was conducting this unexpectedly protracted campaign against the enemy, he feuded with the Federal Chancellor, Otto von Bismarck, as to who controlled wartime grand strategy. Bismarck, for his part, was waging a political struggle to persuade Prussia's South German allies to join in the creation of a German Empire.

Within Paris itself meanwhile another struggle for power was taking place between the moderate republicans who formed the government and the far Left: a contest with deep implications for the conduct of the defence. Nor was this the limit of French divisions. The wartime republican government could not count on the loyalty of the imperial generals blockaded in Metz, who conducted their own negotiations with the Germans. Outside Paris, the government's representative, Léon Gambetta, became virtual dictator of France and pursued a policy increasingly divergent from that of his cabinet colleagues isolated in the freezing and slowly starving capital. Finally, in January 1871, Paris had to surrender, not because its people had lost the will to resist but because food was running out and every effort to break the German blockade had been defeated. Gambetta railed against the armistice, but the great majority of French voters in the provinces accepted peace with relief.

The cessation of hostilities proved to be a false awakening from a nightmare, for France's troubles had yet to reach their bloody denouement. In the capital outraged patriotism at the loss of the war combined with fears of a monarchist restoration and economic grievances to spark insurrection. Bitter divisions over the conduct of the war that had festered between Frenchmen spilled over into horrific civil strife in the streets of Paris. France was left internally scarred by the trauma of the Commune, and externally by the amputation of her two eastern provinces, Alsace and Lorraine.

The latter stages of the Franco-German struggle, the so-called 'republican phase' of the war after the downfall of the Second Empire following Sedan, have been variously considered (or dismissed) as a mere prelude to the Paris Commune, as the background to the creation of the German Empire in January 1871, or as supposedly exemplifying a 'People's War' with troubling implications for military strategists. First and foremost, however, this was a desperate conflict between nations, worthy of attention both in its own right and for its consequences for European history.

The importance which the Franco-German War had for contemporaries has been diminished not only by the passage of time but by the vastly greater scale of the world conflicts of the twentieth century. Yet for France this was the first in a tragedy of three acts spanning three-quarters of a century. Just as in historical perspective the Second World War is viewed as having grown out of the First, so the First World War had roots in that earlier struggle. Among the Great Powers that went to war in 1914, only France and Germany did so in the spirit of a long anticipated resumption of hostilities against the national enemy.

That rancorous mutual sense of an unresolved feud, transcending even the issue of Alsace-Lorraine, was the bitter legacy of 1870–71.

This narrative, which is a sequel to *Sedan 1870*, attempts simply to weave the story of victory and defeat, both military and political, into a reasonably compact introduction to events. Rather than focusing exclusively on the siege of Paris, it sets that episode within the context of the wider struggle extending over several theatres of war. Why the French pursued the strategy they did, why they failed, and why various attempts to end the war by negotiation proved abortive are questions integral to the story of one of the darkest hours in the history of France.

Douglas Fermer
2010

Acknowledgements

My initial debt, once more, is to Rupert Harding of Pen & Sword, without whom this retelling of the story of a momentous but now comparatively neglected conflict would not have seen the light of day. For help at various stages of research my thanks go the staffs of the British Library, the Institute of Historical Research, The Wellcome Library for the History and Understanding of Medicine, The Maughan Library & Information Services Centre of King's College London, Leeds University Library, Croydon Central Library, to Vanessa Corrick and Christine Mason of the Bodleian Library, University of Oxford, and to Nick Stansfeld and William Bellchambers. In France, I am indebted to staff of the Centre d'Acceuil et de Recherche des Archives Nationales (C.A.R.A.N.), the Service Historique de l'Armée de Terre at Vincennes, the Université Louis Pasteur at Strasbourg, and the late Madame Hélène Bergé of Montpellier. In the United States, I am grateful to Lisa Starzyk-Weldon of the Library of the Boston Athenæum, the staff of the Imaging Services Department of the Widener Library, Harvard University Library, Cambridge, Mass., and Clara Latham and Nadine Stowe of the Moffett Library, Midwestern State University, Wichita Falls, Texas. I owe special thanks to Pamela Covey for her editorial skills in guiding this book through to publication. I am also immensely grateful to Tony Weller for photography, to John Cook for giving so generously of his time and skills in drawing the maps from my sketches, and to his son, Matthew Cook, for processing them digitally. As ever, these thanks imply no liability for any error or shortcoming in this book, which is mine alone.

Errata

In the preceding volume, *Sedan 1870: The Eclipse of France*, please note the following:

Of the two illustrations bearing the caption 'Main street of Bazeilles after the battle', that at top left of the double-page spread in question (the twenty-second in the plate section) should be captioned 'Fighting in a courtyard near Bazeilles, 1 September 1870, by Lançon.'

Page 104:

The number given for French casualties at Borny, including 205 officers, should read 3,614.

Page 123:

For 'the Grand Duke of Mecklenburg' read 'Duke Wilhelm of Mecklenburg' and the index reference similarly.

Page 187:

For 'In 1876' in the last sentence of the second paragraph read 'In 1878'.

Chapter 1

The Germans are Coming

Revolution

The crowd had been growing all morning as people poured down the Rue de Rivoli and the Rue Royale in the early autumn sunshine and filled the Place de la Concorde to overflowing. The protestors, working people and bourgeois alike, were shouting that they wanted no more of the Empire: only a Republic would satisfy them, and they would not be denied. Many men wore a kepi, signifying membership of the National Guard. For a while mounted gendarmes held them at the bridge over the Seine, but the elderly General de Caussade, responsible for guarding the Legislature in the Palais-Bourbon, proved irresolute, knowing that the Empress wanted no bloodshed in defence of the regime. When an armed contingent of National Guards appeared he was persuaded to order his men to let them through. But, far from having come to help protect the Legislature, these militiamen were the vanguard of revolution, and were soon jostling the police cordon guarding the palace gates.

A suspiciously large number of people had already got through the gates, brandishing press passes or claiming to be the relatives of Deputies. After some haggling between palace officials and Left-wing Deputies who hoped for some vocal support from the public galleries, it was agreed that some National Guardsmen could pass through on condition that they first put aside their rifles. However, once the gate was ajar the dam was breached, and hundreds of men poured through. At about 2.15 p.m. France's elected representatives became aware that the crowd had invaded their building.

The Chamber on this Sunday, 4 September 1870, had been debating how power might be legally transferred to a new government in the wake of the shocking news of the Emperor's capture. For the government, Count Palikao proposed a Regency Council with himself as Lieutenant General – a continuation of the Empire under another name. Its chances of acceptance were minimal. For the republican opposition, Jules Favre had introduced a motion deposing the Bonapartes and transferring power to a parliamentary commission, while maintaining in post the Military Governor of Paris, General Trochu; a popular favourite whom the opposition had been cultivating. The motion for deposition was too much for many moderate Deputies, who recognized that the Empire was finished but had tender consciences about breaking their oaths of allegiance to it. Veteran statesman Adolphe Thiers put forward a compromise proposal that would transfer power to a parliamentary commission without mentioning deposition. These proposals were under consideration in committee when the Deputies were overtaken by events.

An estimated 700 or 800 people burst into the Chamber, including some of the more extreme elements of the crowd who began smashing windows and furniture. Speaker Eugène Schneider soon abandoned the effort to conduct business and suspended the session. Recognized as the proprietor of the Le Creusot ironworks, scene of a violent strike the previous January, Schneider was punched and knocked down as he left the building amid shouts of 'Exploiter of the workers!' and 'Kill him!'[1] Although the threat was not carried out, further violence seemed imminent. Deputies of the Left tried to calm the mob. Léon Gambetta with his stentorian voice pleaded for order, but eventually, to satisfy the impatient crowd, remounted the tribune and declared Napoleon III deposed. Jules Favre could barely make himself heard above the hubbub, but to insistent shouts for the Republic he responded, 'This is not the place to proclaim it. To the Hôtel de Ville! Follow me, I shall lead you!'[2] By signs and gesticulation the crowd was made to understand, and a triumphal procession began down both sides of the Seine towards the city hall. For in Paris, as all parties knew, revolution had its traditions, and the republican leaders seized their opportunity to ride the popular wave. When they reached the Hôtel de Ville towards 4.00 p.m. even the officers of the guard shook their hands and imperial officials withdrew with good grace.

These republican Deputies, of whom Favre was the most prominent, had led the parliamentary opposition to Napoleon III and his regime. They welcomed political revolution, but had no wish to see it spill over into violent social upheaval. They believed that if they did not take the initiative in leading the crowds then more radical agitators would take control. This revolution could not have succeeded so easily had it not been for the widespread, overwhelming and largely spontaneous desire amongst the people of Paris for a change of government: and not only of Paris, for Lyon had pre-empted the capital by proclaiming a Republic that morning, and Marseille would not be far behind. Yet since the previous evening there had been planning and preparation amongst Left-wing militants in the working-class suburbs of Paris who had been watching for an opportunity to overthrow the hated Empire. *Le Siècle* that morning had carried a notice calling on National Guardsmen to rally outside the Legislature at 2.00 p.m.[3] When Favre and his colleagues reached the Hôtel de Ville they were perturbed to see hard-line revolutionaries already present, including Jean-Baptiste Millière, Félix Pyat and the old Jacobin Charles Delescluze. On the scene too were followers of Auguste Blanqui, an apostle of violent revolution who had first taken part in a Parisian insurrection in 1827 and whose plots had since earned him more years behind bars than even Delescluze. Revered by his disciples as 'The Old Man', the name of the gaunt, intense Blanqui was a bogey to property-owning bourgeois. The extremists were busily drawing up their own lists for a government and throwing the written paper slips out of the window to the crowd below. Red flags were in evidence.

After proclaiming the Republic to enthusiastic cheers, the republican Deputies withdrew to the telegraph office in the Hôtel de Ville and devised a formula that would legitimize their own claim to power. The new government, they agreed, should consist only of those Deputies who had been elected in Paris constituencies in the last parliamentary elections – those of 1869. This conveniently included those of them who, like Gambetta, had been elected in Paris but had opted to sit for other constituencies where their names had also headed the list. It would exclude all the men of the far Left except Henri Rochefort, a journalist whose satirical darts had brought Napoleon III's reputation low. Yet Rochefort was immensely popular, and the mob had just liberated him from prison; far better to have that gadfly inside the government than turning his talents against it. Favre made another shrewd move by sending a deputation to invite General Trochu, Military Governor of Paris, to join the new government.

Louis Jules Trochu received the deputation at his headquarters at the Louvre, donned civilian clothes and made his way through the jubilant crowds. His popularity made him the man of the hour, though his influence on the day's events had been curiously negative. A liberal monarchist by sentiment, he had no love for the imperial regime, which had treated him as an outsider and had made clear its mistrust by bypassing him when giving orders for defence of the Legislature. Small wonder that this day Trochu concluded, with his habitual philosophical detachment, that the Empire was beyond any man's power to save. A staunchly Catholic Breton, he saw himself as ordained to prevent power from falling into the hands of radicals with an anti-clerical, socialist agenda. When he met Favre he asked him to guarantee that 'religion, family and property' would be respected under the new regime.[4] Favre and his colleagues willingly agreed, for the government must have the army's support if it were to survive and maintain order. (Rochefort's membership was temporarily kept from Trochu lest it prove an obstacle to his acceptance.) Favre also willingly acceded when Trochu asked to head the new government, with full control over military matters. Such an arrangement would help rally moderate support for the new regime, and none of the civilians in the new government had any military experience. Indeed, most had distinguished themselves by their eloquent pre-war opposition to army reform and re-armament, and several had voted against the war in July.

Nor had the new men, mostly lawyers and journalists, any significant min-
isterial experience. They had been in opposition for years, having refused on
principle to serve the Empire. All, Trochu included, owed their popularity to
their opposition to the Empire, and their talents lay in their destructive skill
with words, for which they were admired in an age that valued oratory highly.
Favre, who with his lined face and ash-coloured beard resembled an Old
Testament prophet, had made his name as a barrister by defending the silk-
workers of Lyon against their employers in the 1830s, but had become
nationally famous for his defence of Orsini, the Italian who had tried to kill
Napoleon III with bombs in 1858. Since then Favre had been the leading spirit
of the republicans in the Chamber. On the basis of a brief role at the Foreign
Ministry during the 1848 revolution, he now became Foreign Minister of
France. The sceptical and witty Ernest Picard, one of the original five republican opponents of the Empire in the Chamber in the 1850s, had dared there in
1864 to brand Napoleon's coup d'état of 1851 'a crime'. Skilled in debate but
more pragmatic than his colleagues, it was Picard who suggested the title
'Government of National Defence' for the new Cabinet, precisely expressing
its overriding task and the popular mood. The rather feline Jules Simon
became Minister of Education. He had been forced to give up his professorial
chair at the Sorbonne after refusing to take the oath of allegiance following the
coup, but his speeches and writings on liberty had inspired a generation of
students in the Latin Quarter. Gambetta was a spellbinding orator with great
natural authority. Since his indictment of the regime when defending
Delescluze at the Baudin trial of 1868 he had been the idol of the Left. Like
Gambetta, Jules Ferry, another lawyer, was still in his thirties, and was second
only to him amongst the younger generation of republicans. The son of a
wealthy Alsatian manufacturer, Ferry was as cold and crabbed as Gambetta was
warm and impulsive. He took over the considerable powers hitherto wielded by
the imperial Prefect of the Seine.

Thus the new government had no shortage of brains, but it was a group of
talented and highly competitive individuals rather than a team. Gambetta beat
the more moderate Picard to the key post of Minister of the Interior by rushing
over to the Ministry and taking possession. He telegraphed news of the
Republic to the Departments, signing himself Minister of the Interior. Picard
had to be content with the Ministry of Finance, to which his talents were
nevertheless well suited. There were other instances where ministers would
take initiatives without consulting their colleagues. When the perennially popular Étienne Arago, who was acclaimed as Mayor of Paris on 4 September,
proceeded to appoint radicals as mayors of the Paris *arrondissements*, Gambetta
endorsed his action without consulting the Cabinet, much to the indignation of
its more moderate members. Gambetta and Ferry had such a violent dispute on

12 September that Ferry was narrowly restrained from breaking a chair over Gambetta's head.[5]

Outside the inner circle of what was subsequently dubbed the 'Government of Jules' (after the forename shared by Favre, Ferry, Simon and Trochu), the other ministers were veteran opponents of the Empire. Like Favre, Louis Garnier-Pagès, Adolphe Crémieux and Eugène Pelletan had been active in the 1848 revolution that had overthrown the Orléans monarchy, as had Emmanuel Arago (Étienne's nephew). Famed for his defence of Berezowski, the would-be assassin of the Tsar in 1867, Arago became Attorney General. Alexandre Glais-Bizoin, a stalwart of the Left, was known as 'the great interrupter' for his sprightly debating style. Frédéric Dorian, by contrast, was a successful manufacturer with solid business ability who became Minister of Public Works. Trochu picked the War and Navy Ministers. General Adolphe Le Flô was a fellow Breton who had been exiled for his courageous opposition to the 1851 coup. Vice Admiral Léon Fourichon, commander of the Mediterranean squadron before the war, was a friend of Trochu's known for his liberal views.

Notwithstanding their liberal credentials, the new government did what they had for years belaboured Napoleon III for doing in 1851: they closed down the elected Legislature. A few Deputies met to protest this violation, but Thiers advised them that 'In the presence of the enemy, who will soon be outside Paris, I believe that we can do only one thing: retire with dignity.'[6]

The new government recognized the need to legitimize itself in the country by holding elections, which were initially set for 16 October. For the moment, the national emergency ensured it widespread acceptance in France, though the support of the far Left would prove highly conditional and short-lived. In the countryside, where the mass of peasantry had been loyal to Napoleon III, there was some suspicion of the new regime imposed by the capital and notified to them by telegraph. Memories of high taxes levied by the republican revolutionaries of 1848 were long, and there was no desire to see local officials replaced by inexperienced strangers from the towns. No one, however, fired a shot in defence of the discredited Empire, whose leading figures – including the Empress – were allowed to slip into exile without pursuit. In Paris, popular violence was largely limited to smashing imperial symbols on buildings.

By the morning of 5 September the joyful capital had returned to its business confidently, though not calmly. Favre thought 'it believed itself saved because it had recovered its liberty'.[7] The very name of Republic conjured visions of the armies of the Great Revolution driving back the foreign invader eight decades previously. A Parisian editor observed that the population of the capital 'truly believed that at this word Republic the Prussians would be terrified and halt in their tracks. It imagined that it was one of those magic spells that drive away demons and calm tempests.'[8]

High hopes were placed in the new government, whose revolutionary origins would nevertheless return to haunt it, especially once holding elections proved impracticable in the face of enemy invasion. The very fact that the new men derived their power and popular support from Paris tied them to it. Moreover, Paris was the nerve centre of the highly centralized French administrative system; and for a government to abandon it seemed unthinkable. Expecting that a great battle was about to be fought beneath its walls, they felt honour-bound not to desert it. 'In the present crisis, the seat of battle should be the seat of power,' they proclaimed.[9] There would be no submission to the enemy as in 1815. In their view Paris was the heart of France and of the national resistance. If they left for the provinces, where they had less support, would not radicals seize power in Paris by the same right of revolution that they themselves had claimed? Gambetta alone, concerned that the rest of the country was being 'somewhat forgotten'[10] urged removal of the government to the provinces: though more from anxiety about the volatile political situation in Lyon and southern France than from fear of strategic isolation.[11] The Cabinet, however, decided on 11 September merely to send the elderly Crémieux, Minister of Justice, to represent them at Tours, to spare him the perils of a siege.[12] Parts of some government departments were also told to transfer to Tours. The decision of the government itself to remain in Paris was to have a profound and crippling effect on French strategy, but it would soon be too late for second thoughts.

The German Advance

In the immediate aftermath of his stupendous victory of Sedan the priority of General Helmuth von Moltke, Chief of the German General Staff, was to realign his two armies, which had been concentrated for the battle, and to set them on the road to Paris, some 210 kilometres distant. Two corps were temporarily left at Sedan to deal with the huge numbers of French prisoners. Meanwhile, after disentangling their supply lines, his 150,000-strong forces began their advance on 3 September on a 90-kilometre front. Third Army, commanded by Crown Prince Friedrich Wilhelm of Prussia, constituted the left wing. To its north moved the right wing, Fourth Army (also called the Army of the Meuse) commanded by Crown Prince Albert of Saxony. They marched by easy stages, confident of meeting little opposition.

The only significant body of French troops remaining at large in the vicinity was 13 Corps, commanded by General Vinoy. Having reached Mézières, north-west of Sedan, with his leading division, Vinoy had listened all day on 1 September to the sound of battle, and the 10,000 French fugitives who reached the town by nightfall left him in no doubt of its disastrous outcome. For one French division to attempt to attack the German flank would have

The German Advance
SEPTEMBER - OCTOBER 1870

German Advance →
French Retreat ⇨
28 SEPT. = Date Captured by Germans

N

BELGIUM
Brussels
LILLE
ARRAS
Calais
Hastings
0 20 40 60 80 100
KILOMETRES

PRUSSIA
LUX.
Bitche
Phalsbourg
METZ 29 OCT.
Montmédy
Sedan
MÉZIÈRES
St. Quentin
Rethel
RHEIMS
LAON 9 SEPT.
Soissons
Compiègne 15 OCT.
VINOY
Meaux
Château Thierry
Ferrières
PARIS
Versailles 19 SEPT.
R. Aisne
R. Oise
R. Marne
CHÂLONS
BAR-LE-DUC
Verdun 8 NOV.
Toul 23 SEPT.
La Bourgonce
NANCY
St. Dié
Sélestat 24 OCT.
STRASBOURG 28 SEPT.
Colmar
Neuf Brisach 10 NOV.
Mulhouse
BELFORT
BADEN
SWITZERLAND
Besançon
Gray
Vesoul
ÉPINAL
CHAUMONT
Langres
DIJON 31 OCT.
WEDER
CAMBRIELS
I ARMY
II ARMY
III ARMY
R. Seine
MELUN
TROYES
AUXERRE
Montargis
Pithiviers
Étampes
Arténay
ORLÉANS 11 OCT.
LA MOTTE ROUGE
Salbris
Vierzon
BOURGES
TANN
WITTICH
Châteaudun 18 OCT.
CHARTRES 21 OCT.
Ablis
Dreux
EVREUX
ROUEN
BEAUVAIS
AMIENS
Montdidier
CAEN
ALENÇON
LE MANS
Vendôme
BLOIS
TOURS
R. Loire

St. Quentin

been suicidal, and Vinoy took the only sensible decision – to retreat. Leaving a garrison in Mézières and wiring his two other divisions to turn back towards Laon, he set his men in motion south-westward after midnight. To muffle sound, they were told to strap their mess-tins to their knapsacks, and were ordered to keep marching even if attacked.

The Germans should have caught and overwhelmed Vinoy. They had VI Corps and two cavalry divisions operating west of Sedan to watch for any French activity in that direction, and they soon picked up the trail of 13 Corps. By 6.00 a.m. on 2 September Vinoy encountered German cavalry which, however, kept its distance after a skirmish.

Unlike so many French generals in this campaign, Joseph Vinoy kept his nerve in the face of superior numbers. He was a tough old regular soldier, born in 1800 and educated at a seminary before joining the army. Years of campaigning in Algeria had been followed by brigade command in the Crimea, where his performance at the storming of Sebastopol won him divisional rank. He had also played a key role in the victory of Magenta in Italy in 1859. A solid Bonapartist, he had supported the coup d'état in 1851, and following his retirement in 1865 had become a senator before being recalled to service in 1870. Despite his age, he had a surer grasp of the art of command than some of his younger colleagues, even though his troops were no better or worse than those who had just met with disaster in the Sedan campaign – a mixture of regulars and half-trained reservists.

With the Germans shadowing him, Vinoy headed for Rethel. Learning that it was occupied, he posted a rearguard to hold the Germans at bay and swung his weary column off to the north-west. It did not take the Germans long to pick up his new direction and to set off in pursuit, while preparing to block his passage of the Aisne. Although his men were near the end of their tether, Vinoy had campfires lit, then, taking advantage of a moonless night of torrential rain, set out at 2.00 a.m. on 3 September. Making a detour, he slipped past the Germans. It was afternoon before he again heard their cannon to his rear. Luckily for him, the Germans misjudged his position after the bulk of their cavalry was called away to deal with a reported French concentration at Rheims. Realizing that they had lost the chance of overtaking Vinoy, the German infantry ceased pursuit. After covering 48 kilometres in sixteen hours that day over muddy roads, Vinoy's exhausted men were safe. On 5 September they reached the railway at Laon. By 9 September the whole of 13 Corps, plus the column of fugitives from Sedan who had been directed via a more northerly route, were assembled in Paris. Together, they numbered 43,068 men and 13,567 horses, together with artillery and wagons.[13] It was a priceless reinforcement for the threatened capital, and Vinoy's troops included two good regular regiments, the 35th and 42nd Line. They had been part of the French garrison of Rome, and would be one of the most reliable elements in the defence of Paris.

The rumoured French concentration at Rheims did not materialize. German troops entered the city, and on 5 September King Wilhelm of Prussia moved his headquarters there. German officers took the opportunity to visit the great Gothic cathedral, the traditional coronation site of the kings of France, and notably of Charles VII, who had been crowned there in 1429 in the presence of Joan of Arc at another time of foreign invasion. It seemed unlikely that the French could now mount a comparable revival of national fortunes. For the most part the German advance had the air of 'a military promenade' or 'pleasure trip', with no major forces in front of them.[14] Yet evidently French resistance had not quite been extinguished. A detachment sent to mop up the French garrison at Montmédy had to give up the attempt when the garrison proved determined to resist, even after bombardment. Soissons too declined a summons to surrender.

What happened at Laon demonstrated both extremes of French reaction to invasion. Like Montmédy, the citadel sat high on a pinnacle of rock commanding the surrounding area. Its garrison was small, consisting of a half company of the 55th Regiment and 2,000 Gardes Mobiles. The fortress was in disrepair and poorly supplied, but it could have resisted, and such was the intention of its commander, General Théremin d'Hame, when the Germans first summonsed him to surrender. The townspeople, demoralized by the earlier retreat of Vinoy's men and fearing imminent bombardment, had other ideas. A crowd cornered Théremin in a restaurant and threatened to kill him unless he surrendered. The Prefect was also put under pressure. Instead of wiring orders to hold out at all costs, Paris was telling garrison commanders to act according to circumstances. Théremin yielded. On the morning of 9 September, in pouring rain, Duke Wilhelm of Mecklenburg-Schwerin rode into town at the head of a German column. Laon's regular garrison was taken prisoner, and the Gardes Mobiles were disarmed and paroled. Théremin was surrendering his sword to the Duke when suddenly the citadel erupted in two huge explosions. Laon was enveloped in a great black cloud, from which rained rocks, timbers and bloody human fragments.

Théremin fell, mortally wounded. The Duke, wounded in the foot and covered in yellow mud, rushed into the town council, accusing them at gunpoint of treachery and furiously swearing vengeance as his surviving men fell to massacring the Gardes Mobiles in the street. When a reckoning was made of the carnage it was found that forty-two Germans had been killed and seventy-two wounded, but there were also 369 French casualties.[15]

The French authorities, as they protested, had not been complicit in the ambush. One French NCO, the custodian of the citadel's artillery, had evidently felt such rage and despair at the shameful surrender of the garrison that he had blown up the powder store rather than surrender. Dieudonné Henriot, decorated for his service in the Crimea and Italy, had become what a later age would call a suicide-bomber, so serving notice on the Germans of the depths of hostility they might tap as they penetrated deeper into France.

There were other signs of that hostility as peasants and local National Guards sniped at German cavalry patrols entering their villages. King Wilhelm was reminded of the campaign of 1814 over this very ground, in which he had taken part. He took a more sober view of warfare than many of his subjects. Even as they had cheered him at the outbreak of war in July, he told Queen Augusta that he was filled 'with utter dread by this enthusiasm; for what may be the chances of war, by which all this rejoicing must, and will, be silenced?'[16] On 7 September he told a confidant, 'Only now is the war beginning. Their leaders will preach the *levée en masse*, as in 1814; the armed uprising of the peasants that gave us much trouble then ... We shall perhaps have some difficult days; but nobody wants to believe it, because all are dazzled by our unparalleled success.'[17] More typical was the correspondent of the *Cologne Gazette*, who assured his readers that the dramatic interest of the war had finished with Sedan, and that the vaunted 'national defence' would 'last no longer than a straw fire'.[18]

Brushing aside sporadic local resistance and rapidly replacing destroyed bridges, the German armies moved inexorably towards the Marne, its green waters winding between hills covered with ripening grapes. Orders for the encirclement of Paris were given from Royal Headquarters at Château-Thierry on 15 September. Fourth Army then swung north of Paris while Third Army advanced south of it, both cutting railways and telegraph wires as they went. From high ground German troops caught glimpses of Paris spread under a radiant sun, and could not help but be impressed by 'the great city, with its infinite sea of houses, its hundreds of spires and towers'.[19] Distinguishing the gilded dome of Les Invalides, Guards officer Paul von Hindenburg felt sure that 'when the Crusaders gazed for the first time on Jerusalem their feelings were the same as ours when we saw Paris lying at our feet'.[20] None suspected how long they would stay, nor how they would tire of that initially exhilarating view.

Châtillon

The defences of Paris, constructed in 1840, had not been kept in good repair in recent years, and had been cut through in numerous places for the passage of roads, canals and railways. The development of more powerful artillery had left them outmoded, but maintenance funds had not been voted by the Legislature. Only since news of the first defeats had arrived on 7 August had repair work been pressed forward in earnest, but much had been achieved, and the restored defences would prove sufficiently formidable to deter the Germans from a frontal assault. A wall 10 metres high and 3.5 metres thick ran for 34 kilometres around the city and incorporated ninety-four bastions. Before it gaped a 15-metre wide ditch, while behind it ran a military road. Beyond this defensive perimeter were fifteen large, detached forts, some with redoubts in between, forming a defensive circumference of 53 kilometres. Together, these defences bristled with 2,627 guns and mortars, some of the heaviest having been brought in by the navy, which also provided garrisons for many of the forts. Paris industries would prove equal to supplying sufficient ammunition to remedy an initial shortage, and to manufacturing more cannon.

Approximately 80,000 men had been set to work repairing the defences, constructing 61 kilometres of palisades, levelling buildings and felling trees to open lines of fire. The forts were equipped with electric searchlights and connected to Trochu's headquarters by telegraph. Sandbags, gabions and fascines were prepared in huge quantities. A further 12,000 men were employed in closing or narrowing the gaps in the perimeter wall, though this created huge traffic jams at the very time when it was vital to bring supplies into the city. Experience showed that the labour would have been better employed in improving the defences of the forts – work which had to be carried on after the siege had begun.

Meanwhile, the imperial authorities had taken essential steps to provision the city. Unsung heroes of this effort were Deputy Intendant Victor Perrier and his assistant commissaries at the War Department, who bought in immense quantities of foodstuffs and salt from England and elsewhere.[21] Clément Duvernois, the imperial Minister of Commerce, arranged during August for 250,000 sheep and 40,000 cattle to be brought into the city, where they grazed in its green spaces. These efforts, and purchases by the municipality and private enterprise, ensured that Paris was stocked to withstand a siege of months rather than weeks. The Empress had directed important artworks to be sent to the provinces or packed away in cellars.

Far from bringing new energy to preparations, in some respects the Revolution of 4 September brought an unfortunate interruption. Amid the ensuing political excitement, many workers on the fortifications went off to join the National Guard or to look after their families in the suburbs, leaving the works unfinished. Quantities of food that had been amassed outside Paris were not brought within its defences. Trochu's order to burn the forests around the city to deny the Germans cover, fuel and timber produced palls of choking smoke by day and illuminated the horizon at night; but there was neither time enough nor sufficient petroleum in Paris to complete the job.

Trochu's political role proved a distraction from his military duties. The government inevitably was much preoccupied with political appointments, for the republican faithful expected Bonapartist officials throughout France to be purged in their own favour. Amid a barrage of proclamations, the government asserted its libertarian principles and its triumph over the fallen regime by such measures as republicanizing the police force and removing stamp duty on newspapers – the symbol of censorship – despite its need for funds. A commission busied itself with renaming streets, while another set about publishing secret imperial correspondence left behind in the Tuileries.

With government encouragement, possibly 100,000 people who could afford to do so left the city. The police expelled 1,400 prostitutes and 3,600 vagrants, and 4,640 terminally ill patients were evacuated from hospices. German citizens were ordered to leave.[22] However, these modest attempts at partial evacuation were counteracted by an influx of over 200,000 country people, suburban dwellers and refugees from eastern France who deserted their homes at the German approach and made for the supposed safety of the city.[23] The population of the capital swelled to over 2 million people, and the number of mouths to feed would directly determine the length of time it could withstand a siege. Yet the government at this stage had no idea that a siege might last more than a few weeks at most and, being good liberals, they did not impose rationing.

The mood in the city was one of mounting excitement rather than dread. Uniforms were everywhere: 100,000 Gardes Mobiles had arrived from the provinces, while almost every Parisian male – even the fishermen by the Seine – seemed to be sporting the kepi of the National Guard, though many lacked other items of uniform. On 13 September, to enthusiastic cheers, Trochu reviewed their massed ranks, totalling some 300,000 men. Among the National Guardsmen bourgeois frock-coats mingled with workmen's smocks, men with grey beards stood shoulder to shoulder with beardless boys, and flowers adorned rifle barrels.[24] It was an impressive show of unity that was to prove all too fleeting, but for the moment Parisians could feel confidence in their numbers. How could the Germans overcome such resolute patriots? Although the theatres had closed their doors, cafés were overflowing and the city seemed as vibrant as ever. There was public disbelief that the Germans could ever take the city: 'The capture of Paris,' wrote Francisque Sarcey, 'seemed to us such a monstrous sacrilege, such a terrible affront to all laws, divine and human, that it didn't enter our imagination that this crime could be accomplished; no, it was not possible.' The same message was thundered by the newspaper rodomontade of Victor Hugo, who had returned from nineteen years of exile and was the idol of the moment. Hugo believed that, once unsheathed, the 'sword of revolution' was invincible.[25]

General Trochu's professional estimate of the situation was more pessimistic. He had at most 85,000 regular soldiers, of whom scarcely a third were worthy of the name. The Gardes Mobiles needed more training before they could operate effectively with the field force. The National Guard was an untrained mass, fit only to garrison the ramparts. Trochu had told Jules Favre on 21 August that the defence of Paris could be only a 'heroic folly'.[26] He expected the Germans to make a direct assault on Paris, and privately believed that their superiority in numbers would give them every chance of success.[27] Without help from outside, he judged, Paris 'must infallibly ... succumb sooner or later, like all fortresses subjected to this law of isolation ...'[28] He was convinced that it was unwise to hold any line beyond the fortresses.

However, on 15 September he acquired a collaborator of a very different temperament. General Auguste Ducrot had briefly commanded the army at Sedan after MacMahon's wounding. Taken prisoner, he had escaped while waiting to be embarked on a train to Germany and had made his way back to Paris – by breaking his parole, declared the Germans; by legitimate escape from armed guards, insisted Ducrot.[29]

Though very different in their outlook and politics, Ducrot and Trochu were old friends from Algerian days. Admiring Ducrot's vigour as a man of action, Trochu gave him overall command of both Renault's 14 Corps and Vinoy's 13 Corps (Trochu made clear his disdain for the Bonapartist Vinoy, who was incensed by this humiliation). Ducrot argued that allowing the Germans to occupy the Châtillon heights south-west of Paris would yield them an excellent artillery position, overlooking not only the forts in that sector but the city itself. After Sedan, Ducrot had developed a strong aversion to sitting still while the enemy surrounded him, and now he proposed going over to the offensive. He would strike the German Third Army as it moved westwards.

Trochu gave reluctant permission to 'feel the enemy's flank', but cautioned that any move beyond the forts might lose 'a significant part of our advantages'.[30] The sanguine Ducrot determined to attack nevertheless. The Prussian V Corps was moving west towards Versailles, having skirmished lightly with Vinoy's men on the 17th and Ducrot's on the 18th. At dawn on 19 September Ducrot sent two of the three infantry divisions of 14 Corps south-westwards to intercept the Germans. It was a bold plan, and if successful might have given republican France its first victory and restored the morale of the regular troops. But the 30,000 men of 14 Corps were not a seasoned unit: rather a hotchpotch of temporary regiments hastily composed of fragments of others, with officers and men unfamiliar to each other. Many men were reservists, while others were fugitives from Sedan who had still not recovered their nerve.

Such was the case with the Zouaves of Ducrot's right-hand column. Not long into the engagement they were unwisely called together near the Trivaux

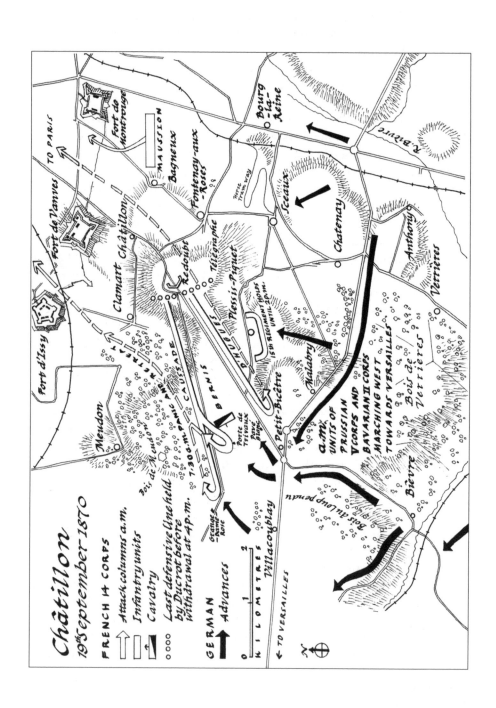

Châtillon
19th September 1870

FRENCH 14 CORPS

Attack columns a.m.

Infantry units

Cavalry

o o o o Last defensive line held by Ducrot before withdrawal at 4p.m.

GERMAN

Advances

KILOMETRES

0   1   2

← TO VERSAILLES

N

Fort d'Issy

Fort de Vanves

TO PARIS

Fort de Montrouge

MAUSSION

Bagneux

Fontenay-aux-Roses

Clamart Châtillon

Redoubt

Télégraphe

Plessis-Piquet

Meudon

Bois de Meudon

CHAUSSADE

BERNIS

7.30a.m.

7.30a.m.

Porte de Trivaux Pavé Slope

Petit-Bicêtre

15th REGIMENT HOLDS UNTIL 2p.m.

Malabry

a.m. UNITS OF PRUSSIAN V CORPS AND BAVARIAN II CORPS MARCHING WEST TOWARDS VERSAILLES

Bois du loup pendu

Villacoublay

Granges - Rose

Bièvre

Bois de Verrières

Anthony

Verrières

Chatenay

Sceaux

Porte Tram way

Bourg-la-Reine

R. Bièvre

Farm for an issue of ammunition. While they were gathered, a volley of shells burst among them, killing and wounding relatively few men, but sufficient to start a stampede. The Zouaves panicked, some running all the way into Paris before the sun had even burned off the morning mist, spreading alarm with shouts of treason and defeat. Meanwhile the Germans were counter-attacking, with units of Bavarian II Corps hurrying forward to the right of the Prussians. Before long, the whole French line had given way. As one of Ducrot's staff confessed, 'The battle was lost before it had fairly begun.'[31]

Covered by their artillery and *mitrailleuses*, and by a stand around Plessis-Piquet by the 15th Regiment, the French retreated to their starting positions. The right division, Caussade's, kept going all the way into Paris: Ducrot was so furious that he wanted to court-martial the old general, who suffered a fatal stroke a few weeks later. Ducrot's reserve division also withdrew following a mistaken order by his chief of staff. By 4.00 p.m. Ducrot had abandoned the Châtillon heights, together with nine guns, even though the German pursuit was slackening.

Trochu had been proved right about the risks of an offensive with the troops he had; yet almost certainly he had been wrong not to extend his defensive perimeter to cover the Châtillon heights. The engineers, who jealously preserved their autonomy from field commanders, had spent August building a half-finished stone redoubt there which Ducrot had used to cover his retreat. Yet, as French veterans of the siege of Sebastopol like Trochu might have grasped, the time would have been better spent digging fieldworks to defend a wider area. Americans in Paris, with their Civil War experience, were baffled by the French reluctance to entrench.[32] Moreover, Ducrot's alleged reason for abandoning the position, lack of water, was one which engineers could have remedied. As it was, a key strategic position had been lost, greatly easing the Germans' task. French casualties at Châtillon were 723, German 444.[33]

The arrival of fugitives from the battle caused alarm in Paris, where several of the Zouaves were arrested. More redoubts were needlessly abandoned and bridges destroyed. Gambetta issued a dramatic proclamation: 'Citizens, The cannon thunders. The supreme hour has come.'[34] Might the Germans have broken into the city's defences had they pressed hard upon Ducrot's heels? Moltke was unaware of the opportunity, though he pointed out afterwards that the forts were still intact and such an assault would have needed much preparation.[35] Besides, a rebuff would have fortified French spirits. The French offensive had failed to disrupt Moltke's plans. That night of 19 September Third Army reached its objective, Versailles. Fourth Army had also moved west without serious opposition, and joined hands with it. Paris was now invested, with no access by land to the rest of France or the world beyond.

Not an Inch of Our Territory

Even as the cannon boomed at Châtillon, talks were being held to explore whether the war could be ended without further bloodshed. Jules Favre had left Paris on 18 September to meet Count von Bismarck to establish what terms the Germans might offer.

Upon taking office, on 5 September, Favre had drafted a ringing circular for publication abroad and at home. He condemned the imperial regime while extolling 'our heroic army, sacrificed by the incompetence of the high command'. Republicans, he affirmed, had condemned the war and favoured respect for German self-determination, but he threw down a challenge to the invader:

> ... the King of Prussia has declared that he made war not on France, but on the imperial dynasty. The dynasty has fallen. Free France has risen.
>
> Does the King of Prussia wish to continue a wicked war which will be at least as fatal to him as to us?
>
> Does he want to give the world of the nineteenth century this cruel spectacle of two nations destroying each other and, forgetful of humanity, reason and science, heaping up ruins and corpses?
>
> Let him of his own accord assume this responsibility before the world and before history!
>
> If he throws down the gauntlet, we accept it. We shall not yield an inch of our territory, nor a stone of our fortresses.[36]

Rather than submit to a shameful peace, France would accept a war of extermination.

This rousing rhetoric undeniably expressed the Parisian determination to resist and the conviction that under the Empire France had scarcely begun to fight. In vain Ernest Picard had objected that it was unwise to rule out so publicly any surrender of territory or dismantling of fortresses when the enemy held all the military advantages. Experienced diplomats across Europe recognized a *faux pas*: France could scarcely avoid some territorial concessions. Favre was deceived too in believing that Germany was fighting only Napoleon III, not the French nation. That claim had appeared in the proclamations of German army commanders to their troops, but it had never been Prussia's official stance.[37]

Encouraged by growing sympathy for France abroad, Favre hoped that other powers would broker a settlement. The USA and Switzerland hastened to welcome France to the small fraternity of republics by recognizing her new government. Several secondary powers followed suit; but sympathy and recognition did not amount to active support. Favre put most hope in mediation by Britain which, however, was determined to maintain strict neutrality in the face

of French importunity on one hand and on the other strident German complaints that British merchants were selling coal, horses and ammunition to
France. Even had Britain any compelling motive or desire to act, her tiny army
put intervention out of the question. Belgian neutrality, her main concern,
might be jeopardized by intervention, and mediation could only be considered
if both sides requested it. Britain preferred to see the war ended by direct talks
between the belligerents. A mild private letter was drafted for Queen Victoria
to send to King Wilhelm expressing the hope that the terms imposed on
France would not be too harsh.[38] Meanwhile Britain withheld formal recognition from the new French government pending its legitimation through
elections, but maintained day-to-day diplomatic contacts.

To sway the British Government, Favre despatched France's most prestig-
ious statesman. Adolphe Thiers, had he wished, could have been a member of
the Government of National Defence, or even its head, for he had been elected
to the Legislature by a Paris constituency and spoke for a large body of
moderate opinion in the country. But, just as Thiers had resisted the imperial
regime's appeals to its old opponent in its dying hours to save it by heading a
moderate ministry, so he was too canny to become the figurehead of a republican regime which he believed would soon have to sign a humiliating peace.
With an eye to his own political prospects, the former Orleanist minister would
accept no office under the new government. Nevertheless, Favre persuaded
him to go to London to promote European mediation, and accepted Thiers's
suggestion that he should extend his mission to the other neutral great powers.

Thiers left for London on 12 September and received a courteous hearing
from Lord Granville, Gladstone's Foreign Minister. Britain would not budge
from its neutrality, but used its good offices to enquire through diplomatic
channels whether the Prussian government would grant Favre safe-conduct
to enter German lines for a meeting with Bismarck. Through these contacts
Favre was enabled to slip out of Paris on 18 September and pass through the
lines south of the city. Only Trochu and War Minister Le Flô knew of this
approach. Informal soundings of his Cabinet colleagues convinced Favre that
they would firmly oppose such peace-feelers if the matter were put to them
formally, as would the majority of Parisians.

For his part, Bismarck remained sceptical as to whether a revolutionary
government in Paris could sign a binding peace, even when Favre wrote to
assure him that its orders would be obeyed. On 11 September Bismarck
announced that Germany recognized only the French imperial government.[39]
Germany's military advantage was so preponderant that he need be in no hurry
to conclude peace or offer concessions. Every day brought likely German
victory nearer. As the Crown Prince of Prussia wrote, 'no serious, long-
continued resistance is to be expected'.[40] Bismarck was well placed to deflect

any proffered European mediation, and majority opinion in Germany continued to support prosecution of the war. A few dissenting voices from radical socialists and democrats were easily silenced by arrests and imprisonment under martial law. He could listen to what Favre might offer with all the aces in his hand.

Entering German lines, Favre grew despondent at the sight of ruined and pillaged French villages as he crossed roads so thick with German troops that they struck him as 'an armed torrent'.[41] Eventually he saw riding towards him the formidable, already legendary figure of the Chancellor of the North German Confederation, identified by his white cuirassier's uniform and cap with its wide yellow band. As they rode together from the village of Montry towards the nearby château of La Haute-Maison they passed along a narrow road between wooded banks. 'This place,' said Bismarck, 'seems made for the exploits of your *francs-tireurs*. This area is infested with them, and we hunt them down without pity. They aren't soldiers: we treat them as assassins.' Favre objected that the *francs-tireurs* were only defending their homes, and that Germany was abusing the laws of war in not recognizing them as combatants. Bismarck insisted that 'We can only recognize soldiers under regular discipline. The rest are outlaws.' When Favre pointed out that in 1813 Prussia had proclaimed an uprising against the invading French, Bismarck countered, 'That is so, but our trees still bear the marks where your generals hanged our people.'[42]

This exchange set the tone for talks over the next two days, held first at Haute-Maison and then at the luxurious country château of Baron Rothschild at Ferrières, where Bismarck had been a guest at a hunting party in 1856. Favre was quickly disabused of his hope that Germany might be satisfied with a cash indemnity. Bismarck lectured him that France had started the war, and now Germany could find security against her continual aggression only by a cession of territory, principally Alsace and its chief city: 'Strasbourg is a perpetual threat to us. It is the key to our house and we want it.'[43] When Favre protested that such a loss would fill France with the desire for revenge, Bismarck retorted that France had never accepted the verdict of Waterloo nor of Sadowa. No doubt she would want revenge for Sedan too, and her warlike disposition meant that Germany must have guarantees for her defence and tangible compensation for the immense sacrifices she had made in this war. Besides, had France won she undoubtedly would have annexed the Rhineland.

Bismarck's firm line reflected German nationalist opinion, which was clamouring for annexation and would accept nothing less than Alsace. Likewise the German General Staff insisted on having the line of the Vosges as the new military frontier with France. 'We shall in no case let Lorraine and Alsace go; Metz must become a Prussian fortress,' wrote one of Moltke's inner circle.[44]

Some stiff-backed Prussian generals boiled with indignation at any negotiation with French republicans. General von Blumenthal complained to his diary that if 'such a rank democrat' as Favre had appeared at his headquarters, 'at the most, I should have sent my servants to interview him'.[45] Bismarck himself taunted Favre with the possibility that he might prefer to negotiate with a representative of the Empire who had just arrived at his headquarters. Regarding Metz, which remained under German blockade, Bismarck threw in the unsettling observation that 'Bazaine does not belong to you. I have strong reasons to believe that he is still loyal to the Emperor and ... will refuse to obey you.' He reminded Favre that his Government of National Defence 'was born of sedition, and tomorrow you may be overthrown by the populace of Paris'.[46]

Favre proposed an armistice to allow the election of a French National Assembly which would be fully empowered to consider German terms. Bismarck agreed in principle, though he would not allow elections in Alsace or German-occupied Lorraine. However, the negotiations broke down on the question of armistice conditions. Favre requested that French fortresses, including Paris, should be allowed to re-provision during the armistice. This was unacceptable to the Germans, because their military advantages would dwindle while the French gained precious time for reorganization. After consulting the King and Moltke, Bismarck set out the sureties Germany required for an armistice: the surrender of Strasbourg and of Toul and Bitche which were still resisting, plus the fortress of Mont-Valérien, the Gibraltar of the Paris defences, which overlooked the city. For the French to accept these conditions would be tantamount to conceding defeat, for to give up that fortress was to yield Paris.

A tearful Favre broke off the talks and returned to Paris, where the press had published news of his mission, provoking some disturbances. The Cabinet received him coldly, and after he had recounted Bismarck's conditions there was no hesitation. Rather than accept dismemberment, France would fight on. If Favre's diplomatic skills had not shone, he at least snatched a propaganda victory with a circular that stiffened resolve at home and helped generate sympathy for France abroad:

> Prussia responds to our overtures by demanding to keep Alsace and Lorraine by right of conquest. She will not consent even to consult their populations; she wishes to dispose of them like cattle ... Let Europe be the judge! For us the enemy is unmasked. He places us between duty and dishonour. Our choice is made. Paris will resist to the last extremity ...'[47]

Chapter 2

The War Outside Paris

Strasbourg Falls

In Paris the statue representing Strasbourg on the Place de la Concorde, decked with flags and wreaths, had become a symbol of resistance and a focus for demonstrations by the National Guard. That fortress city of 85,000 people lay 400 kilometres away on the eastern frontier, almost on the banks of the Rhine. It had been invested by the Germans since 11 August.

To German nationalists too Strasbourg was deeply symbolic. They had long coveted it and were determined to have it as a matter of historic 'right', and this feeling was even stronger in the South German states than in Prussia. Militarily, too, the Germans could not afford to leave the capital of Alsace in their rear. As a transportation centre and military stronghold it might serve as a base for raids against their communications or even into Germany. Thus, immediately upon the French defeat at Frœschwiller on 6 August, the Baden Division had been detached from the Crown Prince's Third Army and sent south against Strasbourg, meeting only slight opposition as it advanced. It was shortly joined by units fresh from Germany, together forming a siege corps of 40,000 men, 250 guns and 88 mortars under the command of Lieutenant General August von Werder.[1]

Defending Strasbourg was General Uhrich, who had commanded there at the time of Louis-Napoleon's coup in 1851. Emerging from retirement in July 1870, the Bonapartist veteran found the fortress almost wholly unprepared for defence. Few in France had imagined that the war would be fought west of the Rhine or that Strasbourg, supposedly a base for the invasion of Germany, would find itself in the front line. Uhrich had to improvise a garrison from the troops who happened to be present: the 87th Line Regiment, plus assorted battalions and 123 sailors under Rear Admiral Exelmans who had been detailed to defend the Rhine by manning floating batteries which, however, had not arrived from Toulon. In addition there were customs officers, *francs-tireurs*, Gardes Mobiles and 3,000 local National Guards, plus some demoralized fugitives from Frœschwiller. Nominally, this gave Uhrich 21,486 men,[2] but scarcely half were fit for combat. He was reluctant to defend a wide perimeter or to mount more than small actions to harass the German approach. Critically, he lacked sufficient engineers and artillerists to make best use of his 250 guns and mortars, which were far inferior to the German guns and of fourteen different calibres.[3]

Unlike Paris and Metz, Strasbourg had no outlying forts with heavy guns to keep attackers at bay. Plans to build them had been recommended as 'urgent and indispensable' by the fortifications committee in 1867,[4] but little work had been done because funds had not been voted. Strasbourg's citadel and walls had been considered masterpieces of Vauban's art when constructed in 1681, the year Louis XIV had taken possession of the city for France, but by 1870 they were within easy range of German rifled artillery. In their hasty and belated efforts to ready the city's defences after the outbreak of war, the French had dammed streams to flood the low ground south and north-east of the city; but the Germans were able easily to take the higher ground to the north-west and establish batteries there. Uhrich was startled by the range and accuracy of their fire. The Germans also established batteries on their own territory at Kehl on the east bank of the Rhine, whence they could lay a pulverizing fire on Strasbourg's citadel, at the eastern end of the city. When French gunners then targeted Kehl and set it ablaze on 19 August, the Germans declared their outrage that an open town had been bombarded.

The poor state of Strasbourg's defences made it more vulnerable to close siege than Paris or Metz, but Werder wanted to avoid that lengthy procedure if possible. With permission from Royal Headquarters, on the night of 23 August he began an intense bombardment of the city with the aim of terrorizing it into an early submission.

When the first shells had fallen in the city on 14 August there had been incredulity among some citizens that this could happen to a civilized European city in the mid-nineteenth century. Regulations from the 1814 siege were revised and brought back into force. Local fire wardens were appointed, auxiliary firemen were recruited, and fire buckets were placed on every floor. Citizens were banned from high buildings, for fear of spies was rife. Although the majority were loyal to France, espionage was all too easy in a city with strong commercial and social ties across the Rhine and where three-quarters of the people had German surnames and spoke a German dialect.

When all-out bombardment began the city experienced destruction on a scale so many Europeans were to suffer over the next three-quarters of a century. On the night of 24 August the Protestant Temple, the Art Museum and the City Library were destroyed, together with priceless artworks and manuscripts. The city authorities had left protecting cultural treasures too late. A more immediate loss to the defence for lack of deep bomb-proofs was the destruction of 35,000 artillery percussion fuses in the arsenal. The next night the railway station and the cathedral were badly damaged, though out of defer-ence to European opinion the Germans ceased to target the cathedral after the

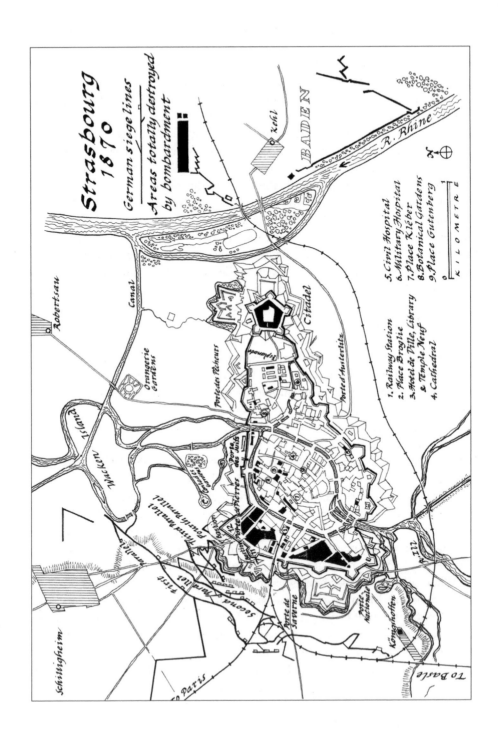

Strasbourg
1870

German siege lines

Areas totally destroyed
by bombardment

BADEN

Kehl

R. Rhine

KILOMETRE

1. Railway Station
2. Place Broglie
3. Hotel de Ville, Library
& Temple Neuf
4. Cathedral

5. Civil Hospital
6. Military Hospital
7. Place Kléber
8. Botanical Gardens
9. Place Gutenberg

Robertsau

Canal

Orangerie
Gardens

Wacken Island

Citadel

Porte des Pêcheurs

Esplanade

Porte d'Austerlitz

Porte des Juifs

First parallel

Second Parallel

Porte de Saverne

Porte Nationale

Königshoffen

Schiltigheim

To Paris

To Basle

Ill

French removed their observation post from its spire. On 27 August the Palais de Justice burned, along with the city's records.

Yet for all this damage to public buildings in the picturesque old city, the working-class districts suffered most. For Strasburgers, the memory of these nightly bombardments fused into one nightmare: the overwhelming noise and concussion of the guns, the sight and unnerving sound of shells falling through the night sky, the crash of masonry, the screams, whole streets seemingly ablaze and the city a giant furnace. By day, a sulphurous dust-cloud hung over Strasbourg, with only the single spire of the cathedral visible above it.

Every neighbourhood had its victims – children slaughtered in their class-room, women dismembered, shopkeepers buried in the rubble of their premises. Thousands of homeless people sought temporary shelter, but no-where in the city was safe from the guns, not even the hospitals which filled with dreadfully wounded victims, but where chloroform had run out. Doctors noted the prevalence of 'nervous delirium' among traumatized victims. Even in this famous centre of medical learning, a doctor confessed that amputations became little more than butchery. Septicaemia and hospital gangrene added to the high mortality.[5]

Yet none of this produced the quick surrender Werder hoped for. Uhrich rejected his summons on 26 August, and Werder resigned himself to regular siege operations. The Germans opened their first parallel north-west of the city on 29 August, 800 yards from the walls. French sorties on 2 and 3 September failed to disrupt their approaches. The bombardment, though not quite at the level of late August, continued relentlessly, sometimes being audible 30 miles away. On the night of 3 September the sound, mingled with the natural violence of a thunderstorm, struck one Strasburger as so terrible that it seemed almost supernatural.[6]

For the thinly stretched garrison conditions were gruelling. At the front, they could make little effective reply to gunfire which swept their ramparts and redoubts. Nor was there any respite for those returning to the citadel or barracks, which were systematically reduced to rubble. There was a steady attrition of officers. Meanwhile civilian morale dipped. At first Werder (or Mörder – murderer – as Strasburgers nicknamed him) refused requests for women and children to pass through German lines, and when the Bishop of Strasbourg attempted to intercede personally for the city with the Grand Duke of Baden he was rebuffed. Eventually, however, Werder yielded to the entreaties of the President of the Swiss Confederation to allow a Swiss delegation to enter the city on 11 September. Over the following week about 2,000 women, children and old men were taken in wagons to the safety of Switzerland.

The Swiss brought news from outside. News of Sedan scotched fevered rumours and hopes of rescue that had circulated since the siege began.

However, news of the revolution in Paris was welcomed, and precipitated a handover of civil authority. The Bonapartist Prefect and mayor resigned, making way for republicans. Professor Émile Küss, a respected veteran of the 1848 revolution, became mayor. He was supported by a 47-man Municipal Commission which included men from a social class that the old oligarchy would never have admitted. They organized the city's wartime administration very effectively.

While sufficient basic foodstuffs remained, the price of many items rose rapidly. However, 'People's restaurants', run by private restaurateurs but subsidized by the municipality, provided cheap meals for the homeless. Epidemic diseases began to appear among exhausted people forced to spend hot nights fully clothed in crowded, damp, unventilated cellars with poor sanitation. As the usual cemeteries outside the city were out of bounds, people wheeled their dead on barrows to the temporary burial ground in the botanical gardens, where hasty funeral services were frequently interrupted by bursting shells.

To some, further resistance seemed pointless. After demonstrations in August, Uhrich had banned public meetings. He dismissed naïve proposals from some civic leaders to buy off the Germans, and on 18 September forbade the publication of a petition from several members of the Municipal Commission requesting talks with the enemy. He did not intend to be pressured into capitulation by a minority of civilians, and most Strasburgers continued to support him and to respect his authority. On 20 September the new republican Prefect, Edmond Valentin, entered the city by the remarkable feat of crossing German lines under fire and swimming the moat. His rousing proclamations heartened the defence but could not change the hopeless military situation. The Prefecture burned down on the morning of his arrival.

Defying wet weather, the Germans worked day and night in muddy or waterlogged trenches to push their saps forward with remarkable speed and ingenuity. Soon they had zigzagged their way up to the glacis, and fighting reached a crescendo in the third week of September. The bombardment intensified, with 8,000 shells a day being hurled into the city, including giant incendiary shells. Citizens who ventured out during the day had to scurry along under the cover of walls. Firing was also concentrated at one point in the defences. Bastion 11 was pounded with 600 shells on 24 September. Bastion 12 had 467 shells fired into it two days later. In military terms the Germans had opened a 'practicable breach', and the imminent taking of the city by storm would lead to large-scale loss of civilian life. On the 27th Uhrich wrote to Werder notifying him that Strasbourg had reached the limit of its resistance and asking for terms. At 5.00 p.m. the white flag was raised followed, after a moment of incredulity, by German cheers and a spontaneous chorus of *The Watch on the Rhine*.

Inside the city there was an angry, disbelieving demonstration, and shots were fired at the white flag, but the crowd dispersed during the night. Next morning, 28 September, the mood was sullen and resigned. French soldiers, some of them drunk, smashed their rifles and threw them into the moat as they marched out of Strasbourg into captivity. A civilian mob pillaged the remaining military stores, and as 8,000 Germans marched into the city there were incidents, with a few deaths on both sides over succeeding days. Much to the disgust of Strasburgers, occupying troops were soon followed by German civilian sightseers.

For Strasbourg, the price of resistance had been high. The Germans had fired 202,099 shells at the city over five weeks (compared with the 110,286 which Paris, a much larger target, would receive).[7] Whole districts had been laid waste. About one tenth of the city's housing was destroyed or un-inhabitable, and the rest more or less badly damaged. About 10,000 people were homeless and dependent on charity, and a relief commission would be working far into 1872.[8]

The garrison had suffered 2,441 casualties, while inflicting 933 on the Germans.[9] The official civilian death toll was given as 279, but deaths from wounds over subsequent months raised it to 341. The real toll, including deaths from disease and deprivation, was higher still. Between 13 August and 31 December 3,023 Strasburgers died, compared with an average of 967 for the same period in the previous four years. The difference, 2,056, approximates the number of civilians whose deaths could be ascribed directly or indirectly to siege conditions.[10] The bombardment of what Moltke styled 'this German city'[11] left a legacy of hatred amongst most Strasburgers, whose French sentiments were strengthened and were to endure through a generation of German rule. 'Could they have treated more stupidly a people whom they had pretensions of attaching to Germany?' asked one resident bitterly.[12]

The Germans were jubilant at gaining their prize. Envisaging the need to rebuild and thoroughly Germanize the city after 189 years of French rule, the Crown Prince of Prussia noted that 'the capitulation of Strasbourg is a specially important success ... We are now in possession of the capital of Alsace, and need no longer include its surrender among possible conditions of peace.'[13] To the shaken inhabitants, the new German Governor of Alsace put the matter more bluntly in a proclamation of 8 October: 'Strassburg is and will remain a German city.'[14]

Gambetta's Mission

The city of Tours, on the Loire 200 kilometres south-west of Paris, had never been so bustling as in September 1870. Its hotels were full to overflowing with government officials, place hunters, officers soliciting commands, contract seekers and hopeful inventors. The streets teemed with military units from all over France, wearing all manner of flamboyant and outlandish uniforms. Here, as throughout provincial France, patriotism and men willing to defend the country were not lacking; but arms, equipment and time to drill and train new levies were in desperately short supply.

On 13 September Adolphe Crémieux arrived in Tours to represent the new republican national government. He had enjoyed a long and distinguished career at the Paris bar. Born in 1796, his first major oration had been a loyal address to Napoleon I in April 1815, soon after the Emperor's return from Elba. Since then, Crémieux had been a lifelong defender of oppressed minorities and champion of civil liberties, particularly of his own Jewish community, and had briefly served as Justice Minister during the 1848 revolution. Incongruously, he took up residence in the Archbishop's Palace at Tours, where he tried to take the reins of government of a country in the throes of invasion and revolution.

The Paris Government, which included some of his former colleagues at the bar and some, like Gambetta, who had served in his chambers, had despatched Crémieux to Tours as its delegate out of consideration for his age and infirmity. Four days later two more members of the government were sent to reinforce him: another septuagenarian, the lawyer, playwright and journalist Alexandre Glais-Bizoin, and the comparatively youthful 61-year-old Navy Minister, Vice Admiral Fourichon, who at least had command experience and an expertise in ordnance.

Crémieux reacted petulantly to the arrival of his two colleagues, and almost resigned. The three-man Delegation of Tours, or 'The Three Fates' as they were derisively nicknamed, failed to work harmoniously. Around a green baize table heaped with memoranda, files, correspondence and telegrams they bickered their way through long-winded and chaotic meetings. These triumvirs were handicapped by a shortage of administrative personnel and by a lack of national reputation. Crémieux was little known outside Parisian opposition circles; Glais-Bizoin, with his Punchinello face, was nobody's idea of a political heavyweight; and Fourichon who took over the War Ministry had a naval officer's impatience with politicians and was driven to distraction by what he saw as meddling in his department by the other two. Criticism of the supposed 'inaction' of the Delegation soon filled the newspapers. Radical young republicans clamoured for a revolutionary *levée en masse* like the one that had saved beleaguered France in 1792–93. Looking for a ruthless Committee of Public Safety to prosecute the war energetically, critics saw only three elderly gentlemen apparently mired in regulations and lacking the authority and drive necessary to conduct a war of national defence.

In fairness, the military situation faced by the Delegation was daunting in the extreme. By one estimate the number of regular troops immediately available for operations in mid-September, excluding those blockaded in Paris, Metz and other fortresses, amounted to just 24,000 of all arms – not nearly enough for any counterstroke against the Germans.[15] Nevertheless, France still possessed deep wells of manpower which the imperial authorities had taken steps to mobilize during July and August with a view to creating a reserve army behind the Loire. With the politician's penchant for self-promoting partisan bombast, Gambetta later claimed sole credit for raising the Republic's new armies. His achievement was certainly formidable, but his assertion that when he took control of the war effort at Tours on 9 October 'nothing existed' need not be taken at face value.[16] Under the Delegation the War Department continued the work of training and equipping the masses of men who had been mustered, including the Garde Mobile, recruits of the class of 1869, older classes of reservists and previously exonerated men not called up in July, and volunteers. One of the first acts of the new government had been to advance the mobilization date of the 160,000 men of the class of 1870 by three months to 1 October 1870. These sources yielded an impressive number of men nominally in military service in provincial France on that date:[17]

	Available for Duty	In Depots	In Algeria	Total
Regular Army	53,992	205,167	37,279	296,438
Garde Mobile	130,386	102,992	9,778	243,156
Francs-tireurs	8,053			8,053
Total	192,431	308,159	47,057	547,647

Admittedly these figures included tens of thousands of men who were not medically fit or who did not report for duty, but the real problem was that scarcely a fifth of those available had had any previous military training, and that often rudimentary. All had to be formed into temporary regiments. The officers available to command them were mostly elderly men dug out of retirement.

The situation regarding armaments was equally challenging. In theory there were enough rifled cannon in store to arm 296 batteries of six guns each, but lack of horses, harness, caissons and, most of all, gunners, meant that only forty-eight batteries could actually be equipped. As for the infantry, 750,000 Chassepot rifles which France had possessed at the start of the war were either captured or in blockaded cities. Local authorities around the country were demanding Chassepots for the troops they were busily organizing, and were ill content when sent only old rifled muskets converted with a 'snuffbox' breech mechanism. Yet Chassepots could not be mass-produced as easily as muskets in the days of the Revolution. French arsenals could produce only 20,000 per month. Contracts to manufacture more were placed in Birmingham, Liège and elsewhere. Moreover, both the firing pins for the Chassepot and the machinery needed to produce its ammunition had been made at specialist factories in Paris, now beyond reach. Only 2 million rounds of Chassepot ammunition were in reserve out of 100 million held when the war began. Since existing workshops could produce only 3 million rounds per month, new workshops had to be created to fill the required capacity. Eventually, a clock factory at Le Tréport on the Normandy coast was found which had the machinery to make firing pins.[18] Similarly, contracts had to be let for the production of uniforms, boots and all the other equipment that the War Ministry needed in vast quantities and quickly.

The Delegation's troubles were deepened by the political situation it faced in central and southern France. At the news of Sedan revolutionary disturbances had broken out in Lyon, Marseille, Toulouse and other cities, bringing to power republican committees well to the Left of the Government of National Defence. The red flag flew at Lyon, though a fresh insurrection on 28 September by extremists including the Russian anarchist Mikhail Bakunin and a French officer, Gustave Cluseret, was quickly suppressed by the local National Guard. When they were not busy persecuting priests and reactionaries, the radicals in control of southern cities began forming 'Leagues' to organize their own defence, and seethed with impatience at the apparent defeatism and passivity of local garrison commanders. These Leagues proclaimed their belief in the unity and indivisibility of the French Republic, and their zeal to relieve Paris. Yet they embodied decentralizing urges that had been repressed by the imperial regime, and while the central government was preoccupied and unable to exert its authority effectively they saw themselves as alternative centres of power. They would co-operate with the Delegation, but on their own terms.

Confrontation loomed as October began. Admiral Fourichon, who was trying to instil much-needed discipline in the army, was appalled when the Prefect at Lyon demanded authority over the unpopular Military Governor, General Mazure, and Crémieux and Glais-Bizoin promptly granted it. When Fourichon declared that he would wire Mazure not to obey orders given by the local civil authority they shouted him down. Mazure, pursued by an angry mob, was imprisoned by the Prefect. Fourichon thereupon resigned the War Ministry, but remained in the Delegation in his capacity as Navy Minister. Crémieux and Glais-Bizoin tried to cover the War Minister's role, but neither had any military knowledge or experience. Both seemed to think that enthusiastic bands of *francs-tireurs* were all that was needed to beat the Germans, and Glais-Bizoin devoted much time to reviewing such troops.

Another problem demanded the Delegation's attention. They had at first opposed holding elections in the midst of invasion, but had come around to the view that only an elected Assembly could master the radical dissidents in the south and make the government respected. On 1 October they decreed that elections should be held on the 16th, the date originally set by the Paris Government, with whom they had now lost telegraphic communication: for on 27 September the Germans had found and severed the submarine cable recently laid in the Seine.

When a carrier pigeon brought news of the Delegation's decree to Paris the government was aghast, for it had reversed its earlier decision on the need for elections. The rationale for them had been to secure recognition of the government by foreign powers, and to elect an Assembly that could authorize the acceptance of peace terms. However, the failure of Favre's peace talks at Ferrières had transformed the situation. Elections were now seen as a distraction from a war that had to be fought to the finish. Besides, German occupation of several eastern Departments made polling there impracticable. Moreover, while some cabinet members had been confident of the results, others harboured fears that, in the words of the London *Times*, 'if the votes of the French people were now taken, it is more than probable that a majority would be found opposed to the establishment of a Republic'.[19] A conservative Assembly elected in the provinces might be a serious handicap to the conduct of the war by the Paris Government.

In all, it was agreed that a Cabinet member must go to Tours to enforce the government's decision to cancel the elections. But who should go? Favre declined. He saw his place as in Paris, and had no appetite for the hazardous voyage by balloon, which was now the only way out of the besieged capital. With feigned initial reluctance, Gambetta volunteered. His remit was to ensure that the 'political direction' of the Delegation conformed to the wishes of the Paris Government. Gambetta would have the casting vote in the Delegation, and full powers over recruiting and organizing the armed forces.[20] Although military operations would remain the responsibility of the War Minister, Gambetta promised Favre that, 'I shall return with an army, and if I reap the glory of delivering Paris, I shall ask nothing more of destiny.'[21] He prepared to depart as soon as a persistent fog cleared and the wind stirred.

The science of ballooning in France was in its ninth decade, but no effective means had yet been found of steering a balloon after its launch. Nonetheless, balloons were the only viable means of carrying mail from the capital to the provinces, so the government entered into contracts with private operators. The first successful balloon flight of the siege was made on 23 September. The deserted Gare du Nord and Gare d'Orléans became balloon factories and, as no return flights were possible, the navy began training picked men as pilots.

After three days of cancellations, the fog cleared on the morning of 7 October. Wrapped in a fur cloak and sporting a fur cap, Léon Gambetta, bearded, barrel-chested and blind in one eye from a childhood accident, climbed into the basket rigged beneath the gas-filled yellow globe of *L'Armand-Barbès*. After its launch from the Place Saint-Pierre on the hill of Montmartre, watched by a large crowd, the balloon hovered perilously low over German lines before drifting north-eastward. Two attempted landings had to be aborted when German patrols appeared and opened fire. Eventually the balloon landed in a tree near Épineuse, west of Compiègne. Gambetta suffered a grazed hand, which republican newspapers enthusiastically attributed to a Prussian bullet. That night he reached Amiens, then made the circuitous trip to Tours by train, telegraphing ahead to announce his coming. At Rouen he paused to make a rousing speech to the National Guard, calling upon every man to do his duty and declaring, 'If we cannot make a pact with victory, let us make a pact with death.'[22] His audience hailed him as a saviour and gave him an ovation, and he was again acclaimed when he reached Tours on the 9th.

The triumvirs resentfully saw that their days of power were over. Tactfully but firmly Gambetta informed them that the elections were cancelled, making it clear that he was now head of the Delegation. As he had done on 4 September in seizing the Interior Ministry, he rapidly saw and took another opportunity, even if it exceeded his instructions from the Cabinet. With Fourichon's support, he took over the War Ministry, thus concentrating civil and military power in his own hands.

During the invasion of 1792 France had found a bold, eloquent leader in Danton. In October 1870 she had at last found another in the 32-year-old son of a Genoese immigrant who ran a successful grocery business in Cahors. Gambetta, who because of his paternity had formally to take French citizenship in 1859, was energetic, determined, boundlessly self-confident and steeped in revolutionary legend. With his arrival the war entered a new phase, and for the first time on the French side would be directed with unrelenting vigour.

Artenay and Orléans

On the day of his arrival in Tours, Gambetta issued a proclamation to French citizens announcing his determination to 'turn to account all our resources, which are immense'. France must 'shake off the torpor of our country regions, put an end to foolish panics, intensify partisan warfare and, against an enemy fertile in ambushes and surprises, set traps, harass his flanks, make surprise attacks on his rear, and at last inaugurate a national war ... It is not possible that the spirit of France should be stifled forever ... Therefore let us rise up in mass, and die rather than suffer the shame of the dismemberment of the country.'[23] Yet over the next two days, even as this stirring rhetoric was being read and digested, France suffered two more defeats and the loss of a major city.

After establishing the blockade of Paris, the Germans had sent cavalry out west and south of the city to requisition food, cut railways and protect their rear. In late September a cavalry division under the King's nephew, Prince Albrecht, probed southward through the fertile but monotonous and sparsely populated ploughed lands of the Beauce region towards Orléans, 110 kilometres south of the capital. As they approached they met unexpectedly spirited resistance from French cavalry and isolated bands of Gardes Mobiles and *francs-tireurs*. Growing apprehensive, the Germans pulled back.

Ironically, they had created sufficient alarm in Orléans to cause the French garrison to withdraw precipitately on 27 September – not the first or last instance in this war of timid generals beating a hasty retreat from each other. Once the danger had abated the French returned to Orléans. Sitting on the north bank of the River Loire where its northerly loop brings it closest to the capital, the city was a road and railway hub of great strategic value, being the obvious bridgehead for any French attempt to relieve Paris. A new commander, 66-year-old veteran General Édouard de la Motte-Rouge, was sent to command the newly-formed 15 Corps which was organizing south of Orléans. He was under pressure to take the offensive as soon as possible in order to protect the city and relieve Paris.

Concerned at reports of French troop concentrations south of the Loire, Moltke took defensive measures. Having completed their work around Sedan, General von der Tann's I Bavarian Corps and General von Wittich's 22nd Division of XI Corps had marched down to join Third Army south of Paris. On 6 October these troops, supported by three cavalry divisions, were set in motion southward across the Beauce. The force under Tann's command totalled 28,000 infantry, 11,000 cavalry and 160 guns.

An incident during their advance illustrated the growing ruthlessness of the war. On the rainy night of 7 October a squadron of hussars from Schleswig-Holstein and a company of Bavarian infantry billeted themselves in the town of Ablis. In the small hours they were surprised by a troop of French *francs-tireurs*, who killed or wounded a dozen Germans and captured sixty-eight before withdrawing. Learning of the surprise from fugitives, the 6th Cavalry Division under General von Schmidt returned to Ablis in force. Six French civilians were killed, twenty-two inhabitants were taken hostage and threatened with death if the German prisoners were not returned and, in the terse phrase of the German official account, 'the place was laid under a contribution and reduced to ashes'. When Bismarck heard of this action he thoroughly approved.[24]

Later that day, 8 October, Tann received orders from Third Army Headquarters to press southward, occupying Orléans and clearing the French from the surrounding region. To meet this threat, General de la Motte-Rouge had on paper nearly 60,000 men of 15 Corps at his command around Orléans.[25] In reality, scarcely 25,000 were ready, and these were 'badly armed, badly equipped' and 'reduced for the most part to carrying in their pockets the few cartridges they could be given'.[26] In trying to funnel these troops from south of the city to its north, bottlenecks developed on the railways and chaos ensued. By nightfall on 9 October French troops north of the Loire were still widely dispersed. Although better defensive positions existed closer to the city, about 10,000 were directed to the crossroads of Artenay, 20 kilometres north of Orléans on the main road to Paris. This was a dangerously exposed position in the face of a superior German force.

On the damp, cold, misty morning of 10 October the French were attacked at Artenay by 14,000 Germans. For five hours the contest was stubborn, but with the Germans bringing 102 guns to bear against just sixteen on the French side there could be but one outcome. By mid-afternoon the German cavalry had lapped around the French flanks to form a great semi-circle around their enemy. Under a demoralizing hail of fire, the French retreat became a rout. Three cannon, sunk up to their hubs in mud, had to be abandoned, together with tents and equipment. French losses were around 1,500, including 800 prisoners. The Germans had suffered 224 casualties,[27] but pushed on next morning, confident of meeting no further opposition before reaching Orléans. In the event, a more obstinate and bloody fight awaited them.

Fearing that Orléans was vulnerable to encirclement by an enemy crossing the Loire above and below it, La Motte-Rouge concluded that he could not hold the city. He prepared to evacuate it and march south, but left 13,000 men to defend its northern approaches: too few for a prolonged defence, but rather too many for a mere rearguard action. Throughout the fine autumn day of 11 October this force made use of the cover provided by villages, vineyards, walls and hedgerows. When driven into the city's suburbs it fought tenaciously behind a railway embankment, in the station of Les Aubrais and the buildings of the nearby gasworks. Moltke paid this rearguard a back-handed compliment, writing that 'In the open field, where skilful handling of masses is possible, it would soon have been defeated; but in street-fighting unflinching personal courage is all that is needed in the defender, and the latest recruits of the newly created French levies did not lack that attribute.'[28] The 5th Battalion of the Foreign Legion defended the village of Les Aydes with a ferocity that reminded the Bavarian attackers of their experience in the ill-fated village of

Bazeilles at Sedan six weeks earlier.[29] Finally though the Germans infiltrated gaps in the French defensive line, taking it in rear, and at dusk they poured through into the cobbled streets and squares of Orléans, where they camped for the night. At a cost of 932 casualties they had killed or wounded perhaps 700 Frenchmen and captured 1,800. Less than a fortnight after the fall of Strasbourg they had captured another historic French city, together with its marshalling yards, ten locomotives and sixty wagons.[30] The French army had disappeared southwards under cover of darkness.

The New Leadership
When Gambetta heard the news of Orléans he instantly dismissed La Motte-Rouge, without even verifying a false report from a political source that the old general had abandoned his men. Gambetta intended to make an example of failed generals, in the spirit of both the French revolutionaries and the Prussian army. His belief that many imperial generals were defeatist reactionaries not up to their job was only strengthened. It was shared by the civilian he appointed to be his Deputy War Minister, who henceforward would be in day-to-day control of the military effort.

Charles de Freycinet, a gifted 42-year-old mining engineer and a committed republican, had sought appointment as a Prefect in a south-western Department following the revolution of 4 September. However, the fact that he had held a minor political post under the Second Empire made him suspect to local radicals, who ousted him. He then offered his services at Tours, where his administrative grasp, diligence and sharp intelligence commended themselves to Crémieux, who recommended him to Gambetta. Freycinet soon earned his new master's confidence, and between them they supplied the directing will and energy that the war effort had been lacking. Within days a succession of decrees poured from Freycinet's office.

Freycinet had been impressed by the citizen armies raised to fight the American Civil War, and he determined to apply the same formula in France. He began by rationalizing the multiplicity of military organizations that had so complicated the war effort. The Garde Mobile, the National Guard and independent volunteer units were all grouped into an Auxiliary Army, which was assimilated to the regular army for the duration of the war. These combined forces would be known as the Army of National Defence (decree of 14 October). For the sake of discipline and effectiveness, all *franc-tireur* companies were placed under military command. Those refusing to accept this would be disarmed and disbanded (decree of 4 November). The normal rules of promotion were suspended for the duration of the war, allowing men of any age or background – including civilians – to be appointed to command. Temporary promotions could be retained after the war only if merited by conspicuous bravery in action (decree of 13 October). Officers allowing their troops to be surprised by the enemy would be court-martialled (decree of 14 October). All Departments within 100 kilometres of the enemy must be put on a war footing by local defence committees, and supplies must be put beyond the enemy's reach (decrees of 14 and 22 October). Already, on 29 September, the Delegation had conscripted all fit single men between the ages of 21 and 40 not yet in military service and made them liable to serve in field battalions of the National Guard. A decree of 2 November extended conscription within that age group to the hitherto exempt married men and widowers with children. Eleven training camps for assembling and drilling the new men were designated around the country (decree of 25 November).[31] Thus under the pressure of invasion France had by stages adopted universal military obligation, which she had strongly resisted in the last years of the Empire.

Simultaneously Freycinet set about reorganizing all the services of the military administration, appointing commissions of experts – military or civilian – to make them fit for purpose. Great resourcefulness was brought to this task. For instance, to remedy the desperate shortage of maps, a photographer in Tours was commissioned to make thousands of copies of those that existed for supply to commanders. An intelligence bureau was created to process information about the enemy that was to be gathered by the civil authorities. Frédéric Steenackers, the Director of Posts and Telegraphs, had lines laid to every general's headquarters. Under the capable direction of Colonel Thoumas, 1,400 cannon were manufactured between 10 October and the end of the war.

Unsurprisingly, amid these formidable efforts to sustain the war, mistakes were made. Gambetta and Freycinet put their faith in mass, and were unduly optimistic as to the fighting potential of the citizen National Guard. Many of the 500,000 men raised in the provinces could not be put to effective use. An unsophisticated exemptions system meant that mobilization sometimes disrupted war industries. Furthermore, the historical precedents that inspired Gambetta proved to be mirages in some respects, concealing harsh truths about the limits to what republican enthusiasm could achieve. In 1792–93 France had faced invaders who were disunited and hesitant and enjoyed no technological superiority in weaponry. The situation in 1870 was starkly different. The citizen armies of America so admired by Freycinet had been able to draw on a strong state militia system and had faced opponents as green as themselves. Even then they had to undergo many months of training and some harsh experiences before they could campaign effectively. By contrast, Gambetta's raw levies would have to be thrown straight against Germany's well trained and battle-hardened veterans. Old army officers were horrified by what many saw as ignorant civilian meddling and blunders, and by their own subordination to men whose politics they detested. They were affronted by the appointment of a swarm of civilian careerists, adventurers and downright charlatans to command troops, sometimes over the heads of better qualified officers of the regular army. As had been the case in America, many such officers proved totally unfit to lead men into battle.

On the procurement side too there would be much to criticize. To make up her shortage of rifles, carbines, swords, pistols and bayonets, France had to look not only to her own state arsenals and private industry but to purchases abroad: to Britain, Belgium, Austria, Italy, Switzerland, and especially to the United States, which had huge stocks of weapons left over from the Civil War. The Armaments Commission purchased over a million weapons, but some of its purchases were ill-advised and ill-co-ordinated, and obsolete firearms were all too willingly offloaded by some foreign vendors. Over forty different types of gun were purchased, with consequent complications when it came to supplying ammunition to troops in the field. More than half these weapons were still in warehouses at French ports at the end of the war.[32]

Gambetta, short of funds, would happily have paid for the war effort by simply printing money, but the Bank of France rejected such an inflationary expedient. Instead it advanced funds, and in addition a loan of 250 million francs at 7 per cent was negotiated in London from the American banker Morgan. Gambetta also obliged local authorities to meet some of the expense of equipping troops. Even so, with the war costing 10 million francs per day the national debt began mounting alarmingly. After the war, parliamentary commissions packed with conservatives would take satisfaction in detailing all the errors, flawed contracts and money wasted that could be laid to the account of the Delegation of Tours.

Yet, with the enemy besieging the capital, Gambetta and Freycinet were prepared to stamp on toes and trample convention to galvanize the war effort and arouse popular support for the struggle, which remained generally high during September and October. They pointed out that even had there been time to check the credentials of everyone who applied for an officer's commission, they had no access to the War Ministry's personnel records, which were still in Paris. They faced a chronic shortage of junior officers, even after doubling the size of infantry companies to 200 men and enlarging regiments by a third to a strength of 3,600. And if bad appointments undeniably were made, there were also some very good ones, and the aim of promoting younger, more committed and vigorous men to command was achieved. Thus men who had been junior officers or NCOs in the regular army found themselves commanding companies, regiments, brigades and divisions in the Auxiliary Army.

Naval officers discovered new talents for leading infantry units and performed admirably.

Moreover, despite Gambetta's frequent attacks on the record of the imperial regime and his constant identification of the Republic with the cause of national defence, he was prepared to take leaders wherever he found them. In the French phrase, he made arrows from every kind of wood. He retained some imperial generals against the advice of his supporters. As Crémieux had welcomed Cathelineau's royalist and Catholic volunteers from the Vendée, much to the horror of pure republicans, so Gambetta welcomed the Papal Zouaves under Charette and gave commissions to other royalists who viewed the Republic only as an expedient. At the other extreme, though with misgivings, he welcomed Italian and other foreign volunteers led by the radical hero Garibaldi and his warrior sons, who had landed at Marseille on 7 October to enthusiastic acclaim.

With the unruly radicals of the southern cities Gambetta used a mixture of firmness and conciliation. His republican credentials lent him authority, and the radicals could hardly complain now that the war lacked energetic direction. To replace the troublesome Prefect of Marseille Alphonse Esquiros, the President of the Southern League and a complaisant tool of the extremists, he sent a more reliable nominee, Alphonse Gent. Surviving an assassination attempt and facing down extremist threats, Gent restored order and was welcomed as a liberator by most citizens. France was in no doubt as to who was the master and, having reasserted the authority of the central government, Gambetta could turn his energies to the relief of Paris.

Châteaudun

After General von der Tann's capture of Orléans on 11 October, the German high command urged him to push on southward to capture Bourges and threaten Tours, so breaking up French attempts to form a new army and disrupting the new government. However, Tann had misgivings about marching so far into enemy territory through wooded, difficult country against hostile forces of unknown strength. If his comparatively small force ran into difficulties against the fortifications of Bourges he would be far from any help, and if he were forced to withdraw the French could claim a victory. He deemed it wiser to remain at Orléans and make himself secure there. The high command accepted his judgement, but ordered him in that case to send back Wittich's 22nd Division, comprising regiments from Thuringia and Hesse, and the 4th Cavalry Division. These troops should not come back to Paris by the direct route but make a detour to the west to clear out French garrisons at Châteaudun and Chartres. They set off on 17 October.

Guerrilla activity on their flanks had continued to annoy the Germans. On 14 October two German cavalry squadrons had been fired on by the National Guard of the villages of Varize and Civry, with the usual consequences: on 15 October the Germans pillaged then burned both villages, killing several inhabitants.[33] The Germans had a particular score to settle with Châteaudun, because it was the base of the Francs-tireurs de Paris under Major Count Ernest de Lipowski, who had been responsible for the surprise raid at Ablis ten days earlier. Lipowski, a former officer of light infantry, had succeeded in imposing his will on his volunteers and in shaping them into a well-disciplined and effective military unit – a most unusual feat amongst *francs-tireurs*, who elected their own officers. His 700 men were joined by *francs-tireurs* from Nantes and Cannes and the National Guard of Châteaudun under Commandant Testanière, a retired cavalry captain. In all, Châteaudun had about 1,300 defenders, but they had no cavalry or artillery.

At the first tidings of the capture of Orléans, Lipowski had advised the town council that the defence of Châteaudun against a large German force would be impossible: 'A few of the enemy would be killed, but without useful purpose for the national defence, and the town would be ravaged and burned.'[34] On the night of 12 October he began to withdraw his men and the National Guard was disarmed. Next morning, everyone recovered their resolve. The town council called Lipowski back, the National Guard were given back their rifles, and Châteaudun was put in a state of defence with barricades of stones, sandbags and timber blocking the entrances to the town. When the bloody corpse of a German cavalryman was paraded around town there were jeers and exultation which horrified more diffident citizens.

Some believed the danger had passed when suddenly, shortly before midday on 18 October, lookouts in a church tower saw masses of Germans advancing from the east down the main road from Orléans and rang the bells to give the alarm. The French began firing from a farm on the outskirts of town and from behind a railway embankment. Though slow to deploy, by 2.00 p.m. the Germans had fought their way to the edge of town. Hours of intense street-fighting followed. Wittich's artillery fired over 2,000 shells into the town during the afternoon, but progress in house-to-house fighting was slow. Only at dusk did the Germans succeed in turning the barricades. By 7.00 p.m., with the 8,000-strong German force near completing its encirclement of the town, Lipowski withdrew with some 300 of his men. Unaware of his departure, the remainder stayed on with Testanière's National Guard and fought it out 'with the stubbornness of despair'.[35] Even after the Germans had reached the main square, the French continued to resist in side-streets, in places nerving themselves by intoning the *Marseillaise* as darkness and the enemy closed in around them.

Even before this savage struggle had died away, the Germans had begun to pillage and burn the conquered town. Paul Montarlot recorded the scenes that followed:

> In an instant doors were smashed in with axes, windows broken, the inhabitants threatened, beaten, pushed out at bayonet point and forced to flee. Fires were started in every building, several of which were not yet empty ... At the Rose Inn in the Rue de Chartres, the Prussians set fire to the bed of a 70-year-old man who, being para-lyzed, perished in the flames. A few yards away, they hammered on the door of a retired captain, Michau, and when the indignant old man confronted them shot him dead. The captain fell back into the arms of a relative, who laid him in an armchair: but fire soon en-gulfed the house, and next day only the charred bones of the victim remained, which I saw being gathered up. At the Grand-Monarque Hotel the soldiers ate and drank from 7.00 p.m. At 11.00 p.m., dis-regarding the desperate entreaties of the proprietor, who had had to bear their demands patiently, they set fire to the hotel by igniting the curtains of the rooms and piles of linen which they had heaped up. In the Route de Vendôme they forced an old man to bring them a lighted candle, and set alight the curtains of his bed before his eyes.[36]

The red glow of Châteaudun burning lit the surrounding area as if it were daylight, and a westerly wind fanned the blaze. Nearly 200 houses were torched: in all 235 were completely destroyed, and the town suffered 5 million francs worth of damage. The Germans took whatever they wanted from the town and destroyed what they did not, sometimes with fastidious thorough-ness. A German doctor billeted on Doctor Anthoine after the battle took his pick of his host's instruments, then broke or bent the rest.[37] Paul Montarlot found the Saxon bandsmen billeted on him decent enough men, homesick fathers of families who wanted the war to end so that they could go home, but, in the way of troops down the ages, they took whatever they needed when they left, down to his blankets and razors.[38]

The fighting had cost each side about 100 men. At least a dozen civilians were asphyxiated in cellars as their houses burned. The Germans took about 150 prisoners.[39]

When news of Châteaudun's dire fate spread it caused great excitement and indignation. Paris extolled the self-sacrifice of republican heroes and named a street for the town. Gambetta decreed that the town had 'deserved well of the country'.[40] Lipowski was promoted to lieutenant colonel and Châteaudun's status as a symbol of national resistance was recognized in 1877 when it was allowed to incorporate the Legion of Honour in its coat of arms. Yet Châteaudun was noted because its heroic bitter-end defence was untypical, and an example more often honoured than emulated. Undoubtedly German methods had their effect. Three days after the destruction of Châteaudun, Wittich's men moved on to Chartres where they made a show of encircling the town. Although there were 7,000 troops inside the city, the civic authorities decided against resistance. An agreement was made whereby the French garrison marched out to the west as German troops entered the city. The German high command, concerned by continuing reports of enemy activity to the west, decided that they should stay in the vicinity rather than return to Paris.

The War in the East

In eastern France too the Germans were plagued by guerrilla attacks. On 30 August one small French group had even created alarm in Baden by a raid across the Rhine. While General Werder was besieging Strasbourg he had to detach columns to deal with guerrilla raids in his rear by independent bands operating from towns in mountainous Upper (southern) Alsace.

French guerrilla activity would have been much more effective had it been properly co-ordinated. From Paris the new War Minister, General Le Flô, saw possibilities for attacks against German lines of communication and, just before the siege of the capital began, designated General Albert Cambriels to take command at Belfort and to co-ordinate all French forces in the south-eastern theatre of war with a view to an offensive against them. Cambriels was suffering agonies from a head wound he had taken at Sedan: an injury so severe that the Germans had not bothered to keep him a prisoner. He reached Belfort on 23 September and set about trying to organize the groups of Gardes Mobiles, National Guard and *francs-tireurs* scattered throughout the region into a force that could strike the Paris–Strasbourg railway, which was vital to the Germans. Captain Varaigne, commanding at Épinal, had already planned a raid to destroy the Lutzelbourg tunnel near Saverne, but the Germans got wind of the attempt and increased their guard. Nevertheless, a larger French force might find promising opportunities.

Unfortunately for Cambriels, the Germans got their blow in first. As soon as Strasbourg fell Werder was tasked with advancing south-westwards across the Vosges Mountains to drive French forces away from the key railway lines, and if possible to secure the railway that ran through Chaumont, Langres and Épinal to provide extra capacity for supplying the forces besieging Paris. A division of fresh troops that had been guarding the North German coast against the possible French landing that had been feared in the summer was brought down to lay siege to the towns of Sélestat and Neuf-Brisach, guerrilla bases in Upper Alsace. Meanwhile Werder's Baden Division and other troops who had been besieging Strasbourg, totalling 36,000 men and now designated XIV Corps, struck across the Vosges, heading first for St Dié.

Seeing the threat, Cambriels called for reinforcements, and Dupré's Brigade of 15 Corps was rushed by rail from the Loire theatre to bar the German advance. On the foggy morning of 6 October it collided with the German vanguard at the village of Nompatelize in the hills above the Meurthe valley north-west of St Dié. The battle, named for the nearby town of La Bourgonce, was a hard-fought seven-hour contest, pitching 9,500 Frenchmen with six guns against 7,000 Germans with ten guns. Amidst charge and counter-charge among blazing hillside villages it was the Germans who received reinforcements as evening came and won the day at a cost of 436 casualties against 846 French, half of whom were prisoners.[41]

Cambriels reached the front next day, intending to use this difficult, heavily forested country to contest the German passage of the Vosges. The reality was that Werder's forces were too strong. They advanced on a broad front, overwhelming opposition, burning villages and shooting inhabitants where they met resistance. By 11 October, with his flanks threatened, Cambriels judged that he was facing 'disaster and complete ruin' if he did not get his ragtag army of 15,000 men away quickly.[42] He decided to trade territory for time. Resisting the temptation to seek safety in Belfort, where he would have been besieged, he broke contact and withdrew over 120 kilometres southward to the entrenched camp of Besançon, destroying bridges behind him. In truth his men had become little more than a mob. They were exhausted, poorly shod, and soaked through by driving rain and snow. Because they had no haversacks, their rations of army biscuit threaded on string and slung over their shoulders had disintegrated in the rain, leaving them hungry. Because they had no cartridge-pouches their paper cartridges had become sodden and unusable.[43] By the time Cambriels' raw troops reached Besançon they were unruly and mutinous, and drunkenness was rife.

Cambriels was suffering terribly from icy snow entering his wound, but he received little sympathy. Threats were made against his life. Patriotic republicans, believing that every inch of French territory must be defended, denounced this suspect imperial general to the government. The Prefect of the Doubs wired Tours on 16 October: 'Is he mad? ... Is he incompetent or culpable? ... Should he be put on trial?'[44] Gambetta took the train to Besançon to see for himself. On 18 October he listened to Cambriels explain the need to discipline, instruct and equip his troops before attempting another offensive. Gambetta urged an early advance, but was sufficiently convinced to leave Cambriels in command. Over the next ten days the general made headway in organizing what would become the French 20 Corps, and was contemplating a new advance when his head wound re-opened. On 28 October he resigned his command.

Werder had been in no great hurry to pursue the French. He occupied Épinal, where he found the railway destroyed, and wanted to drive westward until repeated urgings came from Moltke to resume the pursuit of the enemy. Contact was re-established with some sharp skirmishes along the banks of the River Ognon, north of Besançon, which made Werder wary of launching a direct attack. While weighing his next move he sent reconnaissance patrols probing westwards towards Dijon, the capital of Burgundy.

The German approach alarmed the civil authorities in Dijon, who decided on 28 October that the ill-prepared garrison of the city should evacuate, and that the National Guard should be disarmed. When this news reached Werder, the temptation to seize such a prize proved irresistible. He ordered two brigades of the Baden Division to advance on Dijon. Yet the city had a change of heart, just as had happened at Châteaudun. Citizens took up arms and fired at German patrols while the few French troops who had not gone beyond reach were rushed back to Dijon by rail. On 30 October 3,600 of them under General Fauconnet, a recently promoted colonel of gendarmes, held head against 12,000 Germans. Fauconnet was mortally wounded in the stomach, but the defence was sufficiently determined to give Werder second thoughts about continuing the assault. During the night, however, the civil authorities sent a white flag into German lines, and terms of surrender were agreed. Next day Werder's men marched into Dijon, a base that could provide all their requirements. Just over a month after their capture of Strasbourg, they had established themselves in the heart of France, driving all opposition before them.

Werder's campaign had succeeded in pushing organized French forces well away from the railways the Germans needed to sustain their siege of Paris. Meanwhile in his rear the German grip on Alsace tightened when Sélestat, invested on 11 October, fell on the 24th, and Neuf-Brisach, besieged since 7 October, fell on 10 November.

Here, as elsewhere in the east, the length of time that poorly maintained and equipped French fortresses could hold out behind German lines depended not only upon the determination of the garrison commander but on the morale of the civilian population. Discouragement at news of French defeats elsewhere often made civilians reluctant to sacrifice their city. The testing time came when the Germans had brought up enough heavy guns for a sustained bombardment. Under this ordeal not all commanders waited for a breach to be made in their walls; and several failed, or were unable, to destroy their armaments before surrender. This was a boon to the Germans, who had a limited number of heavy guns. Thus Toul was shelled with the help of French guns captured at Marsal; the bombardment of Soissons was supported by ten

French mortars captured at Toul, while the guns targeting Verdun included French cannon taken from Sedan and Toul.

In Lorraine, Phalsbourg, besieged since 10 August, and Bitche, bombarded since 24 August, were still holding out. But the key fortresses for the Germans were those that blocked important sections of railway, and these began falling into their hands. Toul, besieged from 19 August, fell on 23 September after 4,241 shells had landed in it. Soissons, besieged from 14 September, fell on 15 October. Verdun, besieged since 24 August, surrendered on 8 November. In the case of Metz, the Germans built a section of railway to bypass the blockaded city.

Thus, by railway and road, the stream of men, munitions, rations and supplies between Germany and the armies besieging Paris kept flowing. Certainly there were frequent interruptions and difficulties, and limitations on capacity were a source of irritation to Moltke. Aided by a 'bitterly hostile' population, guerrillas frequently achieved surprise in attacks on German guard posts spaced out along the railways, and disappeared before more troops could arrive.[45] It was not safe for the Germans to run trains by night, and even by day they resorted to forcing local dignitaries whom they had taken hostage to ride on locomotives to deter ambushes. When sabotage occurred they took draconian measures against nearby communities. Large numbers of *Landwehr* troops were required to guard hundreds of kilometres of vulnerable track, and constant effort was needed to maintain the railways. There was a shortage of labour, and reluctant French workers were requisitioned.

Yet, for all this, the Germans kept their grip upon their lines of communication, failing which the siege of Paris would have had to have been abandoned. What was more, at the end of October they took a mighty stride closer to ultimate victory with the capture of the greatest fortress of eastern France – the city of Metz.

Chapter 3

The Enigma of Metz

Blockade

Having fought two huge battles west of Metz under the bronze skies of August, France's first line army had fallen back to its entrenched camp around that great military city. After losses, its combat strength was about 140,000. On 20 August, two days after the Battle of Gravelotte-Saint-Privat, the German First and Second Armies under the command of the King's nephew, Prince Friedrich Karl, had completed their investment of the place. Even though the six great forts protecting the city were incomplete, their heavy guns were sufficient to deter the Germans from a frontal assault. Steep-sided Mont Saint-Quentin, which dominated the city from the west, remained in French hands. The Germans, 170,000 strong, resorted to the spade, beginning three defensive lines around 48 kilometres of front.

Within a few days French troops, rested and re-equipped, expected another battle. Both materially and morally, wrote a lieutenant in the 6th Regiment, 'we were all ready to resume the campaign'.[1] After all, they were France's best regular troops, and still believed that they could beat the Germans in the open field. Their commander, Marshal Achille Bazaine, was on the other hand reluctant to leave the protection of the Metz forts. On learning of the advance of Marshal MacMahon's army to support him, Bazaine had ordered an offensive on the east bank of the Moselle for 26 August. 'My aim,' he explained, 'was to draw the enemy's forces to that bank, and, if the battle went in our favour, to take advantage of it to continue towards Thionville.'[2] But his approach march was abysmally managed, torrential rain began to fall, and in the midst of the operation Bazaine decided to call his corps commanders to a council of war. In the ruined Grimont château as rain lashed down his generals listened as General Soleille, commanding the army's artillery, urged the reasons for staying in Metz that he had rehearsed to Bazaine earlier. To evacuate the city, argued Soleille, was to sacrifice it and Lorraine to the Germans. If the government had to negotiate peace, then continued French possession of the city would be an important asset. Crucially, he claimed that the army had only enough artillery rounds for one battle. If it risked breaking through enemy lines German forces would set upon it in open country 'like a pack of hounds after a stag'. Better both politically and militarily, therefore, to keep the army intact. Soleille went on to argue that, using Metz as its base, the army could usefully mount raids against German lines of communication; though how it would accomplish this without first breaking out he did not explain.

Soleille's information was misleading. The army had over 100,000 artillery shells, ample for four large battles, and abundant Chassepot ammunition, but his advice had a discouraging effect on his colleagues. The council of war, like the others that Bazaine would call, perfectly illustrated Napoleon I's maxim that such meetings 'will terminate in the adoption of the worst course, which, in war, is always the most timid; or, if you will, the most prudent'.[3] General Frossard, commanding 2 Corps, fearing that a retreat would degenerate into a rout, agreed that the offensive should be called off. Marshal Canrobert, commanding 6 Corps, thought that the army 'must not be compromised by an offensive', but should keep the enemy under pressure by continual raids. Marshal Le Bœuf, the former imperial War Minister now commanding 3 Corps, considered that 'To conserve the army intact is the great and best service we could render the country, but how can it be done without food supplies?' General Bourbaki, commanding the Imperial Guard, wanted a breakout, but like Ladmirault of 4 Corps conceded that insufficient ammunition would make one impossible.

General Coffinières, the army's chief engineer and commander of the Metz garrison, insisted that on its own the fortress could not hold out more than a fortnight. Therefore the army should stay and protect it. The decision rested with Bazaine, who seemingly had already made up his mind. He concluded that his army was performing a great service by pinning down large numbers of enemy troops, 'giving time for France to organize resistance'.[4] He cancelled the offensive. Disorganized, soaked to the skin and baffled, his troops blundered their way back to their encampments in the dark.

On 29 and 30 August Bazaine received confirmation of the approach of MacMahon's army – an eventuality that had not even been discussed on the 26th. He ordered another offensive east of the Moselle for the 31st, but once again deployment was protracted for hours while the Germans watched the leisurely spectacle and put their reserves in motion for the threatened sector. It was late afternoon before the ill-co-ordinated French assault began. Although the troops achieved some of their objectives with élan, the offensive petered out in the dark. Bazaine showed not the slightest sense of urgency or determination to reinforce success before retiring for the night. Next morning, 1 September, despite a fog that could have favoured the French, he gave characteristically ambiguous orders that allowed for retreat, while the Germans counter-attacked with equally characteristic vigour. The Battle of Noisseville or Servigny ended with the French back where they started, less 3,547 casualties to the German 2,978.[5] Surprise, good staff work and more resolute leadership might not have guaranteed success, but assuredly would have given the French a much better fighting chance, and might have allowed a significant portion of the army to break through while leaving sufficient men to defend Metz. After 1 September the French would never be so strong, nor the Germans so weak on the eastern bank.

After the battle Bazaine occasionally spoke of the possibility of another sortie, but did not act on the idea. One week later news began to filter through of the destruction of MacMahon's army at Sedan. As part of a prisoner exchange on 6 September Friedrich Karl deliberately sent captives from MacMahon's army into Metz to spread the demoralizing news, and details were garnered from various sources over the next few days. There was no longer an army of rescue. Bazaine waited until 16 September, when the news was already well known, to announce officially to the army in measured terms the Emperor's capture and the change of government:

> Our obligations to the country in its peril remain the same. Let us therefore continue to serve her with the same devotion and the same energy, defending her territory against the foreigner, and the social order against evil passions.[6]

Initially he ordered imperial symbols to be removed from the army's stationery, but changed his mind four days later, convinced that the Empire remained the legal government of France. He and his generals had sworn their loyalty to the Emperor, by whom they had been well rewarded. They regarded the revolution in Paris in the midst of an enemy invasion as a criminal insurrection led by a few radical lawyers who were known opponents of the army. They despised Trochu as a disloyal schemer who had failed to protect the Empress. Bazaine regarded the attempt to defend Paris as 'an absurdity', and the French high command in Metz had no faith in the capacity of hastily raised and ill-trained levies to mount any serious resistance.[7] If, as Bazaine expected, Paris fell before Metz, it seemed all the more important to him to preserve his fine army as the last constituted force in France that could negotiate terms with the enemy and perhaps 'restore order' in the country.[8]

On 12 September Bazaine reiterated at a council of war that there would be no further attempt to break out; only raids to gather food from nearby villages and keep the troops fit. Yet such raids were slow to materialize. The first, at Lauvallier east of the city on 22 September, achieved modest success, but put the Germans on their guard. A further effort next day bore no fruit. On the 27th a raid south-eastwards towards Peltre failed to achieve surprise and the

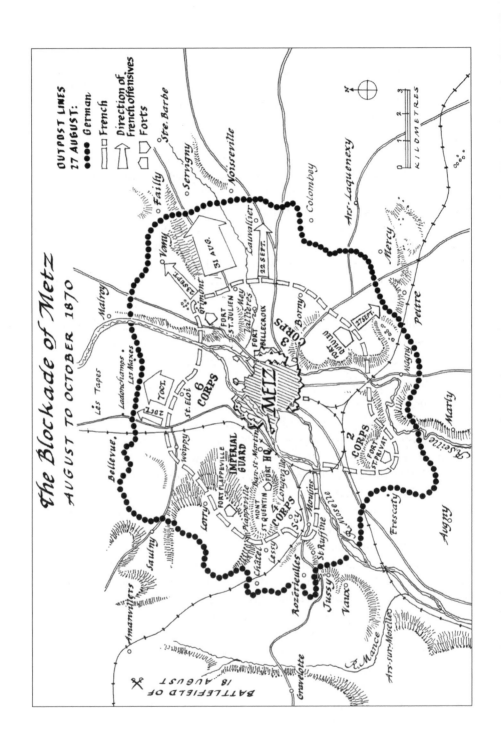

The Blockade of Metz

AUGUST TO OCTOBER 1870

OUTPOST LINES
27 AUGUST:
●●● German
⊏⊐ French
⇑ Direction of
French offensives
⬠ Forts

N

0 1 2 3
KILOMETRES

Ste. Barbe
Noisseville
Failly
Serigny
Lauvallier
Colombey
31 AUG.
23 SEPT.
22 SEPT.
27 SEPT.
Vrémy
Grimont
Fort
St. Julien
La Tières
May
Fort
BELLECROIX
Borny
Ars-Laquenexy
Mercy
Peltre
Fort
QUEULEU
Malroy
3 CORPS
Les Tapes
Ladonchamps
Les Maxes
Metz
Nouilly
Marly
2 OCT.
1 OCT.
St. Eloi
6
CORPS
Moselle
2
CORPS
FORT
ST. PRIVAT
Wagny
R. Seille
Bellevue
Woippy
FORT PLAPPEVILLE
Frescaty
Augny
IMPERIAL
GUARD
Plappeville
St. Quentin
Devant-les-Ponts
HQ
Fort
St. Martin
4
CORPS
Fort
Queuleu
Sauley
Lorry
Lessy
Châtel
Moulins
St. Ruffine
Amanvillers
Rozérieulles
Jussy
Vaux
Ars-sur-Moselle
Gravelotte
R. Mance
BATTLEFIELD OF
18 AUGUST ⚔

gains made were lost. To thwart further French attempts, Friedrich Karl ordered all food stocks in villages around the perimeter to be destroyed. The inhabitants were given two hours to leave before their villages were torched.

Bazaine briefly contemplated another sortie, and ordered preparations. The château of Ladonchamps north of the city was seized on the night of 1 October. Coffinières was sufficiently alarmed to plead with Bazaine to reconsider: 'God grant,' he wrote, that the citizens of Metz and the army 'do not fall victim to the decision that you are about to take.'[9] In the event Bazaine confined his plans to a large-scale raid. The action of 7 October, launched northward from Ladonchamps, was mounted by 6 Corps with support from units of the Guard while neighbouring corps created diversions. The main attack reached its objectives, but brought down such a German barrage that transporting forage back to Metz proved impossible. By evening the French had retreated over shell-swept terrain, having suffered 1,257 casualties to the German 1,782.[10]

Ladonchamps was the last French offensive at Metz. The army was growing progressively weaker. In August Bazaine had been so anxious to withdraw under the protection of the Metz forts that he had neglected the opportunity for his army to hold a wider perimeter incorporating some of the villages which later were raided unsuccessfully for food. Whilst the Metz storehouses were adequately stocked to keep its garrison for six months, they could feed a large army for only a few weeks. Beef cattle, salt for baking bread and cooking, and forage for horses were in particularly short supply. The lack of beef meant that from 4 September the army had to live on horsemeat, which without salt was bland and indigestible and could not be preserved. From 18 September 250 horses were butchered daily. Many of the weaker animals were already in a near skeletal state and were reduced to gnawing each other's manes and tails in desperation. They began dropping dead by the dozen, then by the hundred. With every passing day the army was devouring its strength in cavalry and eating up the means of pulling its wagons and guns. By early October the remaining animals barely had the strength to pull the loads necessary either for a battle or to feed the army in open country after a breakout.

Bazaine had at first been reluctant to weaken his army by reducing the daily bread ration, but it became unavoidable. The ration, originally 750 grammes, was cut to 500 on 15 September, to 300 on 8 October and 250 two days later, though the horsemeat ration was increased to compensate. The bread itself reflected the declining quality of available ingredients. Coffee and sugar too were rationed. Vegetables were so scarce that men foraged for potatoes between the lines. Soldiers supplemented their rations by trying to buy food in Metz, which sent prices in the city's shops and restaurants rocketing and created shortages there.

The population of the city had been swelled from 50,000 to 70,000 by an influx of refugees who had fled there in the first month of the war, adding to the mouths to feed. Metz was also overflowing with sick and wounded. The Place Royale and the Esplanade, the city's great public space, were covered with hospital tents and railway carriages which, having no other current use, served as makeshift wards. On 24 September Bazaine's medical director reported over 14,000 sick and wounded in the hospitals. Around 2,000 more were being tended in private homes. A diet deficient in salt and vegetables was producing a great increase in cases of diarrhoea; and scurvy, smallpox and typhoid fever had appeared.[11] Sickness was aggravated by the cold, wet weather that prevailed in the first half of September and returned in early October. The fields around Metz where the army shivered in its tents became dismal oceans of mud, littered with ordure and horse carcasses. Bazaine's hope of keeping his army intact was being remorselessly eroded as its morale and physical state sank lower. A wounded lieutenant would later lament, 'Metz was becoming a tomb in which our admirable army was buried alive.'[12]

The blockading Germans were better sheltered, three-quarters of them being billeted under roofs of some description, and they could be re-supplied from Germany. Even so, they endured great discomforts, and many German soldiers remembered their service at Metz in September and October 1870 as the bleakest days of their lives. The supply of fresh meat from Germany was restricted by an outbreak of cattle plague, meaning that much tinned meat had to be consumed. Foraging unripe grapes from local vineyards brought its inevitable consequences. Although the strength of Friedrich Karl's army had risen to nearly 200,000 by late September, its state of health was no better than that of the French. During the blockade 22,090 men fell sick from gastric fever and typhus, 1,328 of whom died. A further 27,959 contracted dysentery, 829 of whom died. Many villages remained full of men too badly wounded in the August battles to be moved to Germany, while in the air hung a pestilential stench from corpses buried in shallow graves and sometimes exposed by the heavy autumn rains. By late October nearly 40,000 men of the German army surrounding Metz were hospitalized.[13]

The work of blockade went forward nevertheless, with men in the front line learning to be wary of the superior range of the Chassepot. An elaborate web of breastworks, shelter trenches and fortified villages was spun around Metz, protected by abattis of felled trees and wire. Although cleverly concealed German batteries could not reach the city of Metz itself, starting from 9 September they periodically bombarded the French camps and front lines by night, making life even more wretched for the defenders. With the German lines all but impregnable by the end of September, it could only be a matter of time before the French were forced to capitulate.

Negotiations

In the French camps rumours multiplied about secret comings and goings at the outposts. On the same day that he announced the change of government to his army, Bazaine entered into correspondence with Friedrich Karl, 'under pretence' as he put it, 'of learning the position after Sedan'.[14] He asked for information about events, but also whether his aide-de-camp, Baron Napoleon Boyer, could be given a safe-conduct to King Wilhelm's royal headquarters.

Friedrich Karl, courteously replying to Bazaine as 'Marshal of the French Empire', obliged with a summary of recent events, including confirmation that the new French government had not been sanctioned by the Legislature. Although the German commander ignored the proposition regarding Boyer, he declared himself 'ever ready and authorized' to make further communications. Bazaine replied on 17 September with an unctuousness exceeding both the formal courtesies of the day and the scope of communications with an enemy permitted by regulations:

> Sire, I have the honour to thank your Royal Highness for the most interesting communication which he has deigned to make to me, and I am most grateful to him for it.
>
> What sad events! How they afflict me! France may fall into anarchy, and all Europe will feel the effects. May God guide us and protect society![15]

There was further correspondence, which Boyer later destroyed.

On 22 September, by his own account, Bazaine received a copy of the newspaper containing Bismarck's communiqué of the 11th, declaring that the Germans recognized only Napoleon III as the legitimate ruler of France, and therefore could treat only with the Emperor or Empress, or with 'Marshal Bazaine, who holds his appointment from the Emperor'.[16] So concerned was Bismarck to find someone in France prepared to accept his peace terms that at this juncture he made use of a strange amateur negotiator who offered himself as an intermediary.

Victor Régnier, a self-important land-owner who had fled to England in late August, was an imperial loyalist with a taste for melodrama who took upon himself a mission to restore the Empire and end the war. Under his plan, the Empress would return to France under the protection of the French navy and declare herself the sole legal government. He importuned the Empress's household at Hastings to be allowed to visit the captive Emperor with a view to initiating negotiations with the Germans. Empress Eugénie would not see this insistent busybody, whose pet scheme would inaugurate civil war. Régnier then latched on to the Prince Imperial's tutor, Augustin Filon, to whom he provided postcards of Hastings with the request that the Prince sign them with a message to the Emperor. Next day, 17 September, Régnier was handed the cards with the Prince's autograph message:

> Dear Papa,
> I send you these views of Hastings, hoping they will please you.
> Louis-Napoleon

It was enough for Régnier, whose intention of travelling to see Napoleon III at Wilhelmshöhe was modified when he read of the peace talks about to take place between Bismarck and Jules Favre. Desperate to forestall any German agreement with the revolutionaries, Régnier rushed from England to Ferrières, where on 20 September he plausibly presented himself to Bismarck as Eugénie's emissary.

His arrival was opportune for Bismarck, who delighted in showing Favre the signed postcard and telling him that he had a representative of the Empire in the next room. Sowing dissension among the French might encourage both parties to come to terms, for fear of being outbid by the other. Bismarck's preference would have been to deal with the Empire, and he listened while the garrulous Régnier developed his ideas for a restoration of the Regency, backed by Bazaine's army, which could guarantee the execution of a peace treaty and maintain social order. Régnier took it as read that the war was lost and that some territorial concession by France was inevitable. Bismarck gave him a safe-conduct to Metz, saying 'Do what you can to bring before us some one with power to treat with us, and you will have rendered a great service to your country.'[17] So it was that on the evening of 23 September, as he was playing his habitual game of billiards at his headquarters in the village of Ban-Saint-Martin outside Metz, Bazaine was told that an envoy from the Empress had arrived.

Like Bismarck, Bazaine accepted a postcard as Régnier's credentials because his arrival seemed to offer some way out of his impasse. He was broadly in sympathy with Régnier's views, and when Régnier urged that either Marshal Canrobert or General Bourbaki should go back through the lines with him to see Eugénie – which was entirely his own idea – Bazaine took it as a command from the Empress. Canrobert being unwilling, there followed the farce of Bourbaki, commander of the Imperial Guard, being smuggled out of Metz with German connivance disguised as a Red Cross worker from Luxembourg and wearing a pair of outsize trousers lent him by the corpulent, thick-set Bazaine.

When Bourbaki reached England he was humiliated to find that Eugénie was not expecting him and knew nothing of his mission. The affair was soon all over the English press. Bismarck recognized that this initiative could bear no fruit. He wired a message to Friedrich Karl for conveyance to Bazaine asking if Régnier was empowered to treat for the surrender of his army. Bazaine had been having his own doubts about Régnier's authenticity, fearing that he might have been duped by a Prussian spy. He responded in the negative, whereupon Bismarck refused to see Régnier again. Complaining that a golden opportunity had been lost by the obtuseness of the Empress and Bourbaki, Régnier returned to England. Whilst he was not, as many Frenchmen believed, a paid Prussian spy, he had willingly given the Germans useful information about the state of Bazaine's army. In 1874 he was sentenced to death in his absence for espionage and negotiating with the enemy, but avoided execution by settling in Ramsgate where he ended his days running a laundry.

As a result of this bizarre interlude, Bazaine was deprived of Bourbaki's services. Bismarck was quite prepared to let the general back into Metz, and it was so ordered from Royal Headquarters (which had moved from Ferrières to Versailles on 5 October). Friedrich Karl, known as 'the Red Prince' because of the hussar jacket he customarily wore (definitely not for his politics) had other ideas. He wanted nothing to spoil his impending military triumph in capturing Metz, which must assuredly be drawing closer daily. The prospect of one of Bismarck's diplomatic gambits leading to some kind of deal with the French that would allow Bazaine's troops to march out and escape captivity exasperated him. He made difficulties about re-admitting Bourbaki, who lost patience and returned to France via Belgium, offering his services to the Government of National Defence.

Inside Metz outlandish rumours circulated about Bourbaki's fate, including suspicions that the secretive Bazaine had had him shot or imprisoned for urging a sortie. After Bourbaki's failure to return and the repulse at Ladonchamps it was evident that Bazaine's options were shrinking. The army had scarcely a fortnight's supply of food remaining, even after orders were belatedly given, over Coffinières' strong objections, that all food stores in Metz must be shared with the army. On 10 October, as icy rain streamed down, Bazaine called another council of war. It agreed unanimously that Metz should be held as long as possible, but that an envoy should be sent to Prussian headquarters to seek a military convention. A sortie would be attempted only if the enemy failed to offer honourable terms. Meantime, further small operations had become pointless and would cease. Boyer, Bazaine's confidant since the days when the Marshal had commanded the French expedition in Mexico, and newly promoted from colonel to general, would be his envoy.

Boyer had borrowed books on past capitulations from the military library in Metz. That of Kléber at Mainz in 1793 provided a promising precedent. The Prussians had allowed the French to march away with full military honours, under oath not to fight against them again. Kept intact, Kléber's army had then been employed to suppress rebellion in western France. Bazaine hoped that the Germans would be so concerned to uphold the forces of conservatism and order in France that they would allow his army to march out upon an oath to take no further part in the war. He also hoped to avoid surrendering the fortress of Metz itself, on the grounds that since its governor, Coffinières, had been appointed by the Emperor, Bazaine as army commander had no authority to order its surrender. The letter he sent with Boyer sought to persuade the Germans that generosity was in their interest:

> At a moment when [French] society is menaced by the attitude adopted by a violent party, whose inclinations cannot bring about a solution desired by right-thinking people, the Marshal commanding the Army of the Rhine, motivated by the desire to save his country and protect it from its own excesses, examines his conscience and asks himself if the army under his orders is destined to become the safeguard of society.
>
> The military issue is settled; the German armies are victorious, and H.M. the King of Prussia will set no great value on a triumph he will obtain by eliminating the only force that can today master the anarchy in our unhappy country, and assure France and Europe the calm that has become so necessary after the violent commotions that have stirred it.

He argued that the intervention of German armies in French internal affairs could only worsen disorder, whereas his well-organized army could restore stability and legality, and guarantee Prussia that her demands would be faithfully executed.[18]

Yet Friedrich Karl at first refused to let Boyer pass. Only a royal order, inspired by Bismarck, compelled him to do so, illustrating the growing tensions between the Chancellor and the military high command. During Boyer's trip to Versailles the Germans took care that he learned only what they wanted him to know of the situation in France, and Bismarck ensured that Boyer was seen in full uniform riding in an open carriage. The news that Bazaine was treating separately with the Germans incensed republicans. Although Bazaine and the Tours government had made sporadic efforts to contact each other, no messages got through; and even had Boyer been free to do so he had no inclination to contact 'those people'.[19]

Bismarck sought to exploit this discord. Drawing Boyer into the garden of his quarters at Versailles so that they could not be overheard, he offered a bargain similar to Régnier's scheme. If Bazaine wanted to march his army out of Metz with its weapons and full military honours, he must first publicly declare the army's allegiance to the Empire (so opening an irreconcilable divide between him and the Government of National Defence). But this must be linked to the Empress signing peace preliminaries accepting German terms, 'however exorbitant they might appear'.[20]

When Boyer returned to Metz on 17 October he painted a dark picture of the state of France based on the exaggerations Bismarck had fed him: the Army of the Loire destroyed at Artenay and Orléans; France in such a chronic state of anarchy and disintegration that French cities supposedly were appealing to the Germans to provide garrisons and maintain order. Bazaine swallowed this avidly, and the news was communicated to the army. Meeting on 18 and 19 October, a council of war agreed with Bazaine that Boyer should proceed to England to put Bismarck's terms to the Empress. In an apparent attempt to fulfil the first German requirement, Bazaine wrote confidentially to Friedrich Karl on 20 October assuring him that the council of war had agreed 'to uphold the government of the Regency', and that his generals considered themselves bound to 'the rightful government' by their oaths to the Emperor.[21] This fell short of the public declaration Bismarck required.

On 22 October Boyer reached Camden Place at Chislehurst, Kent, where Eugénie had settled. He bore a letter from Bazaine assuring her of his loyalty, and another from Frossard, former tutor to the Prince Imperial, urging her to make contact with the Prussian government and to accept its terms 'if they are not completely unacceptable'.[22] However, through contacts with the Prussian embassy in London, Eugénie soon learned that they were 'completely unacceptable'. Bismarck was asking her to sign a blank cheque for an unspecified territorial concession as the price of her return to power.

Bonapartist hopes rested on the belief that they would be offered significantly more lenient terms than the republicans. There were informal feelers as to whether Bismarck might accept part of Alsace becoming a buffer state, coupled with the demolition of Strasbourg's fortifications, a large indemnity and France's colony of Cochin China. Bismarck dismissed such ideas. Germany was not rich enough, he sneered, to maintain that colony. He later told his circle, 'I want no colonies ... For us in Germany, this colonial business would be just like the silken sables in the noble families of Poland, who have no shirts on their back.'[23]

Shattering Bonapartist hopes, Bismarck made clear that his price to the imperialists was the same as to the republicans: Alsace and Lorraine. Eugénie's desperate plea to Bismarck to let Metz be re-supplied while she appointed Bazaine Lieutenant General of the Empire with full powers to negotiate was rejected. Germany had no interest in conceding re-supply on any terms, and the territorial demand was the rock upon which negotiations foundered. In a confidential letter to Eugénie, King Wilhelm explained that 'after having made immense sacrifices for her defence, Germany wishes to be assured that the next war will find her better prepared to repel the aggression upon which we can count as soon as France has recovered her strength and gained allies. It is this sad consideration alone, and not the desire to enlarge my country, whose territory is great enough, which compels me to insist on these territorial concessions, which have no other object than pushing back the starting line of French armies that will come to attack us in the future.'[24]

This letter would be useful to France in 1918, when an aged Eugénie sent it to Georges Clemenceau to support France's claims at the end of the Great War, but in October 1870 it signalled the failure of negotiations. The Empress earned a grudging gratitude from the new republican government for her refusal to buy a restoration with French territory, and she struck her favourite pose as a romantic heroine who would never betray France. In reality, to have accepted the German terms would have been political suicide for the dynasty.

Even before Wilhelm's explanatory letter had reached England, Bismarck had notified Bazaine that, none of his preconditions having been met, the attempt to negotiate a politically acceptable solution had failed.

Capitulation

Bazaine shared this news with a council of war on 24 October, where it was received 'with painful surprise'.[25] A last effort to break out was ruled out: the majority view was that it could lead only to a disastrous defeat followed by the disintegration of the army. Canrobert considered that it would be 'an act of despair [which], without adding to the honour of our flag, would give the Prussians one more triumph and be a cause of demoralization to France'. To General Soleille a sortie would be 'not only useless but even culpable' – the soldiers would not follow their officers.[26] Bazaine later argued that offering the enemy such an easy victory would have been 'a veritable suicide' and 'a crime to sacrifice uselessly so many thousand lives'.[27] Very little food remained. It was decided to ask the Germans for terms.

Still Bazaine clutched at straws. General Changarnier, an old–school royalist who had attached himself to headquarters in August, was sent to Friedrich Karl to ask if a local armistice could be arranged, with the French army being re-supplied in Metz while the French Legislature was summoned there. Failing that, could the army be interned on French soil, or perhaps sent to Algeria? Friedrich Karl was the soul of politeness to the elderly Changarnier, but quickly disillusioned him: he would not even communicate such terms to Versailles. Nor would he countenance separation of the French army's fate from that of the fortress of Metz. It must surrender on the same terms as the French army at Sedan, with all its arms and material. Over the following days details were hammered out by the respective chiefs of staff: Stiehle for the Germans and Jarras for the French – an officer whom Bazaine despised and had treated throughout as a clerk. They met at the château of Frescaty, where the capitulation was signed late on 27 October. Jarras's heart was pounding so hard that he could scarcely sign his name.[28]

How would the army react? During September the bonds of discipline, reinforced by the habits of military routine, had held firm. Rumours of political negotiations during October, coupled with physical miseries and waning confidence in Bazaine's leadership, had created a deep undercurrent of discontent. When the question of supporting an imperial restoration had been discussed, the high command had reckoned that the Imperial Guard, with its higher pay and privileges, could be counted on; so probably could the largely royalist cavalry and a substantial proportion of the infantry. Yet, despite Bazaine's calculated liberality with decorations, promotions and allowances, a question mark hung over whether some units would remain solid if given such orders, particularly in 3 and 4 Corps and the engineers. Discontent was brewing among certain junior officers of Bazaine's staff, who would later publish the most vehement attacks on him. His own chief of staff had grave doubts, fearing that had Bazaine's negotiations to restore the Empire succeeded they would have caused 'division in the army, leading to an atrocious civil war', while their failure led to an irreparable loss of time.[29] Another staff officer judged restoration 'an impossible solution. Victorious armies have indeed been known to impose a sovereign on a country, but can one imagine a beaten army having the pretension to restore a dynasty rejected by the country only a few weeks ago?'[30] Dr Quesnoy, although by no means inclined to join in the chorus of criticism of Bazaine, found himself wondering 'Whether it would not be better to be prisoners than to be reduced perhaps to playing policemen at home?'[31]

The prospect of capitulation without a fight pushed a minority of officers, many of them with republican sentiments, to the edge of mutiny. Bazaine was alerted that the leading spirits were two engineer officers, Boyenval and Rossel, and called both before him. He imprisoned Boyenval but, impressed by Louis Rossel's frankness, and having known his father in Algeria, let him off with a reprimand. On 26–27 October angry meetings of junior officers mooted the idea of either deposing Bazaine or asking him to stand aside in favour of another leader willing to lead a last desperate breakout. Several brigadiers were known to be sympathetic, notably General Justin Clinchant, who was willing to command an attack if 15,000 to 20,000 men could be mustered. But by next morning, 28 October, scarcely 6,000 had signed up for the attempt, and Clinchant was called to Bazaine's headquarters to be given a dressing-down by a near apoplectic Changarnier while his troops were quietly disarmed. Any violation of the capitulation agreement would have invited German reprisals. In any case, open disobedience was a step too far for most French officers, and the most ardent spirits seem to have been those with staff jobs rather than front-line duties.[32] The proposed breakout came to nothing, though a few units signed solemn protests against the capitulation. Notwithstanding their later claims, many men seem to have been reluctant to sacrifice themselves in a hopeless attempt. For several days prior to the capitulation hostilities had all but ceased, continuous rainstorms discouraged any activity, and the Germans had noted an increase in the number of deserters. The great majority of the troops seem to have accepted the capitulation with resignation and even relief, largely oblivious, an officer noted ruefully, to 'the slur cast upon our military honour'.[33]

In Metz, civilian anger had been mounting steadily during the blockade. Bazaine had become so unpopular that he kept clear of the city. The citizens of Metz, including its 5,000-strong National Guard, were ardently republican, and were indignant that Bazaine not only refused to recognize the Paris Government but was keeping their city an imperialist island while the rest of France had thrown off the Bonapartes. The city's newspapers were so critical that Bazaine had them censored. Letters and petitions had demanded that the army go out and fight the enemy, and Bazaine's passivity was denounced as treason. In mid-October there were violent demonstrations by the National Guard, in which imperial emblems were smashed. Even General Coffinières, who as Military Governor of the city was deeply unpopular, bowed to this pressure and recognized the Government of National Defence while Bazaine still refused to do so. Coffinières had already sent out of Metz by balloon a letter critical of Bazaine intended for Tours, only for the Germans to intercept it and return it to Bazaine. Coffinières was bitterly criticized at councils of war for apparently tolerating subversion and disorder in 'the Republic of Metz'.[34] On 15 October Bazaine summoned the commanders of the National Guard to his headquarters and, in response to their frank criticisms of his inaction and their suspicions of his plans to restore the Empire, declared untruthfully that 'he had no thought of serving the imperial power, which had fallen through its own fault [and] . . . that his relations with Prince Friedrich Karl concerned only prisoner exchanges, and nothing more'.[35]

When the signing of the capitulation became known on 28 October there were tumultuous scenes in the streets of Metz. Furious crowds, including National Guards and soldiers, joined in noisy demonstrations in which shots were fired. One group barricaded themselves in the cathedral and tolled its famous bell, La Mutte, as a call to action. Disturbances continued into the night, and Bazaine had to send two battalions of the Imperial Guard to restore order.

Meanwhile most of the army had been disarmed, though a few units disobeyed orders by smashing their weapons and burning their flags rather than surrender them. This question of the flags, as symbols of the army's honour, became a focus of post-war recrimination. In his characteristically casual way

Bazaine had, as an afterthought, given verbal orders on 26 October to have the flags sent to the arsenal for burning. Since the Germans insisted that the flags be handed over, and there were German spies in Metz, he avoided giving written orders and specified that the flags must be transported in covered wagons. Equally characteristically, he took little care to see that his orders were clearly understood and carried out; for all that he would afterwards complain that his subordinates had failed to obey them. Few flags had been destroyed when, on the morning of the 28th, the Germans got wind of what was happening. Unlike Sedan, where the French had destroyed nearly all their flags, Friedrich Karl did not intend to be cheated of these highly prized trophies. He sent Bazaine a note threatening that the terms of the capitulation would become void if the flags were not handed over intact. Thereupon Bazaine had little choice but to order the destruction to cease.[36]

Ignorant of the German threat, most of his men believed to the end of their days that Bazaine had deliberately lulled them into sending their flags to the arsenal under false pretences with the intention of surrendering them to the Germans. Certainly he had not made their destruction a priority, and General Soleille who was in charge of the process had written out an order several hours before the German ultimatum specifying that the flags must be inventoried and surrendered.

Soleille and Changarnier, whose counsels exercised a baleful influence over Bazaine, held such a fanatically narrow concept of military 'honour' that, even before the capitulation was signed, they believed themselves bound to surrender every last item of arms and material intact to their German brother officers. Soleille fiercely rebuked a general who tried to destroy some *mitrailleuses*, and Bazaine and Canrobert were similarly abrupt with junior officers who dared suggest such steps. Bazaine went so far as to declare in his farewell proclamation to his men that the material had to be kept intact because Metz was to be returned to France after the war – an entirely unfounded claim.[37]

For the French high command, with their 'Better Bismarck than Blanqui' mentality, fear of indiscipline among their own men and hatred of republicans far outweighed any animus towards the national enemy. Their assertiveness was limited to demanding that French officers be permitted to keep their swords and personal possessions, which the Germans granted.

Thus occurred one of the most humiliating capitulations in French history, involving more men even than Sedan. The Germans thought they had blockaded perhaps 80,000 troops and were incredulous when they counted 173,000, comprising 137,670 men of the field army, 15,157 of the garrison, 15,462 sick and wounded, plus Gardes Mobiles, customs officers and sick in private homes.[38] The 6,000 officers captured included three Marshals of France –

Le Bœuf, Canrobert and Bazaine – enough, Bismarck joked, to make up a whist party with the Emperor.[39] Shipping all these prisoners to camps in Germany was a major operation. In addition to the intact fortifications of Metz, the Germans had captured 622 field guns, 876 fortress guns, over 3,000,000 rounds of gun ammunition, 420,000 kilograms of gunpowder, 137,000 Chassepots with over 13,000,000 cartridges, 72 *mitrailleuses* and 123,000 other small arms. They made a triumphant display of the fifty-three flags surrendered out of a possible eighty-four.[40]

Bazaine refused the formal honours of war offered by the Germans: there would be no parades and salutes. Instead, on a bleak, rain-swept 29 October long columns of his hungry and weakened men tramped out of Metz across fields that had become cesspools on their way into captivity. 'What a Calvary to climb!' thought one captain as he tried to avoid looking at the black and white German flag flying from a French fort.[41] Approximately 11,000 of these prisoners would die of sickness in Germany over the winter.

Meanwhile the victorious Germans marched into Metz, past the statue of Marshal Fabert (1599–1662), which the citizens had draped in black. Fabert's words inscribed on the plinth were shaming:

> If, to prevent a place entrusted to me by the King from falling to the enemy, I had to throw my life, my family and all my goods into the breach, I should not hesitate to do so.

To avoid any incident, Bazaine had slipped away from his army at dawn. On reaching the outposts, he received a note from the Germans telling him not to enter their lines until evening. He spent the day in virtual hiding in a house near Moulins, and when he finally set out his cavalcade received such a hail of insults and brickbats from the villagers of Ars-sur-Moselle that he had to be protected by German military police. To his companions he said, 'This business will at least have a good side: it will put an end to the resistance of Paris and bring peace to our unhappy country.'[42] He bade them farewell with 'See you in Paris in a month.'[43]

How news of the capitulation was received in Paris, and the momentous impact it had upon the course of the war, will be told in due course. Playing to the French penchant for attributing any defeat to treason, and to unrealistic expectations of how long Metz could have held out, Gambetta issued a proclamation on 30 October which struck a deep chord. Denouncing Bazaine's 'treason', he ascribed France's disasters to twenty years' rule by a corrupt regime, and declared that the heroism of French soldiers had been betrayed by 'the treason of their commanders'.[44] Crémieux and Glais-Bizoin added their signatures, but Admiral Fourichon, shocked by this violent attack on the high command, refused. His distaste was widely shared by conservatives and officers of the imperial army who were now serving the Republic.

Gambetta's proclamation ignited the public feeling that would make Bazaine the scapegoat for French national humiliation, culminating in his trial in 1873. Though fearless under fire, Bazaine had been a remote and inscrutable commander, lacking the common touch, and had become a focus of hatred.[45] At his court martial he frequently gave lame answers or tried to shuffle blame onto his subordinates. To public satisfaction, he was stripped of his rank, titles and decorations and sentenced to death, though the sentence was immediately commuted to twenty years' imprisonment. He was not accused of treason, and a stream of dubious witnesses failed to produce any proof of it. Many of the villainies imputed to him by contemporaries were absurd, and defenders have portrayed him rather as a realist who recognized that his position was hopeless and that the war was lost. He might have managed his resources better, but even so it is doubtful whether he could have held out more than another fortnight, and arguable whether that would have made much difference to the war's outcome. As it was, he held out until his food was exhausted, and in that respect did no worse than many other French fortress commanders, including Trochu at Paris. His misfortune, it has been argued, was to remain loyal to his oath to a failed regime. Rather than revealing the Machiavellian ambition of a selfish intriguer to play a political role, his contacts with the enemy can be interpreted as forlorn attempts to save his army by any means.[46] For all that has been written about them, Bazaine's intentions and ambitions remain an enigma.

Yet it is hard even for Bazaine's defenders to contend that he played a skilful hand as a strategist, tactician or negotiator. His contacts with an enemy who had everything to gain by stalling him in negotiations were begun before he had exhausted his military options and did him no honour. His political allegiance fed his defeatism, which seems also to have been rooted in a reluctance to take responsibility or risk his reputation. He went out of his way to disseminate rumours of French defeats throughout his army. The various assurances he gave that there would be no capitulation, and hints that a breakout was imminent, added to the odour of duplicity that clung to him, as did his management of councils of war to suppress opinions or information that might have called into question his do-nothing strategy.

As a commander, Bazaine undoubtedly was sluggish, irresolute, and unequal to the heavy responsibility he bore. His passivity, evident even before Sedan, caused him to become trapped in Metz and remain there rather than risk a battle in open country. He accepted all too readily the supposed impossibility of a successful sortie, of re-supply outside Metz, and of escaping the inevitable German pursuit with at least a significant portion of his force. He failed to execute a well-planned, co-ordinated and aggressive attempt to break out before the odds made it impossible. Always he temporized, opting by default for the most prudent course and so, in seeking to avoid risk, doomed his army ineluctably to destruction. His pusillanimous surrender of vast quantities of arms and ammunition in the conviction that the war was over contrasted with the sense of duty exhibited by junior officers like Second Lieutenant Archer, who on 9 August had defended the blazing small fortress of Lichtenberg against great odds, but managed to destroy his ammunition stores and spike his guns before raising the white flag; or NCOs like Sergeant Major Bœltz, who when summoned to surrender the tiny fortress of Petite-Pierre on 8 August had with great coolness immersed his store of gunpowder, destroyed his guns, and marched his men to safety through German lines by night.[47] No less a degree of military competence, fighting spirit and determination might surely have been expected of a Marshal of France.

Bazaine's court martial found him guilty of capitulating 'without having exhausted all the means of defence available to him, and without having done all that duty and honour prescribed'.[48] Although he escaped from captivity on the Mediterranean island fortress of Sainte-Marguerite in August 1874, he ended his days miserably, abandoned by his young Mexican wife and eking out an impoverished exile in Madrid. He wrote an incoherent defence which incensed veterans by its slur that his soldiers had not been up to the standards of Napoleonic times.[49] In 1887 a demented ex-Communard stabbed him in the face, and was applauded by elements of the French press. Until his death in 1888 Bazaine remained haunted by the dark autumn days of 1870 at Metz,[50] which had ruined his life as surely as they had ruined the formidable army that had been entrusted to his command.

Chapter 4

Paris Resists

The Revolutionary Spirit

Paris had seen great changes since the Revolution of 1789. In the last two decades Napoleon III had set Baron Georges Haussmann, his Prefect of the Seine from 1853 to 1869, the task of modernizing the city. Haussmann had opened up Paris, sweeping away its picturesque but insanitary alleys and buildings that had survived since medieval times. New bridges, railway stations, markets and wide boulevards lined with uniform stone façades had produced a spectacular transformation. Green spaces and better water and sewerage systems brought much needed improvements in public health. These immense works had created plentiful employment and profits for many.

Paris had also grown phenomenally, and was now six times more populous than its nearest rivals, Lyon and Marseille. High wages in the capital compared to the rest of France had attracted large-scale immigration from the provinces, so that by 1870 only one Parisian in three had been born in the capital[1]. In 1860 Paris had incorporated its outer ring of suburbs, adding eight more *arrondissements* to the twelve of the inner city. When the siege began in September 1870 approximately 2 million people were living within its limits, compared to 1.2 million twenty years earlier.

Expansion and improvement had come at a high price, socially as well as financially. The demolition of much cheap housing in the city centre and rising rents had pushed more workers out to the southern and north-eastern suburbs, where overcrowded tenements and shanty towns with poor sanitation stood in glaring contrast to the bourgeois opulence of western Paris and its comfortable suburbs. Whether workers were employed in the traditional small workshops or in the growing number of factories, the cost of living made their livelihoods precarious. If only a minority lived in outright poverty, most of the working class scraped an existence which left no money to spare after food, rent and clothing had been paid for – and then often only by recourse to the pawnshop.

Social changes had only fortified the stubborn spirit of opposition within the metropolis which drew its inspiration from the Great Revolution and its creed of liberty, equality and fraternity. No government could forget that riots in Paris had overthrown the Bourbon monarchy in July 1830 and the Orléans monarchy in February 1848. Rioting workers had been bloodily suppressed by troops in 1831, 1834, June 1848, 1849 and 1851. In vain Napoleon III had tried to win over the working class by a paternalistic policy: for instance by relaxing the penalties for forming workmen's associations and going on strike. Official sponsorship of a French workers' delegation to the Universal Exhibition in London in 1862 facilitated the formation of the International Working Men's Association two years later; but when the French section opened offices in Paris in 1865 it proved hostile to the government and was dissolved after the trial of its leaders in 1868. Paris remained staunchly attached to its republican traditions. The greater freedom of the press and rights to hold public meetings allowed by Napoleon from 1868 only fuelled militant opposition to his regime at a lean time for the French economy. The elections of 1869 and the plebiscite of 1870 produced a large majority in Paris against the Empire, accompanied by riots and a wave of strikes. Yet a widespread belief in the eventual coming of a universal republic went hand in hand with fierce patriotism, ever ready to confront foreign despots. Young working men had been prominent in the crowds who had shouted for war with Prussia in July. The Government of National Defence appealed to the deepest convictions of its audience when it declared on taking power: 'The Republic saved us from invasion in 1792: The Republic is proclaimed.'[2]

The politicians in the new government had come to power on the crest of the revolutionary wave that had swept away the Empire on 4 September, and were all too keen to gratify the demand for arms from those on whom their power depended. Given its revolutionary history, Napoleon III had curtailed the size and role of the Paris National Guard, confining its membership to the wealthier districts which could be relied upon to furnish 'good' battalions whose limited role was to maintain civic order. Before the war these volunteer part-time citizen-soldiers numbered 24,000 men. Following the outbreak of war the Imperial Government, goaded by Favre, had allowed a limited expansion of this force, doubling the size of battalions to 1,500 men and authorizing the raising of another ten battalions on 12 August, bringing the total to sixty battalions. Some of these battalions had spearheaded the Revolution of 4 September.

A belief in the superiority of citizen militias to standing armies was ingrained amongst republican politicians. On coming to power, Gambetta, with his faith in the masses to defend the Republic, immediately called for another sixty battalions, to be mustered by the mayors of the *arrondissements*. It was the opening of a floodgate. In three weeks 254 battalions were raised. Just as an exodus of middle-class people from western Paris was reducing the strength of the original battalions, so the strength of battalions recruited in north-eastern working-class districts that were hotbeds of radicalism – particularly Belleville, La Villette and Montmartre – mushroomed out of control. The contraction of trade caused by the war made the 1.5 franc per day awarded to Guardsmen from 9 September a vital dole for thousands of unemployed men. The introduction of additional daily allowance of 75 centimes for their wives on 28 November sent the number of marriages soaring.[3]

By 30 September the Paris National Guard had swollen to 343,000 men, 60,000 of whom had no arms. Yet, having heedlessly raised this citizen militia which the generals did not want, the government was at a loss how to employ it. For it refused to work on the defences and by law the National Guard could not be used beyond the ramparts. The government tried to get around this restriction by calling on 16 October for volunteers for field service. Elaborate ceremonies were organized involving flag-bedecked 'altars of the country' for those willing to step forward. Yet, for all their strident patriotic demands to be led against the enemy, most National Guardsmen hesitated to put themselves under full military authority and to leave their families. Many saw the war in terms of defending their own quarter – each Paris *arrondissement* was divided into quarters – against the expected German attack, and were reluctant to be separated from the local unit they had volunteered to serve in. The radical press was critical and suspicious. In three weeks 26,700 men did sign up for field service, but the government concluded that the voluntary principle alone had proved insufficient.[4]

Mostly poorly trained and ill-disciplined, with the right to elect its own officers, the National Guard spent its days manning the ramparts well behind the French front line, drinking wine or absinthe, playing pitch-and-toss, talking politics, illegally searching the homes of 'suspects' and arbitrarily arresting anyone they suspected of being a spy. In the prevailing atmosphere of wartime paranoia this could mean anyone rash enough to place a lamp near an upper window or whose dress or politics they disliked. Marshal Vaillant and General Ambert were amongst those manhandled into jail. One disgruntled victim was struck by the 'ridiculously despotic, interfering, suspicious and bureaucratic mentality of these men who talked everlastingly about liberty'.[5] With the theatres closed, guardsmen typically spent their evenings in clubs listening to orators who became increasingly critical of the government, and passed grandiose resolutions about all aspects of the conduct of the war. In their own eyes the club orators were patriotic guardians of democracy whose duty was to hold a backsliding government to account. To horrified conservatives and regular army officers they were loud-mouthed braggarts who were undermining discipline and unity.

Political pressure from the Left was expressed through other channels. On the morrow of the 4 September Revolution radicals formed vigilance committees in every *arrondissement* and sent representatives to a Central Committee of the Twenty Arrondissements housed in the same building as the International Working Men's Association in the Place de la Corderie. The Committee's leaders had been prominent in radical politics before the war and, whatever their doctrinal differences, all saw themselves as the true heirs of the Great Revolution. In the first glow of republican unity after the September Revolution they declared their eagerness to support and assist the new government. Even Auguste Blanqui, the inveterate conspirator and high-priest of violent revolution, declared on 5 September that 'In the presence of the enemy, there must be no parties ... All opposition, all contradiction, must disappear for the public safety.'[6] Nevertheless, the Central Committee very soon seemed to be posing as a rival government. On 15 September it published a 'Red Poster' setting out its demands, which included the arming of all citizens, local police powers for the National Guard, and local powers to requisition food and impose rationing. In demanding democratic control of defence measures it employed a formula that was becoming common currency: 'The republicans of Paris are resolved to bury themselves beneath its ruins rather than surrender.'[7]

On 20 September 230 delegates from local vigilance committees called for elections to be held for the 'Commune', a semi-mystical term conjuring up self-government for Paris (long denied by successive French governments) which was expected to fulfil the democratic and egalitarian aspirations of every shade of Left-wing opinion. Yet, as a bourgeois orator warned, there was 'blood on that word',[8] redolent of the Terror of 1793–94 and the dictatorship of Parisian revolutionaries over the rest of France.

Favre's negotiations with Bismarck at Ferrières stirred the radicals' mistrust of the government. Over the next three days there were small demonstrations by elements of the National Guard protesting at the negotiations. Jules Simon placated them with the assurance that the government would die rather than surrender. A more serious demonstration occurred a fortnight later, led by the flamboyant adventurer Gustave Flourens, who sported a voluminous blond beard and mustachios, and a bizarre uniform festooned with gold braid. Flourens, the son of a Professor at the Collège de France, had taught there himself until dismissed for his political activities. In the best romantic style, he had gone to fight for Cretan independence in 1867 and on his return was in continual trouble with the imperial authorities for his revolutionary embroilments. He had recently been elected to command no less than five National Guard battalions, and had lobbied Trochu for the rank of colonel on the strength of it. Trochu demurred, but granted him the honorary title of 'Major of the Ramparts'. On 5 October Flourens led his battalions from the ultra-radical districts of Belleville and Ménilmontant to the Hôtel de Ville, bands playing at their head. He demanded Chassepots, a sortie against the enemy and municipal elections. Trochu was conciliatory, reasoning with him like a father, and eventually Flourens, brandishing his sabre and shouting 'Long Live the Commune!'[9] amid the cheers of his men, was persuaded to lead them away.

Emboldened by the day's events, Blanqui attempted to lead his Montmartre battalion against the government on 7 October, but his men were unenthusiastic and shortly elected a new commander. However, the government's announcement that it was postponing municipal elections until after the siege provoked calls from the vigilance committees and the radical press for an insurrection. On 8 October – the day after Gambetta's departure by balloon – crowds chanting for the Commune gathered at the Hôtel de Ville. They hissed Trochu, but the number of spectators cheering for the General outnumbered them. This time several battalions of National Guard favourable to the government were on hand and the demonstrators, seeing that they could not get their way, dispersed by late afternoon, and Jules Favre addressed the 'good' battalions which passed in review. Next day, when the demented ex-soldier Théodore Sapia attempted to lead his battalion in insurrection, his men arrested him.

The government was inclined to rely on 'moral authority'[10] when dealing with radicals: after all, they were all republicans, and the extremists represented only a small minority. Kératry, the chief of police, resigned on 11 October when Trochu, anxious to avoid provocation, refused to let him arrest Flourens and other ringleaders. For the moment a policy of appeasement seemed necessary to maintain unity in the face of the enemy. Sincerely attached to libertarian principles, the government had readily conceded the radicals' demands for the removal of all remaining restrictions on liberty of the press and the right of assembly, and had packed off the hated but effective imperial police to fight at the front, replacing them with a weaker force of unarmed 'peacekeepers'. In doing so it had greatly empowered dissent at its own expense. The parliamentary republican leaders had used the Parisian spirit of opposition to overthrow the Empire. They were learning that that spirit was no respecter of persons, and could be turned against even the best-intentioned government: particularly as prices rose, food shortages began to bring real suffering, and the government failed to meet popular expectations for a decisive military blow against the enemy.

Offensive Reconnaissances
Leaving aside the mass of the National Guard, portions of which were to prove more dangerous to the government than they ever were to the Germans, General Trochu commanded a motley collection of forces for the defence of

Paris. The naval troops and regular army regiments provided a kernel of trained professionals, but there were too few of them. Even among the regulars, a large proportion were conscripts and depot battalions hastily formed into temporary regiments lacking cohesion and experience. There were in addition thirty-three independent volunteer units that too often were composed of men averse to regular army discipline – indeed to any discipline whatever – but with a predilection for fancy uniforms and military titles. With a few honourable exceptions, they would be of little use to the defence and merely absorbed former soldiers and officers who would have been more use in the regular army. More reliable were well-disciplined units of gendarmes, customs officers, forest-rangers, firemen and the former imperial constabulary. Trochu chose to keep these government battalions as an elite reserve, though they would have provided excellent officer and NCO material to bolster the temporary regiments and the Garde Mobile, which was the other mainstay of the defence.

However, the government – particularly Gambetta and Ernest Picard – insisted that the Garde Mobile must have the right to elect its own officers even in wartime, in accordance with republican principles. Their aim was to purge it of Bonapartist appointees and sympathizers. Thus, even as fighting raged at Châtillon on 19 September, electioneering was in progress and the Garde Mobile were casting their ballots. Ironically, many Bonapartists retained their posts, but overall the results saw trained officers and effective disciplinarians displaced by men whose main talents were political, including some notorious rabble-rousers and drunkards. Moreover, until they could be quartered in barracks beyond the ramparts, where discipline could be better preserved, the 116,000 Gardes Mobiles were billeted in the capital, where they could imbibe freely both alcohol and the political excitement of the day, and were prey to the temptations of the city. By December 8,000 had contracted venereal disease.[11] These circumstances combined to reduce the effectiveness of troops who could have been more useful had they been brigaded with regular army regiments, as was done in the provinces.

Nevertheless, many of these young provincial *moblots*, as they were nicknamed, showed 'an excellent spirit and remarkable willingness',[12] and would give a good account of themselves despite their lack of expertise. The Breton Garde Mobile, in particular, remained largely immune to anti-government propaganda: partly because their Catholic and royalist background made them resistant to the militant atheism and anti-clericalism of the Paris clubs, but also because many of them spoke only the Breton language and did not understand French. Being a Breton himself, Trochu had some claim on their loyalty.

In all, the men at Trochu's command were more impressive in quantity than quality. Approximate totals on 21 October were[13]:

Regular army		130,700
		(infantry present for duty = 83,888)
Garde Mobile		116,400
		(infantry present for duty = 98,419)
Naval troops		14,300
Gendarmes, customs officers, firemen, forest-rangers, etc.		11,000
Auxilliary gunners		3,000
Independent units		18,000
	Sub-total	293,400
National Guard		343,000
Total		636,400

Surrounded by a German army with a combat strength of 181,667 men and 672 guns by the end of October,[14] what was Trochu to do? His initial conception was that the defence should be modelled on the siege of Zaragoza in 1809, where the French had suffered high casualties in attempting to assault a city defended by ardent Spanish patriots. He thought that unacceptable losses could be inflicted on the Germans if they attempted to fight their way into Paris.[15] For a fortnight Parisians lived in expectation of bombardment and attack at any moment: exactly the course of action advocated by Bismarck. Popular enthusiasm for building barricades of sandbags and paving-stones outran attempts at control by the Barricades Commission chaired by Rochefort.[16]

The problem for Trochu was that Moltke, who controlled German strategy, agreed with his assessment, and had no intention of obliging him. The Germans did not have the luxury of overwhelming numbers to mount an assault. Their forces formed a cordon, thin in places, extending nearly 90 kilometres around Paris, the largest fortress in the world. Nevertheless, by fortifying deserted villages around the capital, which incidentally provided good shelter for their troops, and by extending a system of breastworks and shelter trenches protected by abattis behind their outpost line, they soon made their positions secure and the blockade effective. Behind this defensive line they began a series of blockhouses and redoubts from which their artillery could mow down attackers.

Moltke was confident that starvation, aided by dissension amongst the French, would produce surrender within weeks. On 21 September he mused wistfully to his brother Adolf that the leaves on his country estate would be turning red and yellow. He reflected that 'such a campaign tries the strength severely when a man has seventy years on his shoulders, as I have. But I cherish a private hope that I may be shooting hares at Kreisau by the end of October.'[17]

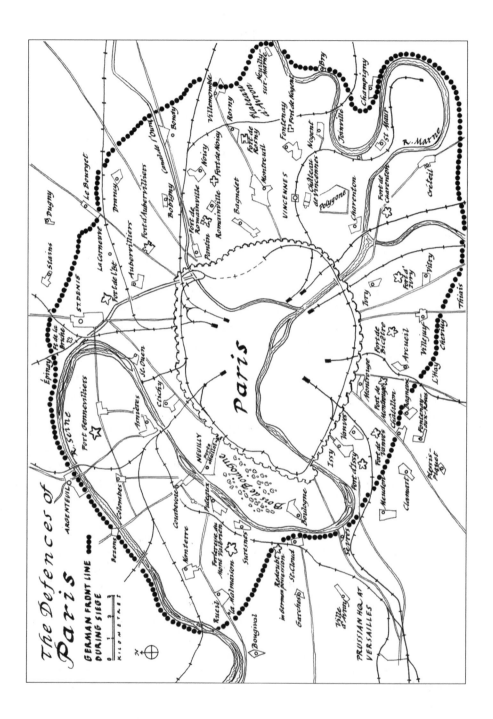

The Defences of Paris

GERMAN FRONT LINE ●●●●
DURING SIEGE

0 1 2 3
KILOMETRE

Paris

In the face of the enemy's immobility, Trochu was nonplussed. He later confessed that he had 'no idea of strategy or tactics ... My first conception of the siege of Paris was not replaced in my mind by any other.'[18] General Tripier, an elderly, round-faced, bespectacled engineer officer, was more imaginative. Drawing on Russian techniques at Sebastopol, he proposed that the French should dig parallels to recover key points from the Germans. The French would in effect lay siege to the besiegers, using their advantage in manpower and the protection afforded by their fortress guns to stretch and weaken the German lines, making them vulnerable to assault. Trochu approved a limited trial south-east of Paris which gave promising results in early October, but he failed to grasp the strategic possibilities of this form of active defence. Instead, he demonstrated the poverty of his generalship by a series of futile 'offensive reconnaissances'.

Firstly, however, the French had to recover strategic points that had been evacuated in panic following Châtillon. A battalion of the notoriously unruly Paris Garde Mobile had needlessly abandoned the vital fortress on Mont-Valérien west of Paris, fleeing back to the city in disorder. They were replaced by two provincial battalions without the Germans discovering their opportunity. Similarly on 22–23 September it proved possible to recover the Villejuif plateau and the abandoned redoubts of Moulin-Saquet and Hautes-Bruyères south of Paris, protecting the forts in that sector. The guns of the forts enabled the French to beat off a German counter-attack and achieve a small but useful victory which, much inflated by the Paris press, helped restore morale after Châtillon.

General Vinoy, commanding 13 Corps, planned to use the Villejuif plateau as the jumping-off point for a further small operation to recover ground and damage German communications. Trochu, dismissive of his subordinate's plan, intervened to turn the operation into something quite different. He drew up detailed instructions for 20,000 men to attack southward in three columns. This force was too large for a reconnaissance yet too small for a serious assault, and the preparations were obvious to the enemy. A half-hour bombardment preceding the attack merely served to alert the Germans without doing them significant damage. Then at 6.00 a.m. on 30 September the infantry went forward. Within three hours the right-hand column had been beaten back from the village of L'Hay by a storm of German rifle fire delivered from behind the solid walls of parks and a cemetery, while the left column met a similar fate at Thiais. The centre brigade, including the two best regular regiments, the 35th and 42nd, fought its way into Chevilly, but could not dislodge the Germans from the southern end of the village. Its brigadier, General Guilhem, was felled by ten bullets in the chest as he tried to lead an assault. His men, their flanks exposed, were forced eventually to withdraw. In contrast to the speed with which the Germans brought up reinforcements, Trochu had given orders that the reserve was not to be committed. Beyond demonstrating that the French still had some fight left in them, the only result of the Chevilly operation was the loss of over 2,000 men to a German loss of fewer than 500.

A fortnight later, to establish whether the Germans had detached significant forces to the Loire, Trochu ordered Vinoy to attack south-west of Paris, where their lines were close to the Paris forts. Aproximately 25,000 French troops mounted the assault on a sunny 13 October. The right-hand column easily occupied Clamart, while the left-hand column captured Bagneux after a brisk fight. Between them lay the village of Châtillon, hastily abandoned the previous month, which the French found a tougher nut to crack. They fought their way in, only to find that the Germans, though fewer in number, had used barricades to turn the centre of the village around the church into a fortress that could not be taken or outflanked despite fierce street-fighting. German reinforcements began appearing from the Châtillon heights. Vinoy wrote a note asking Trochu if he at least wanted to retain Bagneux, which would be a useful extension of the French position. Trochu, with characteristic caution, ordered a withdrawal, abandoning all the ground his troops had gained at the cost of over 400 of their comrades – fifty more casualties than the Germans suffered.

The next major action occurred a week later west of Paris, in the Gennevilliers peninsula formed by a loop of the Seine. The wooded heights at the base of the peninsula towards Bougival, an area so recently favoured by Parisians for a Sunday excursion and the haunt of little-known artists like Renoir, Monet and Pissarro, were now fortified by the Germans. However, German access to the peninsula itself was barred by the guns of Mont-Valérien. On 13 October shells from the fort started a fire that gutted Napoleon III's palace of Saint-Cloud, which the Germans were using as an observation post. The chamber where the French decision for war had been taken on 14 July was reduced to ashes, along with many artworks. Although the French preferred to blame Prussian arsonists, the destruction of Saint-Cloud was the work of their own artillery. The nearby Sèvres porcelain factory also suffered damage.

General Ducrot was concerned that German patrols were infiltrating towards Rueil, taking advantage of dead ground, and he wanted to drive them away from French lines. He was insistent, too, that his men must be exposed to combat to recover their nerve after the rout of Châtillon. He got Trochu's permission for a foray against German lines, for which he drew up characteristically elaborate and detailed orders that allowed his subordinates no initiative. The attack, involving 11,000 men, was launched on 21 October, another fine autumn day. Although Parisians ascribed the failure to achieve surprise to the sinister ubiquity of enemy spies, signs of the impending offensive were as usual easy for the Germans to read: the city gates closed, a red and white pennon flying from atop Mont-Valérien, and the firing of signal guns.

The assault was made through the park of La Malmaison, formerly the favourite residence of Napoleon I, then of Josephine. It was spearheaded by four companies of Zouaves under Major Charles-Auguste Jacquot. They more than redeemed the honour lost by their comrades at Châtillon, dashing very close to German lines on the La Jonchère height under a hail of lead. But the French assault was badly disjointed, supports were not close at hand, and when some Gardes Mobiles arrived they fired so wildly into the backs of other French troops that an officer had their bugler sound 'Cease fire!' This emboldened the Germans, whose supports were soon on the scene. Before long Jacquot was mortally wounded and French units who had entered the park and the neighbouring enclosures of Longboyau and Buzenval were forced to evacuate through breaches made in their walls. One group desperately held back onrushing Germans in hand-to-hand fighting at the Longboyau Gate while French artillery limbered up under fire and retreated. By the end of the afternoon's fighting the French were back where they had started, at the cost of over 500 men to over 400 Germans. The inhabitants of Bougival, who had started firing at the Germans in anticipation of their liberation, were severely punished: three men executed and everyone else heavily fined and expelled.

Though his men had been repelled at all points, Ducrot claimed success at La Malmaison. Yet German patrols could have been pushed away from Rueil far more economically. As for inuring his men to battle, by which Ducrot set such store, he had sacrificed some of his best troops. The Zouaves 'could never forgive General Ducrot for having allowed their comrades to be uselessly and stupidly slaughtered'.[19] Moreover, the Germans were spurred into strengthening their defences in that sector.

To impatient Parisians it appeared that Trochu's strategy consisted of marching men out to fight in the morning, committing only a fraction of them, then retreating in the evening and proclaiming success in verbose bulletins. His much-touted 'plan' became the butt of jokes and mocking songs,[20] while in the clubs orators who had no intention of facing enemy bullets and shells themselves angrily demanded a 'torrential sortie' to break the German lines.

The First Battle of Le Bourget
The agitated state of Paris, cut off from the outside world for six weeks, manifested itself on 27 October when Félix Pyat, most quarrelsome of revolutionary veterans, reported in his paper, *Le Combat*, that Bazaine was negotiating with the Prussians for the surrender of Metz and for peace in the name of Napoleon III. Pyat indignantly denounced this as high treason and accused the government of concealing it. Henri Rochefort had confided

rumours of General Boyer's mission to Flourens, who had passed it on to Pyat. Incredulous Parisians turned their wrath not on the government but on Pyat, whom they suspected of malicious fabrication. A mob ransacked the office of *Le Combat* and copies of the paper were seized from news kiosks and burned in the streets. The government, intent as usual on placating public opinion with high-flown phrases, promptly denied the news. Jules Favre unwisely rushed to defend 'the glorious soldier of Metz ... who has not ceased to harry the besieging army by brilliant sorties', and denounced Pyat's 'odious' invention as a deliberate device to undermine the government in the face of the enemy.[21]

The day Favre's denial appeared, 28 October, brought news of a victory that turned the volatile Parisian mood to one of rejoicing. Before dawn the Francs-tireurs de la Presse, a small company reduced to 260 men by desertions, sallied out from French lines and successfully rushed the village of Le Bourget, north of Paris, which had been lightly held by a company of the Prussian Royal Guard. The attack had been ordered by General Alexandre Carrey de Bellemare, who had opposed capitulation at Sedan and had subsequently escaped captivity and been given command of the Saint-Denis sector north of the capital. An ambitious man, Bellemare went into Paris next day to ask Trochu not only for reinforcements but for divisional command on the strength of the success and the fact that he was commanding three brigades.

Trochu, however, was displeased that the attack had been made without his knowledge or authority. Insistent that it was unwise to hold any ground beyond the line of forts, he thought the Le Bourget position so exposed as to be strategically worthless. Nevertheless, given the state of public opinion, he dared not order a retreat.

The responsibility for what happened next became a bone of contention between Trochu and Bellemare.[22] Some reinforcements were sent to the sector, but not enough to hold it effectively. Being a fatalist about the value of defending Le Bourget, as about so much else, Trochu belatedly ordered only a single battery of artillery to strengthen the village, and there was such a lack of urgency that it had not arrived two days later. About 2,000 of Bellemare's men settled into the village in the pouring rain, but they were left largely to their own devices and even food was slow to reach them.

Meanwhile, it became clear that the Germans did not intend to let the matter rest. Although a weak German counter-attack was sharply repulsed on the night of the 28th, next day they bombarded Le Bourget from their lines on rising ground to the north, where columns of Prussian infantry were observed gathering. Ironically, the commander of the Prussian Guard, Prince August von Württemberg, felt much as Trochu did about the value of Le Bourget, fearing that it would be difficult to defend if recaptured. However, he was overruled by his army commander, Crown Prince Albert of Saxony, who insisted that the French must not be allowed to keep the ground they had won.

The German assault was made on the morning of 30 October by Lieutenant General von Budritzki's Second Guards Division, employing tactics adapted to recent experience of facing murderous Chassepot fire over open ground. Approximately 8,000 infantry advanced in three columns in a concentric attack on Le Bourget, a string of houses oriented north-west along the Lille Road and once home to 700 people. The assault troops left their packs behind and advanced in dispersed formation to reduce casualties, preceded by swarms of skirmishers who advanced in short rushes until they were close to the enemy, who was firing from behind thick walls. Under cover of their artillery, the Guardsmen dashed forward across sodden potato fields under a leaden sky. While the centre column charged into the northern tip of the village, taking the heaviest losses, the two flanking columns made a pincer movement to seize its southern end. The plan worked, thanks to good artillery support and to the ill-co-ordinated command of the French line on either side of Le Bourget. French counter-attacks to relieve the garrison of the village were piecemeal and ineffective, and were hampered by a horde of fleeing Gardes Mobiles who panicked when they saw themselves being surrounded. Although French fortress guns began targeting the village, they caused as much harm to their own troops holding out there as to the enemy.

Within Le Bourget there was desperate but unco-ordinated resistance. The remaining French defenders included battalions of the Imperial Guard that had remained in Paris at the outbreak of war, and they fought it out for over three hours with their opposite numbers in the Prussian Queen Elizabeth and Kaiser Franz Regiments. Budritzki himself grabbed a flag and led the storming of the first French barricade; then fighting was house-to-house, on staircases, landings and in cellars using bayonets and clubbed rifles. To make progress down the main street Prussian pioneers used pickaxes to knock holes in dividing walls. By about 11.00 a.m. the three German columns had joined hands in the village, but pockets of French troops held out until after midday in a glass factory, in stout farm buildings and in the church. Here a macabre contest was fought out in the nave, with the French using stacked pews as barricades and the Germans firing down through the church windows until the French survivors under Major Brasseur finally surrendered.

Officer casualties on both sides were particularly high, the Germans having two colonels killed. Total French losses were about 1,850, over 1,200 of whom were prisoners, while German losses were 468.[23] At the end of the battle the streets of the smashed village of Le Bourget were littered with discarded weapons, and its bullet-pocked walls were spattered with blood and brains.

The desolate scene, thought one correspondent, ought to cure anyone of enthusiasm for war.[24]

Though each blamed the other for the debacle, both Bellemare and Trochu had lost reputation. Trochu had given his trademark vague and ambiguous orders during the crisis. It was becoming painfully evident that his talents as a talker and writer, and his popularity as a pre-war critic of the army's failings, did not translate into any real capacity for field command. His proclamation dogmatizing on the small strategic importance of Le Bourget had a lame ring as lines of ambulance wagons trundled into Paris. The shock, disillusion and anger felt in the city at the incompetence that had led to the defeat were compounded by two other items of news that were borne through German lines that afternoon by Adolphe Thiers.

The Return of Thiers
Thiers, aged 73, white-haired, bespectacled and gnome-like, had completed a 5,000-mile trip around Europe in six weeks, and had come to report the results of his mission to the Cabinet.

He had volunteered to continue his search for international mediation, begun in London in September, by visiting the capitals of the other European Great Powers. For all its desire for peace, and Prime Minister Gladstone's personal distaste for the German annexation of Alsace without consulting the population, the British Government could not be budged from neutrality. It held to the view that, whilst it wished to see an armistice, it could not offer mediation until both belligerents requested it. Thiers put greater hopes in Russia, where he travelled next by way of Tours, Vienna and Warsaw.

Tsar Alexander II had greeted the news of Sedan by crossing himself and exclaiming, 'Thank God, Sebastopol is now avenged,' a reference to Russia's defeat at the hands of Napoleon III in the Crimean War.[25] Yet the new republican government in Paris was disagreeable to him, both on principle and because it included vocal advocates of Polish freedom, particularly Emmanuel Arago, defender of the Pole Berezowski who had attempted to assassinate Alexander in Paris in 1867. Venerating his uncle, King Wilhelm I of Prussia, Alexander did not share the disquiet of the Russian press at growing German power. Rather, his government covertly saw the war as an opportunity to free itself of the prohibition on maintaining a fleet in the Black Sea imposed on Russia by Britain and France by the Treaty of Paris of 1856 at the close of the Crimean War. With this end in view, Russia had no wish to antagonize Bismarck by offering mediation, and no interest in active intervention in the conflict. For all the courtesies lavished upon him at St Petersburg, the best Thiers obtained was a letter from the Tsar to the Prussian King encouraging the Germans to talk to Thiers, and requesting a safe-conduct for him to consult the government in Paris.[26]

On his return to Vienna on 11 October Thiers likewise received only polite expressions of goodwill from an Austro-Hungarian government which had no intention of becoming embroiled in a war that France clearly was losing. At his Vienna hotel Thiers by chance encountered a fellow historian, Leopold von Ranke, and exchanged ideas with his eminent old German friend on how peace might be made. Thiers insisted that, now Napoleon III was gone, France posed no threat to Germany, but that no French government could willingly cede Alsace. Ranke objected that French governments changed so often that Germany could not feel safe from attack, and that Alsace was German-speaking. 'The King of Prussia,' Ranke explained, 'is no longer fighting against Napoleon, who is a prisoner, nor against France as such; he is fighting the spirit of Louis XIV, who, at a time when Germany was weak and torn asunder, seized Strasbourg and Alsace without any right. We have contemplated this national demand since 1814–15.'[27]

In Florence Thiers, long an opponent of Italian unification, vainly tried to persuade the Italian Government that it was in its interest to intervene by sending troops to help France. But the Italians had already got what they wanted from this war, having taken advantage of France's troubles to occupy the long coveted Papal City of Rome. The only Italians who would fight in France were Garibaldi's volunteers, who would be beyond the control of both governments.

At the end of his mission Thiers returned to France on 21 October with nothing to show but the promise of the Tsar's letter. Reaching Tours, he learned that Britain had offered to broker an armistice, but he believed that a direct approach was required. Confident in his own abilities, he sought government authorization to negotiate directly with Bismarck. In his view there was little point in France fighting on alone, and every need for elections for a government that could be formally recognized by the Great Powers and empowered to negotiate a peace settlement. Thiers was impatient both of Gambetta's bitter-end rhetoric and the idea that the provincial armies could achieve anything. News of the fall of Metz further convinced him of the necessity of peace. On 30 October he reached German headquarters at Versailles and, after speaking briefly with Bismarck, crossed the lines into Paris under a safe-conduct.

The Cabinet was thunderstruck that night when Thiers brought news of the capitulation of Metz, only Trochu maintaining a philosophical calm. It was agreed that Thiers should return to German lines next day to seek an armistice with a view to elections on certain conditions; though publication of the fact should emphasize that this was at the wish of the neutral powers rather than a French initiative.

Thus next day, 31 October, Parisians had three government bulletins to digest at once, confirming rumours that were already current. To fury over Le Bourget was added the calamity of Metz, news of which made it appear that the government's earlier denials had been calculated lies. Whilst rumours of an armistice had kindled hope among many shopkeepers and bourgeois, radicals were confirmed in their worst fears that the Republic was being betrayed by incompetent cowards who did not share the popular determination to resist. Georges Clemenceau, a radical young doctor who was mayor of the 18th Arrondissement, posted a notice protesting 'with indignation against an armistice which the Government cannot grant without committing treason'.[28] Under the triple blow of the day's news, wrote one of Trochu's staff officers, 'the public spirit caught fire like a powder train'.[29]

Insurrection

Monday, 31 October, a dismal autumn day of cold rain, recalled those sinister, tempestuous days of the Great Revolution when the Paris mob had dictated its will to those attempting to govern France. Crowds gathered shouting 'No armistice!', 'Down with Trochu!' and 'Long live the Commune!'[30] After two months of crushed hopes, the moderate republicans who had seized power on 4 September confronted the self-same prospect of overthrow that the despised Imperial Government had faced that day at their hands.

The Committee of the Twenty Arrondissements was quick to see its opportunity, and early in the day two leading revolutionaries, the socialists Lefrançais and Millière, were calling for the invasion of the Hôtel de Ville, the overthrow of the government and proclamation of the Commune. By midday the crowd, including many National Guards, had forced their way into the Hôtel de Ville. The government, slow to realize its danger, had taken no effective measures to defend itself. Even those battalions of the National Guard in the vicinity who took no active part in the demonstration were either sympathetic or indifferent to the overthrow of the government, turning their rifle butts upward in the traditional gesture indicating that they would not defend it. Trochu, confident that speeches would calm matters, tried to address the invading crowd, but found himself angrily denounced for treason by a deputation of citizens. Matters had gone beyond speeches; Trochu was overborne and unable to make himself heard. Soon the government found itself virtually under siege in the Council Chamber.

Elsewhere in the building Étienne Arago, Mayor of Paris, was chairing a meeting of the mayors of the *arrondissements*. They wanted an end to armistice talks and immediate elections for an independent municipal government, which would have given them the authority of universal suffrage which the government signally lacked. When an emotional Arago took this proposition to the beleaguered government, it eventually agreed in principle but would not specify a day for the elections. When Arago went out to tell the crowd what had been agreed he found that he too had been overtaken by events: he was manhandled, insulted, and violent hands tugged at his sash of office. An armed mob burst into the Council Chamber and took the government hostage.

All evening there was pandemonium in the Hôtel de Ville, with neither members of the government nor anyone else able to make themselves heard above the cacophony of shouting. The air in the darkening, overcrowded room became foul with the stench of tobacco smoke, sweat, wet uniforms and alcohol, large amounts of which were being consumed by some rioters. Paris seemed briefly to live up to the American General Sheridan's disdainful characterization of it as 'a madhouse inhabited by monkeys'.[31] Around four o'clock Flourens arrived at the head of his Belleville troop, announced to the government that they were his prisoners, and began striding up and down, booted and spurred, on the Cabinet table. He and several others were drawing up lists for a new government which included the names of the revolutionary stalwarts Delescluze, Millière, Ranvier and Pyat, plus popular heroes like Victor Hugo. Flourens's list inevitably began with his own name, which drew derision even from some revolutionaries. Amid the chaos, he too began to grow hoarse, and Trochu heard the sergeant guarding him mock his slightly effeminate commander with the gibe, 'Florence, my dear, you're flagging.'[32] Surprised by events, the revolutionaries could not agree amongst themselves exactly what they proposed to do next; some wanted a Committee of Public Safety, as in 1793, some wanted a government led by Dorian, the Minister whose capacity for producing armaments efficiently made him the only popular member of the Cabinet. Meanwhile in another room a latecomer, Auguste Blanqui, set to work purposefully without engaging in debate, making appointments and issuing clear-headed orders which, if executed, would have secured the building against counter-attack.[33] If the exact constitution of the new government remained to be settled, it seemed evident that the revolutionaries had carried the day. While the interior of the Hôtel de Ville remained thronged, as the night wore on supporters of the revolutionaries began to drift away from the square, assuming that the day had been a success and that elections for the Commune would be held next day. Notices were being posted announcing them.

In the confusion one member of the government, Ernest Picard, had managed to slip away. He reached his office at the Finance Ministry by 5.00 p.m.

and began summoning help. Trochu's headquarters had taken no initiative all afternoon, feeling bound by the General's parting instructions to do nothing without an order from him. Picard ordered General Ducrot in western Paris to bring his troops into the city, and Ducrot, itching to settle matters with the revolutionaries once and for all, gave orders for an infantry division to be set in motion, accompanied by cannon and *mitrailleuses*. Meanwhile at approximately 8.00 p.m. a loyal battalion of the National Guard, under Major Ibos, succeeded in forcing its way into the Hôtel de Ville. So crowded was the Council Chamber, however, that only a few men could push their way in. For a while there was a slanging match between Flourens and Ibos, whose men managed amid the hubbub to spirit three members of the government out of the room: Jules Ferry, Emmanuel Arago and Trochu, whose staff secreted his epaulettes, decorations and gold-braided kepi to prevent him being recognized. When the revolutionaries realized what was happening they became enraged, and the remaining five members of the government, including Jules Favre and Jules Simon, were herded into a window recess at gunpoint. Bloodshed seemed imminent, yet, although a shot was fired accidentally, both sides were reluctant to begin a civil war. Even under intimidation, Cabinet members showed considerable personal courage by stolidly refusing to resign.

Avoiding bloodshed was Trochu's priority, and once at liberty he ordered Ducrot to halt his troops. Trochu wanted order to be restored by loyal battalions of the National Guard, though he yielded to Ducrot's insistence that it must have a reliable commander, the royalist Roger du Nord. Many of the National Guard seemed to be having second thoughts, for though they had no love for the government, nor were they willing to tolerate the rule of extremist revolutionaries. As Jules Simon candidly admitted, they marched, 'not for us, but only against Blanqui, Flourens and Delescluze'.[34] In the face of Trochu's reluctance to order any effective action, Jules Ferry took command for the government, displacing Roger du Nord and leading the loyal National Guard contingent to the Hôtel de Ville himself with drums beating. Great caution was necessary, for the lives of the ministers who remained hostages were in imminent peril. Ferry therefore negotiated with the revolutionaries inside, who realized that the balance of forces had been reversed. Thanks to an initiative by Major Legge of the Garde Mobile, the ground floor of the Hôtel de Ville was back under government control. Legge had led his battalion from the Napoleon Barracks through an underground passage into the basement of the building, and had disarmed and captured about 300 largely drunk National Guards and locked them in the cellars. Gradually Legge's Bretons recovered control of the building, and the revolutionaries, as hungry and exhausted as their captives, realized that their best gambit was to bargain for their own immunity from prosecution. This was accepted, and in the small hours the leading revolutionaries left the building together with the members of the government. Jules Ferry mounted the table and dismissed the remaining insurgents with the warning that 'if you attempt another coup we shall show no mercy'.[35]

Trochu was cheered by loyal battalions of the National Guard. That civil war had been avoided owed something to his calm and humanity. Yet it was mostly thanks to Picard, Ferry, Ibos and Legge, and to hesitations among the revolutionaries themselves, that the government had survived the day and found itself still in power.

The Cabinet would henceforth meet at the Quai d'Orsay or the Louvre rather than the vulnerable Hôtel de Ville. When its weary members convened on 1 November they were divided on whether they were bound by promises of immunity made to the insurgents under duress, and whether it was practicable to arrest the leaders. Picard, Ferry, Favre and Trochu spoke for strong measures, but were outvoted six to four. However, continuing insurrectionary activity in northern Paris shortly produced a reversal of the vote after a stormy debate. Next day a new attempt by Flourens and Millière to proclaim the Commune at Ménilmontant and to march on the Hôtel de Ville was prevented by a show of force, and they and other leaders were stripped of their National Guard commands. Twenty-two indictments were brought in connection with the events of 31 October, but the justice system was to prove both slow and indulgent. Blanqui went quickly to ground. One of his disciples, Gabriel Ranvier, was soon released from prison and was heard boasting in the clubs that the government lacked the courage to shoot him, but he would have the courage to shoot the government.[36]

The government went to the polls, but not in the way expected by the revolutionaries or the mayors. On 3 November Parisians were asked simply whether they wished to uphold the Government of National Defence. This was a plebiscite in the style of Napoleon III, which the men of 4 September had so decried, but they gladly employed the device to secure a mandate. The result endorsed them and was a sharp rebuff to the insurrectionary Left, which nevertheless remained a powerful force in Belleville and the neighbouring districts:

	Yes	No
Civilian voters	321,373	53,585
Armed forces	236,623	9,053
Total[37]	557,996	62,638

Elections were held on 5 and 7 November for the mayors and their deputies; a very different proposition to the elections for an independent municipal government demanded by the revolutionaries. This time the turnout was smaller but the Left did better, returning its trusted leaders in the working-class *arrondissements*.

Differences over repression of the insurgents and the elections led to the resignation of Rochefort from the government and of Étienne Arago as Mayor of Paris, his powers being assumed by Jules Ferry. The Liberal Edmond Adam was superseded as police chief by Ernest Cresson, while the ineffectual General Tamisier was replaced as commander of the National Guard by General Clément Thomas, hated by the extreme Left for his part in the bloody repression of the uprising of June 1848, which remained a vivid memory in Paris.

The government had emerged from the crisis strengthened, and Trochu sought to convince the National Guard that the armistice negotiations were not a prelude to capitulation but 'a tribute [by the neutral powers] to the attitude of the population of Paris and to the tenacity of the defence'.[38] Fortunately for the government, this inflammatory issue was about to be defused, temporarily at least.

Negotiations Fail
On 5 November Thiers returned from his talks with Bismarck. In the wake of the disturbances in Paris, Trochu judged it unwise to be seen meeting with him. Instead he sent Favre and General Ducrot out to Sèvres, the agreed point for flags of truce. The bridge having been dynamited by the French in September, Thiers was rowed across the Seine and met with Favre and Ducrot in the ruins of a house destroyed by shellfire.

Thiers's discussions with Bismarck, whom he considered 'a savage of genius',[39] had begun promisingly on 1 November. Thiers, confident in his diplomatic ability to arrange an armistice from which peace might follow, had brushed aside Bismarck's usual gambit of applying pressure by threatening to treat with the Bonapartes. The two men had agreed in principle to an armistice of twenty-five days for the French to hold elections, and Bismarck had even seemed willing to allow some token representation of Alsace and Lorraine. This appeared to be an advance on both the talks at Ferrières and on the two-day truce to organize elections which Bismarck had proffered through the good offices of the American General Burnside, who had acted as an intermediary between the two governments in the first fortnight of October. In the evening Bismarck, professing gratitude at having civilized company, had encouraged Thiers to talk informally.

But on 3 November Bismarck's tone, like the weather, had turned frostier. He had learned of the riots in Paris, and challenged Thiers to confirm that he still had powers to negotiate. Bismarck claimed too that King Wilhelm was in high dudgeon at reading Gambetta's proclamation of 30 October declaring Bazaine a traitor and inciting French resistance to the bitter end. To suggest that Metz might have been yielded through treachery was insulting to German military pride, and Gambetta's tone hardly indicated that the French were sincere in seeking peace. Taking these German complaints at face value, French conservatives would allege that Gambetta and the Paris revolutionaries between them had cost France the chance of an early peace on better terms than she later received. Thiers himself believed that had France made peace in November 1870 she might have kept a substantial part of Lorraine and paid a war indemnity of only 2 billion francs instead of 5 billion.[40] But Bismarck never formally offered such terms, and it is likely that Thiers's notorious vanity and eagerness to make peace led him to exaggerate what he might have obtained. The German generals certainly would have opposed any reduction of their territorial demands, and a possible mitigation of the financial penalty rested on no more than wishful thinking on Thiers's part.

In reality, the peace talks foundered on the question of the re-supply of Paris, just as they had in September. The French Government had stipulated that any armistice was conditional upon Paris being supplied with sufficient extra food for its duration, otherwise the Germans would be gaining an unfair military advantage. The Germans countered that they would be yielding the French a military advantage if they kept their armies stationary with winter coming on while the French used the cease-fire to improve their defences and train their armies. Moltke and the General Staff were adamant against an armistice on such terms. Their armies clearly held the upper hand and, with Metz in their pocket, what interest had they in postponing the inevitable capitulation of the French capital? Quite possibly, in any case, Bismarck was talking to Thiers only to sound him out and to give the neutral powers – particularly Russia – the appearance of being reasonable. He insisted that if re-supply were allowed the French must yield at least one of the Paris forts. 'You're asking me for Paris,' Thiers protested.[41] An impasse had been reached.

Thus when Thiers met Favre and Ducrot in the ruined house at Sèvres he reported that Bismarck would offer only an armistice without re-provisioning, or facilitation of elections in the occupied Departments without an armistice. Thiers suggested that it would be better to accept these conditions, harsh as they were, because there was little chance of military success and 'to continue the struggle ... would mean the complete ruination of France' and eventually even crueller conditions.[42] Ducrot took the opposite view: that military honour required France to fight on, to prolong the defence of Paris as long as possible, and to give the provincial armies time to organize.

'You're talking like a soldier, not a statesman,' Thiers objected.

Ducrot begged to differ, insisting that 'a great nation like France can always recover from material losses, but will never recover from moral ruin'.[43]

It did not take the government long to reach a decision. It unanimously rejected an armistice without re-supply as 'a covert means of reducing Paris without firing a shot',[44] and elections without an armistice as impossible. Public opinion in Paris would hardly let it do otherwise.

Both governments issued bulletins blaming the other for making totally un-reasonable demands. Bismarck, who apparently had been seeking pretexts to break off talks, expressed satisfaction at being 'rid of any more negotiations with Thiers'.[45] Thiers departed for Tours, his confidence in Russian support having proved illusory. The Russian Government had shown its real pre-occupation while the talks at Versailles were in progress, announcing to the other powers in a circular that it was abrogating the 1856 'Black Sea Clauses'. Seizing its opportunity while the West was preoccupied with the Franco-German War, it had nullified one of the main Allied achievements of the Crimean War. The Tsar then showed his continuing goodwill to Prussia by creating Crown Prince Friedrich Wilhelm and Prince Friedrich Karl honorary Field Marshals in his army: the same rank to which those jealous cousins had just been elevated in the Prussian service. 'I no longer see any Europe!' lamented the Austrian Chancellor.[46] France could look for no succour in her struggle with an enemy who now had her in a stranglehold.

Ducrot's Plan

Could the stranglehold be broken? General Ducrot thought so, and since early October had been developing plans for a breakout. He believed that the German lines were thinnest in the north-western sector, where the Seine wound its way from Paris towards the Normandy coast. He planned to launch an assault column of 50,000 men across the river on the western side of the Gennevilliers peninsula, around Bezons and Argenteuil. Preceded by a heavy bombardment of the German positions and aided by substantial diversionary attacks on other parts of the line, his troops would cross the Seine on pontoons and punch a hole in the German defences, then make forced marches up the right bank of the Seine towards Rouen through country as yet little touched by the war. The Norman capital, easily supplied by sea and rail, would become Ducrot's base and a rallying point for national resistance. By concentrating the forces being assembled in the North and the greater part of the Army of the Loire, Ducrot projected that 'we could assemble nearly 250,000 men between Dieppe, Rouen and Caen'. This feat would produce 'a most powerful effect upon morale'.[47]

Ducrot, who felt suffocated in the political hothouse of Paris, had initially yearned to leave the capital by balloon to lead the provincial armies, but was dissuaded by Trochu. His breakout plan would achieve the same end. At the head of a large relief army, he professed confidence that he could inaugurate a new phase of the war and defeat the German forces that inevitably would be sent against him, in all probability forcing them to raise the siege of Paris.

The ardent Ducrot's imaginative plan was open to several objections. He might well succeed in piercing the German front line, but if the Germans brought up their available reinforcements quickly they could use the high ground overlooking the Seine valley to decimate his column and possibly surround it as it tried to fight its way through. Vinoy thought the operation 'most perilous'.[48] Even if Ducrot reached Rouen with a substantial body of troops, he underestimated the speed and force with which the Germans could react, bringing their seasoned troops available after the fall of Metz to bear against his raw levies.

Ducrot's plan represented a reversal of French strategy. In August and September thousands of troops had been rushed into the capital to defend it, yet great energy and ingenuity were now devoted to contriving how to get a portion of them out again. Still, it was a plan, and Trochu gave it his blessing, albeit with some scepticism as to its chances of success. Neither he nor Ducrot apparently considered the possibility of isolating and destroying a portion of the besieging forces. Yet at least Trochu could feel more confident about the strength of the capital's defences. For if the German lines were growing more formidable with every passing week, so were his, making it at least as hard for the Germans to break in as for the French to break out.

Trochu put little faith in the ability of the provincial armies to aid Ducrot's attempt. Unaware of the prodigies being performed at Tours, he thought it would be a long time yet before they could take the field.[49] In any case, given the uncertainty and insecurity of communications with the Delegation by balloon, he was reluctant to commit details to paper. The idea of co-operation with the provincial armies was proposed by a civilian, Jules Favre, the only member of the government to whom Trochu had confided Ducrot's intentions. Favre realized that 'we could no longer limit ourselves to minor operations, or to the outpost actions that had inured our troops to combat during October', and urged upon Trochu the political necessity of 'striking a decisive blow'.[50] He suggested that Trochu confide in Arthur Ranc, a political associate of Gambetta's who was about to leave by balloon. Trochu did so, explaining the concept of shifting the Army of the Loire to Normandy in general terms. Ranc left Paris on 14 October and reached Tours safely, but Gambetta took Trochu's plan as only a suggestion, and one that presented logistical problems at that. He was unconvinced that Trochu had the resolution necessary for an offensive; an impression strengthened by the ambiguity of a later communication from Trochu which spoke of the Army of the Loire standing on the defensive. In sum, there was no clear plan for a co-ordinated offensive with mutually understood dates and objectives.

Ducrot carried forward his preparations with a view to launching his attack in the third week of November. Gun emplacements were dug, cannon and mortars were brought up ready for the bombardment, and he began concentrating troops west of Paris in readiness for the offensive. He justified the action at La Malmaison on 21 October partly by the need to keep the Germans away from his concentration area.

Secrecy was for once closely observed, though the related reorganization of the army was publicly announced on 6 November. Ducrot was given command of the main field army – designated Second Army – consisting of three corps and numbering 105,000 men and 288 guns. Trochu had intended Vinoy to command one of these corps, subordinating him to Ducrot. Trochu himself intended to command the 70,000-strong Third Army, largely composed of Gardes Mobiles, with the role of mounting diversionary attacks. On Ducrot's advice, however, Vinoy was given command of Third Army.

The entire National Guard, now 266 battalions strong, was formed into First Army under General Clément Thomas. Its role would be defensive. A decree of 8 November required each battalion to form four companies for field service, either from volunteers or, failing that, in turn from five categories of men classed by age and marital status, commencing with bachelors or widowers without children aged 20 to 35. It was a departure from the failed voluntary principle that could with advantage have come two months sooner. It produced 104,000 men eligible for field service, despite an outcry from the radical press and clubs that the government intended to lead its citizen soldiers to the slaughter.[51]

In fact Trochu, apparently more concerned with managing public opinion than the war against the Germans, continued to pander to the National Guard and to flatter it extravagantly. Instead of integrating the defence forces, as Gambetta was attempting in the provinces, Trochu's approach deepened the gulf between the different armed forces defending Paris – the army, the Garde Mobile and the National Guard – which was such a debilitating inheritance of the pre-war military system. The National Guard was encouraged to regard itself as superior to the regulars holding the front line. The army, conversely, had come to view the 'bitter enders' of the National Guard with smouldering contempt. Regulars resented seeing the half-trained, unreliable National Guard mollycoddled and kept away from real soldiering. Yet the prejudices of the generals – notably Ducrot – against using citizen soldiers on grounds of their unfitness were partly self-fulfilling. The great fund of patriotism and goodwill that undeniably had existed initially among the better elements of the National Guard was being squandered by its inactivity and inadequate training.[52]

Inter-service rivalries were but one symptom of the inaction that tried the nerves of soldiers and civilians alike as the weeks passed. The holiday atmosphere of September had evaporated as the privations of siege life bit deeper. By 9 November items of poultry and smoked ham were selling at four or five times their pre-war prices. Fresh fish, bacon and dried fruit had all but disappeared, and the price of eggs, butter and cheese put them beyond most purses.[53] Only alcohol seemed to be in bountiful supply: 'hideous drunkenness was the bane of a good part of the National Guard,' and the cause of public apprehension and complaint.[54]

Scarcity emboldened hundreds of scavengers – male and female, military and civilian – to venture out daily to forage for vegetables between the lines, either for their own use or for sale in the markets at inflated prices. Sometimes the Germans turned a blind eye in return for newspapers. On other occasions they shot scavengers – ten were killed and thirty wounded on 17 November – but neither the risks nor orders from Trochu curbed the practice. Meanwhile marauders profited from looting suburban houses that were either ruined or had been abandoned by the owner.

Paris was becoming a dirty and gloomy place. Litter accumulated because many of the city's pre-war street cleaners were Germans who had been expelled. From 1 November all use of gas lighting in public buildings and private homes had to be cut by half, and all gas lamps were to be extinguished by 10.30 p.m. Stocks of coal gas, already running low, were being further depleted by the need to inflate the balloons that were leaving Paris on average every other day. On 16 November all cafés and restaurants were ordered to extinguish gas lighting by 7.00 p.m., leaving customers to while away the hours playing cards or dominoes by candlelight or oil lamp. From the end of the month gas to private customers and public establishments was cut off to conserve supplies for street lighting and industry.[55] The boredom of dark evenings encouraged many to take more notice of striking autumn sunsets; and particularly of the spectacular natural display of the aurora borealis on the evenings of 24 and 25 October. Sightseeing tours of the ramparts on the perimeter railway remained a popular Sunday entertainment, while in the evenings the closure of the theatres had only swelled attendance at the political clubs. In late October theatres and concert halls began to reopen their doors: though in keeping with the puritanical public mood they played mostly patriotic or classical pieces, advertised as charity fund-raising events in aid of the wounded, widows and orphans, or the founding of more cannon.

The discomforts of the siege were compounded by the lack of reliable news. On the military front Parisians had only outpost skirmishes to divert them, including the exploits of Sergeant Hoff. An Alsatian of the 107th Regiment who believed that his elderly father had been shot by the Prussians, Hoff killed twenty-seven Germans in night raids. Otherwise the newspapers were full of the wildest rumours: Moltke and members of the Prussian royal family died regularly in their columns. The press also published military information of great potential value to the enemy. More than once, after divisive internal debate, the government announced measures of censorship and warned of harsh penalties. This had little effect, though police chief Cresson, after threatening to resign over the issue, did clamp down on the trade in obscene political cartoons, many featuring the imperial family, that had been rife since the September revolution.

The public was avid for any scrap of news from the outside. 'If by great good luck an edition of the *Journal de Rouen* should reach the city, it was reprinted as the most priceless of rarities,' wrote Edmond de Goncourt: 'Never have 2 million people been so completely imprisoned.'[56] Balloons could not return from the provinces to the capital, but the first flights had carried homing pigeons which were released on landing to notify Paris of the balloon's safe arrival. It was only a short step from there to writing short messages on strips of thin paper which were inserted in a tube and tied to the pigeon's wings; and from 10 October to an organized postal system whereby official despatches were set in print at Tours and photographically reduced, so that one pigeon could carry hundreds of messages that could be transcribed in Paris by clerks with magnifying lenses and delivered to the addressee. This increase in capacity allowed the service to be opened to the public from 10 November, enabling Parisians to receive replies to short messages sent out by balloon. The arrival of a carrier pigeon became an eagerly awaited event, and crowds would gather to follow, and even try to capture, any bird suspected of being a carrier. Nine birds arrived in September, twenty-one in October and twenty-four in November.[57]

Important as it was to the morale of the city, pigeon post was hazardous. Balloons carried 407 birds out of the city, but only seventy-three successful return flights with despatches were made during the siege. Newspapers made play of the ravages supposedly inflicted by German-trained birds of prey; but adverse winds, cold, predators, accidents and misadventures – including hungry French farmers – accounted for most of the birds that went astray. Twenty-four were captured by the Germans. Several copies of each despatch had to be made and entrusted to different birds to ensure safe arrival.

On 14 November a pigeon reached Paris bearing a despatch from Gambetta dated the 11th that electrified the city. It told of a victory over the Germans on the 9th at Coulmiers. 'How can I describe the intensity of emotions, the explosion of rejoicing, the extent of hope that this victorious clarion call created in Paris?' asked Trochu: 'The provincial armies existed, and could not only fight the Germans but beat them! All the doubts that had tormented people's minds were dispelled at once!'[58]

Gambetta had taken the strategic initiative and Trochu, who had taken so long to develop any plan of his own, would be forced to react to it.

Chapter 5

The Army of the Loire

Coulmiers

Following its defeats of 10 and 11 October at Artenay and Orléans, the French 15 Corps withdrew south of the Loire. There on 12 October it got a new commander, General Louis Jean-Baptiste d'Aurelle de Paladines, a 66-year-old retired veteran who had been recalled to service in the national emergency. Beyond a deep patriotism, the devoutly Catholic marquis had little in common with the ardent republicans controlling the government at Tours, but he quickly proved his competence at commanding an army. Within a fortnight d'Aurelle had produced a transformation which even Freycinet, with his mistrust of the old imperial officer corps, was forced to admire.[1]

D'Aurelle withdrew his men well to the south, to Salbris 50 kilometres from Orléans. Encamped on the commanding south bank of the River Sauldre, they were safe from immediate pursuit. He organized a proper system of pickets and cavalry patrols so that he knew where the enemy was and could not be surprised. He visited his troops and encouraged them, doing his best to see that necessary supplies of food, clothing and equipment were procured and distributed. He also instilled the discipline so conspicuously lacking hitherto, not only by plenty of drilling and instruction but by ruthless use of the new system of courts martial decreed by Admiral Fourichon at Tours on 2 October. Among the offences punishable by death under this draconian decree were not only espionage, murder and desertion but theft, marauding, wilful destruction of arms and ammunition, incitement to indiscipline and refusal to obey an order, with or without physical threats to a superior. Any man accused of one of these offences was to be court-martialled the same evening. Witnesses were to be heard and the defendant could speak, but there could be no counsel, no appeal and no revision. The court martial could vote only yes or no on the factual question of whether the offence had been committed. If 'yes' the mandatory death sentence must be carried out before the unit marched next morning.[2]

D'Aurelle expected his generals to make exemplary use of the decree in the face of the enemy. Quartermaster Corporal Amédée Delorme witnessed its application. A Corporal Tillot, slightly drunk, responded to a sharp word from his sergeant-major by shaking him violently by the lapels in front of 150 witnesses. Tillot was the father of a family, a middle-aged man who had joined up voluntarily to fight the invader, and when he sobered up he was apologetic and contrite: to no avail. As Delorme observed, 'he was caught up in the cogs of military justice, a terrible machine which the necessity of common security rendered pitiless'. The court martial had no option but to find him guilty as charged.

At dawn the whole brigade was drawn up in a forest clearing to see the condemned man alight from a carriage and walk, supported by a chaplain, to the place of execution where he was blindfolded and knelt ten paces from the firing squad. A funereal drum roll was succeeded by a silence more dismal still. 'In this space where 8,000 men were breathing in the open air, you could hear the laboured respiration of the condemned man like a death-rattle.' A lieutenant had barely finished reading the death sentence when 'the final word was smothered by a detonation that re-echoed in the forest like thunder. Then came a single shot, dry and sinister – the coup de grace – as a cloud of white smoke drifted upwards.' The troops were marched past the corpse to see the jacket perforated with holes, the pale face lying in a dark red pool. Delorme recorded that while one of his comrades declared the execution barbarous and stupid, others considered that Tillot had in his way been a martyr for the country, dying 'without glory but not uselessly', becoming a victim a few days before many of his fellows in order to exorcise the demons of fear and indiscipline.[3] Only a score of men were shot in this way, but the effect was profound, and discipline undeniably improved.

In addition to his 15 Corps d'Aurelle had under his authority 16 Corps, which was organizing north of Blois but was not yet in a state of readiness. His forces constituted the core of the Army of the Loire and formed a screen protecting both the arsenal at Bourges and the political capital at Tours. Gambetta and Freycinet were eager for the army to take the offensive and recover Orléans as a prelude to an advance to relieve Paris. We have seen that they discounted Trochu's idea of shifting the army to Normandy by rail as impracticable. It would leave central France open to invasion and General Bourbaki, who following his adventure in England had been appointed to command in Northern France, recommended against its adoption. Nevertheless, Gambetta was mindful of the need to relieve Paris quickly. According to his information the capital could not be expected to hold out beyond mid-December, and he was urged on by messages from Jules Favre. One, dated 23 October, insisted that 'Once Paris is relieved, the war is over! To march on Paris is therefore a necessity, and must be your objective.'[4] With the inexperienced army at Gambetta's disposal, the direct route to Paris via Orléans seemed the only feasible one.

Freycinet visited d'Aurelle at Salbris on 24 October to discuss an offensive. Next day the conference resumed at Tours with Gambetta presiding and a plan was agreed. It aimed at trapping Tann's I Bavarian Corps in Orléans by a pincer movement. A force of 30,000 men under General Martin des Pallières (another wounded veteran of Sedan) would cross the Loire to the east at Gien and advance up the right bank to Orléans. Meanwhile, leaving a screening force on the south bank of the Loire, d'Aurelle would cross the river to the west with 74,000 men and advance towards Orléans, where the two columns would join hands to cut off the Bavarians' retreat.

The movement began on 27 October with a view to a combined attack on Orléans on the 31st. The transfer of d'Aurelle's forces westwards from Salbris by rail was given out to be reinforcements for Le Mans, a plausible cover that confirmed German apprehensions of a French build-up in that direction. In fact, from Tours his troops were bound not north-west but north-east, to Blois and Mer, but transportation arrangements soon became chaotic, with units separated from their supplies and batteries from their ammunition. Days of heavy rain turned the roads into quagmires.[5] D'Aurelle, feeling that his units – particularly 16 Corps – needed more time to organize, asked for an adjournment of the offensive, which Freycinet grudgingly conceded. The right-hand column under Martin des Pallières, which had already begun its advance, was recalled across the Loire to its starting point.

The profoundly discouraging news of the fall of Metz reached d'Aurelle on 28 October under a flag of truce. He and his generals seethed with indignation at Gambetta's subsequent proclamation denouncing the 'treason' of Bazaine and his officers. Meanwhile Gambetta and Freycinet champed with impatience at the pause imposed by Thiers's armistice talks at Versailles and at d'Aurelle's apparent reluctance to advance. When Freycinet expressed his frustration at the thwarting of their military projects, Gambetta agreed emphatically that 'my mandate and my duty are to make all-out war'.[6] On 5 November d'Aurelle was ordered to resume the interrupted offensive. The new rendezvous with Martin des Pallières's column was set for the 11th at Orléans.

The advance of d'Aurelle's main force northwards was at first screened by the Forest of Marchenoir, and French confidence was greatly boosted when on 7 November they met and roundly trounced a German reconnaissance force under General von Stolberg at Vallière. However, this engagement dispelled General von der Tann's uncertainty as to French movements, and he had no intention of allowing his small force to become trapped in Orléans. Although the French reckoned his strength at 60,000, in reality it was scarcely 26,000. To keep his line of retreat open Tann reacted on 8 November as Bazaine should have done at Metz in August: under cover of darkness he moved west into open country with a clear road behind him, leaving only a small garrison in

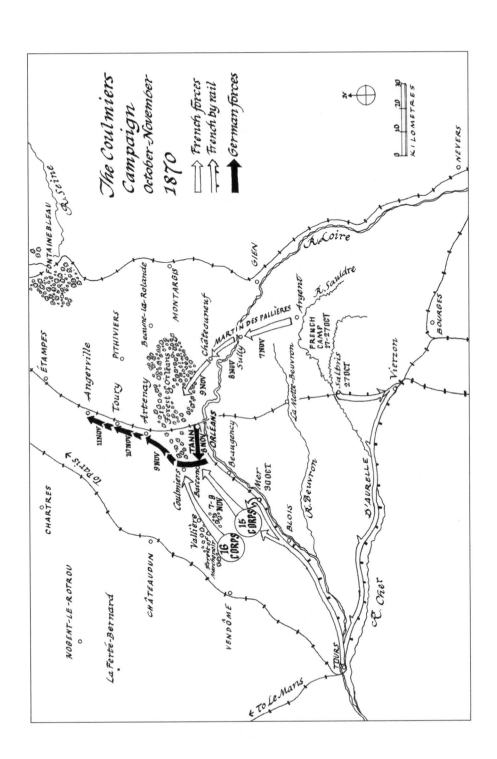

The Coulmiers Campaign October–November 1870

→ French forces
⇒ French by rail
➡ German forces

KILOMETRES
0 10 20 30

N

FONTAINEBLEAU
R. Seine
ÉTAMPES
CHARTRES
To Paris
NOGENT-LE-ROTROU
La Ferté-Bernard
CHÂTEAUDUN
VENDÔME
Angerville
Toury
PITHIVIERS
Beaune-la-Rolande
MONTARGIS
GIEN
R. Loire
R. Sauldre
NEVERS
BOURGES
VIERZON
Salbris 27 OCT
FRENCH CAMP 17–27 OCT
Argent
La Motte-Beuvron
MARTIN DES PALLIÈRES
7 NOV
Sully
8 NOV
Châteauneuf
9 NOV
Forest of Orléans
Artenay
11 NOV
10 NOV
9 NOV
ORLÉANS
TANN
8 NOV
Coulmiers
Baccon
9 NOV
Vallière
Forêt de Marchenoir
7–8 NOV
Beaugency
Mer 30 OCT
BLOIS
R. Beuvron
R. Beuvron
D'AURELLE
R. Cher
15 CORPS
16 CORPS
TOURS
← To Le Mans

Orléans. He improvised a defensive line anchored on the village and château of Coulmiers and its neighbouring villages, with his back to the Montpipeau Forest. There he awaited d'Aurelle's attack.

On the chilly, grey morning of 9 November the French advanced northwards along the wide plain that sloped gradually towards the Loire to their right. The good order of the long double line of his army moving silently as if on parade filled d'Aurelle with pride,[7] and for once the French had a more than two-to-one superiority. There was no tactical subtlety on display, but they attacked with spirit and their artillery, running forward boldly and firing shells with percussion fuses, showed German gunners that they could no longer have things all their own way as they had in the first weeks of the war. The commanding village of Baccon and the high-walled château of La Renardière were taken by 15 Corps on the French right; then during the afternoon the struggle focused on Coulmiers, which was assaulted by Barry's Division of 16 Corps. A young telegraphist arrived at the front at about 3.00 p.m. amid a maelstrom of cannon, *mitrailleuse* and Chassepot fire and watched awestruck as a French bayonet charge through a vineyard penetrated the blazing village in the face of a murderous fire: 'With what hatred Germans and Frenchmen lay about each other and fell to mutual slaughter! What exclamations of savage joy when the enemy fell, his chest pierced or his skull cleft, and the victor finished him off where he lay with a last blow accompanied by a grunt like that of a woodcutter felling a tree! How pitiful too when some young soldier, mortally wounded, lay in a ditch calling quietly and plaintively for his mother.'[8]

His troops overwhelmed, exhausted and low on ammunition, Tann retreated after Coulmiers had been lost and drew off northwards. He had lost 1,308 men to the French 1,800.[9] The initiative of one of his subordinates in directing reserves and the ineptitude of the French cavalry had combined to save his western flank from being turned. D'Aurelle's cavalry chief, General Michel, formerly head of the cavalry school at Saumur, had been sent off to the eastern theatre to replace General Cambriels, leaving command of the French cavalry at Coulmiers to General Reyau. Reyau ignored orders to cut off the German retreat. Instead he attacked in the wrong place, suffering unnecessary casualties; then turned tail and withdrew entirely when off to his left he thought he saw enemy forces that turned out to be Lipowski's *francs-tireurs*, who were under his orders. As a result the Bavarians made good their escape with little pursuit through a night of heavy rain mixed with snow. Meantime, off to the east, Martin des Pallières's column had heard the gunfire of Coulmiers but was too far away to close the trap.

Incomplete victory as it was, Coulmiers was an immense fillip to French morale, and the bells of Orléans rang out to celebrate the liberation of the city as French troops re-entered it. For the first time since war was declared, the

French army had squarely won a pitched battle. But could that victory be exploited?

The Fog of War

A bold general commanding troops flushed with their first victory might have pursued the exhausted Bavarian I Corps after Coulmiers and made a second attempt to destroy it. General Alfred Chanzy, who since 2 November had commanded 16 Corps, favoured making the attempt. D'Aurelle, however, was thinking in purely defensive terms. To continue to advance towards Paris after Coulmiers, he judged, would have been 'a hare-brained and rash attempt, exposing the army to certain destruction'.[10] Convinced that the Germans hoped to lure him into a trap if he advanced further, he proceeded to make Orléans a vast entrenched camp. He spread his corps out like a fan north of the city, partially concealed by the Forest of Orléans and protected in front by the *francs-tireurs* of Cathelineau and Lipowski. To his rear, labourers worked on a double line of defences, bristling with redoubts and palisades and backed by fifty-four naval guns. The rawness of his troops and the desperate shortage of experienced officers deepened d'Aurelle's conviction that standing on the defensive was his only option. Meanwhile, organization and equipment could be completed as reinforcements arrived.

Keeping an army stationary had its drawbacks, nevertheless. Since taking command d'Aurelle had insisted, for the sake of discipline, that his men should always sleep under canvas rather than be billeted in villages and farm buildings. French camps soon became seas of mud, and the November wet and cold took their toll on men who often lacked adequate clothing and nutrition. The hospitals became overcrowded with men suffering from diarrhoea and bronchial complaints, and the death rate rose alarmingly as smallpox spread. Many hospitalized men were slow to return to service.[11]

Whatever its justification, d'Aurelle's passivity allowed the Germans to recover the strategic initiative they had lost temporarily at Coulmiers. Even before the battle, on 7 November, Grand Duke Friedrich Franz of Mecklenburg-Schwerin had been given command of a large army detachment with the mission of protecting German siege lines around Paris against any French thrust from the west or south-west. His force included not only Tann's I Bavarian Corps – in disfavour at Versailles after their defeat – but a Prussian infantry division, Tresckow's 17th, plus Wittich's 22nd, and three cavalry divisions: in all about 45,500 combat troops and 208 guns.[12]

Crucially, too, Moltke could now bring the army that had captured Metz into play. One corps had already been brought from Metz to reinforce German lines around Paris. Three more were detached as First Army under General von Manteuffel to counter any French threat to the investment of Paris from the north. The balance, constituting Second Army under Prince Friedrich Karl, had started from Metz soon after its fall, bound for the Loire front and relieved to be away from the bleakness and squalor of the blockade. By the time Coulmiers was fought the seasoned troops of the German III, IX and X Corps and 1st Cavalry Division – 60,000 combat troops and 276 guns – had covered half the distance between Metz and the Loire. Moltke undoubtedly had under-estimated the likely extent of French resistance in the provinces, and at first intended Second Army to make straight for Bourges and central France. Upon the disquieting news of Tann's defeat, however, he ordered its advance to be angled more to the west, to cover Paris from the south. He also ordered the pace of the advance to be quickened, and German infantry began averaging 33 kilometres per day on a 70-kilometre front. This inexorable approach of the German Second Army from the north-east was a major reason for d'Aurelle's reluctance to leave his lines. To venture out, he reasoned, would invite being caught between the two fires of Mecklenburg and Friedrich Karl.

Yet for the moment those two forces were widely separated. Clashes between cavalry patrols and outposts occurred daily across the late autumn landscape, but neither side could quite dispel the fog of war that hid the other's intentions. Until late November the campaign in the Loire theatre, extending 200 kilo-metres from Le Mans in the west to Montargis east of Orléans, was governed by misconceptions on both sides.

The Germans were at first unaware of d'Aurelle's concentration at Orléans. Alarmed by hostile activity only two days' march west of headquarters at Versailles, they believed that the bulk of French forces were concentrating in that direction, around Le Mans. As a result, Mecklenburg led the bulk of his force not towards but away from Friedrich Karl's army for a week from 16 November, leaving only a cavalry screen covering the Paris–Orléans road. Heading first north to take Dreux, he then moved on a south-westerly axis through Nogent-le-Rotrou and La Ferté-Bernard on the road to Le Mans. The campaign was gruelling. Tann's men in particular craved rest after their defeat. The roads were bad, and many men had worn-out boots and sore feet. As the lame could not be left in such hostile country, they had to ride in a long convoy of requisitioned carts. The wooded and hilly Perche region, with its confined vistas, walls and thick hedges, was well-suited to defence and for once the Germans did not possess good maps of the country. The risk of ambush was constant, and the troops were under strain. Every day they had to deploy and fight, and though they won every action and pushed their enemy before them, every night in darkness and fog they had to fight again to secure their billets. They were a long way from home – and from the excitement and triumphs of the early days of the war. As they marched onward, their clothing and gear drenched by rain and caked in mud, little of the usual singing was heard.[13]

Although there were possibly 30,000 French troops west of Paris they were widely dispersed and ill-co-ordinated. Their daily combats with the oncoming German columns were not an orchestrated guerrilla campaign: rather, disparate local defence forces and Garde Mobile battalions who had never been under fire made piecemeal and vain attempts to block the road. Roger de Mauni, a junior officer in a battalion of Mobiles from Mortain in Normandy, described their baptism of fire in a forest near Thiron-Gardais on 21 November. His men were 'expiring with hunger and thirst' when news came of the German approach. They were formed into line of battle, 'straining our eyes in the endeavour to penetrate the depths of the woods'. Suddenly a party of German cavalry appeared, but turned and fled when fired upon. During the ensuing pause a chaplain pronounced absolution for the men, who 'were trying the hammers of their muskets – everyone thought the hour was come'. The soldiers waited in suspense as the cannonade drew closer. A peasant arrived claiming that some German cavalry could easily be captured at a nearby farm, and a company was detailed for the task. Whether through stupidity or treachery, the peasant led them into an ambush. The rest of the battalion heard intense firing but could see nothing, meanwhile experiencing being shelled for the first time:

> At last the bushes 200 paces ahead of us began to stir, and I saw emerge two men in long great-coats and shiny helmets. I had hardly sighted them before several of our men opened fired on them, and at the same moment the first Prussian bullets came whistling smartly about our ears ... The fight was now joined along the whole line, and our firing at will must certainly have destroyed a large number of the enemy, for the range was short and they were an easy target. But the gaps we made in their ranks were rapidly filled up, and when occasionally the smoke cleared we could see ever denser masses overflowing the road and the fields and threatening to overwhelm us.

To avoid being outflanked the French were forced to withdraw, having suffered significant losses.[14] Such scenes were repeated many times during the German advance on Le Mans. Such was the fear that the city would fall that Gambetta rushed there by train to inspire and organize the defence. But the Germans turned away. It had become evident at Versailles that the main French army was not to the west after all, but before Orléans. On 23 November Mecklenburg was ordered to shift front to the south-east, and to head for the Loire to link up with the right of Second Army. His intended day's rest for his weary men was overruled, and impatience at Versailles with the speed of his operations was signalled by the despatch of General von Stosch to replace his chief of staff.

The operational picture had become clearer to Moltke when General Werder had reported from eastern France on 22 November that the French army facing him was being transported westwards by rail. This was the army formerly commanded by General Cambriels, and for a few days after his departure by the cavalryman General Michel, who had immediately despaired at the prospect of commanding such a motley force and had been recalled. Leaving only 15,000 men to face Werder, the other 40,000 troops of the Army of the East became 20 Corps of the Army of the Loire, commanded by General Crouzat. They detrained at Gien on d'Aurelle's right flank on 19 November.[15] Also reinforcing d'Aurelle's right wing was the newly-raised 18 Corps, provisionally commanded by its chief of staff, Colonel Billot, an escapee from Metz. Meanwhile on d'Aurelle's left wing 17 Corps was in the process of formation under the command of Gaston de Sonis, a 45-year-old cavalryman with an aggressive reputation from his African service.

Thus, while the Germans were slowly concentrating their forces before Orléans, the French had brought up greater manpower to confront them. Freycinet asserted that the Army of the Loire was 250,000 strong, double its strength a month previously: though d'Aurelle protested that such a figure was 'exaggerated and partly fictitious ... It would be dangerous to trust in the deceiving mirage of figures on paper, and to mistake them for reality.'[16] He thought the actual figure nearer 145,000[17] and judged the new levies unfit to take the field. Many of them lacked items of uniform, haversacks, boots, tents and cooking pots, and they carried a bewildering variety of antique, converted or foreign weapons.[18]

Disagreements between the civilian and military leadership as to how the army should be used had become acute. In thanking the army for its victory at Coulmiers, Gambetta proclaimed,

> You are today on the road to Paris. Let us never forget that Paris awaits us, and that our honour demands that we wrest it from the clutches of the barbarians who threaten it with pillage and fire.[19]

But d'Aurelle had literally and figuratively entrenched himself before Orléans, and resisted all attempts by Gambetta and Freycinet to prod him into taking the offensive. Having emulated the mobilization of manpower in the American Civil War, the two republican politicians ironically found themselves facing the same dilemma as President Lincoln in 1862: how to prompt a conservative and cautious general who disapproved of radical war aims into using the immense army entrusted to his command. They reasoned and pleaded to no effect. 'Paris is starving and demands rescue' wrote Freycinet on 19 November, inviting d'Aurelle to join hands with Trochu. Next day Gambetta himself wrote, urging d'Aurelle to draw up a plan for the advance on

Paris.[20] D'Aurelle's obduracy provoked Freycinet into drawing up his own orders for an advance, and the general's criticisms drew from him an acid rejoinder:

> If you bring me a better plan than mine, or indeed if you bring me any plan at all, I can abandon mine and revoke my orders. But, during the twelve days since you have been at Orléans, despite the reiterated invitations of Monsieur Gambetta and me, you have proposed no plan whatever ... Necessities of a superior order oblige us to *do something*, and consequently to advance from Orléans.

He emphasized that spending the winter at Orléans was not an acceptable political option, and that the bad roads of which d'Aurelle complained were equally difficult for the Germans. The military difficulties would remain long after Paris had run out of food: 'Therefore we must stir from our immobility, which the salvation of the country will no longer permit.'[21]

D'Aurelle's evasive reply was the last straw. Freycinet began issuing orders direct to corps commanders, merely copying them to d'Aurelle. If the commanding general was not going to use his army, Freycinet would, working out moves on a map in his office and telegraphing them from day to day. His conception of the military situation was shaped by Mecklenburg's advance, which apparently threatened the seat of government at Tours, where panic took hold. An attempted northward counter-thrust by Sonis's 17 Corps backfired when that general thought himself about to be outflanked at Châteaudun and on 26 November ordered a night retreat that ended with thousands of his troops scattered and disorganized. To relieve the pressure on the threatened French left, Freycinet believed, required a blow launched at the opposite end of the German line, east of Orléans. An attack in that direction could also open a path towards Fontainebleau to join hands with the imminent breakout from Paris. Accordingly, he ordered 18 and 20 Corps on the French right wing to advance and attack Friedrich Karl's left flank.[22]

Unknown to Freycinet, the immediate threat to Tours had passed. Friedrich Karl, daily more convinced of French strength in front of Orléans, had wheeled his army round to confront it. His urgings, combined as we have seen with intelligence of the reinforcement of d'Aurelle's right flank, had induced Moltke to order Mecklenburg to shift eastwards to make junction with Second Army. As d'Aurelle pointed out, Freycinet's plan would pitch a fraction of the French army against a strongly-placed enemy, risking defeat outside his carefully prepared lines.[23]

Even so, the offensive almost succeeded. On 28 November, 63,000 French troops bore down on 14,000 Germans of X Corps posted on the hills around Beaune-la-Rolande. The plan was to encircle them, with Crouzat's 20 Corps attacking from the west and south while Billot's 18 Corps attacked the enemy's rear around Juranville to the east. But stubborn German resistance prevented the French pincers from closing. On the eastern sector Billot was held up all day, condemning Crouzat to fight a separate battle. On the 20 Corps' front the town of Beaune-la-Rolande proved a veritable fortress. Having arrived in the town on 24 November, the Germans had prepared its stone houses and cemetery for defence, loopholing walls, building barricades, and erecting firing platforms behind the partly ruined but still thick and high medieval defensive perimeter wall. The French, advancing in dense swarms with what a German described as 'a sort of savage enthusiasm',[24] met 'a real hurricane of lead and iron' at close range.[25] Yet despite suffering heavy casualties they almost surrounded the town. The German situation looked desperate during the afternoon until they were reinforced by a division from III Corps. General Stülpnagel, commanding 5th Division, had anticipated his orders by marching towards the sound of the guns, while nearby French commanders took no such initiative. Crouzat was reluctant to use his artillery to bombard an occupied French town, and the Germans could not be dislodged. In desperation, Crouzat had bugles sounded and led the last charge at dusk:

> We reached the first houses, and were greeted there by a most intense fire at point-blank range. Our horses started at the red flames from rifles; revolvers cracked ... It was futile ... The street was blocked by a burning timber barricade, and by now only a few officers were following me. We had to return to our point of departure, which we did at a walk. The road was covered with my poor dead or wounded Gardes Mobiles and Zouaves.[26]

Among the dying Zouaves was Frédéric Bazille, one of the most promising artists of his generation.

As night fell the first units of 18 Corps finally arrived, but in the darkness and confusion began firing on Crouzat's men. It was enough. Crouzat pulled his troops back, their shaken morale further depressed by the sound of German victory chants. In the darkness near Juranville medical teams went out with lanterns to gather the wounded who, wrote Dr Henri Beaunis, 'were nearly all young, and nearly all experiencing battle for the first time'. He noted disapprovingly that 'some of them were crying like babies' with pain.[27]

Freycinet claimed a strategic success.[28] In reality, the hard-fought battle of Beaune-la-Rolande was a bloody repulse which cost the French over 3,000 men to 900 German casualties. The failure of d'Aurelle and Freycinet to work together, combined with a lack of co-ordination on the battlefield, had lost any chance there might have been for a victory before the Germans had fully concentrated their forces.

The Road to Paris is Blocked

Improbably, the next French offensive, and the crisis of the war in the Loire theatre, was triggered by a telegram from Norway.

On 24 November General Trochu in Paris had written a despatch to the Delegation in response to the tidings of Coulmiers:

> The news received from the Army of the Loire has naturally prompted me to decide to break out to the south and to go to meet it, at any cost.

The breakout, under General Ducrot, would be launched on 29 November and the Paris army would head for the Loire, probably towards Gien.[29] Trochu's despatch was put aboard the balloon *La Ville d'Orléans*, which took off from Paris at twenty minutes to midnight.

Night flights for balloons had recently been introduced as a security measure. It was not that German patrols blazing away at passing balloons had done much harm, nor that the small cannon being designed by Krupp to bring them down had yet claimed any successes. It was rather that the Germans had developed a system for observing the balloons and reporting their position by telegraph, leading to three recent captures. Hence night departures to foil daylight observation. Yet the new routine carried its own risks, including higher winds and loss of visibility. When darkness and fog had dissipated sufficiently to see what lay below, the novice pilot of *La Ville d'Orléans* broke into a cold sweat on realizing that he was moving fast above the North Sea. After a nerve-wracking journey he and his companion managed to jump to ground as the balloon passed low over a snow-covered mountainside nearly fifteen hours after leaving Paris. With wolves but no humans in evidence, they slept that night in an abandoned cabin. Only next day, 26 November, did they find an occupied habitation and learn that they were in Norway. Their balloon had travelled 1,246 kilometres, an unwanted record among the sixty-seven launched during the Siege of Paris.

While they were travelling from the remote region where they had landed to Oslo, Trochu sent a duplicate message by another balloon, *Le Jacquard*. It proved even more ill-fated, being driven north-west and lost at sea with its pilot.[30] The earlier message was finally transmitted from the French embassy at Oslo on 29 November, via London, reaching Tours at 5.20 a.m. on the 30th. Freycinet took the train to Orléans, and at a council of war with d'Aurelle and his generals that evening ordered an advance without delay to join hands with Ducrot, who must already have begun his sortie.

The plan was for the Army of the Loire to concentrate around Pithiviers, then to strike north-east for Fontainebleau to rendezvous with Ducrot. As Chanzy's 16 Corps on the army's left had the furthest to go it would start first,

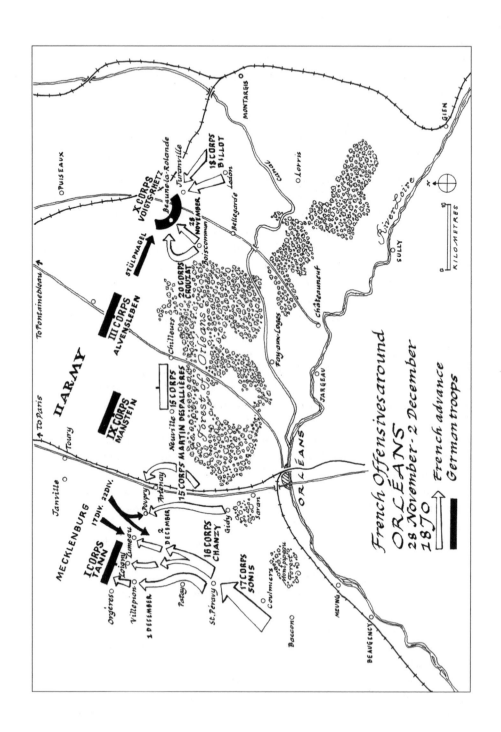

French Offensives around
ORLÉANS
28 November - 2 December
1870

⇧ French advance

▬ German troops

wheeling to the right towards Pithiviers. As Chanzy was well aware, in doing so he would expose his left flank to German forces to his north, around Janville and Toury on the main road from Orléans to Paris. Freycinet was impatient. He thought Chanzy strong enough to drive off the Germans in that direction, and reiterated that the government's orders were irrevocable.[31]

Next morning, 1 December, Chanzy began his march in clear weather across the snow-covered plains of the Beauce. The ground had frozen hard overnight, making it easier than of late to move men and guns. When Chanzy reached Patay, scene of Joan of Arc's victory over the English in 1429, he received confirmation that there were Germans to his north. He had his left division – Admiral Jauréguiberry's – peel off to drive them away, and arranged for cavalry and artillery to support it. The fighting was brisk, lasting from early afternoon until after dark. Jauréguiberry was everywhere on his little horse, leading by example and encouraging his men with shouts of 'Come on boys! Get your hands out of your pockets! You can warm them on your rifle barrels later.'[32] His opponents were first one brigade, then another of Tann's Bavarians who, though caught in the open before they could concentrate, did their best to hold out until nightfall against the impetus of the French assault. Finally a French bayonet charge took the village of Faverolles, and the substantial château of Villepion and its tree-lined park were captured. The Battle of Villepion had seen some 17,000 Frenchmen drive 16,000 Germans from the field at a cost of 1,100 casualties for 936 German.[33]

This victory was not the sole cause of rejoicing in the French camp that night. A balloon landing at Belle-Ile off the Brittany coast that day had brought great news from Paris. Freycinet assured d'Aurelle that 'Paris has made a supreme effort. The lines of investment have been broken and thrown back with admirable heroism.' The general must therefore 'Fly to Ducrot's assistance without losing an hour.'[34] Accordingly, d'Aurelle exhorted his soldiers to attack with the same ardour as the Paris army: if they did so, 'We can save France!'[35]

The bulletin from Paris, and its bearers, had given the impression that the battle on 30 November had succeeded, and included the statement that French troops had 'advanced upon Longjumeau and brilliantly seized the fortified positions of Épinay'. Longjumeau, 18 kilometres south of Paris, was within German lines. From the juxtaposition of names, Gambetta reasonably assumed that the Épinay in question was nearby Épinay-sur-Orge, which is further south still, and that the German lines had therefore been broken. Amid wild celebrations at Tours, nobody suspected that it was actually Épinay-sur-Seine, north of Paris, that had been taken in a diversionary attack. Gambetta and Freycinet were convinced that German forces facing d'Aurelle must pull back towards the capital to help contain the French breakout.

They were mistaken. Chanzy's men, ordered not to reveal their positions by lighting bivouac fires, spent the long, freezing night without warmth. Yet they could see that the Germans north of Villepion had no such inhibitions, and the extent of their campfires was disquieting. The Grand Duke of Mecklenburg was not withdrawing at all, but concentrating his forces west of the Paris road. His front line encompassed the villages of Loigny and Lumeau, in close proximity to the French, and he was determined to fight. 'In every campaign,' wrote a German general to his wife, 'there are moments when the outcome of the war hangs in the balance. It is so now, but the balance seems to tip in our favour.'[36]

On the bitterly cold morning of 2 December, under a winter sun appropriate to the anniversary of Austerlitz, Chanzy ordered the whole of 16 Corps forward in the hope of 'pursuing the enemy vigorously'.[37] His men advanced with the same spirit they had shown at Coulmiers against the same enemy, Tann's Bavarians. But this time the Germans were in strength and enjoyed good fields of fire for their rifles and artillery over open terrain. After driving in the German outpost line the French struggled to make headway amid a hail of shellfire that unnerved several regiments. Even local successes could not be exploited when German reserves made a timely appearance. The open country allowed German cavalry to menace the French left, until a battery of *mitrailleuses* and Chassepot fire proved more effective than French cavalry in keeping them at bay. However, it was on the French right that the attack began to unravel with the intervention of Tresckow's 17th Prussian Division and Wittich's 22nd. Chanzy's right division attacking Lumeau disintegrated under the impact of a flank attack; some of its men fleeing all the way back to the Orléans defences. His second Division, Barry's, sorely mauled in the early attacks, had also withdrawn, leaving Jauréguiberry's to bear the brunt of the fighting. By early afternoon the Germans had moved over to the counter-attack, and it was all the French could do to hold their ground in Loigny itself and around Villepion. Dense bodies of German troops could be seen from the turret windows of the château. Chanzy sent an urgent appeal for help to General de Sonis of 17 Corps.

De Sonis had little confidence in his raw and unsteady troops, who had been following in Chanzy's rear in a supporting role. He sent forward his reserve artillery, which helped stabilize the French line, but his leading infantry brigade quickly gave way under heavy fire. Seeing that the situation was desperate, Sonis, an ardent Catholic, brought forward his favoured elite troops, 300 of Charette's volunteers from western France, formerly the Papal Zouaves, together with two companies of Mobiles from the Côtes-du-Nord and *francs-tireurs* from Tours and from Blidah in Algeria, some 800 men in all. At about 4.00 p.m. they charged from Villepion towards Loigny, the Papal Zouaves following not the tricolour but their banner of the Sacred Heart of Jesus. It was an epic but forlorn bayonet charge.[38] Charette and Sonis were shot from their horses and 380 of their men, including two-thirds of the Zouaves, became casualties. Although survivors reached the first houses of Loigny, a German counter-attack in the winter's dusk drove them out again. Elsewhere in that blazing village the 37th Regiment was still holding in the cemetery as night fell, its wounded and captured commander replying to a German general's invitation to order his men to lay down their arms with, 'Monsieur, it's your job to make my men stop firing, not mine.'[39] Their grim battle among the tombstones finally ended with their being taken prisoner.

About 8 kilometres east of Loigny, a separate battle was being fought that afternoon. A division of 15 Corps, moving northward in accordance with orders, encountered Germans around the village of Poupry and attacked. This initiative might have ensured Chanzy's men success had it occurred in the morning, but by the time it was launched the right of 16 Corps had already been broken, and with their usual skill in moving reinforcements to the threatened point the outnumbered Germans were able to rush units from Wittich's Division to meet the new threat at Poupry. That, and the failure of another division of 15 Corps even to reach the battlefield, ensured that the fighting there ended in bloody stalemate.

Since Coulmiers the obvious strategy for the French had been to try to bring the bulk of the Army of the Loire against some fraction of the German forces facing them. D'Aurelle's caution both before and after Coulmiers had combined with Freycinet's meddling to sacrifice that chance. On 2 December 16 Corps had fought alone all morning, while in the afternoon only fractions of 17 and 15 Corps had come belatedly to its support. Meanwhile at the far right of the French line 18 and 20 Corps, battered by their repulse at Beaune-la-Rolande, together with half of 15 Corps, had been too far away to help. At most the French had brought 45,000 men disjointedly into action and had failed to find a German weak spot.

The Germans had suffered 4,142 casualties,[40] but the French had lost nearly 7,000, including 2,500 prisoners. This was more than a setback. The Army of the Loire had shot its bolt against an enemy who was just too strong. Morale dropped, and the state of his forces convinced d'Aurelle that he had no option but to pull his army back in order to save it.[41] The Battle of Loigny was the high-water mark of the French offensive, and Mecklenburg's troops were the rock against which the tide broke before rolling back.

Conditions at the front were dreadful as more snow fell during the night, covering the dead and dying as burning villages illuminated the landscape. French wounded died in the blazing church of Loigny whilst within sight of its steeple wounded of both sides froze to death. General de Sonis, his left leg shattered by a shot at close range, was amongst thousands who lay out in the snow. Resting his head on his saddle, he survived, though with a frost-bitten right foot, and following amputation lived until 1887.

An overblown proclamation to the country penned by Gambetta under the previous day's impression of victory convinced few in the camps with its claim that Prussian tactics had proved 'impotent against the solidity of our troops'. Its closing paean to 'the heroic spirit of the Revolution' and to 'the Republic one and indivisible' struck a flat note in this army where many men were royalist and Catholic in sentiment and were officered by local nobles. According to d'Aurelle, soldiers' comments on the orator's exhortations were 'picturesque and caustic'.[42] Their disillusion would have been greater had they known that, Gambetta's fanfaronade notwithstanding, the great sortie from Paris had been a failure.

Chapter 6

The Pinnacle of Hope

The Eve of the Great Sortie

The Army of the Loire's latest offensive had been improvised in response to Trochu's announcement of a sortie from Paris; a sortie which, ironically, had been improvised in response to the news of Coulmiers. On 19 November Trochu took the decision to abandon Ducrot's projected breakout west of Paris and instead to attempt one southwards to join hands with the Army of the Loire. Although he later claimed to have been pressured into changing his objective by messages from Gambetta, actually he was carried along by a tide of press enthusiasm, the urgings of Cabinet members, and the simple logic of the popular cry 'They are coming to us, we must go to them!'[1]

After all his preparations, General Ducrot was bitterly disappointed. He had no faith in what the Army of the Loire might achieve, and he abandoned his plans on the lower Seine with great reluctance. Nor, after a reconnaissance south of Paris, was he impressed with the chances of success on that part of the front. Then a staff officer, Colonel de Miribel, suggested that the Germans might be less on their guard in the south-eastern sector, where the River Marne loops its way towards its junction with the Seine, forming a natural moat. Here the French could cross the Marne under cover of their fortress guns and, with their flanks protected by the river, perhaps establish themselves on the heights beyond before the Germans could react. From there they could push on towards Fontainebleau.

Ducrot, whom Thiers once described as 'a man with one pint of blood too many'[2] was enthused by the possibilities and from 23 November threw himself into planning and organizing the new operation. During 27 and 28 November he smoothly transferred his Second Army from the western outskirts of Paris to the south-eastern: some troops marching through the city, others being transported by the perimeter railway. About 80,000 men were massed in the plain outside the Fort of Vincennes on the west bank of the Marne ready for the attack. In his usual style Ducrot drew up elaborately detailed orders specifying the movements of every unit. The essentials of his plan were for two of his three corps to cross the Marne between Joinville and Nogent, then to seize the heights overlooking the east bank around Champigny, Villiers and Bry. Meanwhile, Exéa's 3 Corps would cross the Marne further to the north-east to outflank the Germans defending Bry. The offensive would be supported by six diversionary attacks around the defensive perimeter of Paris designed to confuse the Germans as to where the main blow would fall.

The success of the operation would depend on speed and surprise. Each infantryman would carry 108 rounds of ammunition and six days' rations but would otherwise travel light; blankets and the sheepskins that some troops had obtained as body-warmers were to be left behind. When junction was made with the Army of the Loire, Ducrot would take command of both forces.

Troop movements for the intended offensive on the Marne could hardly be kept secret in Paris, and were widely discussed. Any doubts about the date set by Trochu were dispelled by the announcement in the *Journal Officiel* of 25 November of the closure of the city gates on the 29th. On the eve of the offensive, 28 November, General Ducrot issued a stirring proclamation to his army to nerve his troops for the struggle. Trying to impart the 'thirst for vengeance and rage beyond words that fill me', he included the oath that was to hang around him like an albatross:

> I swear before you and the entire nation that I shall not return to Paris save dead or victorious; you may see me fall, but you will not see me retreat. In that event don't stop, but avenge me.[3]

Though much derided for his boast after the event, there can be no doubting Ducrot's passionate sincerity. Probably his words were a conscious echo of the Duc de Montmorency's vow to return as 'victor or dead' when sallying from Paris to fight Condé's besieging Protestant army in November 1567, an attempt in which Montmorency died. A legend, originating in the patchily reliable memoirs of the Comte d'Hérisson in 1885, claimed that these famous words had been inserted in the manuscript by the promoter of the Suez Canal, Ferdinand de Lesseps, who supposedly was dining with Ducrot when the proofs of the proclamation arrived from the printer. (During the siege de Lesseps busied himself with organizing one of the city's many private ambulance services. His son Victor was on Ducrot's staff and was closely involved in preparations for the sortie.) This canard was mischievously taken up by the Paris press in 1892 when it was in full cry after de Lesseps during the Panama scandal, and has been repeated since. Like most good anecdotes, it was baseless. During the controversy Ducrot's children produced the draft of the proclamation, including the disputed phrase, entirely in the general's handwriting. He had consulted Trochu about the draft, and even that addict of windy rhetoric had cautioned against giving a hostage to fortune with the 'dead or victorious' phrase; but Ducrot insisted on retaining it. The only alteration he made at Trochu's behest was to change a reference to the 'outrage' of French women to 'desolation'.[4]

When Ducrot issued his proclamation it undoubtedly caught the mood of many at a moment of intense patriotic fervour. All felt that the fate not only of Paris but of France hung on this long anticipated effort to break the German lines of investment. 'You had to have lived through those unforgettable hours to understand the effect,' wrote one officer,[5] while a veteran colonel agreed that 'It is with such stage effects that one motivates men. Let them all be convinced that tomorrow we must break through or die, and they will break through.'[6] A Zouave testified that when his unit first heard the words they produced genuine enthusiasm.[7]

The operation began on the night of 28 November but went awry from the outset, giving rise to another enduring myth about the Great Sortie. Following the report of Chief Engineer Krantz, Trochu and Ducrot swore to the end of their days that their plans had been thwarted only by an unpredictable natural event – a sudden rise in the waters of the Marne. In reality, no such rise occurred. Rather than being in spate, the waters of the Marne were relatively low that night and the weather was calm.[8] The violent current that prevented the laying of pontoons was certainly no illusion, but its causes were man-made. At the approach of the Germans in September the bridge at Joinville had been blown up, even though it was easily commanded by French fortress guns. The debris of the bridge formed channels in mid-river where the current ran very fast, and the problem had unwittingly been aggravated by adjustments the engineers had recently made to a barrage they had constructed upstream to protect a trestle bridge.

Thus when the leading tug of the pontoon flotilla, *La Persévérance* under Commander Rieunier, attempted to pass upstream through the ruined Joinville Bridge, it found itself struggling desperately against the current and battered against the remaining piers. During a second attempt at full speed ahead three of the pontoons it was towing sank, together with their crews and equipment. Finally, with every valve straining, *La Persévérance* succeeded in passing beyond the bridge, but much too late for the pontoons to be completed before dawn as planned. Nor had Krantz's engineers got the downstream pontoons in place. On learning the news in the small hours of 29 November a furious Ducrot went to confer with Trochu. After considering alternatives they reluctantly concluded that they had to delay the operation for twenty-four hours. However, Ducrot insisted that the diversionary attacks should go ahead as planned to distract the Germans' attention. Apparently Trochu had some misgivings, for at about 7.00 a.m. he sent a characteristically ambiguous message to the commanders of the diversions advising them that the main offensive was adjourned, but leaving the course to be pursued to their discretion.[9]

By the time Trochu's telegram arrived, three of the diversionary attacks had commenced. The most important, the seizure of the Avron plateau by Rear

Admiral Saisset's sailors, had met no opposition. Possession of the detached plateau, which projected eastward from beyond Fort Rosny towards German lines, would allow French artillery to cover the more northerly river crossings that Ducrot would be using. Saisset quickly established ten batteries on it. Meanwhile south of Paris naval troops scored another smart success with Rear Admiral Pothuau's seizure of the Gare-aux-Bœufs Farm. However, to the west of this action an attack by one of Vinoy's brigades against the fortified village of L'Hay became mired in a costly fire-fight. German positions had been insufficiently prepared by artillery and the promised entrenching tools failed to arrive. When Vinoy received Trochu's telegram at 8.35 a.m. he ordered a retreat, including the evacuation of Gare-aux-Bœufs. The contempt in which Trochu and Ducrot held Vinoy's military abilities was cordially reciprocated. Vinoy was livid that he had needlessly lost nearly 1,000 men.

The Germans had suspected for some time that a sortie was being prepared – so much was evident from their habitual analysis of the Paris press, from spies and the interrogation of deserters. By 28 November these sources, together with increased French artillery fire, suggested that it was coming in the south-eastern sector. Next morning news of the Battle of Beaune-la-Rolande and French occupation of the Avron plateau added to the intelligence picture indicating such an attempt. Moltke took needful precautions, wiring Fourth Army Headquarters to support 'with all available forces' the Württemberg Division which held the neck of the Marne peninsula. One division of XII (Royal Saxon) Corps was ordered to the threatened sector, while the other and the corps artillery stood ready in support.[10] The day's delay to the French bridging operation had cost any chance that might have existed of catching the Germans at a disadvantage.

Champigny

With the pontoons now in place, Ducrot's men began crossing the Marne before dawn on 30 November. Behind them a great arc of French artillery pounded the peninsula they were entering. The morning was clear and cold and the guns made 'an infernal uproar'. 'What a spectacle! What a setting! What an orchestra!' thought Ducrot's medical director.[11] Yet for all its noise and visual grandeur, and Ducrot's promise that it would sweep away all obstacles, this bombardment by over 300 cannon was hitting ground held only by the German outpost line – a few companies of Saxons who had relieved the Württembergers at the front line overnight. French artillery was not damaging the main German defensive line on the hills at the neck of the peninsula.

This was not evident at first as French troops made rapid progress. The Saxons were pushed out of Champigny by the division of Joseph Faron, a Marine general who had campaigned in Senegal and had been commanding in

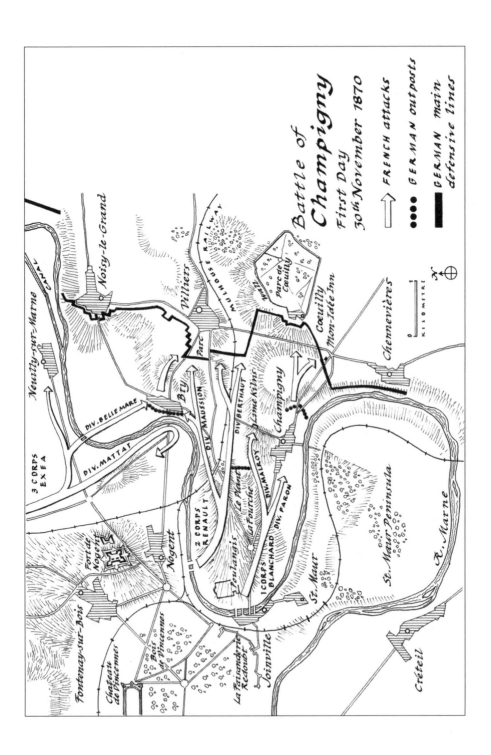

Battle of
Champigny
First Day
30ᵗʰ November 1870

⟶ FRENCH attacks

●●●● GERMAN outposts

▬▬ GERMAN main
defensive lines

0   1
KILOMETRE

Cochin-China on the outbreak of war. To its north Malroy's Division captured a landmark cluster of limekilns, while further north still 2 Corps seized the railway embankment and Bry. By 10.00 a.m. the French were established in a line across the peninsula. From this point onward, however, the ground rose steeply and German resistance stiffened.

The Germans had fortified the high ground using the long park walls of two châteaux, Cœuilly to the south facing 1 Corps and Villiers to its north barring the way to 2 Corps. Solidly dug in, with their second line well in rear of the crest, they had created formidable killing grounds raked by artillery, particularly from a redoubt by an inn named *Mon-Idée* – called the Jägerhof in German accounts. German percussion fuses bursting on the hard-frozen ground were cruelly effective against French troops who mounted successive charges in close formation, but who had insufficient field artillery to hand to support them. Casualties in this lethal blizzard of fire were frightful as regiments of scared Gardes Mobiles went forward 'huddled together like sheep'.[12] Amongst the high proportion of officers brought down as the hours passed was the commander of 2 Corps, General Renault, who had an outstanding reputation for bravery in Africa. His thigh smashed by a shell, he died a few days later, allegedly cursing Trochu.[13]

On the right against Cœuilly even the two regular regiments, the 35th and 42nd Line, could not break the German lines. The 42nd alone lost 800 men on the Cœuilly plateau, reinforcing the regulars' laconic complaint in this war that 'it's always the same men who get killed'.[14] After suffering severe losses French units became inextricably confused and the Germans mounted local counterattacks – the Saxons in the north towards Bry, the Württembergers towards Champigny. They were driven back only after a flurry of ferocious fighting, some of it hand-to-hand. Ducrot himself was on the front line, and drove the sword which he had had blessed at the Holy Sepulchre of Jerusalem while on pilgrimage in 1861 into the body of a Saxon. In desperation Ducrot kept throwing his men forward because the only alternatives seemed to be to withdraw or stay pinned under fire suffering casualties while waiting for more artillery to arrive. He sent urgent messages to General Exéa of 3 Corps, who by this time should have broken the impasse by taking the German position to the north in reverse.

Despite a 5.00 a.m. start, Exéa's progress towards the Marne had been dilatory. His men approached Neuilly on the north bank warily and bombarded it for some while before entering the undefended town. Another hour was consumed in putting it in a state of defence, and it was 11.00 a.m. before pontoons began to be laid between Bry and Neuilly. They were unfinished when the Saxon counter-attack at midday got a foothold in Bry and the civilians working on the nearest pontoons were driven off in panic by heavy German fire. At

Neuilly the pontoons were completed and Bellemare's division started to cross; but with the Germans in strength on the heights above Exéa feared that his bridgehead would be cut off and destroyed. He ordered Bellemare to return and pulled his other division, Mattat's, well back from the river. Exéa confined himself to turning artillery and *mitrailleuse* fire on the Germans on the far bank, which at least provided useful support to 2 Corps.

Even when Ducrot's staff officer arrived at 1.00 p.m. with orders to cross urgently, Exéa hesitated before finally yielding to Bellemare's entreaties for permission. Yet once on the south bank Bellemare saw that he might find himself fighting an isolated battle against strong German forces if he turned left towards Noisy, his objective. Moreover, to his right he could see 2 Corps hard pressed in and around Bry, so he turned right to support it. It was 2.30 p.m. before his leading brigade of Zouaves and Gardes Mobiles got into action and secured Bry. They then made frontal assaults on the Villiers Park, merely adding greatly to the French corpses strewn there. What should have been a wide turning movement by a whole corps had been reduced to a belated reinforcement of the main attack by part of one division.

By this time most of 1 and 2 Corps were a spent force, and some units had given way in disorder. General Blanchard of 1 Corps had even ordered a withdrawal, which Ducrot angrily countermanded on pain of death when he got wind of it. But if Ducrot would not retreat, evidently he could not move forward against immovable German resistance. As night fell he had his men dig in below the heights they had been unable to take by storm. The day's battle resembled General Burnside's débâcle at Fredericksburg in December 1862 during the American Civil War. In both cases charge upon forlorn charge had served only to demonstrate the futility of employing antiquated massed infantry tactics against well-protected riflemen and artillery.

During the day diversionary attacks had been mounted without any effect on the main action. Susbielle's Division of 2 Corps had been kept back to launch an offensive 5 kilometres south-west of the main battlefield, between the Marne and the Seine. Striking south from Créteil, it captured the hill of Montmesly, but during the afternoon was forced back to its starting point in disorder by German counter-attacks round its flanks. Seeing this action on his left General Vinoy, who had received no orders or information whatever, launched a supporting demonstration that was too late to be of help. North of Paris the success of General Hanrion's brigade in seizing Épinay-sur-Seine was, as we have seen, to cause an unfortunate misunderstanding when communicated to Tours, but had no other result: that evening orders came from Trochu to evacuate the town.

Ducrot might have renewed the main attack next day with the fresh troops at hand, or have withdrawn to try again elsewhere. He later blamed the government's fear of insurrection in the capital for preventing a withdrawal.[15] There had indeed been exasperation in the city on the 29th at the delayed river crossing, and the offices of *La Liberté* had been sacked by a mob when the paper reported that the operation had failed. However, the mood on the 30th had been one of tense expectation as anxious crowds listened to the constant rumble of the cannonade and grasped at contradictory rumours about progress. The extremists had been relatively quiet following the proceedings against their leaders in the wake of 31 October. Flourens had been deprived of his command and was in hiding.

The fact was that Ducrot did not propose withdrawal to Trochu or anyone else on the night of the battle. Trochu was probably closer to the truth in suggesting that Ducrot was reluctant to admit defeat by abandoning the ground gained; and there remained the hope that the Army of the Loire might arrive.[16] When Exéa and Bellemare took it upon themselves to withdraw across the Marne in the face of German reinforcements on the morning of 1 December Ducrot sharply ordered them to return to their positions. Both sides spent the day fortifying their lines, replenishing their ammunition and bringing up reinforcements, taking advantage of a truce to collect such wounded as had survived a night of glacial cold. Some French units dug themselves in more effectively than others, and a combination of tired troops, frozen ground, insufficient entrenching tools, inexperienced officers and unverified assumptions that neighbouring troops were covering their flanks left vulnerable gaps in the defences.

To secure unified direction on the German side Moltke appointed General von Fransecky of II Corps to command the threatened sector. Fransecky was inclined to stand on the defensive, but he had been placed under the orders of Crown Prince Albert of Saxony, commanding Fourth Army. Just as he had after Le Bourget, Albert insisted that the French must not be allowed to keep any of the ground they had occupied. His orders to attack reached Fransecky too late to be executed on 1 December but, aided by darkness and freezing fog, the Germans achieved surprise before dawn on Friday 2 December.

At his headquarters in the ruined château of Poulangis, Ducrot was alerted by the boom of cannon and the long, continuous crackle of rifle fire mingled with the bugle calls of French infantry and the whistle blasts of the Germans. Then from out of the mist emerged a horde of fugitives, thousands of men throwing away rifles and knapsacks in a race for the river crossings. It appeared that the Germans were about to succeed in their objective of driving the French into the Marne. Quickly Colonel Aimé Lambert, the army's Provost Marshal, had his gendarmes guard the bridges while artillery officers blocked the road with wagons. Thanks to their exertions and Ducrot's the panic of these men who 'would rather have suffered death than go back under fire'[17] was overcome, and they were herded back towards the front. Enough of their comrades had stayed and fought to prevent the French line from breaking completely.

French outposts in front of Champigny had assumed until it was too late that the moving figures they could discern were their own engineers, and were quickly overrun. The German battle-tide surged in, capturing the eastern half of the town, and the streets, houses and gardens of Champigny became the arena of furious infantry fighting as the Württembergers struggled to eject Faron's men. It was the same story in Bry, where the Saxons broke in and threatened to cut Exéa's men off from the bridges. Once again Exéa thought to regain the safety of the north bank, and the danger seemed so great that Ducrot was prepared to allow it. General Trochu, however, was on the spot and foresaw disaster if the Germans were enabled to turn the French left. He ordered Exéa's men to stay, and the situation was stabilized.

In the centre, across a bare landscape swept by rifle and *mitrailleuse* fire, fighting swirled around the railway embankment and limekilns. General Paturel hastily pulled his small brigade together and launched two counterattacks before being wounded, buying time for reinforcements to arrive. By mid-morning the French had everywhere recovered from the initial shock of the German assault, and beat off repeated attempts to renew the offensive. Once the mist had cleared French batteries were able to stem German progress, though in doing so French field gunners exposed themselves to heavy losses at the hands of their German counterparts. The Germans in Champigny might have been driven off sooner had General Favé, commanding the artillery on the St Maur peninsula south of the Marne, opened fire. In a particularly crass example of the habit of the French technical arms of regarding themselves as independent of field commanders, Favé obstinately refused to obey orders from Trochu and Ducrot to do so, for which he was dismissed that night.

By 3.00 p.m. on 2 December the battle had become an artillery duel, with the French holding approximately the line they had held on the night of 30 November. If they had failed to break out, the Germans had failed to destroy them, and were not eager to renew such a murderous contest.

That night Trochu and Ducrot agreed to try another attack next day, but when Ducrot rode out next morning under a doleful grey sky he changed his mind. He found 'our poor soldiers crouched on the frozen earth, exhausted, shivering, body and soul weakened by fatigue, lack of food and suffering'.[18] His men had spent four nights in the open, and that they were numb with cold after a night when the temperature touched −14 degrees centigrade owed much to Ducrot's refusal to let them carry a blanket. News had arrived that the Army of the Loire could not reach Fontainebleau until 6 December at the earliest, and even the prospect of pinning down German reserves could not persuade

Ducrot that it was worth staying. Without consulting Trochu he withdrew his men across the Marne in good order by nightfall on 3 December, taking advantage of fog and covering his retreat with a bombardment that led the Germans to believe that another assault was coming.

Next day Ducrot issued a proclamation to his army explaining frankly that to persist on the Marne peninsula would have been to sacrifice more lives vainly, but urging them to prepare for an early resumption of the attack.[19] However, when he met with his generals at Vincennes there were strong objections to his plan for another reorganization of the army to be carried out within forty-eight hours. Characteristically, the choleric Ducrot began shouting the odds and became involved in a scene with General Blanchard of 1 Corps in front of the assembled officer corps. Trochu entered the room in time to break them up as Blanchard challenged Ducrot to a duel with, 'Let's see if your sword is as long as your tongue.'[20] It was a sorry illustration of the divisions among the French high command, with a consequent impact upon the army's morale.

The disappointment of so many high hopes, which had been fuelled by Trochu's deceptively optimistic bulletins during the battle, provoked public anger at the 'laxity and incompetence' of the generals, but there were no disturbances.[21] The prevailing mood was disbelief and despondency at the failure of the sortie which, for the moment at least, 'destroyed in nearly all hearts the hope that Paris could free itself by its own efforts'.[22] The city was dismayed at the number of wounded arriving by riverboat at the quays, or in requisitioned carriages and omnibuses:

> All felt a painful shudder, mingled with avid curiosity, at these pale and ghastly faces, these bloodstains and tattered uniforms; at the restrained and smothered sufferings of these wounded who knew that all eyes were upon them and strove to be worthy of the spectacle ... Their vague smiles to passers-by made you want to weep. The faces of some betrayed horrible anxiety about their wounds, and their uncertainty as to whether amputation, or life or death awaited them.[23]

Ducrot, once the man of the hour, suffered the obloquy of failing to fulfil his 'dead or victorious' promise. Yet his personal courage had been conspicuous: indeed, his continual presence at the front was arguably a fault, for he had thereby sacrificed overall control of the battle. If he had received only a slight neck wound, no fewer than ten of his staff had been hit, including Léo Berthier, grandson of Napoleon I's chief of staff, who suffered hideous disfigurement when the fuse of a German shell embedded itself in his face, shattering his upper jaw. Two were dead, including the handsome, wealthy young Jewish socialite, Franchetti, daring leader of a cavalry troop and a great favourite of Ducrot's. Ducrot's medical director had repeatedly warned his staff:

> If you are wounded ask for me. I shall put you in a tent in an isolated spot, where you will be in effect in the open air, exposed to the breeze. You will be cold and lack creature comforts, but you will get better. Never allow yourself to be carried to the big, comfortable hospitals of central Paris. You could catch an infection there: it's raging amongst the crowds of sick, and I can't answer for what might happen.[24]

Yet when Franchetti was brought in with a smashed hip he insisted on being treated by the renowned Dr Auguste Nélaton who presided over the Red Cross hospital at the Grand-Hôtel, mordantly described by Dr Léon Le Fort as 'the celebrated Necropolis'.[25] Franchetti, a popular idol, died on 5 December, and his funeral two days later at the Père-Lachaise Cemetery, presided over by the Chief Rabbi, became a focus of mourning.[26]

For most of the dead there was little ceremony. They remained on the battlefield for a few days until a truce was arranged for burial. Parties of French labourers went out accompanied by Christian Brethren – lay teachers in Catholic schools who, in their distinctive cassocks and broad-brimmed tricorn hats, served the Press Ambulance Association, the best organized ambulance corps in France during the war. Dr Sarazin, who acted as interpreter, described the desolate scene:

> The sky was dark, it was very cold, and the countryside was covered in snow. What a melancholy task! ... Down that long, dreary, straight, frozen road, under a mournful sky, they brought us cart-loads of corpses. Long rows of bodies were lined up along the edge of the pits: gunners, Zouaves, regular infantry, Mobiles, in serried ranks on the frozen ground, themselves frozen in the eerie contortions of their death agony. Officers of all arms formed the front rank of this parade of honour. The Christian Brethren, with their long black robes that stood out sharply against the white snow, came and went among the dead. There was a horrible symmetry in these dismal affairs. The pits were long, wide and deep. Nearly 700 bodies had to be found a place in them, and perhaps those men would find there too the eternal rest that is the due of all those who die for their country.[27]

According to Ducrot's figures, the Marne fighting had cost the French 1,666 dead, 6,100 wounded and 1,716 missing, for a total of 9,482. Yet, if casualties in the futile diversionary attacks on 29–30 November are added, the 'Great

Sortie' cost over 12,000 men.[28] Amongst the 1,586 French prisoners on their way to Germany was the fabled Sergeant Hoff, who survived by concealing his identity.[29]

The Germans lost 5,235 men on the Marne peninsula, or 6,200 including the diversions. The French offensive had caused them some anxiety, and contingency plans had been drawn up for temporarily raising the siege if necessary to contain the threat. But, as Bismarck observed during the fighting, 'Where could [the French] go? They would put their heads in a sack. Such an attempt would be the best thing that could happen for us. Where they came on with eight battalions we should meet them with ten: and better troops too.' And, as Bismarck remarked, Paris had yet to learn that hopes of a relieving force were vain: the Army of the Loire had been defeated.[30]

Orléans Falls

While fighting raged at Champigny on 2 December Moltke sought to force matters to a conclusion in the Loire theatre. That afternoon, even as the Army of the Loire was suffering its repulse at Loigny, Moltke wired orders to Prince Friedrich Karl, commanding both Second Army and the Grand Duke of Mecklenburg's detachment, to launch an offensive southward against Orléans.

The German offensive was launched next morning, 3 December, well prepared and supported by a massed artillery bombardment. The dispersal of the Army of the Loire over 60 kilometres that had so hampered its offensive operations now vitiated its defensive efforts. Only General Martin des Pallières' 15 Corps guarded the approaches to Orléans, and the brunt of the concentric German attack fell upon it alone. Its divisions were widely separated, with two on the main Paris–Orléans highway around Artenay and the other nearly 20 kilometres away around Chilleurs on the road running northeast from Orléans to Pithiviers. Thus the French fought two separate delaying actions while trying to carry out d'Aurelle's orders to fall back on their defensive lines. The Germans penetrated the gaps between French units, forcing them back. By late afternoon, as snow and freezing rain cruelly tested endurance, outgunned French troops had given way everywhere and were falling back towards Orléans. The German advance had entered the northern fringes of the Forest of Orléans and was set to resume next morning.

On the Paris road d'Aurelle and his staff made vain efforts to halt groups of disbanded, demoralized men who were heading back to Orléans in search of food and shelter in temperatures of 7 degrees below zero. Convinced that his army could not hold, that night the general took the decision to evacuate the city. At 4.00 a.m. on 4 December he telegraphed to Gambetta that 'I consider the defence of Orléans impossible' and that retreat was the only way to avoid a great disaster.[31]

Gambetta and Freycinet were incredulous. Only five hours previously Freycinet had ordered the general to concentrate at Orléans, lecturing him unblushingly about the dispersal of his corps: a situation for which Freycinet's own directives were largely responsible. He now repeated those orders, unable to see the desperate necessity for evacuation. Why could the army not resist behind the defensive works constructed with so much labour?[32]

D'Aurelle's reply was sharp: 'I am on the spot and better able than you to judge the situation.' The German advance had been so rapid and his troops were so disorganized that to make a stand at Orléans would expose the army to destruction.[33] Gambetta reluctantly assented, though he spread the responsibility by the unusual step of convening all members of the Delegation to endorse the permission to withdraw, and emphasized that it was given solely on d'Aurelle's recommendation.

Then d'Aurelle wavered; influenced, he said, by the safe arrival from Chilleurs of the largest and most reliable division of 15 Corps, but probably also by Freycinet's reproaches. Shortly before midday he called on 16 and 17 Corps on the left and 18 and 20 Corps on the right to concentrate for the defence of Orléans. It was far too late: the Germans already barred the roads into the city on the north bank of the Loire. Following their previous orders, both wings of the French army were withdrawing in divergent directions, the left wing to the south-west and the right to the south-east: instructions d'Aurelle had given to avoid creating a bottleneck at Orléans. On the right, 20 Corps made a desultory attempt to reach Orléans during the afternoon, but a skirmish with a German division was sufficient to persuade it to double back and cross to the south bank of the Loire that night at Jargeau, while upstream 18 Corps likewise crossed to safety at Sully. On the army's left, Chanzy had tried to cover his own retreat and to relieve pressure on the collapsing 15 Corps by a stand against Tann's Bavarians, but two of his divisions had crumbled under the German advance. Chanzy judged that d'Aurelle's latest orders could not be executed, and soon the sound of the cannonade at Orléans told him that he was too far away to help. He continued his retreat southward.

Meanwhile in Orléans on this cold, clear Sunday the situation was chaotic, and deteriorating by the hour. The hospitals were filling with wounded and the ground in the city was shaking with the sound of gunfire on its northern outskirts. The evacuation order given that morning had hardly stiffened the will to resist among troops in the city, some of whom were exhausted by marching all night in the snow and biting east wind in obedience to d'Aurelle's orders. Many could be found 'in cabarets, in private homes, or lying drunk in the public squares and in front of houses. Officers had left their soldiers, and filled the hotels and cafés. Discouragement reigned.'[34] Officers declared that their men 'could not and would not do more'.[35] At 4.00 p.m. d'Aurelle reverted to his orders for immediate evacuation.

A few thousand French troops were still steadfastly defending the northern approaches to the city, supported by sailors who manned their heavy guns until forced to spike them by the exultant German advance. Amongst the volunteers assisting them, under an assumed name, was the Prince de Joinville, a son of the former King Louis-Philippe of the House of Orléans. While this rearguard fighting was in progress during the afternoon Gambetta attempted to reach the city, but his train turned back when it came under German artillery fire.

All evening thousands of French troops streamed across the bridges over the Loire by moonlight. An Irish doctor watched the remnants of several regiments pass:

> Most of them were without arms, and all went limping along, evidently quite foot-sore, while numbers were slightly wounded, to judge from the various bandages which they displayed round their heads, legs and arms. They looked more like a procession of invalids out for a walk than soldiers still capable of fighting. The poor fellows were dead beat, and did not so much march as shuffle along.[36]

So great was the crush of men on the footbridge constructed by the Bavarians during their occupation that a few men were lost in the dark waters of the river, while their comrades tramped on, hungry, haggard and apathetic. Finally, when nearly all the men, guns and wagons were across, engineers destroyed the footbridge and set fire to the pontoon bridge, sections of which made an unearthly groaning and creaking noise as they collided with giant ice floes in the Loire. Engineers failed to find sufficient powder to destroy the historic stone bridge, which stood silhouetted by the fires, but probably its destruction would have slowed the Germans for only a few hours. They had already entered the northern suburbs of Orléans, but were not eager for a night assault and entered into negotiations, threatening to bombard the city if the French did not evacuate. The French were only too glad of an agreement that allowed them to disengage. The Germans entered the city at half past midnight, skirmishing with a few remaining French who were determined to resist, but taking prisoner hundreds who had preferred to linger rather than to follow their own army.

The two-day Second Battle of Orléans had cost the Germans 1,747 casualties. The extent of the French disaster was measured in a loss of 20,000 men, of whom approximately 2,000 were killed or wounded, the rest prisoners; plus seventy-four guns and much material.[37]

Thus in a week of fighting, from Beaune-la-Rolande fought on 28 November to the fall of Orléans on 4 December, all hopes that the Army of the Loire was on the brink of rescuing Paris were extinguished. Its component parts were in retreat in three different directions, the shattered 15 Corps trudging directly south to the camp at Salbris, whence it had set forth in mid-October on the road that led to Coulmiers. When d'Aurelle had been a victorious general Freycinet and Gambetta had been reluctant to dismiss him. In the shadow of a defeat which they were at pains to attribute publicly to his failures, they informed him on 6 December that his post was suppressed and ordered him to take charge of the defences at Cherbourg. D'Aurelle declined such a lowly appointment and went home, burning with resentment at the politicians whom he blamed for ruining his army.

D'Aurelle had indeed suffered many slights at Freycinet's hands: slights he might have spared himself had he been less reluctant to accept command of the newly-formed army corps which Freycinet originally offered him, had he been more positive and forthcoming in proposing his own plans, and had he threatened to resign rather than consent to operations that he knew to be unsound. D'Aurelle was a talented organizer, but he was not the bold, self-confident commander-in-chief and resourceful strategist that Gambetta hoped for and France craved. With the loss of Orléans disappeared the belief that the armies of the Republic could miraculously reverse the defeats suffered by the imperial army. And, if the major defeats at Paris and Orléans in the first week of December were not enough to depress French morale, there were bleak tidings from the north as well.

The Germans Enter Normandy

Unoccupied Northern France – the country lying north of the corridor of invasion that extended between the frontier and Paris – had been left in dis-array by the news of Sedan and the severance of communications with the capital. For several weeks there had been little co-ordination between Depart-ments or between civil and military authorities. Bewildered elderly generals doing their best to muster troops and forward them to Tours frequently found themselves at odds with local defence committees and self-appointed 'vigilance committees' who wanted to see more energetic efforts to defend their own districts and to strike at the nearest enemy forces. As a step towards more unified direction, on 30 September the Delegation of Tours appointed Dr Armand Testelin, a prominent republican of Lille, as Defence Commis-sioner for the four most northerly Departments: Aisne, Somme, Pas-de-Calais and Nord. Testelin, knowing little of military matters, turned to the colonel of engineers in charge of the Lille fortifications. Like many engineers, Albert Farre was a convinced republican, and threw himself into organizing a new army corps – 22 Corps – of which he became chief of staff with the rank of general. The great cities of the region, Lille and Amiens, their civilian populations already swollen by refugees from Paris and the invaded areas, became hives of military preparation.

As at Tours, the human material for this new force was very raw indeed – Gardes Mobiles, depot troops who had not reached the front in August, new recruits from the class of 1870, volunteers, gendarmes, firemen and sailors who had to learn infantry drill. There were only forty-two serviceable field guns, and hardly any cavalry. Yet this embryo Army of the North had an invaluable asset in the number of regular soldiers who had escaped from Sedan or Metz and rallied to it. In particular, the experience and exertions of 279 regular officers who had evaded or escaped captivity helped impart the rudiments of training, discipline and handling firearms to a force which by late November could muster about 25,000 men.[38]

Nevertheless, their new commander was unimpressed. General Bourbaki, following his misadventure in England, was appointed by Gambetta to command in the north on 17 October, and reached his new headquarters on the 21st. Bourbaki had been used to commanding the finest soldiers in France, the Imperial Guard, and the contrast with his new charges made him quail. There were only 1,587 Chassepot rifles to go around,[39] meaning that most men had to be armed with old, converted weapons or foreign purchases. Munitions, clothing and equipment were in inadequate supply, though the industry of the region was working hard to fulfil contracts and the ports of the north and the Belgian frontier both remained open. Bourbaki could not see how he could possibly do more than stand on the defensive with such troops, using the great fortresses of the north as strongpoints for manoeuvre. Such a pessimistic assessment was poorly received in the staunchly republican cities of the north, where Bourbaki's attachment to the imperial regime made him suspect. He got a hostile reception in Douai, and newspaper articles questioned his loyalty. At a conference with Testelin and the Prefects on 8 November Bourbaki was pressed to adopt a more aggressive policy, and his objections that such demands were unrealistic did not find favour. A breaking point came over Testelin's insistence that Amiens must be defended. On 19 November Bourbaki learned that he had been recalled by Gambetta and left, taking key staff officers with him.

At this juncture the threat of a German advance materialized. Hitherto the Germans had been able to spare few troops to protect their lines in this direction, though cavalry patrols from Fourth Army had probed northward from Paris to secure supplies and glean information about any possible threat from the north. In both Normandy and the north-east this had led to sharp skirmishes as the Germans clashed with local bands of Gardes Mobiles and National Guards. Sometimes too bands of *francs-tireurs*, who were as much a menace to French peasants as to the Germans, would ambush enemy patrols, with predictable results. The Germans sought with significant success to encourage co-operation by paying for goods they requisitioned, but reacted ruthlessly wherever they met opposition by imposing heavy fines, burning villages, hostage-taking and summary executions. In a typical proclamation, the German commandant at Soissons promised on 19 October that any *franc-tireur* caught with arms would be 'treated as a traitor and hanged or shot without trial'.[40]

The fall of Metz, which so shook French morale, at last gave Moltke sufficient disposable forces to deal with any potential threat to the siege of Paris from the north. First Army, under the ultra-reactionary former chief of the Prussian military cabinet and veteran diplomat, General Edwin von Manteuffel, was tasked with this role. Manteuffel commanded three army corps and 3rd Cavalry Division, but he had immediately to detach VII Corps to handle the transportation of French prisoners from Metz and to garrison the city, and to try to force to a conclusion the sieges of French cities whose resistance was impeding German rail communications: Verdun (which fell on 8 November), Thionville (which fell on the 24th) and Montmédy. Thus it was with only I and VIII Corps and his cavalry – 39,304 troops and 174 guns[41] – that Manteuffel began his northward advance, and he had to make further detachments to besiege Mézières and La Fère. Setting out from the Moselle on 7 November, he had reached Rheims and Rethel by the 15th and the line of the River Oise by the 20th. From there he headed for Amiens, where he expected to find the French.

Well informed of the German advance, General Farre led his troops out to form a long protective curtain south and east of the city, where on 27 November the German army collided with them and fought what became known as the Battle of Amiens. Although over-extended and heavily outgunned, the French fought tenaciously for six hours. Their three brigade commanders, Lecointe, Du Bessol and Derroja, all regular colonels escaped from Metz, directed the defence capably, but late in the day the Germans broke through in the east, seizing commanding ground at Villers-Bretonneux. The fight cost the Germans 1,292 casualties and the French 1,383 killed and wounded plus over 1,000 missing.[42] That night the French generals concluded that they could not risk another day's battle: ammunition was low and the Garde Mobile had proved notably less steady than the regulars. They decided to abandon Amiens and withdraw across the Somme towards Arras. As their men evacuated Amiens they panicked at the sound of a volley, which proved to be only the National Guard following orders to disarm themselves by unloading their old-fashioned rifles in the only possible way. The retreat became a rout, and when the Germans entered Amiens the following morning with bands playing they found only the citadel holding out against them. But the Garde Mobile

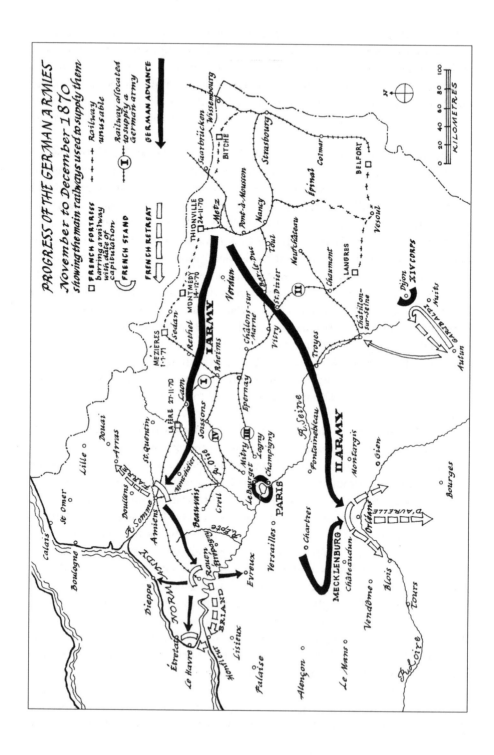

PROGRESS OF THE GERMAN ARMIES
November to December 1870
showing the main railways used to supply them

□ FRENCH FORTRESS barring a railway with date of capitulation
·+·+· Railway unusable
Ⓘ Railway allocated to supply a German army

⌒ FRENCH STAND

FRENCH RETREAT ⇨

⬛ GERMAN ADVANCE

KILOMETRES
0 20 40 60 80 100

N

Calais
Boulogne
St Omer
Lille
Douai
Arras
Dieppe
Étretat
Le Havre
Honfleur
Lisieux
Falaise
Alençon
Le Mans
Tours
Blois
Vendôme
Châteaudun
Orléans
Chartres
Versailles
Évreux
Rouen
Amiens
Doullens
St Quentin
Beauvais
Creil
Le Bourget
PARIS
Champigny
Montargis
Gien
Bourges
Fontainebleau
Soissons
Épernay
Rheims
La Fère 27·11·70
Laon
Mézières 1·1·71
Sedan
Rethel
Montmédy 14·12·70
Verdun
Châlons-sur-Marne
Vitry
Troyes
Chaumont
Langres
Châtillon-sur-Seine
Bar-le-Duc
St Dizier
Toul
Neuf-Château
Nancy
Pont-à-Mousson
Metz 24·11·70
Thionville
Saarbrücken
Bitche
Wissembourg
Strasbourg
Épinal
Colmar
Belfort
Vesoul
Dijon XIV CORPS
Autun
Muits
GARIBALDI
D'AURELLE
MECKLENBURG
I ARMY
II ARMY
III ARMY
Ⓘ
Ⓘ
ⒾⒾ
Ⓘ
Ⓘ NORM... BRIAND
R. Somme
R. Oise
R. Aisne
R. Seine
R. Loire

gunners of the garrison were unhappy at the prospect of having to fire on their own homes, and after an exchange of fire next day which killed the French commandant, Captain Vogel, the citadel surrendered on the 30th with its stores and weapons intact. La Fère had surrendered on the 27th, yielding 2,300 prisoners.

Having fulfilled his first objective, of driving off the French Army of the North and occupying Amiens, Manteuffel left a detachment under General von der Gröben to occupy the city and moved to carry out the next stage of his orders from Moltke. On 1 December his troops marched south-west into Normandy, where military preparations had been proceeding under General Briand independently of those in the north-east.

German overestimates of French strength in Normandy seemed to be confirmed by Briand's successful night raid in the early hours of 30 November against Saxon cavalry from Fourth Army billeted in Étrépagny: a defeat the Saxons avenged by burning sixty houses and disembowelling farm-horses with their bayonets.[43] Yet this was a small affair, and the scattered French were ill-positioned to meet the threat from the east. From Tours, Freycinet, adamant that the Germans were being kept far too busy elsewhere to take 'a promenade in Normandy', ordered Briand to advance south towards Paris.[44] Thus the French were wrong-footed when Manteuffel's rapidly advancing columns crossed the River Epte on 3 December. A hastily collected force of 12,000 which tried to bar the German advance next day at Buchy was quickly routed, opening the road to Rouen, a city easily dominated from the hills to its east. Briand abandoned any thought of defending it, and pulled his disorganized and demoralized troops across the Seine. There was a violent demonstration against the unpopular city council by local 'Reds', who cried treason and fired shots at the town hall, but the angry mob dispersed when the Germans triumphantly marched into the ancient capital of Normandy on the afternoon of 5 December. The only gesture of resistance was by a grocer named Derotte, who fired a shot at the Germans billeted on him and was executed.[45]

Meanwhile the disintegrating French army of 20,000 retreated north towards Honfleur through a night of such brutal cold that men's hands froze to their rifles and exhausted soldiers who stopped to rest in the snow froze to death. After tramping 90 kilometres in thirty hours Briand's troops were ferried across the mouth of the Seine to Le Havre.[46]

With both Rouen and Amiens occupied, Manteuffel sent out a column to feel the defences of Le Havre, another to occupy Evreux, and a third to Dieppe, where it destroyed coastal batteries and telegraph apparatus on 9 December. It was the first time in the campaign the Germans had reached the sea, and on sighting the Channel shore their cavalrymen gave three resounding cheers for King and Fatherland.[47]

Thus in the first few days of December it seemed that German armies could move almost at will in France. Rouen in the north had fallen on the same day as Orléans in the south. Was it time, finally, for the French to concede defeat? On 5 December Moltke sent a courteous note to Trochu in Paris informing him of the fall of Orléans and inviting him to send an officer to verify it. Simultaneously, German officers on the outpost line at Paris let it be known that Trochu might receive honourable peace terms if he were to address King Wilhelm directly.[48]

Chapter Seven

Failure and Frustration

The Day of Reserves: The Second Battle of Le Bourget

Trochu, for whom 'to write and to talk' were 'a perfect mania', told anyone who would listen that he was not taken in by the German invitation, which he saw as a trap.[1] He had privately referred to the siege several times as a 'heroic folly', but both his sense of military honour and fear of the popular reaction dictated that the capital should continue to resist until food stocks were exhausted. There seemed danger too in accepting German accounts of the situation in the provinces; a few days after Moltke's letter two messages arrived by carrier pigeon, purportedly from French officials, painting a dark picture of military disaster and of peasants welcoming the Germans, and insisting on the futility of further resistance. These were clearly bogus: not only were the messages attached to the pigeons in an unusual way but the phrasing was odd and the signatory of one despatch was supposedly André Lavertujon, a Cabinet secretary, who was still in Paris.[2] As it happened, Moltke's note was genuine, but Trochu's fears that 'These people are mocking me; they want to compromise me as they compromised Bazaine'[3] were understandable. In any case, the matter was not decided on Trochu's whim. Moltke's invitation was thoroughly debated in Cabinet, where only Favre and Ernest Picard believed that the opportunity of further negotiations should be pursued now that ultimate capitulation was inevitable. The rest of the Cabinet were strongly of the view that they had a duty to continue to resist while there remained the remotest chance that the provincial armies could mount a rescue attempt. Trochu returned a courteous refusal to Moltke, and published the correspondence in a proclamation concluding that the government had but one resolve: 'To fight!'[4]

Trochu's stance was later to be bitterly criticized by the political Right for unnecessarily prolonging France's agony now that the Army of the Loire had been defeated (a fact shortly confirmed by a despatch from Gambetta). This had become the view of General Ducrot, who believed that if he could not break through no one could. Yet Ducrot's contention that France could have secured better terms at this point, after she had made an honourable but vain military effort, remained unproven. Like his assertion that Moltke's note was evidence of German war-weariness, it contained a large measure of wishful thinking.[5] At any rate, the issue was not tested. The duration of the war would continue to be measured in the number of days that Paris could hold out.

The capital was assured of one staple of life, for German efforts to disrupt the water supply had not seriously diminished the city's ability to draw sufficient fresh water. However, stocks of food and fuel were dwindling, and privations that had seemed bearable in November while there was hope of relief cut more deeply in the darkness and cold of a winter of deepening discouragement.

Food stocks were not expected to last beyond the end of January.[6] The government had begun fixing the price of fresh meat from mid-September, and meat rationing had been introduced during October. Government ministries organized the requisition of livestock at a set price, slaughter and distribution, while the town halls of the twenty *arrondissements* administered rationing. Every citizen was issued with a ration card for presentation to a designated local butcher. Even with these controls, supplies of fresh beef, mutton and pork were exhausted by late November, and for ten days rations had to be made up with salted meat, herring or cod, or with rice and beans. Following a census of privately owned horses, donkeys and mules in the capital on 29 November – there were 45,000 – the government began to requisition and slaughter them at a rate of 500 animals per day, furnishing a daily horse-meat ration of 30 grammes per person.[7]

The government had fixed bread prices at the start of the siege, and soon requisitioned flour and cereals to ensure the city's bread supply. But, despite the clamour of the radical press and clubs, the Cabinet was very reluctant to introduce bread rationing, so permitting significant wastage in the early weeks.[8] A proclamation by Jules Ferry on 11 December forbidding bakers to sell flour or to use it in products other than bread provoked such panic-buying and disturbances that next day the government sought to restore calm by proclaiming that 'bread will not be rationed'.[9] Nevertheless, diminishing wheat stocks meant that the standard loaf was progressively adulterated by the admixture of oats, rice, starch, wheat bran and rye, making it dark, stodgy and 'as disagreeable to the taste as it was unpleasant to the sight'.[10] Moreover, before the war Paris had no flour mills, and despite ingenious feats by private industry to improvise them in railway stations and warehouses there were insufficient millstones. Much bread was coarse through imperfect flour-milling, and its taste betrayed whether the mill was installed in a tobacco warehouse. Nothing caused more frequent and bitter complaints than siege bread.

Food shortage was an obsessive topic of popular concern, and newspapers did their best to divert and entertain on the subject. Humour offered a palliative for hardship: for instance, the image of a gentleman disconsolately contemplating the remains of his pet on his dinner plate and lamenting 'Poor old dog! How he would have loved these bones' – a joke probably as old as the history of sieges. Yet anecdote and cartoon should not be confused with reality. In the Paris markets the meat of cats, dogs, crow, sparrows and even rats were for sale, though their importance as a food source – particularly rats – loomed rather larger in newspaper columns and legend than they did in the daily diet of the majority of Parisians. It was observed that the purchasers of such curiosities were typically not the poor but the wealthy acting out of 'bravado and dilettantism'.[11]

Amongst the items requisitioned were animal bones, which were converted into gelatine, stock and a broth certified by scientists to be nutritious but wryly nicknamed by consumers 'gaiter-button soup'.[12] Government requisitioning and price-setting were not always successful. They caused some commodities, notably potatoes, to disappear from the shops and become available only at black-market prices. Yet unregulated foodstuffs fetched exorbitant prices, reaching seven or eight times their pre-war levels or even higher.[13] Even items in good supply, such as coffee and sugar, saw marked increases. Around 500,000 francs were made available for poor relief, with which the town halls of the twenty *arrondissements* organized municipal canteens where 190,000 Parisians daily ate cheap meals.[14] Charities too were active, supported notably by the wealthy English benefactor Richard Wallace.

At the other end of the scale the rich were able to provide for themselves, even if they had to dig into their savings. Some of the restaurants in the wealthier quarters continued throughout to serve meals which the working classes could only dream of. Ernest Renan and his literary friends later presented the restaurateur Paul Brébant with an inscribed gold medal for having fed them well every fortnight quite as if they were not 'in a city of 2 million besieged souls'.[15] The much publicized slaughter of zoo animals, culminating with that of the elephants Castor and Pollux on 29 and 30 December, was undertaken because they could no longer be provided with fodder. The elephants were bought by the fashionable *boucherie anglaise* at 9,000 francs each, and the meat resold as novelty dishes in exclusive restaurants at fabulous prices.[16]

Between the extremes of wealth and the more than one in five Parisians in need of assistance (471,754 from a civilian population of 2,005,709)[17] were the mass of working people and the lower middle classes, who often suffered unadmitted privations behind closed doors. Particularly hard hit were the unemployed, elderly and infirm. If many members of the National Guard gambled or drank away their pay, the housewives of Paris bore the brunt of trying to feed their families. Francisque Sarcey wrote feelingly of:

> The poor women, who queued all day in the abominable December
> cold at the baker's, the butcher's, the grocer's, the firewood

merchant's and the town hall ... Yet they were the ones most
passionate that the city should hold out to the last morsel of bread.[18]

He heard no complaints, but like other male bourgeois commentators who
praised the quiet heroism of the queues of pale, huddled, shivering women, he
underestimated the resentments being laid up among the 'have nots' of Paris.
Within districts there was much good humour and camaraderie, yet there was
also deep anger which found a partial outlet in the clubs in heated diatribes
against food hoarders and speculators. Doubtless much of this rhetoric,
resonant of 1793, was wildly exaggerated in imagining vast food stores being
secreted by the rich, but profiteering was sufficiently evident to incubate a
festering sense of injustice. The unequally borne sufferings of Paris were
storing up potential tinder for revolution.

At least the city's defenders, the army and the navy, had sufficient stores of
food. The news from Orléans had taken the urgency out of the need to make
another sortie to meet a relieving force. Ducrot took the opportunity to reorganize his army once more, and insisted successfully on his right to nominate
officers, abolishing elections in the Garde Mobile. On 6 December Trochu
declared that the time had come to cease following a strategy dictated by public
opinion and instead to 'make war seriously, based on true scientific principles'.[19] The Cabinet would have been only too glad had he taken his own
advice. The previous day it had forbidden him to issue a proclamation
explaining the reasons for inaction since Champigny. Jules Simon pointedly
demanded action, not proclamations. Over the following week Favre and
others pressed Trochu to communicate a plan of campaign.[20]

Trochu and Ducrot devised a plan for an attack north of Paris, which might
lead to a junction with the Army of the North. The ground east of the Lille
road was an open plain where French troops could advance under the protective fire of fortress guns and field artillery. Trochu's conception was strangely
antique: he sought to draw the Germans into a set-piece battle, where instead
of 'a succession of murderous assaults against almost invisible troops posted
behind obstacles', French infantry could show its mettle out in the open against
'real lines of battle'.[21]

Before the French could advance over the plain, however, they must take Le
Bourget on their left flank. Trochu, who had insisted six weeks earlier that the
village was of no strategic value whatever, now held that the success of his plan
depended upon its capture.[22] This sector of front was held by Vice Admiral de
La Roncière's mixed army and naval corps, which was tasked with capturing
Le Bourget. Not until it was safely in French possession, as signalled by a flag
to be flown from the church steeple, was Ducrot's Second Army to advance on
the right.

As usual the offensive was heralded by Trochu's announcement of the closure of the city gates. The Germans were put on their guard by signs of activity and by information from French deserters and brought up reserves behind their lines. Nevertheless, Le Bourget itself was held by only five companies of the Prussian Guard: about 750 men.

The French assault on 21 December was delayed until 8.00 a.m. by dense fog. The bombardment of Le Bourget, supported by the nearest forts and an armoured railway battery, did not last even the inadequate half hour prescribed. When the first assault column under General Lavoignet went forward from the south it was soon halted by devastating fire from the loop-holed walls of the fortified village, and the attackers were forced to take cover along the railway embankment and in outbuildings. Meanwhile, the second column under Commander Lamothe-Tenet had better success in storming the northwestern face of Le Bourget, taking the cemetery and establishing itself around the church before eventually being contained by German reinforcements hurrying up from their main line. Once again the streets of Le Bourget became a cockpit of bloody close-quarter fighting.

Frustrated by Lavoignet's lack of progress, Trochu ordered up a battery which breached the whitewashed boundary wall of a gasworks that had proved a strongpoint of resistance, but the defending German infantry merely re-formed in a trench to its rear. The fight became a stalemate, with the French trying to pulverize German positions within Le Bourget with artillery. Unaware that Lamothe-Tenet's men were holding out in the centre of the village, the fortress guns did more damage to them than to the Germans. Severely bombarded by friend and foe alike and facing determined counter-attacks, Lamothe-Tenet withdrew at 11.30 a.m., having lost 635 men. Hanrion's reserve brigade was only then deploying west of the village, arriving too late to do more than protect the retreat.

To the east Ducrot impatiently awaited the signal to advance that never came. He shifted his divisions forward, and Bellemare's men drove in German outposts at Groslay Farm before advancing to the line of the Soissons railway. Otherwise the engagement became a deafening artillery contest, with Ducrot's gunners suffering shelling from German guns visible only by their smoke. German infantry failed to oblige by presenting itself in the open for the setpiece battle Trochu had hoped for. About midday orders came from Trochu cancelling Ducrot's advance because Le Bourget could not be taken.[23] With 70,000 men on the field at his command, Trochu had committed against Le Bourget only 5,200, who had been defeated in detail while the rest of the army waited in reserve.

East of Paris, Vinoy had proposed a supporting attack with Third Army, but Trochu had once again reduced his role to that of an insignificant demon-

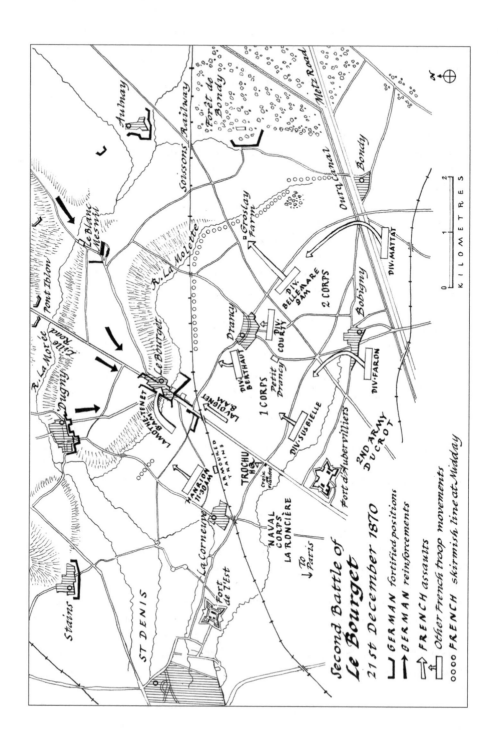

Second Battle of
Le Bourget
21st December 1870

⊐ GERMAN fortified positions
⟹ GERMAN reinforcements
⇧ FRENCH assaults
⇧ Other French troop movements
oooo FRENCH skirmish line at Midday

stration. Vinoy's men took their objectives of Maison-Blanche and Ville-Évrard, but exhibited the besetting sin of French troops by failing to follow orders to secure their positions adequately. After dark their Saxon opponents counter-attacked, joined by comrades who had taken refuge in the cellars of Ville-Évrard during the earlier engagement. The French brigade commander was killed, and after a wildly confused mêlée in the streets the Germans withdrew with over 600 French prisoners. A lieutenant named Schang had deserted to the Germans during the fight, and Vinoy had seven junior officers court-martialled for abandoning their posts and spreading panic.

The day of Second Le Bourget was a fiasco which saw the French back at their starting positions at a cost of some 1,800 casualties to 519 German.[24] The high command, observed the engineer Viollet-le-Duc, had once again demonstrated 'that indecision in the direction of operations that had been so fatal to us since the start of the siege'.[25] 'We had hoped for a decisive battle,' wrote Favre, 'what we got was a mere skirmish.'[26] If Trochu thought that his miserably co-ordinated token effort would satisfy Parisians he was quickly disabused by a torrent of recrimination in the press and clubs. An official bulletin absurdly blamed the weather for the setback and slipped beyond 'spin' into outright falsehood in claiming that French artillery had overpowered the German guns. The National Guard were praised for their 'excellent bearing', though they had been far from the fighting.[27]

At Fort d'Aubervilliers on 22 December Trochu held 'one of those councils of war which are the last resort of commanders who have run out of expedients'.[28] Public opinion would cry treason if the army withdrew, therefore he must give it 'legitimate satisfaction'.[29] Rather than admit failure Trochu decided, three months too late, to try Tripier's method by digging parallels and laying siege to Le Bourget. But on the night of the 21st the temperature had plummeted to −15 degrees centigrade, freezing the ground so hard that entrenching tools broke in it. It was all his inadequately clad troops could do to keep alive. Although this time they had been allowed to carry blankets slung bandolier-style over the shoulder and to bring tents, tent pegs could not be driven into the rock-hard ground. Water froze solid as it was being carried from the Ourcq Canal to camp and ration bread had to be broken up with axes. Next morning there were 980 cases of frostbite,[30] and chest complaints and diarrhoea became widespread. When Jules Favre and Jules Simon rode out in a carriage to seek information from Trochu they were appalled by the pitiful state of the troops who, lashed by a razor-like north wind, had wrapped their heads and limbs in whatever rags they could find. 'Moscow has come to the gates of Paris,' said Simon dejectedly, adding, 'which of us could have foreseen that we would be witnesses to such a dreadful scene?'[31]

A collapse in morale was indicated by a rise in desertions and incidences of fraternization with the enemy. One staff officer heard men saying openly, 'We have had enough of this', while another heard cries of 'Peace! Peace!' as Ducrot rode by.[32] There was a bitter feeling in the army that men were being needlessly sacrificed because their leaders were afraid of Parisian opinion.[33] Trochu, now as unpopular in the army as he was in the city, eventually pulled the bulk of his suffering troops back into their quarters around the capital on 26 December.

The Infernal Retreat

After their victory at Orléans it seemed that the Germans had only to pursue a beaten enemy. The French 15 Corps, which had borne the brunt of that defeat, was in a wretched and demoralized state, made worse by nervous commanders who kept their men retreating all night at the slightest hint of German cavalry, denying them the chance to rest or cook a meal. The Army of the Loire had been split into fractions by the defeat, and rather than retain one unwieldy command the Government at Tours decided to reorganize it as two distinct forces. The eastern portion, comprising 15, 18 and 20 Corps, was to be commanded by General Bourbaki, recently arrived from his ill-starred tenure in the north. For a few days, until confirmation came of Ducrot's failure at Champigny, Gambetta urged Bourbaki to resume the offensive towards Paris, via Gien, Montargis and Fontainebleau. But Bourbaki sent back the despondent reports that were becoming his trademark, insisting on the impossibility of an offensive and the urgent need to rest and re-equip his troops. His chief concern was to put distance between himself and the enemy, and by 11 December he had withdrawn to a position covering Bourges, 100 kilometres south of Orléans. When Gambetta went to see the situation for himself he found the troops 'in a deplorable state of disorganization', conceding privately to Freycinet that they presented 'the saddest sight'.[34]

Markedly different was the experience of the western portion of the army, which was now designated the Second Army of the Loire under General Alfred Chanzy, hitherto commander of 16 Corps. Two divisions of that corps had been severely shaken at Loigny and on the succeeding days, and had retreated to Blois and Mer to reorganize. But one sound division remained, as well as 17 Corps, formerly commanded by Sonis. In addition, Chanzy received the timely reinforcement from the west of the recently-formed 21 Corps, plus a newly-formed division under General Camô. This gave him 120,000 men, of whom about 75,000 could be called fit for combat.

These fresh troops had been entrusted to a commander who did not lack the will to use them. As strict a disciplinarian as d'Aurelle, Chanzy did not share his former commander's prejudice against allowing his men to be billeted overnight in villages, as was the German practice. He also spared his troops night marches so far as possible, and had a realistic sense of what could be asked of them. He ran an efficient staff, and like Ducrot concerned himself with every detail of troop movements and logistics; yet he had a coolness of judgement that never lost sight of the wider strategic picture or gave way to despair after setbacks. Save for an unhappy teenage year as a ship's boy, there was little to distinguish Chanzy's military education and experience from that of many of his more senior colleagues. He had served in Algeria, the Italian War, Syria and Rome, and in the spring of 1870 as a brigadier had taken part in Wimpffen's expedition against dissident North African tribes. Yet he had an aggression and determination to hurt the invader conspicuously lacking in Bazaine, Trochu, d'Aurelle and Bourbaki, and this spirit communicated itself to his officers. When Moltke, not a man given to idle compliments, came to write his history of the war, he stated simply that Chanzy was 'probably the most capable of all the leaders whom the Germans had to encounter'.[35]

Realizing that headlong retreat would only cause his fragile and inexperienced divisions to disintegrate, Chanzy had them turn and make a stand a few kilometres south of the Coulmiers battlefield, crossing which, confessed one Mobile, 'struck a chill into our hearts'.[36] On 7 December Chanzy drew up his army to bar the road to Tours, with its right anchored on the Loire in front of Beaugency and its left a dozen kilometres north-westward in the Forest of Marchenoir. Here for four days, across snow-covered fields and vineyards, it fought a series of stubborn actions which cost the pursuing German detachment an eighth of its strength – 3,395 casualties – though at a cost to the French of perhaps 5,000.[37] French artillery, *mitrailleuses* and rifles had full play across the undulating landscape, inflicting 'fearful loss of life' and giving French troops cause to complain of the Chassepot's tendency to overheat and become foul with repeated firing, so that it could only be cleared with a cleaning rod after it had cooled.[38]

Nor were French troops held solely to the defensive. Divisions counter-attacked, re-took villages and captured prisoners. In 17 Corps Amédée Delorme recalled the fear and heightened senses of men in combat for the first time, trying to make themselves as small as possible while seeing comrades suffer death and wounds, and experiencing the unnerving effects of being pinned down under fire with bullets 'whistling and buzzing around our ears'. 'If lead could grow,' he mused, 'what a terrible harvest the field we occupied would have yielded!' Yet once the enemy could be seen and the order to fire came, he and his comrades lost their fear and fired with a will, realizing that 'Danger can be faced without terror once you can look it in the face.' Only a gunshot wound which broke his forearm compelled Delorme to leave the line.[39]

Conversely, in 16 Corps Corporal Denis Érard was struck by how well his men of the 33rd Garde Mobile sustained a fire-fight in the open at Le Mée Farm, which was captured by a French bayonet charge. Yet, shortly afterwards, having lost all their officers and lying stationary under a hail of German fire, an anonymous cry of 'Save yourselves!' was enough to start a contagious stampede. As he retreated Érard registered sights that would stay with him for a lifetime: men blown apart by shells, an officer with a ripped belly vainly trying to hold in his own entrails. At dusk he reached the village of Villorceau, where chaos reigned. Screeching German shells set fire to the thatched roofs of houses crammed with wounded, who had to be evacuated. The bells of the church, which was also a refuge for the wounded, were ringing wildly:

> Soldiers of all arms packed the single street. They were in disorder and had lost their hats and knapsacks. They struck the ground with their rifle-butts, with gestures of discouragement or rage. All had fought; all had seen death at close-hand under fire; their features were convulsed, their faces and hands black with powder.

Outside the village their officers succeeded in rallying them, but they took no further part in the battle.[40]

This day, 8 December, Chanzy's right wing had been compromised by a direct order from Freycinet to General Camô to withdraw his division southward through Beaugency to avoid being flanked by German troops advancing on the far bank of the Loire. A French attempt to retake Beaugency on the 9th failed, but Chanzy withstood German pressure for another two days. By then he no longer had to worry about protecting the Government at Tours. Although Gambetta stayed close to the front, the rest of the Delegation and their administrative personnel evacuated the city on 8–9 December, reestablishing the government far away at Bordeaux.

Chanzy's unexpected resistance compelled the Germans to change their dispositions. Prince Friedrich Karl at Orléans had expected any French threat to come from Bourbaki, and he was at first contemptuous of the Grand Duke of Mecklenburg's reports that his heavily outnumbered detachment was engaged in fierce fighting. In fact Bourbaki attempted little more than a demonstration towards Vierzon in response to Chanzy's desperate pleas for a supporting advance. Recognizing that Chanzy was the immediate problem, Friedrich Karl despatched the bulk of his Second Army westward, both to give direct support to Mecklenburg and to take Chanzy in rear by crossing the Loire to his south. Anticipating that he would be encircled if he remained, on 11 December Chanzy swung his army back like a door, pivoting on his left, to a position covering Vendôme. From here he could strike the Germans in flank if they tried to advance on Tours.

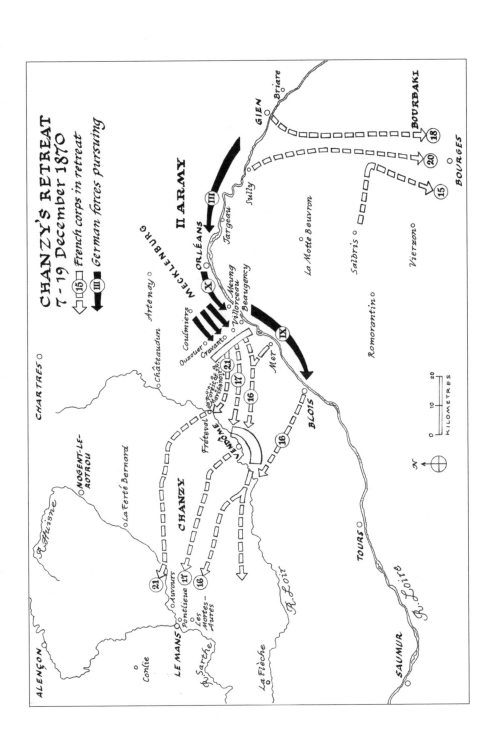

CHANZY'S RETREAT
7 – 19 December 1870

⟦15⟧ French corps in retreat
◀III German forces pursuing

The retreat took three days, in dire conditions. A temporary thaw made the roads slick with ice, then torrential rain turned them into apparently bottomless mud in which many horses and wagons had to be abandoned. The rain-lashed infantry trudged its way laboriously across sodden fields, while the Germans proved unable to mount a speedy pursuit in such conditions. Following in the wake of the retreating French, they encountered thousands of stragglers who had lost the will to resist, as well as unburied bodies in the fields, houses packed to overflowing with sick and wounded who had been left behind without food or medical attention, and roadsides littered with cast-away rifles and dead or dying horses from which famished men had cut strips of meat. French troops trying to buy food from peasants had in some cases been refused or charged exorbitant prices.

Reaching Vendôme, Chanzy held an extended line protecting the city east of the River Loir – a tributary of the Loire – and skirmished heavily with the oncoming Germans on 14–15 December. It was painfully evident, nevertheless, that his army could not withstand another major battle once the Germans had concentrated against it, and on the morning of the 16th his troops slipped across the river under cover of fog. Despite Chanzy's planning, it was not quite a clean escape. The Germans quickly repaired an imperfectly destroyed bridge in Vendôme and captured two batteries and a convoy. Fortunately for Chanzy, the pursuit was not pressed hard otherwise, and a couple of sharp rearguard actions over succeeding days sufficed to keep German cavalry at bay. Discipline was fraying amongst some French soldiers and junior officers. Bands of men, evading the mounted gendarmes who had been posted to turn back stragglers, left the ranks and made their own way through heavy snow squalls to Le Mans, intent only on finding shelter, warmth and food. But most men stuck to their duty as Chanzy's columns continued their retreat over the next three days, going into camp in positions covering Le Mans on 19 December.

Prince Friedrich Karl had lost opportunities to destroy Chanzy, but he decided against being drawn into a long pursuit. After all, provided that German forces could repel any attempt to relieve Paris from the south or west, the capital must eventually fall. News just received suggested that Bourbaki was advancing on Gien, and the prospect that the French might score a propaganda coup by reoccupying Orléans was not to be countenanced. Friedrich Karl headed back to the city on the 18th. A small column was sent to capture Tours, but was recalled from the city's outskirts at the rumour of an approaching French force.

There was a further reason for German reluctance to pursue Chanzy. While discipline among their troops remained sound, months of campaigning were taking their toll, and the army was no longer the instrument it had been. Tann's I Bavarian Corps had been so reduced in recent weeks of marching and continuous fighting that it had to be sent back to Orléans to recoup itself, and from there would be sent to the Paris front as a reserve. Army corps were now little stronger than divisions had been at the start of the war, and divisions had shrunk to the size of brigades. Since August many of the best officers had been killed or wounded, leaving units to be commanded by junior officers and gaps in the ranks to be filled by reservists. Recent operations on the Loire in foul weather had reduced uniforms and boots to tatters. For many in the German ranks, wrote Captain von der Goltz, 'The warrior spirit now burned with only a flickering flame; the desire to enjoy at last a moment of rest was very widespread.'[41]

Burgundy, Belfort, and a Bold Plan

While the main armies clashed on the Loire, General Werder had maintained his position at Dijon, the capital of Burgundy, with the mission of guarding against any French attempt to disrupt the lines of communication of Friedrich Karl's Second Army. His XIV Corps occupied key towns in the upper Saône valley, and his cavalry patrolled for any sign of French activity. The war in this well-forested region was one of small skirmishes between the Germans and groups of *francs-tireurs*, Gardes Mobiles and National Guards.

If the difficulties of Werder's task were underestimated at Versailles, they were at least tempered by the absence of any unified command on the French side. Partly this lack of unity stemmed from political turmoil in Lyon, where many of the units originated and where authority was disputed between several military leaders, the Prefect Challemel-Lacour and the National Guard. The civil authorities were focused on local defence, giving lower priority to any strategy devised at Tours, where Gambetta and Freycinet were anyway preoccupied with the struggle on the Loire. Then there was Garibaldi.

Giuseppe Garibaldi, aging hero of the Italian unification movement and world-renowned warrior, had been in retirement on the island of Caprera writing rather bad anti-clerical novels when war broke out in 1870. He had been a sworn enemy of Napoleon III whom, like most radicals, he blamed for 'betraying' the Italian nationalist cause. In 1867 Garibaldi had fought French imperial troops defending Rome and been worsted at Mentana, but the revolution of 4 September 1870 had aroused his enthusiasm to defend the sacred cause of republicanism, and he had offered his sword to France. Such was his prestige and the enthusiasm he aroused among French radicals that the Delegation of Tours felt bound to accept his offer, albeit with reservations. Garibaldi was a native of Nice, a city annexed to France by Napoleon III as the price of his support for the Kingdom of Piedmont in the Italian war of 1859, and there was apprehension lest Garibaldi reclaim the city for the new Kingdom of Italy as the reward for his support.

Garibaldi excited strong opinions. To radicals he was a hero of the embattled republican cause, the embodiment of the ideal of the universal brotherhood of nations, and the inspirational foe of tyranny wherever he encountered it. Bands of exotically uniformed *francs-tireurs* flocked to serve under him. French conservatives, on the other hand, abhorred him as an atheist, anarchist and foreigner. Their worst fears seemed to be confirmed when his fantastically uniformed Italian, Spanish and Polish volunteers showed as much enthusiasm for desecrating churches and persecuting clergy and members of religious orders as for fighting Germans, and treated French towns they passed through as though they owned them.

Garibaldi established his Army of the Vosges, about 16,000 strong, at Autun, 70 kilometres south-west of Dijon. His celebrity and volunteer status made it awkward for the Delegation to give him direct orders, which in any case he was unlikely to obey. Garibaldi had not achieved all that he had for Italian unity by obeying anybody's orders, and was too old to break the habit of a lifetime. Yet, despite the lobbying of Joseph Bordone, Garibaldi's overweening chief of staff who sought supreme command in the region for his master, the Delegation was wary of placing French generals under his orders. Indeed, some French generals and troops were adamant that they would not serve under a foreigner, and proved reluctant to send Garibaldi the arms and equipment he requested. The Delegation was reduced to making suggestions to Garibaldi, urging him and the French commanders to co-operate.

The Italians commanding the Army of the Vosges had no monopoly on self-willed independence in a theatre where all wanted to command but few to obey. Leaders of *franc-tireur* bands were apt to lead their men away if they did not approve of their orders or of their commander, while four French generals in the region wrangled over who was subordinate to whom. Despite attempts to ensure co-ordination, the lack of an overall commander to direct operations against Werder proved crippling.

Garibaldi's campaign got off to a spectacular start. A brigade led by his son Ricciotti pounced on the German garrison of Châtillon-sur-Seine in the early hours of 19 November, driving it away and capturing 169 prisoners. Upon Ricciotti's withdrawal, however, the Germans returned and subjected the town to reprisals. Two days after this success Garibaldi advanced from Autun, planning to take Dijon by a surprise night attack, supported perhaps by a rising in the city. But this time the Germans were not so easily surprised, and on 26 November they repulsed repeated charges by Garibaldi's men with destructive volleys. Never in his career, Garibaldi admitted, had he encountered such a storm of fire.[42] Retreat was turned into rout by the German pursuit, which continued to the outskirts of Autun. Crippled with arthritis though he was, Garibaldi organized an energetic defence of the town on 1 December. This, and a report of other French forces approaching, induced the German vanguard to withdraw to Dijon, which it reached on 3 December after beating off an attempted French trap at Châteauneuf.

Garibaldi was disinclined to resume the offensive, insisting that he must have more artillery and time to reorganize. Werder too might have been inclined to hold his isolated position, had not Moltke ordered him to make 'vigorous offensive movements' against the forces facing him. And if guerrillas proved a problem, Moltke specified, whether 'there has been open resistance with armed force, or whether obstacles have been created by the malevolent and frequent destruction of communications, the very severest treatment of the guilty as regards life and property can alone be recommended to your Excellency, whole parishes being held responsible for the deeds of its individual members when such cannot be discovered'.[43]

The day after receiving this from Versailles, 14 December, Werder despatched a Prussian brigade north-eastward to try to reduce the troublesome garrison of Langres. On 18 December General Glümer's 11,000-strong Baden Division, accompanied by Werder, advanced south from Dijon. By late morning it was in combat, not with Garibaldi's army but with the 12,000-strong division of General Camille Cremer around the little town of Nuits St Georges.

Cremer, formerly General Clinchant's chief of staff at Metz and an escaper from Germany, posted his men behind a deep railway cutting east of the town and on the vine-covered slopes of the Chaux plateau dominating it to the west. Here was fought one of the stiffest small battles of the war. Only in late afternoon did the Germans take the railway cutting by storm. They were then able to bring up guns to rake the French retreating through the streets of Nuits and to gain possession of the town. The French, meanwhile, could not be dislodged from the Chaux plateau. In this gruelling fight the Germans lost 940 men and the French 2,360, including 650 unwounded prisoners.[44] Glümer was hit, and Prince Wilhelm of Baden, younger brother of the Grand Duke, was severely wounded by a Chassepot bullet that passed through his cheeks. Both sides were so spent that they withdrew – Cremer south to Beaune, Werder north to Dijon.

So the war in Burgundy remained a stalemate, with neither side able to muster the strength and skill to defeat the other. Yet strategically the Germans retained the upper hand. Not only had Werder kept hold of Dijon, but his presence there provided a shield for German operations 140 kilometres to the east.

French possession of the fortress of Belfort, which dominated the mountain gap between the southern end of the Vosges and the Swiss frontier, denied the Germans use of the Paris-Mulhouse railway. Its capture would greatly facilitate the supply of German armies operating on the Loire and around Paris, and on 3 November a 15,000-strong German force under General von Tresckow bore down upon it.

Belfort, however, was to prove the toughest of nuts. Its citadel towered 50 metres above the town, seeming to grow out of a sheer rock face, and was protected by a ring of modern outlying forts and the masonry wall of an entrenched camp. Not only were Belfort's defences unusually formidable, but the commander of its 17,700-strong garrison proved to be an exceptionally able and determined soldier. Colonel Aristide Denfert-Rochereau had been chief engineer of the fortress for six years, so knew the ground thoroughly, and he conducted a model active defence. So energetic was he in taking the fight to the enemy that it was 21 November before Tresckow could complete his line of investment, and then only at a distance of 4 kilometres from the fortress, which meant that his men were thinly stretched. The Germans began a bombardment on 3 December, but had to fight for every advance, and were subjected to frequent French sorties and raids. Even with the arrival of reinforcements, it was clear to them that no early decision was to be expected.

Thus the war in the east, from Burgundy to Belfort, seemed deadlocked in mid-December, but it was in this theatre that Gambetta and Freycinet thought they saw the opportunity for a blow that might yet reverse the fortunes of war. Twice in recent despatches to Favre Gambetta had alluded vaguely to the possibility of concentrating all the forces in Burgundy to relieve Belfort and to strike against German communications in eastern France. General Crouzat and Denfert-Rochereau had been amongst those who had advocated such an operation in early November.[45] Yet the Delegation had remained fixated on breaking through to relieve Paris by the direct route. Even now Gambetta saw Bourbaki's next move as an advance directly northward to Montargis and Fontainebleau towards the besieged capital, which must have only a few weeks' food remaining. It was Freycinet who persuaded him that there was a better alternative. With Ducrot's defeat and the loss of Orléans, Freycinet reasoned, they had to accept that there was no longer any realistic chance for the direct relief of Paris; and if Bourbaki headed straight north he would simply be defeated by Friedrich Karl.

Freycinet proposed that, leaving 15 Corps to cover Bourges, Bourbaki should take the 70,000 men of 18 and 20 Corps east to join with Garibaldi and Cremer to drive Werder out of Dijon. Meanwhile, General de Bressolles with his newly-formed 24 Corps at Lyon would go by rail to join the garrison of Besançon. These troops, combined with Bourbaki's, would then form a mass of 110,000 men capable of relieving Belfort and cutting off the German troops besieging Paris from their supplies.[46] If the Germans could not be driven away from the capital, a French manoeuvre to sever the vital communication artery of the Paris-Strasbourg railway might force them to relinquish their grip.

Gambetta and Bourbaki were quickly persuaded. Orders for the operation to begin were given on 19 December.

Stand-Off in the North

Simultaneously, the Army of the North was demonstrating how sensitive the Germans were to any threat to their supply lines. That army apparently had been put out of action by its defeat at Amiens, but recovered remarkably quickly under the impetus of a new commander.

General Louis Léon Faidherbe had been appointed to succeed Bourbaki on 18 November, but his journey from Algeria meant that it was 3 December before he assumed command of the Army of the North, with General Farre reverting to chief of staff. Faidherbe was a native of the region, the son of a Lille hosiery merchant. Educated as a military engineer, he had made a reputation for himself by extending French territory in West Africa at the expense of native tribes. Twice Governor of Senegal, where the climate had ruined his health, in recent years he had been commanding a military sub-division in Algeria. Like other generals of pronounced republican views he had been held back in Algeria by the imperial authorities at the outbreak of war. With Gambetta and Testelin in power, he got his chance. Energetic, irascible and dedicated, he announced his arrival to his troops by relaying Gambetta's expectation that to save the country they must show 'contempt for death, discipline and austerity of morals'.[47]

Declaring his intention to impose discipline 'pitilessly', Faidherbe pressed the reorganization of his army and within days sent columns of his best troops ahead to harass the Germans and menace the railway between Amiens and Laon that supplied First Army in Normandy. From Arras, General Lecointe led a column south-east to Saint-Quentin, which had been shelled by a German flying column. His troops were welcomed there as liberators, and were reliably informed that the German garrison at Ham, 18 kilometres to the south-west on the railway, was vulnerable. Lecointe issued his officers with maps and briefed them carefully for what was to prove one of the most successful raids of the war.

The fortress of Ham had long been declassified, its only recent claim to fame having been as the prison of Louis-Napoleon, later Napoleon III, who had been confined within its dank walls from 1840 until his escape in 1846. Approaching in thick-falling snow on the afternoon of 9 December, French troops quietly surrounded the town and after dark burst through its three gates and into its gas-lit streets, capturing startled German troops in taverns or their billets. The remainder of the garrison took refuge in the citadel but were bluffed into surrender by the threat that they were surrounded by the whole French army. At the cost of twenty-one killed or wounded, the French had captured the entire German garrison of 220 men: a small victory, but one mortifying to the German high command.[48]

General Manteuffel's First Army was seeking to extinguish French resistance in Normandy when news came of Faidherbe's offensive. One division of VIII Corps, which was en route to Le Havre, was sent back towards the Somme. The other division, finding that the defences of Le Havre, occupied by General Briand with an estimated 40,000 men, were too strong to be taken by assault, shortly followed. Only I Corps was left to hold Rouen and deal with continuing French activity west of the Seine.

Faidherbe's exact whereabouts and intentions were at first unclear to the German high command, though increased resistance by French local defence forces in the Somme region seemed a sure indicator that a French army was in the vicinity, as did the refusal of French railwaymen and postal workers to co-operate with the occupation forces at Amiens.[49] On 13 December Moltke issued orders designating Beauvais, midway between Rouen and Amiens, as the concentration point should it prove necessary for Manteuffel to evacuate some conquered territory in order to protect the forces besieging Paris from a French advance from the north.[50] At Amiens, General von der Gröben was sufficiently alarmed by Faidherbe's approach that he evacuated the city on 16 December, much to Manteuffel's irritation, though he left a garrison in the citadel.

After the success at Ham Faidherbe had moved south-east to retake La Fère but, finding the Germans on their guard, struck north-west towards Amiens. However, upon approaching it he learned that the German commander of the citadel had threatened to bombard the city if French troops entered it. Faidherbe was unwilling to risk the destruction of the city, particularly as he had no heavy artillery with him to reduce the citadel, and Manteuffel was closing in from the west. Bypassing Amiens, on 19 December Faidherbe took up an excellent defensive position on the east bank of the River Hallue, which was just wide and deep enough to form a military obstacle. Here he awaited an attack and completed the reorganization of his army, which now consisted of two corps of two divisions each, 22 Corps under Lecointe and 23 Corps under Paulze d'Ivoy. It counted over 40,000 men and seventy-eight guns, but a quarter of its infantry were a division of National Guard, who were as yet unready for combat. Faidherbe might have used the time available to him to fortify the villages along the marshy valley of the Hallue, but he preferred that these should be held only lightly. He believed that his raw troops would do better defending positions on the commanding heights of the east bank, where his line extended for 12 kilometres.

1. General Trochu reviews the National Guard. Immensely popular in Paris on 4 September 1870, Jules Trochu (1815–96) proved to be, in Gambetta's words, 'A tireless talker, but an irresolute and self-important soldier.'

2. Jules Favre (1809–80). Vice-President and Foreign Minister in the Government of National Defence, and in effect its political head.

3. Léon Gambetta (1838–82). The passionate defender of the Republic who urged war to the bitter end.

4. The French garrison march out of Strasbourg, 28 Septemb 1870. Some soldiers threw the weapons into the moat rather than surrender them.

The Hostages, by Paul Émile Boutigny (1854–1929). French local dignitaries commonly suffered ...ys or weeks of detention as a surety against guerrilla attacks or to enforce compliance with the ...nands of the occupier.

6. Marshal Achille Bazaine (1811–88), Commander of the Army of the Rhine at Metz.

7. The Esplanade at Metz, showing railway wagons in use as temporary hospital wards during the blockade.

8. French troops attack at the château of Ladonchamps, north of Metz. Engraving after a painting by Édouard Detaille (1848–1912).

9. Le Bourget, 30 October 1870. Engraving after a painting by Alphonse de Neuville (1835–85). The last French defenders are carried from the Church of Saint-Nicolas.

10. The Cabinet held hostage at the Hôtel de Ville, 31 October 1870. Flourens bestrides the table. Favre and Simon are visible behind the lamp at right while at left Trochu is spirited away by the 106th Battalion of the National Guard.

11. Meeting by the bridge at Sèvres, 5 November 1870. Thiers (with cane) discusses the armistice terms offered by Bismarck with Favre, while General Ducrot smokes a cigar.

12. General J.-B. d'Aurelle de Paladines (1804–77), Commander of the First Army of the Loire.

13. A French regiment on the march. Drawing by Detaille.

14. A Convoy of Wounded at Janville, on the road from Orléans to Paris, by Paul Grolleron (1848–1901). This was the first war in which both sides were signatories to the 1864 Geneva Convention.

15. General Auguste Ducrot (1817–82) had this photograph taken for his wife and children on 23 November 1870 in case he did not survive the imminent Marne offensive. Having lost his uniform during his escape following Sedan, he wears military insignia sewn onto a civilian coat.

6. Fighting around the limekilns near Champigny, 2 December 1870. After a lost fragment of the Champigny cyclorama by de Neuville.

7. Gathering the wounded after Champigny, by Boutigny. Christian Brethren – teachers in Catholic schools – acted as an ambulance corps during the Siege of Paris. They are seen here at work in the streets of Bry-sur-Marne.

18. German hussars destroying a telegraph line at the Normandy coast, December 1870. Engraving after a painting by de Neuville.

19. German assault on the railway station at Nuits, 18 December 1870. Engraving after a painting by Wilhelm Emélé (1830–1905).

20. General Louis Faidherbe (1818–89), Commander of the Army of the North.

21. French sailors fighting as infantry. Drawing by Detaille. France was well served by her navy in 1870–71. Whether as artillerists or infantry, sailors gave backbone to the national defence in Paris and the provinces.

22. French Gardes Mobiles engaged along a railway embankment. Engraving after a painting by de Neuville.

3. In the trenches outside Paris. Engraving after a painting by de Neuville. Like his fellow artist Édouard Detaille, Alphonse de Neuville served as a staff officer in the Garde Mobile during the siege. They became pre-eminent among French painters who bore witness to the war.

4. Preparing for the attack. Engraving after a painting by Detaille.

25. *Francs-tireurs* sabotaging
a railway line, by Alexandre
Bloch (1857–1919). Such
raids invariably provoked
German reprisals.

26. General Charles Bourbaki
(1816–97), Commander of
the Army of the East.

27. Villersexel, 9 January 1871. French troops burn out defending Germans. Engraving after a painting by de Neuville.

28. General Alfred Chanzy (1823–83), Commander of the Second Army of the Loire.

29. On the Retreat (The Army of the Loire). Engraving after a painting by Detaille.

30. Bismarck proclaims the German Empire in the Hall of Mirrors at Versailles, 18 January 1871. Sketch by Anton von Werner (1843–1915). In the background are Moltke (left) and Roon (right).

Back in possession of Amiens, on 20 December Manteuffel sent out a reconnaissance which ran into the French centre at Querrieux and was driven off, but at least discovered that Faidherbe was awaiting attack. Manteuffel, mustering 22,622 infantry, 2,314 cavalry and 108 guns, was happy to oblige him, announcing to his troops with Prussian brevity on 22 December, 'Tomorrow we shall march against the enemy who stands close before us. I need say no more to the First Army.'[51] His columns advanced from Amiens on the bright morning of 23 December across a landscape of snow made crisp by eight degrees of frost.

The Battle of the Hallue (called Pont-Noyelles by the French) did not go according to plan for either commander. Manteuffel planned to assault the French left, nearest to Amiens, with one division of VIII Corps while the other marched around to attack Faidherbe's right (northern) flank. Kummer's 15th Division, charged with the first of these tasks, made good initial progress in seizing villages along the west bank of the Hallue, but encountered stiffer opposition at Pont-Noyelles in the French centre and also in Vecquemont and Daours at the confluence of the Hallue with the Somme, defended by the Naval Division. Even when these villages were secured, the Germans could make no headway against tiers of French riflemen lining the terraced slopes beyond and laying down a murderous fire. Meanwhile, Barnekow's 16th Division had followed too circuitous a route on its flanking march, and when eventually it did reach the battlefield in mid-afternoon found itself not beyond the French right but attacking it frontally. Although it took some villages in the valley it could make no further progress in the face of artillery and rifle fire from the slopes above, and even found its own left flank threatened.

Faidherbe had counted on the Germans being sufficiently worn out by the day's fighting that they could be driven back by a counter-attack at nightfall. In the early dusk French gunners on high ground had easy targets in the burning villages held by the Germans, while their own positions were less easy to pinpoint. But when French infantry stormed back into Pont-Noyelles and Daours they met bitter resistance, and after fierce fighting by the glow of blazing houses were ejected. Neither side had been able to defeat the other. Faidherbe, shivering with tropical fever, was almost captured, while Manteuffel, who had been campaigning for weeks with a broken foot suffered in a fall from his horse, retired to sleep in Amiens.

Next morning, 24 December, saw only outpost skirmishes and sporadic shelling by both sides. Manteuffel made plans for crossing the Somme to the east to attack the French in rear, but Faidherbe concluded that he could not await such an eventuality. Although it had been his practice to billet his men, all had been forced to remain exposed to freezing winds on the bare downland on the night following the battle, poorly clad and with only a little frozen army bread to eat. Judging that they could not endure another night in such

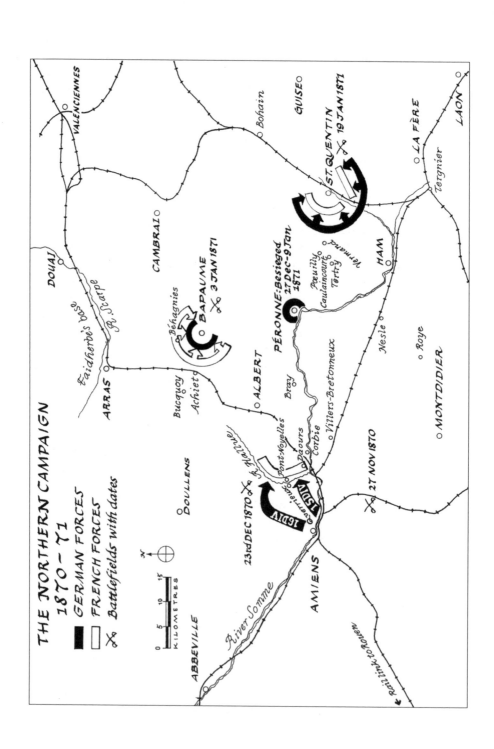

THE NORTHERN CAMPAIGN
1870-71

GERMAN FORCES
FRENCH FORCES
✗ Battlefields with dates

N

0   5   10   15
KILOMETRES

conditions, that afternoon he marched them back to Albert, and thence next day to their old billets south of Arras.

The battle had cost the Germans 955 casualties to 1,226 French, but the French had in addition lost over 1,000 prisoners.[52] Though a tactical stalemate, it had been a strategic victory for the Germans, who had seen off Faidherbe's challenge and held on to Amiens.

Quarrels at Versailles

At German headquarters none doubted ultimate victory, but after five months of war frustration was mounting at the time it was taking to achieve it in the face of the French 'insane determination to resist'.[53] Following the war council each morning, King Wilhelm, who had his headquarters at the Prefecture, passed his days in a round of troop reviews, royal audiences, and formal dinners that filled the winter afternoons. Versailles was packed with foreign dignitaries, German princelings and politicians, reporters, government officials, staff officers and servants, stuck far from home when all had expected the war to be over weeks ago. In this atmosphere intrigues and personal quarrels multiplied at the temporary seat of government.

Bismarck, whose quarters were in the secluded Rue de Provence, was in mid-December tortured by an attack of gout and his nerves were severely strained.[54] It was small wonder, for, in addition to the normal run of business that he had to conduct as Chancellor of the North German Confederation, he was striving to construct a German Empire incorporating Prussia's South German allies, which required all his formidable political skills in managing the southern royal houses and governments, the Reichstag, and not least King Wilhelm. In addition he was watchful against any possibility of European intervention before Germany had defeated France and achieved her war aims: a concern which fed an increasingly bitter feud with the General Staff as to who ultimately controlled state policy.

The South German states, and particularly the most important of them, Bavaria, had played their full part in the war against France. Their continued participation was assured by their military alliances with Prussia, which had been activated by the French declaration of war in July. But, now a joint victory was in sight, what should be the terms of union between the Prussian-dominated North German Confederation and South Germany?

For Bismarck, the rationale of the war against the common enemy had been to secure the accession of the southern states to the Confederation while the tide of German patriotism was running high. In the process he sought to elevate King Wilhelm of Prussia to the imperial dignity: a move the southern states had resisted as recently as February and which Wilhelm himself still affected to regard as 'simply a cross for him to bear'.[55] With varying degrees of reluctance, the southern governments now accommodated themselves to the prevailing German nationalist sentiment. They would need Prussian protection in any future war with France, and the annexation of Alsace and Loraine as a common German imperial territory would provide a welcome defensive barrier. In the wake of Sedan, Baden was the first to apply for admission to the Confederation and be welcomed by Bismarck, while tiny Hesse-Darmstadt, with half its territories already within the Confederation, had little option but to follow suit. But the adhesion of the kingdoms of Württemberg and Bavaria was by no means a foregone conclusion, and their governments exploited their strong bargaining position. Negotiations in October and November proved taxing, and in the end both won significant concessions from Bismarck.

Whilst Bismarck put pressure on the southern governments by inspiring attacks in the nationalist press against the claims of local particularism at such an auspicious moment in German history, he avoided overt coercion. He resisted attempts to renegotiate the basis of the Confederation formed in 1867 in the wake of Prussia's victory over Austria, but he wanted the union with the south to be voluntary and lasting. He also wanted a union created by princes, not one forced upon him by Liberal nationalists. He conceded that, in return for her adhesion, Bavaria would keep wide powers over her army in peacetime and over such matters as immigration, her railway, postal and telegraph services, and the right to maintain her own diplomatic service. Württemberg received only slightly less generous concessions to local autonomy and tradition.[56] Furthermore, the constitution of the North German Confederation would be amended to allow the smaller states the possibility of combining to veto unwelcome measures in the Federal Council or *Bundesrat*, which gained more extensive powers in some areas – notably the right to approve any declaration of war which did not result from an attack on Germany. In the event, Bismarck's concessions were to prove more apparent than real: his own powers remained untrammelled and Prussia retained the strength to exercise a veto in the Federal Council. Yet the southern state governments had achieved what seemed a good bargain in the circumstances, and the treaties with them were signed by 25 November.

Bismarck had in fact paid a higher price for Bavaria's complaisance than was known at the time. The wealth of the exiled King of Hanover, seized after his defeat in 1866, was used to provide the young King Ludwig II of Bavaria with a generous personal income for life. This so-called Guelph fund thus secretly eased the way to German unity and subsidized Ludwig's fantasy castle in Bavaria. In return, Ludwig copied out in his own hand and signed a letter drafted by Bismarck requesting King Wilhelm to assume the German imperial title, so redolent of medieval Germanic power.

There remained the Reichstag in Berlin to convince, and Bismarck spared no effort to secure the ratification of the treaties with the South and the necessary changes to the constitution. The National Liberals and Progressives would have preferred a more unified and centralized federal state, but in meetings at Versailles Bismarck argued that this was the best arrangement that could be had, even threatening to resign if he did not get his way. The Reichstag gave its approval by a substantial majority, and sent a delegation to Versailles to petition Wilhelm to accept the imperial crown. Symbolically, the delegation was led by Dr Eduard Simson, who in 1849 had submitted the same request to King Friedrich Wilhelm IV in very different circumstances and been refused.

King Wilhelm was in one of his depressed and petulant moods. The Crown Prince, acutely aware that his father did not share his idealistic enthusiasm for the panoply and symbolism of the imperial title, noted that the old man was 'in great excitement and ill-humour not less over the military situation than over the course of politics ... His Majesty's outlook on the immediate future is of the blackest.'[57] Yet, though Wilhelm complained at the form of both King Ludwig's letter and the Reichstag address, on 18 December he read out a favourable response prepared by Bismarck to an impromptu assembly of dignitaries, who were moved by the historic significance of the occasion. Wilhelm's mood that evening was noticeably lighter. Although he refused any formal celebration until written consents from all the princes had been received, the new Reich would come into being from 1 January 1871.

Having achieved a major goal of his policy, Bismarck was more anxious for the war to end while the diplomatic situation remained favourable to Germany. Russia's unilateral denunciation of the limitations imposed on her Black Sea fleet by the 1856 Treaty of Paris presented a potential danger. Although Bismarck had previously assured Russia of German support for such a move, its timing was awkward for him. The flouting of the treaty, notified to the other powers in early November, provoked an outcry in England, the prime mover of the restrictions imposed at the close of the Crimean War. A war between Britain and Russia, perhaps involving Austria-Hungary on the western side, could merge with the Franco-German conflict to produce a general European war that might put German gains in question. To forestall such an eventuality Bismarck proposed an international conference to settle the Black Sea dispute. Since Britain was not prepared to fight alone and would welcome a face-saving agreement, she accepted the proposal, as did Russia. It was agreed that a conference should convene in London.

Yet this solution too presented Bismarck with a challenge, for France was a signatory of the 1856 treaty, and the other powers were unanimous in wishing to see French representation at the conference. An astute French representative would have opportunities to try to draw the neutrals into the settlement of the Franco–German war and to mitigate the peace terms imposed on France. Fortunately for Bismarck, the French proved anything but astute. The prevailing sentiment among French republicans was that the Crimean War had been a dynastic adventure by Napoleon III, who had been duped into serving the interests of the perfidious English who were now failing to support their former ally. Jules Favre baulked at the idea of leaving Paris at her hour of crisis to discuss the Black Sea. Even when his able deputy at Bordeaux, the Count de Chaudordy, persuaded him and Gambetta that the opportunity should be taken, Favre betrayed his inexperience by proposing that before France could consent to attend the neutrals must insist on an armistice and the re-supply of Paris during the conference, or even give a prior guarantee of French territorial integrity.

Such inept French tactics and changes of mind, combined with delays to the pigeon post, played into Bismarck's hands. When in late December Britain requested a safe-conduct for Favre to leave Paris Bismarck delayed the news reaching him by alleging the violation of a parliamentary flag at the outposts as a pretext for suspending communication with Paris. He made further difficulties over technicalities, and pointed out that the Government of National Defence had no legitimacy. The net result was that the French Foreign Minister was still bottled up in Paris when the London conference convened in mid-January. Favre had failed to take an earlier opportunity to nominate a deputy who might easily have thwarted Bismarck's stalling tactics by sailing straight from Bordeaux to England.[58]

Bismarck's obstructionism was intended to buy time for Germany to force the surrender of Paris. As the siege dragged on he had become critical of the management of the war by the 'demi-gods' of the General Staff, insisting that they should shorten it by bombarding the city.[59] His table-talk was shot through with contempt for the French, and in the evenings he would vent his spleen by advocating at various times hanging or shooting all male inhabitants of villages where German troops were fired upon, street urchins who insulted German officers, French officers who allegedly had broken their parole (principally Ducrot), anyone escaping from Paris by balloon, and prisoners of war generally.[60] On the principle that the harder war was made upon the French the quicker they would tire of it, he was impatient at the delay in shelling their capital, so keeping in step with public opinion in Germany where there was a deep desire to inflict punishment on Parisians as the instigators of the war. Bismarck encouraged the German press in its cry that only bombardment of 'the modern Babylon' could shorten the war, and shared civilian confidence that the degenerate French could not take much of such medicine before caving in.

The General Staff, on the other hand, had no faith in the efficacy of a bombardment to reduce Paris, considering it at most a last resort. From late September they had taken steps to bring up 235 heavy guns for the bombardment of the perimeter forts in case a regular siege became necessary, but with little urgency. The practical difficulties were greater than imagined by Berliners clamouring for bombardment. The transport of guns and ammunition took up railway capacity at the expense of food and equipment for the 200,000 troops blockading Paris.[61] The siege material then had to be transported miles from the nearest railheads to the front over muddy roads, and there were not enough sturdy four-wheeled carts to do this quickly. It would be worse than useless to commence a bombardment that could not be sustained against such an extensive target for lack of adequate reserves of ammunition. Besides, what was the point of mounting a regular siege and an assault that would sacrifice German lives needlessly when starvation would achieve the same aim just as surely – as it had at Metz. The crusty Chief of Staff of Third Army, General Blumenthal, frequently condemned in his diary the 'foolish', 'absurd' and 'infantile' assumption 'that the bursting of a few shells in the suburbs of Paris will bring about a capitulation'.[62] His views were shared by many senior German commanders, including Moltke.

The issue of whether to bombard became the focus of a power struggle between the General Staff and Bismarck. The senior military men had not forgiven Bismarck's pretension to give orders to the chief of military police in September, nor his interference with troop movements in western Germany during the war of 1866 against Austria. His political negotiations during the blockade of Metz had seemed to the generals unpardonable meddling in a purely military matter, just as his haste to end the war of 1866 had in their view cheated them of complete victory. They resented him as a civilian masquerading in a cuirassier's uniform who was trying to lord it over them.[63] Fearing leaks to the press, they starved him of information to such an extent that Bismarck complained to the King about his exclusion from military councils, as he did about Moltke's communication with Trochu in early December without consulting him. Both Moltke and Bismarck, each with some justification, waxed indignant that the other was trespassing on his sphere of responsibility.[64]

It was Bismarck who prevailed. He had an ally in War Minister Roon, whom Blumenthal characterized as 'bloodthirsty'[65]: Roon's father had died at French hands in the Napoleonic wars and he had lately lost a son at Sedan. Together they won over King Wilhelm and through him put pressure on Moltke to hasten preparations for bombardment. A prominent critic of bombardment, Crown Prince Friedrich Wilhelm, husband of the unpopular Princess Victoria, found himself attacked in the Berlin press for supposedly sparing Paris at the behest of his mother-in-law, the Queen of England. The Crown Prince, who privately deplored the 'perfect mania' among civilians for bombardment, suspected Bismarck of being behind such characteristic attacks on the Liberal, anglophile party.[66]

The apparently interminable extension of Parisian resistance and the resilience of the French provincial armies strengthened the popular appeal of Bismarck's arguments. In a phrase that quickly became notorious in the besieged city, a German paper argued that the 'psychological moment' had arrived to put pressure on the starving Parisians.[67]

At a military conference on 17 December presided over by the King it was agreed that there should be a further delay until a reserve of 500 rounds per siege gun had been amassed. After that the bombardment of the city's defences on the southern front must begin. By way of prelude, seventy-six guns would target French positions on Mont Avron, east of Paris. Preparations were expedited and amid a snowstorm on the morning of 27 December the first German heavy guns opened fire.

Chapter Eight

The Final Defeats

Bombardment

Bombardment of the isolated Avron plateau proved highly effective. Despite having occupied the position for a month, French infantry had not been as industrious as their opponents in constantly improving their defences. Heavy shelling of their shallow trenches in rocky and frozen soil caused a momentary panic among Avron's naval defenders, who suffered 100 casualties on the first day. Even after they had been rallied by old General d'Hugues it seemed doubtful that they could hold their exposed position for long. Trochu, never short on physical bravery, rode out among the falling shells to judge for himself, and ordered the evacuation of the plateau. An orderly withdrawal to the line of the eastern forts was carried out on the night of 28 December with the loss of only one gun, and without German interference or pursuit.

Trochu's credibility, already low after Second Le Bourget, plummeted further. Having been told a month earlier that the capture of Mont Avron had been an important victory, angry Parisians now questioned why it had not been occupied in September, and why adequate works had not been constructed in the time available.[1] Already Favre and Picard had thoughts of either replacing Trochu or exercising much closer Cabinet control over him. As Trochu deftly reminded them, however, finding a politically acceptable replacement would not be easy. Both Vinoy, an ex-imperial senator, and Ducrot, a royalist, were hostile to the Republic. Those two generals and other senior commanders attended a stormy but typically indecisive Cabinet meeting on 31 December to discuss military options. Ducrot was adamant that no break-out was possible, except perhaps by small groups. When Vinoy suggested that if columns were launched at several points simultaneously a way through might be found, or the enemy at least seriously damaged, Ducrot flew into his usual rage, asking where these points were that had escaped his attention, and falling into recriminations about responsibility for the failure of the Marne offensive. When General Schmitz suggested that the army should not just sit passively without attempting a supreme effort at some point in the German defences, Ducrot shouted, 'Find that point then! You won't break through with fine phrases!' He became so overbearing that War Minister Le Flô had to ask him to stop interrupting.[2]

Ducrot had convinced himself that the 'irresolution, weakness and blindness' of the republican government were leading to catastrophe, and that prolongation of the war was pointless.[3] The truth, wrote Trochu, was that although at Champigny Ducrot 'had risen superior to all of us', latterly, 'embittered by the common plight, by personal failure and by injustice, obsessed by violent political antipathies, unable to meet trials with a grain of philosophical calm, General Ducrot became unjust in his turn, agitated, unreasonable, and well below his best'.[4] On 6 January the despondent Ducrot wrote privately to Trochu asking to be relieved of his command and to revert to the ranks. Trochu dissuaded him, pointing out the effect his attitude was having on the officers of Second Army. Ducrot agreed to stay, though henceforward he would follow orders but take no further part in command decisions.[5]

Trochu himself seemed to have little left to offer but bombast, which he continued to dole out in generous measure. Alerted to a rumour in the clubs and among the National Guard that he was treating with the enemy, he rushed out a proclamation on 6 January declaring that 'the Governor of Paris will not capitulate', which chimed oddly with his persistent lack of faith in the success of the defence and his private conviction that capitulation was inevitable.[6] A week later, apparently inspired by an article in Louis Veuillot's ultra-Catholic newspaper, he invoked mystic assistance for the capital's defenders, declaring,

> I am a believer, and have asked Saint Geneviève, liberator of Paris at the time of the barbarian invasions, once again to cast her protective mantle over Paris. She has answered my prayer. She has providentially inspired the enemy with the idea of a bombardment that dishonours German arms and civilization, and that stirs the resolve of the people of Paris ...

When Trochu read the proofs to an incredulous Cabinet, he was met at first with icy silence, then with violent denunciation from the anti-clerical Jules Ferry. Although the Cabinet wanted it suppressed, news of the document leaked out.[7] Trochu's stock was now so low, wrote Henry Labouchère, that 'his enemies call him a traitor; his friends defend him from the charge by saying that he is only a vain fool'.[8]

The morale and health of the troops manning the trenches were at a low ebb. On 1 January the regular army had 23,938 men absent out of 100,705; the Garde Mobile 23,565 absent out of 111,999.[9] In the latter good officers were in short supply and morale needed rebuilding.[10] The National Guard, now taking a turn at front-line duty, was so inexperienced that a single shot from an enemy sentry was enough to set off a wild volley, while one unit calmly abandoned the trenches after firing off all its ammunition as quickly as possible.[11]

The bonds of discipline were under strain even among the regulars, who had lost faith in the high command. To understand the state of things, wrote Viollet-le-Duc, you had to move among them, 'grouped around braziers, dirty, dishevelled, covered in filthy rags, sheltered behind remnants of furniture seized from some nearby houses, answering questions only in monosyllables, allowing their clothing and shoes to scorch by the fire, no longer hearing their officers' voices. You had to see the pale glow of a winter dawn illuminating these half dead men, their numbed limbs covered in hoar-frost, their faces expressionless and utterly indifferent.'[12]

To guard against surprises at night electric searchlights had been mounted around the ramparts.[13] By contrast, Paris itself had become a place of darkness, under cover of which saws and axes were taken to fences, wooden sheds and the city's remaining trees. Partly this scavenging was the work of the poor, desperate for a source of heat for cooking, but much was by criminal gangs seeking to profit from the soaring price of firewood by selling wood pillaged from timberyards, construction sites and gardens. The authorities were felling the trees that had lined the city's streets, as well as those in the Bois de Boulogne and the Bois de Vincennes, but even this timber was prey to raids. Government proclamations condemning these practices had no effect.[14]

The shortage of fuel for lighting deepened the general sense of depression in the city, which seemed half deserted:

> Paris without gas in January, all through the short, dark days! At four o'clock all the shops closed. Some rare passers-by could be glimpsed keeping close to the houses, or drunks reeling along singing the *Marseillaise*. There were no more carriages or horses in the streets. The occasional feebly lit window merely deepened the darkness of the high black facades, just as the bombarding cannon emphasised the silence and stillness of these nights of sixteen long hours. Paris, the city of noise, light and movement; Paris, the city where you worked and played with passion; Paris, the city of busy, enterprising, restless people: Paris was like a city that had died.[15]

Meanwhile, in the first days of January, aided by the rock-hard ground, the Germans stealthily moved their heavy siege guns from their artillery park at Villacoublay into battery sites that had been prepared along the heights south of Paris. The bombardment was scheduled to begin on 4 January, but fog necessitated a postponement until next morning. Then over 100 guns on the southern front joined with the thirty-eight already bombarding the eastern forts, firing 12 and 15cm shell mixed with heavier mortar rounds. Not until 21 January were sufficient heavy guns in position to extend the bombardment to St Denis and the north-western forts. In the month up to 26 January German gunners fired 110,286 rounds,[16] nine out of ten of them against the perimeter forts, which began to suffer severely. The German artillery, directed by Prince Hohenlohe, established its dominance, just as German infantry drove off several French forays against the batteries and established control of what a later generation would call no-man's-land between the lines. Nevertheless, the French forts were not completely silenced, Fort Montrouge proving particularly stubborn, and they inflicted over 400 casualties on German siege artillerists.[17] In the hours of respite provided by darkness the defenders of the fortresses worked at repairs to maintain an unbroken front.

The bombardment of the city of Paris was in military terms an irrelevance, daily diverting against civilian targets 300 or 400 shells that might have been expended more usefully against the forts. No formal notice of bombardment had been given to Trochu, and on the afternoon of 5 January some Parisians surmised that shells landing in the city streets must be accidental overshoots. They learned otherwise over succeeding days as German guns firing at 30 degrees of elevation achieved ranges of over 8,000 yards, scoring hits on the Pont St Michel, the Pont de Notre-Dame, the Champ de Mars, the Jardin des Plantes and the Isle de St Louis. Most shells, however, fell squarely within the southern *arrondissements*, including on and around such prominent left bank landmarks as the Panthéon, the Sorbonne, the Luxembourg Palace and the Val-de-Grâce hospital. The domes and spires of the city's cultural monuments, churches and hospitals unfortunately made convenient aiming points for German gunners. When Trochu formally protested against the targeting of hospitals – as did many eminent French doctors – Moltke denied that it was happening, but gave the barbed assurance that as the atmosphere cleared and his batteries moved closer to the city targeting would become more accurate and it would be possible to distinguish Red Cross flags.[18] The protest of foreign diplomatic representatives who had remained in the French capital received similarly short shrift from Bismarck, who argued that since the French had made Paris a fortress it was a legitimate target.[19]

Taking justifiable pride in their city as the jewel of European civilization, Parisians thought it uniquely barbarous that it should be subjected to the horrors of war. Belief in the malign intelligence of German targeting was reinforced when Prefect of Police Cresson, against Trochu's wishes, moved German prisoners of war into the much-shelled La Santé prison, which thereafter was spared.[20] Yet the heaviest shelling of the city took place at night, and consequently was largely indiscriminate.

Parisians adapted to this new hazard to life and limb as best they could. Thousands migrated to the relative safety of the right bank, lodging with relatives, friends, or in government buildings.[21] Otherwise the hiss and explosion of shells aroused more curiosity and indignation than terror or demoralization, during the daylight hours at least. Crowds gathered to watch the spectacle or to gawp at shell damage, while street urchins found a great game in tricking well-dressed bourgeois into flattening themselves on the muddy ground with a mischievously-timed shout of 'Look out! A shell!' During the siege a cottage industry had grown up for the manufacture of bogus souvenirs, particularly Prussian spiked helmets. Now boys could earn money by selling shell fragments which fetched a better price while still warm, and some risked their lives to defuse unexploded shells.[22] Effective fire precautions and prompt action by the fire brigade prevented all but three of the fifty-three reported fires started by shells from causing serious damage.[23]

Yet if German artillerists could not produce anything like the intensity of destruction achieved against more compact targets like Strasbourg, the southern districts of Paris endured a harrowing ordeal. Some 1,158 houses and 103 public buildings were hit in the course of three weeks, the latter including barracks, convents, schools, churches, hospitals, museums, scientific establishments, prisons and gasworks.[24] Naturally it was civilian deaths and mutilations that caused the greatest revulsion and strengthened determination to resist. At least 103 people were killed and 284 wounded, half the victims being women and children.[25] Jules Favre eloquently expressed the city's grief and anger when he spoke at the funeral of five pupils of the Saint-Nicolas boarding school, killed when a shell burst in their dormitory in the Rue de Vaugirard on the night of 8 January.[26]

In sober fact, deaths from shelling were a tiny fraction of the rising death toll of the siege, and funerals were becoming a common sight. Amongst the military wounded, doctors were losing their battle against infection:

> Nearly all bone wounds rapidly developed complications and became fatal. All amputations yielded deplorable results ... Even with the slightest wounds, purulent infections, hospital gangrene and erysipelas carried off our sick.[27]

Amongst soldiers and civilians alike, smallpox, bronchitis, pneumonia and typhoid were claiming ever more victims, and a malignant form of measles appeared, fatal in one third of cases. Although only six people were recorded as having perished from starvation during the siege, thousands died from the cumulative effects of malnutrition and cold, particularly among the old and very young, for whom there was insufficient milk.[28] In the last week of December there were 3,680 deaths in Paris, compared to 838 for the same week before the war. Two weeks later the figure had risen to well above 4,000 weekly, compared to below 1,000 pre-war. Overall, from the start of the siege on 18 September 1870 to 24 February 1871 there were 64,154 civilian deaths in Paris, compared to 21,978 for the equivalent period before the war,[29] suggesting that over 40,000 deaths might be attributed either directly or indirectly to siege conditions. Moltke had been correct that blockade was a more effective weapon than bombardment.

Birth of an Empire

The Palace of Versailles, monument to the Sun King and 'to all the glories of France', served as a military hospital during the German occupation of the town. Yet the high symbolism of proclaiming the new German Empire in its famous Hall of Mirrors could not be resisted. No more humiliating place for France could have been chosen to celebrate German unity and impending triumph.

Even so, the ceremony almost did not happen when its leading actor threw a tantrum on the eve of the great event. King Wilhelm's earlier concerns had been met, for the rulers of all the South German states had given their formal assent to the new union, and all the state parliaments had ratified it save Bavaria, which would do so by a majority of just two on 21 January. What provoked Wilhelm to tears of rage at a meeting on 17 January was a long debate about what title he should bear. He insisted that he should be styled 'King of Prussia, chosen Emperor of Germany', but the tone of Prussian dominion implied in that style threatened to upset Bismarck's patient handiwork, for it was not the formula that he had agreed with the southern governments without consulting the King. The Chancellor managed to persuade Wilhelm that 'chosen' carried unwelcome overtones of election, but could not convince his peevish master that 'German Emperor' preceding the royal title would be far more palatable to the southern princes.

This difference was still unresolved at the ceremony next day, 18 January, chosen because it was the anniversary of the founding of the Prussian monarchy in 1701. Advised of the difficulty by Bismarck, Grand Duke Friedrich of Baden got round it at the close of proceedings by hailing the new Emperor, his father-in-law, with the words, 'Long live his imperial and royal majesty, Kaiser Wilhelm!'[30] Wilhelm was still so furious that he snubbed Bismarck by refusing to shake his hand after the ceremony, while the Chancellor himself, as he wrote to his wife, wished he could be a bomb, to explode among this princely heap.[31]

These private resentments – which were quickly healed – were symptomatic of Wilhelm's fears that the old Prussia would be swallowed up in the new Empire created by Bismarck. Shared by many Prussian conservatives, such suspicions proved well grounded, and were mirrored among southern conservatives who sensed that within an enlarged German nation-state their little kingdoms would never be quite the same again. Thus while one of Moltke's staff officers enthusiastically described the Kaiser ceremony as 'simple and dignified, and all the more impressive for that reason',[32] Prince Otto of Bavaria wrote to his brother, King Ludwig, of 'how infinitely and agonizingly painful I found the scene ... it was all so cold, so proud, so glossy, so strutting and boastful and heartless and empty'.[33] Significantly, in this marriage of Prussian militarism with German nationalism, there were few civilians present; only princes, soldiers and diplomats all assembled in their dress uniforms festooned with decorations amid much display of flags, drums, silk sashes, polished leather boots and belts and burnished sabres and helmets in a scene immortalized for public edification in the official paintings of Anton von Werner.[34]

The tension between military and civilian power that was to haunt the new Reich was present at its birth, for the feud between Moltke and Bismarck came to a head that very week. Moltke's view was in essence that political decision-making should be suspended for the duration of the war, and that it was for the General Staff to take whatever measures it deemed necessary to achieve military victory and then to dictate peace terms. He saw the impending fall of Paris as merely a step towards the goal of permanently defeating and crushing France. After the French army and the Garde Mobile defending the city had been made prisoners of war and the capital occupied – as had happened at Metz – Moltke's forces would be free to follow the French provincial armies far into the interior of the country in pursuit of final submission. During the siege, Bismarck had observed tellingly, Moltke's profile had come to resemble 'more and more every day that of a bird of prey'.[35]

Crown Prince Friedrich Wilhelm, aware that Moltke and Bismarck were at loggerheads over these issues, found the general 'deeply offended at Count Bismarck's arbitrary and despotic attitude. He has the feeling that, in military matters no less than in political, the Federal Chancellor is resolved to decide everything for himself, without paying the smallest heed to what the responsible experts have to say.'[36] Friedrich's attempt to mediate between the two by inviting them to dine with him on 13 January backfired, leading to a blunt exchange of irreconcilable views. It seemed to him that 'Count Bismarck desires peace, but General Count Moltke a war of extermination.'[37]

Both protagonists put their views to their royal master, to whom each reported directly. On the day of the imperial ceremony Bismarck complained to the King about Moltke's failure to involve him in the correspondence with Trochu about the bombardment. However much Wilhelm identified with his generals, he judged that he must once more give way to his forceful Chancellor. Two days later he ruled that Bismarck would take the lead in any armistice negotiations, while royal orders of 25 January obliged Moltke to keep Bismarck fully informed of future military operations and forbade him to correspond with the French authorities without the King's decision as to whether Bismarck should be consulted.

Moltke was so wounded that he thought of resigning, and wrote a stinging draft suggesting that Bismarck should be made responsible for military operations. On mature reflection, however, he submitted only a dignified protest to the King. The bitterness of General Staff officers towards Bismarck was boundless, and the snub so rankled with Moltke that when years later he came to write his history of the war he managed to do so without once mentioning Bismarck by name. Nevertheless, the Chancellor had carried his point, and Wilhelm's backing of him was to be crucial to the settlement of the war.[38]

Parisians, however, were not yet ready to concede defeat, and had determined to make one more military effort. They launched it on the day after the proclamation of Wilhelm as German Kaiser, causing the Hall of Mirrors to be transformed once more into a hospital ward.

Buzenval

The bombardment had increased political pressure on Trochu to take the offensive. The Committee (now styling itself the Delegation) of the Twenty Arrondissements, quiet since the failed insurrection of 31 October, placarded a second 'red poster' around the city on 6 January, signed by 140 Left-wing activists. It berated the 'sloth and indecision' of the Government of National Defence and condemned its military mismanagement: 'We count 500,000 fighting men, yet we are held fast by 200,000 Prussians.' Was Paris to await the shame of capitulation, or fight? Invoking the city's revolutionary tradition, it called for the government to give way to the Commune and for a programme of 'General requisitioning, free rations and an attack in mass.'[39]

No demonstrations accompanied the poster. Flourens had been arrested in December, and his troop had been disbanded by General Clément Thomas for cowardice in the face of the enemy at Créteil on 28 November.[40] (Clément Thomas had lately made himself a marked man by his public denunciations of the rowdier elements of the National Guard under his command.) The government's response to the 'red poster' was to institute proceedings against its authors for inciting insurrection.

But pressure to act was exerted too through the radical press and clubs, and also through the mayors of the *arrondissements* who spoke with the authority of elected officials. Although Favre resisted their pretensions to a share in government, he had taken to consulting them regularly. They pressed for a sortie and some – including the radical Clemenceau and particularly the extremist Delescluze – wanted Trochu to be removed or supervised by a civilian committee.[41]

Expectations of action were also fuelled by news from outside. On 8 January, thanks to a break in the freezing weather that had prevented carrier pigeons from flying, messages from Gambetta dated between 23 December and 5 January got through. (They were among the first despatches received from the provinces to have been photographically reduced onto transparent film rather than paper; an advance which allowed thousands of private messages to be carried by one bird, then transcribed using a projector and screen and delivered as telegrams.) Gambetta painted a rosier picture than the facts warranted of the achievements of Chanzy, Bourbaki and Faidherbe, and exaggerated German losses and demoralization. With a growing tendency to be carried away by his own rhetoric, he depicted a France burning with patriotic ardour to carry on the war even after the fall of Paris.[42]

Trochu had no appetite for another sortie, which he believed was doomed to failure and characterized as an 'act of despair'.[43] To justify his delay in mounting one he pleaded at various times the low morale of the army, the need for further information from the provinces, and the supposed arrival of heavy German reinforcements – though in reality the Germans were detaching troops from their siege lines to combat French offensives in the provinces. Trochu was in any case convinced that the bombardment must be the prelude to the long-awaited German assault, and that his forces should therefore wait on the defensive. But, as Favre pointed out, food supplies were running dangerously short, with the prospect imminent of starvation once January was out.

The first plan Trochu adopted under pressure from Favre was for an attack southwards towards Châtillon, with Versailles as its goal. But on 7 January a council of twenty-eight generals at the Louvre objected that German guns would slaughter their men as they advanced over open ground. Instead, with near unanimity, they preferred an idea proposed by General Schmitz, Trochu's chief of staff, and by General Berthaut, one of Ducrot's division commanders. Assembling under the protection of the guns of Mont-Valérien, French forces would strike south-westwards against the wooded hills at the neck of the Gennevilliers peninsula, aiming at Versailles. Planning proceeded, and in the face of Trochu's endless temporization Favre, backed by Jules Simon and Emmanuel Arago, insisted on 16 January that the operation should go ahead on the 19th.

The attack would be made with 90,000 men in three columns on a front of less than 6 kilometres. Of these troops, 42,000 would be National Guards. For, as General Schmitz expressed it, having been mustered and armed at great expense, they could not be told that the defence had no need of them, but should be allowed the opportunity to defend their homes which were being bombarded.[44] Others suggested more cynically that the government, fearing riots if capitulation occurred without the National Guard having been given its chance to fight, thought a bloodletting necessary 'to cure Paris of her fever'.[45] As for the regular army, its prejudice against citizen soldiers was summed up in the remark of one hard–boiled general that 'these clowns of National Guards insist on getting their heads shot off, and we shall lead them to it'.[46]

The offensive was heralded by the inevitable stirring government proclamation, provoking one newspaper to protest, 'Let public opinion finally make [the authors] understand the dignity of silence, since they cannot grasp it for themselves.'[47] The initial movement of troops to the western outskirts of the capital by road and rail went smoothly, but they then had to cross the Seine by the only three bridges available, at Asnières and Neuilly. Although Trochu had issued detailed instructions for the attack, planning for the routes to be used by each unit was woefully defective, leading to enormous traffic jams and delays on the approach to the battlefield. Although the generals were later to complain bitterly that the politicians had rushed them into battle, it was not unreasonable for the Cabinet to expect competent staff work in an army that had had four months to become thoroughly acquainted with the ground over which it had to operate. Instead, during the night of 18 January and the following dawn infantry columns crossed one another, generals argued over the right of way, and artillery columns, wagon convoys and ambulance trains stalled amid a cold drizzle on roads ankle-deep in mud. As a result some units became engaged with the enemy while others were still marking time awaiting their turn to cross the Seine bridges. In his memoirs Trochu wrote, 'What calculation of march routes, what foresight by the headquarters staff could have prevented these inevitable complications?' As one military critic commented acidly, this was straining philosophy rather too far.[48]

The battle was supposed to start at 6.30 a.m. on Thursday, 19 January, with the firing of signal guns and flares from Mont-Valérien, but at that hour Trochu was still delayed in the traffic snarl. At 7.00 a.m. the fortress commander judged that he should wait no longer and the signal was fired. Trochu then arrived and immediately sent counter-orders, but the leading French troops had already commenced the attack on the left. Thus the battle began as it was to continue, piecemeal and with little co-ordination between French units.

The left column under Vinoy went in first and, aided by dense fog, achieved surprise and some initial success, breaking into the German front line at the Montretout redoubt and pushing into the town of St Cloud. It became involved in hard fighting there and in and around the luxurious residences lying north of the park of the former imperial palace, notably the Villa Pozzo di Borgo and the Villa Zimmermann. Coming into action about an hour after

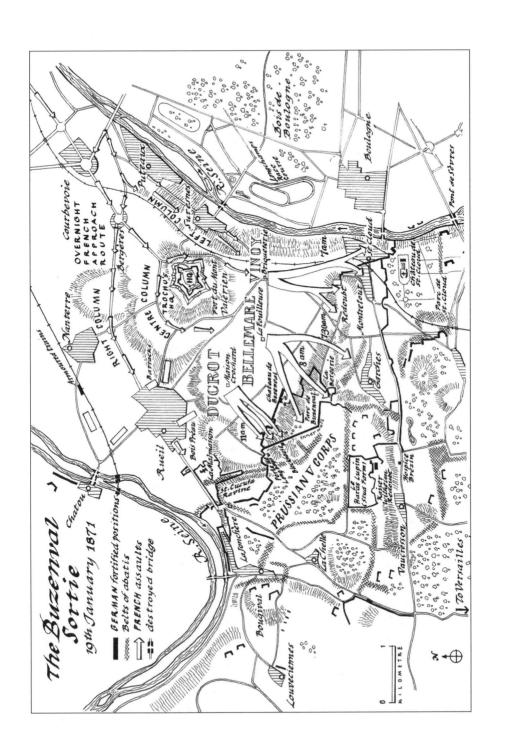

The Buzenval Sortie
19th January 1871

GERMAN fortified positions
Belts of abatis
FRENCH assaults
destroyed bridge

Courbevoie
OVERNIGHT FRENCH APPROACH ROUTE
Nanterre
Bergères
Puteaux
Armoured trains
LEFT COLUMN
CENTRE COLUMN
RIGHT COLUMN
Barracks
TROCHU'S HQ
HQ
Fort du Mont Valérien
Rueil
Bois Préau
La Malmaison
La Cucula Ravine
La Fonchère
Bougival
Louveciennes
VINOY
BELLEMARE
La Fouilleuse
DUCROT
Maison Crochard
Château de Buzenval
Parc de Buzenval
11am
8am
La Bergerie
Inner wall
PRUSSIAN V CORPS
La Chelle
Hariss Lupin Stud Farm
Kaiser Wilhelm
Hospice Brézin
Vaucresson
To Versailles
Briquetterie
7am
La Fouilleuse
130am
Redoute
Montretout
Garches
St Cloud
Château St Cloud
Parc de St Cloud
Pont de Sèvres
Bois de Boulogne
Boulogne
Seine

N

0   1
KILOMETRE

Vinoy's men, General de Bellemare's centre column also drove in the German outposts facing it. On its left its momentum carried it up the ridge defended by the Germans as far as the first houses of the village of Garches, whilst its right-hand units smashed their way through the north wall of the Buzenval Park using pickaxes and dynamite and stormed up the crest. Atop the ridge, however, Bellemare's men encountered an impassable obstacle in the loopholed walls of La Bergerie Farm, from which German rifles vomited a hail of bullets. Despite heroic efforts, a group of French engineers who ran forward to breach this wall were unable to detonate their frozen dynamite before being forced back.

Defending the heights were the 21,000 veterans of General von Kirchbach's V Corps, who had had months to construct three lines of trenches protected by belts of abatis and by blockhouses and redoubts from which infantry and artillery could lay down a devastating fire. By contrast, both Bellemare's and Vinoy's men had insufficient artillery support. Their guns, pulled by under-nourished horses, were bogged in the mud well to the rear. By 11.00 a.m. both the left and centre columns had ceased to make progress and were under heavy German fire.

It was not until then that General Ducrot came into action with the right-hand column. Ducrot's men had had further to march, and he waited to assemble his batteries before attacking across his old battlefield of 21 October. Even so, he committed his infantry disjointedly and in vulnerable mass formations against a concealed enemy. Although Bellemare's men had captured the Buzenval Château, the Germans were still ensconced at the Porte de Longboyau and behind the inner wall of the Buzenval Park, enabling them to shoot down successive waves of French attackers. Amongst those mortally wounded by the terrible fire in front of that 'fatal … accursed wall' was the explorer Gustave Lambert, who had postponed his planned expedition to the North Pole to enlist.[49]

By early afternoon the Germans were mounting local counter-attacks all along the French line, though at first with no success. However, a vigorous effort against the French centre and left at 5.00 p.m. was contained only after a violent struggle amid clouds of thick smoke. Trochu, convinced that the attempt to break through had failed, ordered the retreat at 5.45 p.m.

Although his troops maintained a connected line of battle as a rearguard, it was fortunate for Trochu that darkness and later fog hid the chaotic French withdrawal from the Germans, for in places it was a stampede. Only next morning, as the Germans probed forward expecting a renewal of the battle, did they discover that the French had gone – all except 347 defenders of the Villa Zimmermann who had not received the order to withdraw and were forced to surrender. The victorious German V Corps, with few reinforcements, had barred the road to Versailles at the cost of 610 casualties, having inflicted 4,070 on the defeated French.[50]

The performance of the National Guard in the battle gave rise to widely differing assessments. Ducrot, in his later work *The Defence of Paris* (which might more aptly have been entitled *The Defence of General Ducrot*) made them the scapegoats for failure, citing instances of straggling, cowardice and panic among their ranks, of their ineptly firing into the backs of French troops or taking any opportunity to accompany lightly wounded comrades to the rear.[51] His contempt was heartily reciprocated by men who believed that he was a defeatist who had deliberately delayed his attack and had used them recklessly as cannon-fodder. One radical pamphleteer wrote, 'He has the audacity to blame the National Guard, when he has twice disappointed the legitimate expectations of the people of Paris.'[52] Whilst Ducrot's strictures were true of some battalions, they did not present a balanced picture. Trochu conceded more charitably that such panic as had occurred was not confined to the National Guard, and that despite their inexperience many had done their duty with firmness and patriotism.[53] Another witness saw National Guards making a determined but vain charge into German fire with their heads bent forward as if they were in a hailstorm.[54] They had suffered 1,457 of the French casualties. Amongst its lost citizens fashionable Paris mourned the promising young artist Henri Regnault, who had won plaudits at the Salon for his exotic pictures. In 1868 Regnault had painted an equestrian portrait of Marshal Prim, the Spanish leader who had played a prominent role in the Hohenzollern candidature that had sparked this war in July 1870. Now both artist and subject lay dead: Prim lately assassinated in Madrid and Regnault with a bullet in his head in the mud at Buzenval.[55]

In Paris crowds gathered to learn the progress of the battle through a series of bulletins, which became progressively less reassuring. Mention of masses of German artillery changing the face of the battle provoked anger: 'So didn't we have artillery? What had they done with those hundreds of cannon that had been cast, thanks to our fervently patriotic subscriptions, and offered to the Government of National Defence? Apparently they were being kept to offer the Prussians on the day of surrender.' When next day General Schmitz made public a telegram from Trochu suggesting that truce of two or three days would be necessary to bury the dead and collect the wounded, 'throughout all Paris there was a moment of stupefaction, followed by an infinite sadness'.[56]

Rather than reconciling the city to the necessity of capitulation, the failure of the Buzenval sortie had quite the opposite effect on a population gripped by what observers described as 'siege fever'. Trochu was suspected of exaggerating casualties in order to spread demoralization. There was an upsurge of contempt for 'the Government of National Defeat'[57] amongst the press and clubs, and several Cabinet members agreed with the mayors that a final, all-out attack must be tried, spearheaded by the National Guard. Amongst the mayors there was talk of starvation being better than humiliation, and of dying amidst the ruins of the city.[58] Unconvinced when Trochu told them that a breakout was hopeless, the mayors heard the same message from a council of senior generals on 21 January, and from a meeting of more junior commanders convened by Jules Simon on the 22nd. The mayors had wanted to push the government into action, and shrank from Favre's suggestion that they should be associated with any negotiations for capitulation. They were also reluctant to accept what he confided to them about the city's critical food situation. The government had belatedly introduced bread rationing on 18 January without disturbances. But, even limited to 300 grammes per adult daily, there would be no bread after 1 February, and then only by supplementing the city's supply of grain by drawing on the army's reserves.[59]

For two days the Cabinet and the mayors debated what should be done. The one point all agreed upon was that Trochu must go, but he doggedly refused to resign. Only upon learning in the early hours of 22 January that there were disturbances in Belleville and that a mob shouting 'Death to the Government!' had released Flourens from the Mazas prison did the Cabinet resolve to act. Trochu would stay on as president of the Cabinet, but his title of Governor of Paris was suppressed and command of the army was transferred without prior consultation to Vinoy, who was awoken to be told the news.

The insurrection of Sunday 22 January was less of a spontaneous mass movement than those of 4 September and 31 October. Blanqui's followers were prominent amongst the armed groups who gathered in front of the Hôtel de Ville during the morning, while the old man stationed himself in a café in the Rue de Rivoli, awaiting events. This time there could be no invasion of the Hôtel de Ville, which was guarded by the same Breton Gardes Mobiles who had saved the government on 31 October, and whose royalist sympathies made them the butt of insults from the Paris radicals. The crowd was noisy, though it contained as many spectators as demonstrators. In the afternoon battalions of National Guards supporting the insurrectionists arrived. One – the 101st – advanced towards the railings with drums beating the charge and red pennants tied to its bayonets.[60] It was probably from its ranks that the first shots were fired at 3.15 p.m., killing Adjutant Bernard, one of the Breton officers who were still in the square.[61]

The riposte from the Bretons was immediate. A volley fired from the windows of the Hôtel de Ville cleared the square, where five dead and eighteen wounded were later recovered, some of them simply bystanders.[62] Amongst those killed was the revolutionary activist Théodore Sapia. Firing continued for about twenty minutes until those insurrectionists who had not fled were rounded up from nearby buildings by gendarmes and the troops which Vinoy quickly had on the scene. That evening the government decided on the closure of the clubs and the suspension of two newspapers which had called for revolt, Delescluze's *Le Réveil* and Pyat's *Le Combat*. There was no mass support for the revolutionaries, and the city remained quiet as doctors moved amongst the wounded on the bloodstained pavements to the distant thunder of German cannon.

With order decisively restored, Jules Favre sat down that night to write a note to be carried through the lines next day asking Bismarck for an interview. In doing so he knew that there was no further hope of relief from outside. Late on the 19th he had received a despatch from Gambetta dated the 16th full of bitter reproaches for the Paris Government's inaction, but bearing too the news that Chanzy had been defeated.[63]

Le Mans

General Chanzy had been far from inactive since reaching Le Mans on 19 December. Within a week of his retreat there he sent out columns to harass the enemy and keep his raiding cavalry at bay. One column under General Rousseau struck north-east towards Nogent-le-Rotrou, whilst a larger one under General Jouffroy retraced the army's steps towards Vendôme and fought an engagement on the outskirts of that city on 31 December. With other columns operating between Le Mans and the Loir Chanzy had about 30,000 men – a quarter of his forces – employed in this activity while he remained at Le Mans labouring to improve his fortifications and to bring the bulk of his men up to combat fitness. In his absence, lack of co-ordination between his flying columns enabled the Germans to beat them off in a series of small actions, inflicting at least double the 660 casualties which they suffered themselves. In every encounter the Germans took a high proportion of prisoners.

Worse, the activity of the French columns helped convince the German high command that Prince Friedrich Karl's Second Army should resume its westward pursuit of Chanzy and attack him as a matter of priority. The Germans feared that Chanzy and Bourbaki might act in concert for another offensive towards Paris, which in fact was the strategy advocated by Chanzy in a series of letters to Gambetta. A message from Trochu explaining the critical situation of the capital reached Chanzy on 22 December, prompting him to urge that if he, Bourbaki and Faidherbe advanced concentrically on Paris one of them might have a chance of getting through. By now, however, Gambetta and Freycinet were committed to sending Bourbaki against German communications in the east. Still hopeful that 'we shall throw back these hordes from our soil empty handed', Gambetta replied that the eastern campaign was 'a surer thing and more threatening than the strategy you have in view'.[64]

By this time Friedrich Karl had ascertained that Bourbaki was moving away from Chanzy and, taking advantage of his central position, prepared to deal as expeditiously as possible with his nearest and most dangerous enemy. Having been billeted in and around Chartres, Vendôme and Orléans for a fortnight, German troops were somewhat restored, and like their comrades around Paris had little difficulty in purchasing locally the food they needed, even in the midst of a so-called 'people's war'. With a combat strength of 58,097 infantry, 16,360 cavalry and 324 guns,[65] the German Second Army began its advance towards Le Mans on 4 January, initially on a front of over 80 kilometres.

Over the following days weather conditions made campaigning exceptionally testing for both sides, with fog frequently limiting visibility and ice making the roads treacherous. Snow storms on 9 and 10 January deposited a blanket of snow over a foot deep over the landscape. Contrary to their usual practice, the Germans were compelled to relegate their cavalry to their flanks and many of their guns to the rear of their infantry columns. Yet they kept up relentless pressure, fighting significant actions every day with the retreating French columns, who defended villages, hills, walls, hedges and ditches where they could. The four German corps progressed at different rates, too far separated for mutual support, but Friedrich Karl calculated correctly that the French army was in no state to mount a concerted offensive against him. By nightfall on 10 January the Germans had pushed the French back to their defensive positions in an arc east of Le Mans, running along a chain of heights straddling the River Huisne. When dawn came one French unit found German outposts so close to their trenches that they pelted them with snowballs and insults.[66]

Even though he had been sick for several days Chanzy, in marked contrast to Trochu, breathed the offensive spirit. He rode the lines to instil confidence, accompanied as ever by his escort of spahis, Algerian cavalry conspicuous by their red Arab-style hooded cloaks. He insisted that his troops, shivering in their tents around Le Mans, must take the offensive wherever possible, and that officers who failed to do their duty would be held to account. A draconian order required that any fugitives should be sent back to the front line and shot if they attempted to flee again. He reminded his men that the weather was as bad for the Germans as it was for them, and that 'no-one should think of retreating on Le Mans without having held out to the last extremity'.[67]

The weather cleared on the morning of 11 January but manoeuvre remained difficult across fields and pine woods covered in thick snow. There was little chance here for any grand German flanking movement to encircle the French. North-east of Le Mans, between the Rivers Sarthe and Huisne, the advance of Mecklenburg's XIII Corps (consisting of his stalwart 17th and 22nd Divisions) made only slow progress against Chanzy's left. The heaviest fighting took place east of the city, where Friedrich Karl's two most advanced corps, III and IX, tried to punch their way through the French centre on the Auvours plateau. They almost succeeded, eventually driving off the defenders in disorder, so that by mid-afternoon the French army seemed in danger of being cut in half. The commander of the Breton Division, General Gougeard – one of several naval officers commanding major infantry formations in Chanzy's army – received the order to retake Auvours at all costs. He began by threatening to turn his cannon on French fugitives, some of whom were so terrified that they drowned by falling through the ice as they attempted to flee across the River Huisne. The rest were re-formed with much effort. Gougeard then led a counter-attack with about 2,000 of his Bretons spearheaded by the Papal Zouaves – the same troops who had charged at Loigny – against German positions along a hedge line. Although the first German volley took a terrible toll, after hand-to-hand fighting the attack succeeded.[68] By nightfall Chanzy could take satisfaction that his extended line seemed to have held. News that disaster had overtaken his right did not reach him until after midnight.

The breaking of the French line occurred in a manner unforeseen by Friedrich Karl, thanks to initiatives by German unit commanders. General von Voigts-Rhetz, commanding X Corps, was ordered at dusk to send a division to support the embattled III Corps; yet to do so meant marching a dozen kilometres in the dark down lanes choked with snow while leaving the German left flank exposed. Voigts-Rhetz decided that the best way of supporting the centre was by advancing straight ahead and creating a diversion. His men pressed forward along the slippery main highway to Le Mans until they encountered French trenches near the village of Les Mortes-Aures. While they were brought to a temporary halt by cannon, *mitrailleuse* and rifle fire, a battalion was sent uphill through the forest to find the French flank. It emerged near a spot called La Tuilerie and, making out French troops ahead, fixed bayonets and charged.

La Tuilerie was held by units of the Breton National Guard, whose experience of soldiering had been more than usually miserable. They had been amongst the thousands called up by the Delegation and mustered at Conlie Camp north-west of Le Mans. Count de Kératry, the former Paris police chief who had escaped the capital by balloon, had seen the camp as the base for a new 'Army of Brittany' that would relieve the capital, but Conlie had come to exemplify all the pitfalls of hasty military organization and reliance on mere numbers to make an army. At its peak Conlie held 50,000 men, crammed into tents and barrack huts with an inadequate water supply and scandalous lack of sanitation. Lashed by the autumn and winter weather, the camp had become a fetid quagmire, with inevitable consequences for the sick rate. Scarcely half the recruits had arms, and those issued included eleven different types of rifle, many of them American imports totally unfit for use even when they had ammunition and spare parts. 'Many reproaches were made regarding Conlie Camp,' said General Gougeard, 'all deserved in my opinion.'[69] After Kératry's resignation its commandant wanted to disperse the men and close the ill-sited camp in December, but Gambetta was initially reluctant, fearing political embarrassment because the establishment of such camps was 'one of the most important acts of our administration'.[70] The commandant took it upon himself nevertheless to disperse the unarmed men to sites in Brittany, while about 10,000 armed but poorly trained and equipped men were forwarded to Chanzy's army.

In the darkness at La Tuilerie on the night of 11 January these Breton National Guardsmen were preparing their evening meal, believing that fighting was over for the day, when the first German shells landed. Finding themselves suddenly attacked from the flank, they lost their heads and ran, and their panic spread to neighbouring units. By this coup the Germans seized a key piece of high ground, placing them closer to Le Mans than the bulk of the French army and threatening its ability to retreat. They quickly secured the position. All night and next morning Admiral Jauréguiberry and his officers desperately but vainly attempted to rally enough of their demoralized men to mount a counter-attack. With his troops giving way, at 7.55 a.m. on 12 January Jauréguiberry wired Chanzy, 'I'm sorry to have to say that a prompt retreat seems to me *imperatively* necessary.'[71]

Heartbroken, but reluctantly conceding that the situation on his right was beyond repair, Chanzy gave orders for a retreat that in reality had already begun. Luckily for him the morning was foggy, hiding the full extent of their opportunity from the Germans, who were also hampered by the state of the ground and the condition of their own troops, whose boots and uniforms were frayed and saturated. During the day French troops retreated by stages, keeping up resistance at many points and using all the bridges available to cross the Rivers Huisne and Sarthe. It was afternoon when the Germans reached Pontlieue, just outside Le Mans. French engineers made a determined but hasty attempt to blow up the bridge across the Huisne, with incomplete success. Braving *mitrailleuse* fire, the leading German battalions scrambled their way across the smoking ruins and pressed on into Le Mans, which was still thronged with French troops and convoys. There was a last flare-up of fighting in its streets and squares, particularly around the Café de l'Univers in the Place des Halles which had to be reduced with a cannon; but finally the French disengaged and disappeared westwards, reaching Laval after five days of hard marching, cold, hunger and rearguard fighting. 'We were as near despair as we could be,' confessed one officer, 'the traces of this unhappy army's retreat are lamentable. All along the way we met with stragglers, their faces so drawn, and seeming so exhausted, that you could hardly reproach them for remaining behind.' The Germans captured them by the hundred.[72]

Chanzy had staved off complete rout, but even his iron will and hopes for an eventual return to the offensive could not disguise the calamity that his broken army had suffered. The Germans were almost equally exhausted and had sustained 3,400 casualties since 4 January; but they had inflicted 6,200 casualties on the French and taken 20,000 prisoners and seventeen guns. Despite French efforts to get away as many trains and convoys as they could, the Germans captured six locomotives and 212 railway wagons loaded with provisions, plus great quantities of other material.[73] More than that, they had achieved their objective in putting the Second Army of the Loire out of action, thus effectively finishing the war in the western theatre. One week after Le Mans their comrades in arms would achieve the same feat against Faidherbe in the north.

Bapaume and Saint-Quentin

Following the Battle of the Hallue, Manteuffel had moved east against the French garrison of Péronne, the last important crossing point of the Somme still in French possession. Although that river and its marshes gave the town some protection from assault, its fortifications provided none against modern artillery, and Major Garnier's garrison of 3,500 contained only a small proportion of regular soldiers. By 27 December the Germans had invested the town and over the following three days fired thousands of shells into it from fifty-eight field guns, sending terrified citizens scurrying to their cellars, reducing buildings to rubble and starting fires that could not be controlled because the water in the fire-pumps was frozen. In the intense heat that destroyed a landmark medieval church the molten metal of its bells could be seen pouring down like lava.[74] Although there were acts of heroism, the majority of townspeople were cowed by the violence of this ordeal, which threatened to reduce Péronne to ashes, and the civic authorities urged Garnier to capitulate. Nevertheless he refused the German summons, though knowing that his position was hopeless without rescue from outside.

Faidherbe determined to provide that rescue, and a week after his withdrawal from the Hallue struck south from Arras towards Bapaume, where Kummer's Division had been posted to cover the forces besieging Péronne. Believing that the Army of the North presented little immediate threat, Manteuffel had departed to supervise operations around Rouen, leaving in charge the commander of VIII Corps, General von Göben.

Lacking sufficient cavalry, on 2 January 1871 Faidherbe's army groped its way towards the line of villages held by the Germans north of Bapaume. Marching incautiously into Béhagnies, the Naval Division of 23 Corps found to its cost that the village was still in German hands, and became bogged in a protracted contest with its defenders. To the west, the left division of 22 Corps chased the Germans out of Achiet-le-Grand, but the right division, containing some of the army's steadiest troops, swept wide and encountered only cavalry patrols. Next morning Faidherbe concentrated his forces for an enveloping attack against the German positions.

The Battle of Bapaume, fought on 3 January 1871, was untypical of the war in that it saw nearly 35,000 French troops attacking initially less than half that number of Germans and pushing them to the brink of defeat.[75] Having consolidated their line north and west of Bapaume overnight, the Germans were forced during the morning to yield more ground to the French advancing out of the mist across snow-covered fields. So intense was the cold that the blood of men who were hit quickly froze on their wounds.[76] After a desperate defence of Biefvillers, the threat to their left flank forced the Germans back to a line on the outskirts of Bapaume, which they had fortified and proceeded to defend hotly during the afternoon. Here the French were halted by 'a terrible fire, like hail, which poured from the hedgerows that surrounded the town, from loopholes pierced through the walls of houses, from behind barricades, etc, decimating the assailants from all sides'.[77]

Meanwhile, the National Guard Division under the colourful ex-sailor Anatole Robin had been supposed to turn the German right, but a few shells were enough to drive it back in disarray. Göben urgently called in dispersed units from right and left to bolster his flanks, particularly to drive away the French threatening to cut off his line of retreat to Péronne, 20 kilometres to the south. These reinforcements tipped the balance. Göben's determined and resourceful defence of Bapaume and its nearby villages just enabled him to save the day when combined with Faidherbe's hesitations.

Faidherbe was well-served by his artillery that day. An infantry officer who had witnessed French gunners being consistently outranged and driven off during the Metz battles in August noted admiringly that those of the Army of the North took their guns to within 1,800 metres of the enemy, where they could return shot for shot on equal terms. He observed the artillerists,

> ... so calm in the midst of this tempest of fire and iron, manoeuvring their guns with as much precision as if they were on the practice range; the NCOs directing the movements with perfect regularity, correcting the aim, supervising the bringing up of ammunition; the officers, telescope in hands, never taking their eyes off the enemy except to see if everything was going properly about them, and above all that their instructions concerning distances and allowance for wind were being observed.[78]

Yet Faidherbe would not give his batteries the order to fire on Bapaume. Like General Crouzat at Beaune-la-Rolande, he was reluctant to prepare an infantry attack by bombarding a French town, much to the frustration of his hard-pressed infantry.[79] Closer to victory than he realized, and fearing the effects on his army of a night attack, he ordered his men to withdraw from contact with the enemy after dark. Giving credence to a report that the Germans had raised the siege of Péronne – whereas in fact they had only rushed some troops from there to bolster the defence of Bapaume – he retreated on 4 January, again citing the fatigue of his troops and the extreme cold.[80]

Ironically Göben, low on munitions and fearing defeat next day, had evacuated Bapaume on the night of the 3rd. Having had the best of the battle tactically, Faidherbe by his withdrawal allowed the Germans to claim victory, and would never again have such an opportunity to disable a fraction of their army. The battle had cost him 1,346 killed and wounded. Although over 1,000 men, a large proportion of them National Guards, had gone missing, most rejoined their units. The Germans, who had lost 1,066 men, took about 300 unwounded French prisoners.[81]

Faidherbe intended to make another attempt to relieve Péronne, but by the time he renewed his advance it was too late. The Germans had brought up heavy artillery and recommenced the bombardment. Disease was by now rife in the battered town and Garnier, despairing of relief, allowed himself to be badgered into surrender by the civic authorities. He capitulated on the night of 9 January, so yielding the line of the Somme from Amiens eastwards to German control. Well might Faidherbe condemn Garnier, but his own failure to capitalize on his advantage at Bapaume had contributed as much to German victory.

Renouncing the idea of recapturing Péronne, Faidherbe again manoeuvred towards Amiens, entering the town of Albert. At the nearby village of Pozières on 14 January he received a telegram from Freycinet in Bordeaux asking him to make a diversion to draw German forces from Paris, where the garrison was about to make a supreme effort. With Chanzy defeated, Faidherbe's small but well-officered army was the last hope for creating a serious distraction. Judging the Somme between Amiens and Péronne too well guarded to cross in the face of the enemy, Faidherbe quickly determined to thrust south-east, around the German right, marching beyond Saint-Quentin to cut the rail link to Rheims which the Germans had recently restored.

The manoeuvre might have worked with speed and secrecy, but it was fated to delay and discovery. The Army of the North had to use byroads, which on the first day of the flank march, 16 January, became slick as icy rain fell on frozen surfaces. Then over the following two days a thaw set in, causing streams to overflow their bridges and turning the roads and fields to liquid mud. Although new boots had recently been issued they proved to be badly fitting, with cardboard soles that rapidly turned to mush. An infantry captain observed that his men 'were beginning to have had enough of it. If to that you add intense fatigue and a diet which had become deficient and very irregular, you can understand how little faith we were entitled to place in their resistance or their spirit in case of an encounter, which appeared imminent.'[82]

Despite French feints, the Germans quickly detected the direction of their march from cavalry reports, remarks by prisoners, and the entry of an advance French infantry brigade into Saint-Quentin on 16 January. Manteuffel having been transferred to the east to deal with the threat from Bourbaki, First Army was now commanded by General von Göben, who by the 17th had deduced Faidherbe's true strategy and moved to intercept him. To do so the Germans had a shorter distance to march than the French and could take advantage of the long straight roads which armies had used to cross this region since Roman times. On 18 January the leading German infantry and cavalry units struck the French columns in flank around Tertry, Caulaincourt and Pœuilly, savaging them in fighting that cost the Germans 376 and the French at least 500 casualties.[83] Although the French fended off these attacks, they were so delayed and disrupted that they reached Saint-Quentin only well after dark.

With the enemy so close at his heels, and given his orders, Faidherbe determined to accept battle around Saint-Quentin, an industrial town with a population of about 35,000. General Paulze d'Ivoy's 23 Corps would defend its western approaches, while Lecointe's 22 Corps would take position on the ridges to its south. To face Göben's force, which with reinforcements rushed up from Rouen and Paris numbered 27,000 infantry, 5,580 cavalry and 161 guns, Faidherbe could muster 42,000 men, of whom only 700 were cavalry, with 102 guns.[84] Control of the battle would prove difficult, because Faidherbe's two corps were separated not only by the town but by the Somme with its marshy banks and the Crozat Canal. Moreover, on the dismally rainy and misty morning of 19 January the Germans attacked in the south before 22 Corps had had time to finish deploying or cook a meal.

Even so, Lecointe's men put up a stiff fight, contesting the German advance in a succession of villages on the left bank of the Somme, over sodden sugar-beet fields, around a sugar refinery and a railway cutting, even mounting counter-attacks. Their artillery, sited on high ground by the windmill at Tout-Vent, was used to punishing effect, holding the Germans up all morning. Around midday Göben sent his reserve across the river to break this deadlock, and the French managed to hold on only by funnelling battalions westwards to support the right of their line, so denuding their left. Once fresh German troops, including a battalion sent from Fourth Army around Paris, attacked in that quarter, Lecointe's line began to unravel. Captain Patry, holding a farm on the extreme left of the French position with two companies, testified to the overwhelming power of German gunnery:

> Shells succeeded each other with incredible rapidity, some passing over the courtyard with such a shrill whistling that they made everything shake, others penetrating the roof of the barn, sending its timbers flying, or passing through the house, knocking down dividing walls, making holes in floors, smashing furniture to smithereens, or still more bursting right in the middle of the yard with an infernal uproar ... Our losses, minimal until now, became more and more serious ... directing the fight was becoming difficult.

Having resisted well for two hours, under this 'hurricane of metal and fire' his terrified men soon fled 'like a covey of pigeons', leaving only the wounded in the blazing farm:

> The spectacle inside the courtyard was heart-rending. The men wounded in the course of the action had sought refuge in the house and had taken off some of their clothing in order to tend themselves. Now as the flames reached them they tried to escape by dragging themselves along painfully, all bloody and dishevelled; but the flames overtook them and they were burned alive. A man still in the barn strove to beat a path of escape; he was seized by the flames, blinded by the smoke. He caught fire standing upright like a match and fell into the blazing mass, producing a shower of sparks. Being unable to do anything for these poor men and no longer having the means to defend my post, which had ceased to exist since it had burned down, and having no more soldiers, I chose to make a run for it while there was still time.[85]

Only a counter-attack with the bayonet supported by French artillery deterred the German commander in this sector from immediately exploiting his advantage, but the pounding of Lecointe's line became unrelenting. By late afternoon the whole of 22 Corps was forced back on Saint-Quentin and retreated through the shell-swept town while a rearguard defended barricades on its southern outskirts. The victorious Germans fought their way as far as the railway station soon after 5.00 p.m., but did not pursue the French far into the darkened town, where the inhabitants had taken refuge in their cellars.

Meanwhile west of the town 23 Corps had fought a separate battle that followed a similar pattern. After holding out for several hours it too was forced to retreat, pursued so closely that its commander, General Paulze d'Ivoy, narrowly escaped capture by dashing down an alley guided by an inhabitant.

Nevertheless, German cavalry had proved unenterprising in attempting to turn the French right and cut the roads northward to Cambrai and Bohain. It was up those roads that the defeated Army of the North streamed in retreat all night. Battalions had disintegrated. An officer in the Garde Mobile recalled: 'I still had about thirty men with me. Of my six sergeants, two had been killed, three wounded and one was a prisoner. Marching with us were dismounted dragoons, sailors and regular infantrymen who had lost their boots in the mud and were going barefoot. Yet this motley assemblage presented no contrasts: all our uniforms were the colour of mud.'[86]

After its last stand at Saint-Quentin, the Army of the North was spent as a fighting force. It had sustained 3,384 casualties, but the Germans had captured over 12,000 men, 9,000 of them unwounded, against their own loss of 2,400.[87] Faidherbe distributed the remnants of his army among the fortresses of the North. Although Saint-Quentin had been fought on the same day as Buzenval, it had affected the outcome of the Paris sortie not one whit. Yet, though Faidherbe had made errors of judgement and had been defeated, he would always be remembered with pride and gratitude in the North, where he was credited with saving the region from invasion. He had also earned the respect of the Germans by showing a degree of tenacity and combativeness that had been all too rare among French commanders.

The Lisaine

Unlike Faidherbe and Chanzy, General Charles Bourbaki never enjoyed the full confidence of the government at Bordeaux. Gambetta, to be sure, was glad to have the services of such an illustrious and high-ranking soldier, renowned in the regular army as a hero of the Alma and Inkerman in the Crimean War. Although Bourbaki's intimate connections with the fallen regime made him anathema to radical republicans and fed hostile speculation about his mission to Chislehurst, Gambetta appreciated that his patriotism and devotion to duty were unimpeachable. Much as conservatives were to lambaste Gambetta after the war for his partisan exclusion of Bonapartists from political life, ironically the 'Dictator's' gravest misjudgement may have been to appoint Bourbaki to command the great French offensive in the east, for which he proved tragically unfitted. Freycinet had strong misgivings from the outset, warning Gambetta that 'our veneration of past military glories is what has ruined us'.[88]

Freycinet's conviction that 'Bourbaki is not the man the situation requires'[89] was grounded in more than republican prejudice. For all his immense reputation as a perfect soldier on the parade ground, Bourbaki would demonstrate little gift for army command or as a strategist, and he ran a dysfunctional staff. Bringing with him the bad habits of the old army, he sidelined General Borel, the chief of staff, and the technical service chiefs, relying instead on his old friend and aide-de-camp Colonel Leperche. Moreover, Bourbaki lacked faith in the possibility of victory, having confided to Admiral Fourichon in October that 'if I were paid to think rather than to fight I would vote for an armistice and for peace'. He had recently told Gambetta that 'you are the only man in France who believes that resistance is possible. Currently that resistance is more harmful than useful,' though he accepted Gambetta's response that fighting on could encourage European intervention and obtain better peace terms.[90]

Freycinet had not convinced Gambetta that General Billot, commanding 18 Corps but a colonel as recently as November, would make a better army commander. Instead, as Bourbaki prepared to lead the expedition on which the outcome of the war might hinge, Freycinet determined to supervise operations closely himself by telegraph. In addition, he sent a trusted adviser to Bourbaki's headquarters to keep a close eye on him; and if necessary to date and serve an order relieving the general of command, the existence of which was an open secret.

This emissary was Auguste de Serres, son of a Polish nobleman and a French mother, who had been educated as a civil engineer in Paris and had left a promising career with the Austro-Hungarian railways to return to serve France in September 1870. Not yet 30, the highly intelligent de Serres was burning with zeal to implement a plan of campaign that was as much his brainchild as Freycinet's. His ardour was such that Freycinet had to rein him in from giving direct orders to generals and railway officials; orders which hindered as often as they helped and in one instance led to the execution of a grocer named Arbinet on mere suspicion of being a spy (an act for which de Serres was convicted and sentenced to a month's prison in 1872).[91] Bourbaki nevertheless acknowledged and appreciated de Serres's indefatigable energy and dedication to the success of the campaign.

To Freycinet and de Serres, moving a huge army should have been as straightforward as moving pins on a map. From the agreement of Gambetta and Bourbaki to the eastern campaign on 19 December, they calculated that it should be possible to transport the First Army of the Loire (which, with additional components, would become popularly known as the Army of the East) 248 kilometres by rail in two days.

The reality was far different for an operation launched, as General Chanzy observed, 'at such a season, with raw troops, in mountainous country covered in snow'. Chanzy questioned whether the relief of Belfort could bring timely help to the French army beleaguered in Paris.[92] Yet satisfying public opinion by saving Belfort, where Denfert-Rochereau was still holding out gamely, was given higher priority than cutting German rail communications in the east.

The relief of Belfort was conceived as a lightning stroke, but it took days to gather the necessary rolling stock from neighbouring regions to carry the troops from central to eastern France. The private railway companies were given only a day's notice, and some were initially reluctant to halt commercial traffic. Even so, the first troop trains set off on 22 December, though they had to crawl along at three miles an hour, subject to endless delays caused by bottlenecked rail traffic. As a result it was not until 1 January that Billot's 18 Corps and Clinchant's 20 Corps, having been transported from their camp-grounds around Bourges and Nevers, were fully concentrated around Auxonne and Dôle respectively, while Bressolles' 24 Corps was belatedly transferred from Lyon to Besançon.

The causes of these chronic delays were multiple. The railway companies had to improvise the operation at a time when many of their most able staff had been drafted into the army, and some stretches of line remained single-tracked or incomplete. Furthermore, the very foresight of the *Intendance* – the army supply bureau – complicated the problem because 1,800 wagons had been loaded with food and ammunition ready to supply the army wherever it might move. All these wagons were so many that were unavailable for the urgent transportation of troops, while at the same time they clogged circulation, blocking stations and sidings and causing empty wagons to be returned by a circuitous route. Too many people giving orders, ill-disciplined troops and inexperienced or negligent officers, short station platforms and a lack of ramps for loading horses and cannon all added to delays in embarkation. Not all the impatient harangues and threats of courts martial against railway managers by Freycinet, Gambetta and de Serres could solve these problems by magic, nor remedy the lack of a single directing authority working to a master plan. It was the chaos of the mobilization of July 1870 all over again, but this time in weather that would have made running a railway a nightmare in normal times. Freezing nights caused signals and points to seize up, stuck wheels to rails and solidified water in tanks. For some stages of their route it would have been quicker, easier and healthier for the troops to have marched to their destinations.

While the bulk of the army moved east, 15 Corps was left behind to cover Bourges and to convince the Germans that the main army was still there. In this it succeeded, and for a few days Moltke underrated the extent and significance of French troop movements. As late as 30 December he believed that Bourbaki was still between Bourges and Nevers.[93] In fact by then the cautious Bourbaki had decided that he could not advance until he had 15 Corps with him. To avoid the previous problems, Freycinet took personal charge (by telegraph from Bordeaux) of the transportation of 15 Corps from Vierzon, insisting that no one but he should give any orders regarding it.[94] This time the

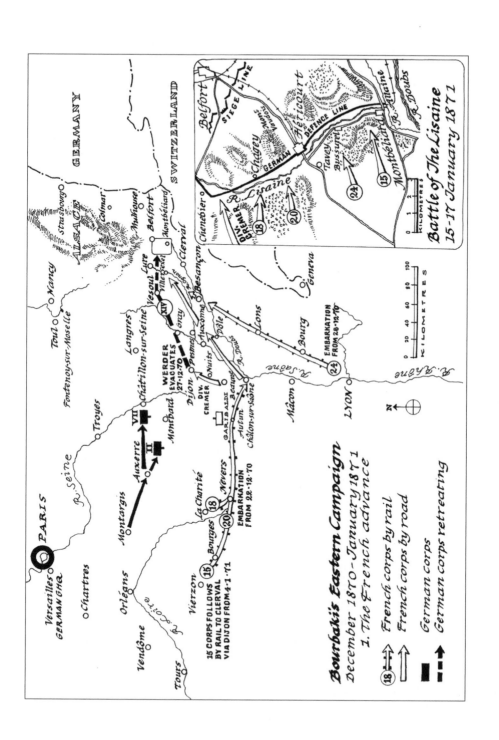

Battle of The Lisaine
15-17 January 1872

Belfort
SIEGE LINE
Chagey · Mont Vaudois
Héricourt
GERMAN DEFENCE LINE
R. Lisaine
R. Doubs
R. Allaine
Montbéliard
DIV. CREMER
CHENEBIER
Tavey
Bussurel
18
20
24
15

KILOMETRES
0 1 2

Bourbaki's Eastern Campaign
December 1870 – January 1871
1. The French advance

GERMANY
ALSACE
SWITZERLAND

Nancy
Toul
Fontenoy-sur-Moselle
Strasbourg
Colmar
Mulhouse
Belfort
Montbéliard
Clerval
Lure
Vesoul
Villersexel
Langres
Châtillon-sur-Seine
R. Saône
Gray
XIV
Pesmes
R. Doubs
Besançon
Auxonne
Dôle
Geneva

Troyes
Auxerre
Montbard
Dijon
WERDER EVACUATES 27·12·70
DIV. CREMER
Nuits
R. Doubs
Battle
Cons

VII
II
Paris
Versailles
GERMAN GHQ
Chartres

R. Seine
Montargis
Orléans
Vendôme
Tours
Vierzon
La Charité
Bourges
Nevers
GARIBALDI
Autun
Châlon-sur-Saône
Beaune
Mâcon
Bourg
18
20
15
EMBARKATION FROM 28·12·70
EMBARKATION FROM 26·12·70
24
LYON
R. Rhône
R. Loire

15 CORPS FOLLOWS BY RAIL TO CLERVAL VIA DIJON FROM 4·1·71

N

KILOMETRES
0 20 40 60 80 100

18   French corps by rail
      French corps by road
      German corps
      German corps retreating

embarkation did indeed run more smoothly, except that a destroyed bridge delayed the operation until 4 January, but debarkation proved a different matter, with dozens of trains backed up in a mighty jam stretching back for miles from Clerval, halfway between Besançon and Belfort, because of inadequate unloading facilities there. In consequence, the move which Freycinet had stipulated should take thirty-six hours took in all twelve days, even longer than that of the other three corps.

The effect of this ordeal by railway on the troops was debilitating in the extreme. Typically, regiments might be camping out in the open for three or four days awaiting their turn to embark before piling into unheated cattle wagons where the smell was so revolting and suffocating, wrote Dr Léon Pissot of the 29th Mobiles, that he wondered how men could breathe in such a pestilent and nauseating atmosphere.[95] Sometimes they were stuck in these wagons for three or four days without warmth or adequate food and drink during interminable halts:

> Their officers, expecting the signal to depart from one moment to another, dared not allow the men to wander off and frequently kept them and the horses inside the wagons. The thermometer stood at 12 to 15 degrees below zero. There were numerous cases of frostbite; many horses died from hunger and cold. Inactive and famished, the troops became demoralized and indiscipline took hold in their ranks. The most alarming rumours circulated: already there was talk of treason.[96]

Units arrived at their debarkation points decimated by sickness and as worn out as if they had been through a battle.[97] For instance, the 42nd (Temporary) Regiment of 18 Corps, leaving Bourges on 19 December with 2,855 men, lost 600 of them en route to the eastern front.[98] Signs of disintegration were visible even as the army advanced. Some soldiers, 'demoralized by their successive defeats and long sufferings, let themselves be led towards Belfort like a flock being led to the slaughter. A great many of them threw away their weapons along the road or abandoned them when they halted. At Besançon station enough were recovered to fill seven or eight wagons.'[99]

News of the cumbersome French advance was reported to General von Werder at Dijon. An intercepted letter from a schoolgirl at Besançon informing her parents that she could not get home for Christmas because the railway had been closed to civilian traffic, that her school was being converted to a hospital and that the town was full of soldiers, was just one piece of an intelligence jigsaw that forewarned Werder that superior forces were concentrating against him.[100] On 27 December he pulled in his detachments and evacuated Dijon, withdrawing his XIV Corps north-eastward towards Vesoul, from where he could cover German forces besieging Belfort whilst observing what direction the French offensive might take.

Bourbaki's army advanced painfully slowly in the first week of January as it tried to organize its supplies. Although adequate food stocks were being accumulated by railway at Clerval, there was a shortage of serviceable wagons and civilian crews to drive supplies to where the troops were; especially as snow and ice made roads with steep gradients scarcely passable and wagons drawn by horses that were not shod for ice could be only half filled. Finally, driven on by the mounting impatience of Freycinet, Bourbaki left his headquarters at Besançon on 6 January heading up the valley of the River Ognon for Belfort. By nightfall on the 8th the vanguard of 20 Corps had reached Villersexel, observed in the bright moonlight by German cavalry. Werder had expected to be attacked at Vesoul but, seeing that possession of the crossroads of Villersexel put the French closer to Belfort than he was, he hastened to intercept them.

The clash of Werder's right wing with the French vanguard at Villersexel on 9 January brought on one of the most savage small battles of the war. It began with the Germans attacking the town from the north-west. Initially held at bay by French troops who had barricaded themselves around the stone bridge over the Ognon, they found a precarious but less strongly guarded footbridge further downstream. Passing men across single file, they were able to capture the château and to take the defenders of the main bridge in flank. By midday Villersexel was in German possession, while in the snow-covered woods and meadows around Moimay to the west they held the heads of advancing French columns in check all afternoon. After dark, however, as a thick mist rose from the river, the French stormed back into Villersexel from the south, and a ferocious struggle raged in its steep winding streets and from house to house. The moon rose on a demonic scene as the flames of fires set by the French to burn out parties of Germans illuminated the pall of black smoke that hung over the town. In furious fighting that surged back and forth in the château park and buildings it was the Germans who resorted to fire. Finding themselves holding the ground floor while the French held the cellars and upper storeys, and unable to make headway in ghoulish fighting on staircases and landings and in darkened rooms, they put the torch to the château and made a bold fighting retreat through the park. By the early hours German forces had evacuated Villersexel. Of 15,000 men engaged, the fight had cost them 579 casualties compared to 1,390 French, of whom roughly half were unwounded prisoners.[101] A French telegraphist who entered the smoking ruins of the town next day was sickened by its sights and smells: large puddles of blood in the snow, disembowelled horses with stiffened legs outstretched, and an over-powering stench of pitch and petroleum mingled with that of charred corpses which were being retrieved from the smouldering debris of homes and the blackened charnel house that had been the château.[102]

During the battle Bourbaki had momentarily recovered his old fighting spirit, spurring his men on to the charge. Nor had they disappointed him, advancing – according to the official bulletin at least – with cries of '*Vive la France! Vive la République!*'[103] Even Freycinet, reading de Serres's enthusiastic report, sent effusive congratulations. In Bordeaux as in the rest of France the significance of this hard-fought but small victory was overestimated. Both Bourbaki and de Serres misread the strategic situation, believing that Werder's route to Belfort was blocked and that they had only to await another German attack. In fact Werder made his way onward unpursued while Bourbaki lost more precious days beset by supply problems. When he did inch forward he spent the whole of 13 January dislodging a German rearguard at Arcey.

Werder made diligent use of the respite to fortify himself strongly along the east bank of the River Lisaine[104] barring the roads to Belfort and beyond it Alsace. The Lisaine was not wide and was frozen along much of its course, but its generally steep and rocky banks made it a formidable defensive position which the Germans worked feverishly to improve. Thirty-four heavy guns were transported from the siege lines at Belfort, only 8 kilometres distant, to supplement Werder's 146 field guns. Trenches and gun emplacements were dug at key points along a 20-kilometre defensive line from Chenebier in the north through Héricourt in the centre to Montbéliard in the south. Telegraph wires were laid to link Werder to his subordinates. Sand and cinders were spread on icy roads to make them passable, while engineers toiled to break up the ice on the Lisaine, to form dams in places and to destroy or mine bridges. Nevertheless, Werder was apprehensive. With 45,000 men,[105] about half of whom were Landwehr whose normal duties were to guard communications, he would face a French army over twice as strong. Momentarily he contemplated abandoning Belfort and withdrawing into Alsace, but even before Moltke's order to stand firm was received he had accepted battle.[106]

Bourbaki's plan of battle for 15 January was for three corps – from south to north the 15th, 24th and 20th – to make demonstrations against the strongest part of Werder's line, while Billot's 18 Corps and Cremer's Division would hook around its northern end and open the road to Belfort. The principle was sound, but its execution failed utterly. Both Billot and Cremer had long distances to march to reach their assigned positions, and received Bourbaki's telegraphed instructions only belatedly, delaying the flank attack. Defective staff work caused French units on the left to cross each other's routes, and then the troops had to advance through deep snow along narrow woodland roads in a freezing wind. When they finally approached their objectives in late afternoon they found themselves not beyond the German right but attacking it frontally, pounded by artillery sited on the natural bastion of Mont Vaudois. Meanwhile in the south 15 Corps fought its way into Montbéliard, the assault on the town being spearheaded with great élan by Paul Déroulède at the head of his company of Turcos. But thereafter the attack stalled and the fortified château remained in German hands. Elsewhere along the line French artillery failed to make much impression on well-concealed German defences, while French infantry silhouetted against the snow as they charged towards the Lisaine were halted with relative ease by German cannon and rifle fire. That night French officers and men huddled around campfires that produced more smoke than heat in an attempt to keep frostbite at bay as the temperature sank to 16 degrees below zero. In contrast, most German troops not on guard duty were able to find some food and rest in the villages they occupied.

Next morning dense fog in the river valley confined the action to a mutual cannonade, but once it cleared the French resumed their attacks. Poorly co-ordinated and pressed with varying degrees of determination, along most of the line they again failed to dent the German defences. Some French divisions were not engaged at all. Of those that were, an artillery officer estimated that scarcely a quarter of the men in each infantry company actually fought. Rear areas teemed with skulkers who spread demoralization and excused their cowardice by traducing their officers.[107] In late afternoon the French did succeed in capturing Chenebier on their left, and probed towards the main road to Belfort, but for lack of initiative and reserves this crucial advantage was not exploited as darkness fell. Bourbaki prepared to try again on 17 January, but before dawn the Germans pre-empted him by mounting a determined counter-attack on their right, around Chenebier, fighting the French hand-to-hand in the pitch darkness. Although the Germans did not have the strength to hold the ground they re-conquered, their initiative helped drain what little remained of the spirit of the French army, which was all but extinguished when falling snow turned to torrents of rain. A doctor who treated twenty-four cases of wounds that morning noted that nine were self-inflicted.[108] French attacks during the afternoon were desultory and feeble.

Profoundly discouraged, Bourbaki had lost faith in his army's ability to continue the offensive in such atrocious conditions. All but two of his generals agreed. Against German losses of 1,646 in the three days of battle, his losses were estimated at 8,000.[109] There were thousands more cases of actual or feigned sickness. Bourbaki decided on retreat, convinced that the Germans were twice as strong as they really were. He feared too that if he persisted in attempting to envelop the German right he would expose his own vital railhead at Clerval to counter-attack. What was more, he had received startling confirmation that a newly-formed German army was moving to cut off his retreat if he delayed withdrawal.

At Versailles on 5 January Moltke had finally become certain that the whole of Bourbaki's force had moved east, and responded with the coolness and logic that were the hallmark of his superiority as a general. The Crown Prince of Prussia had noted admiringly that in every crisis Moltke 'remains always his own calm, clear-headed, matter-of-fact self – a veritable worker of miracles'.[110] He ordered II and VII Corps – currently covering operations south of Paris at Montargis and Auxerre – to concentrate in the upper Seine valley around Châtillon-sur-Seine. They became the South Army, with a combat strength of 48,000 men and 168 guns.[111] To command them Moltke summoned General von Manteuffel from Rouen. After a brief conference at Versailles Manteuffel, under whose orders Werder also was placed, joined his command on 12 January.

At the Lisaine the 54-year-old Bourbaki lamented that at his age he could not share the ardour of a younger officer for an all-out attack.[112] He was about to receive a harsh lesson from Manteuffel, aged 61, at the instigation of Moltke, aged 70, on how to use an army boldly and aggressively. Though his men were tired, cold, and in need of new boots, Manteuffel drove them south-east across the Langres plateau, along glassy roads and through storms of snow and rain at an average pace of 15 kilometres a day. Starting on 14 January, Manteuffel's vanguard reached Gray on the River Saône on the 19th, capturing the bridges there intact. His original objective had been to bring urgent help to Werder; but, learning that on the 18th Bourbaki had begun his retreat from the Lisaine towards Besançon, Manteuffel determined to play a still bolder stroke, aiming to entrap and destroy the French army. It was a daring gamble but, as Moltke assured a nervous Emperor Wilhelm, 'something must be risked when a great success is at stake'.[113] Ordering Werder to pursue Bourbaki's rear, Manteuffel struck south, crossing the Ognon at Pesmes on the 20th and reaching the Doubs at Dôle on the 21st. Struggling back to Besançon next day, Bourbaki learned that his routes westward had been cut.

How had Manteuffel, moving in three columns, been able to advance midway between substantial French garrisons at Langres and Dijon without meeting any resistance other than a few bands of *francs-tireurs*? The question was to give rise to venomous recrimination after the war, with Bourbaki's supporters charging Garibaldi with failing in his duty to protect the army's left flank and making him a scapegoat for the failure of the campaign.

Certainly Garibaldi's Army of the Vosges did nothing effective to stop Manteuffel, whose advance was the subject of much comment in the Dijon press. The inability of either Freycinet or Bourbaki to give Garibaldi binding orders and their reliance on his 'co-operation' now came home to roost. Garibaldi's force had already hindered Bourbaki's advance by commandeering eighteen trains to carry it the short distance from Autun to Dijon at the very

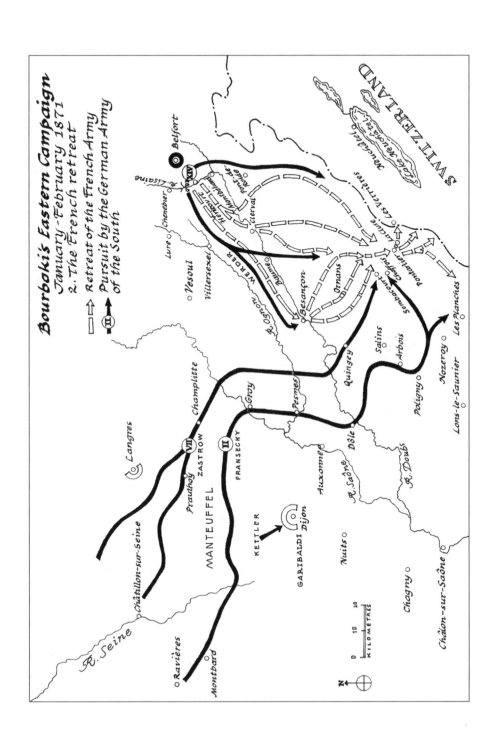

Bourbaki's Eastern Campaign
January-February 1871
2. The French retreat

⇨ Retreat of the French Army
▭ Pursuit by the German Army
of the South

time that those trains were needed to help transport 15 Corps eastward. To objections to this misuse, a colonel on Garibaldi's staff replied that the French Deputy War Minister had 'no right' to countermand Garibaldi's orders.[114] The old adventurer himself was sick, crippled by rheumatism, leaving the management of his army to his irascible chief of staff, Bordone, whose haughty behaviour drove many officers to switch their allegiance to another Italian leader, Colonel Frapolli, who was raising a rival legion at Lyon. Bordone seems to have spent far more time and effort intriguing against commanders whom he considered rivals than in worrying about what the Germans were doing. He blandly assured de Serres and Freycinet that Manteuffel's move was only a 'feint', and that Gray was under no threat.[115] The Italians, whose force was scarcely a manoeuvrable army, saw their role solely in terms of defending Dijon from attack. This, at least, they did valiantly enough.

When he advanced Manteuffel had detached a 4,000-strong brigade under General von Kettler to move against Dijon. Kettler attacked the north-western defences of the city on 21–23 January but was not strong enough to break through well-entrenched defensive lines bristling with cannon. In addition to Garibaldi's 24,000 volunteers of several nationalities, 22,000 National Guards under General Pellissier fought with spirit. In places the contest was murderous. At dusk on 23 January the German 61st Regiment suffered such losses when caught in a cross-fire while trying to storm a factory that its regimental colour fell and was hidden under the corpses of soldiers who tried to recover it. The bloody relic was retrieved next day by the French and became only the second German colour captured during the war (the other, taken at Rezonville on 16 August, had been smuggled out of Metz by Marshal Bazaine after the surrender). Kettler had lost 753 men,[116] but he had convinced the Italians that they were facing a large portion of the German army. In the glow of extravagant self-congratulation, the Army of the Vosges stayed rooted in Dijon, making no move to harass Manteuffel's rear. Freycinet was so thrilled with this defensive victory that he wanted to put Garibaldi, the republican hero and 'our premier soldier', in command of part of Bourbaki's army.[117]

Although Bourbaki complained repeatedly of Garibaldi's failure to guard his flank, he might have done much more himself to detail troops to observe and delay the advancing Germans. Too late he gave orders for key bridges over rivers to be destroyed, but his orders were not carried out. As he endeavoured to assemble his army around Besançon the Germans were already drawing a net around him. While Werder dogged his tracks from the north, Manteuffel's columns not only sealed off the routes westward but those to the south-west. Freycinet, reproaching Bourbaki with the sloth of his movements compared to the 'incredible speed, audacity and success' of the Germans in the same conditions,[118] had been pressing him to get his army quickly on trains to the west and to break his way through the German cordon. After all, Bourbaki still had numerical superiority. Bourbaki had at first agreed, but judged that it was now too late. On 24 January he called his generals together at Château-Farine, south-west of Besançon, to discuss the army's options. To stay at Besançon, where food supplies were limited to eighteen days at most (or so he believed), would invite blockade and the fate of Bazaine at Metz. Of the generals present, only Billot (seconded next day by the engineer Séré de Rivières) thought a breakthrough to the west possible. Bourbaki judged such an attempt a folly, but offered Billot command of the army if he thought he could do it. Billot declined. That left but one desperate resort: a retreat south-eastward across the snow-covered mountains of the Jura towards Pontarlier, whence it might be possible to get back to the Rhône valley and Lyon.

When Freycinet was informed he was thunderstruck. Making it clear that Bourbaki alone must bear the responsibility for such a move, he warned of inevitable disaster. Later that afternoon of 25 January he wired again: 'The more I reflect on your plan of marching on Pontarlier the less I understand it. I have just spoken about it with the generals at the War Ministry, and they share my astonishment. Is there some mistake about the name? Do you really mean Pontarlier? Pontarlier near Switzerland? If that is indeed your objective, have you envisaged the consequences? What will you live on? You will die of hunger for sure. You will be obliged to capitulate or to pass into Switzerland: for I see no way for you to escape.'[119]

Bourbaki had had his fill of Freycinet's strictures. In explaining the need for the retreat he had told Freycinet frankly, 'You have no idea of the sufferings this army has endured since the beginning of December . . . If this plan doesn't suit you then I really don't know what to do. Believe me, at this moment it is a veritable martyrdom to exercise command . . . If you think that one of my corps commanders could do better than me don't hesitate, as I have said already, to replace me.'[120]

Bourbaki challenged Freycinet's assumption that he was leading a properly constituted military force, and estimated that his army included only 30,000 reliable troops.[121] Though not among the reasons he cited, poor leadership at all levels was taking its toll. After the mismanaged battle of the Lisaine, Paul Déroulède realized with disgust, 'we were defeated, disorganized, lost'.[122] During the retreat, wrote Charles Beauquier, many units had degenerated into little more than an armed rabble held together by the need for food: 'Exhausted by cold and malnutrition, they straggled without order or discipline, burning everything they could find to warm themselves and treating the villages they passed through almost like conquered territory.' He described desperate soldiers pillaging a supply train, burning for warmth any food and clothing they did not need.[123] Orders emanating from Bourbaki's headquarters were increasingly confused and contradictory, betraying the all too evident indecision of the high command. Incidences multiplied of units failing to obey orders or to hold designated ground. When attacked by the Germans around Besançon, some regiments gave way in panic, and hundreds of prisoners were being taken in such encounters.

On 26 January the retreat to Pontarlier got under way and the troops struggled up steep icy roads away from Besançon. Increasingly irritable and despondent, Bourbaki watched them pass, convinced that his army was lost and that the government would make him the scapegoat for failure.[124] Again he offered Billot command, but again Billot declined.[125] At dusk Bourbaki returned to Besançon and dictated orders for the next day's movements. Then he retired to his room, lay down on his bed, put a revolver to his temple and fired.[126]

At that moment a telegram from Gambetta was on its way relieving Bourbaki of command on account of the 'hesitations and lack of confidence you have shown in the direction of an enterprise of which we expected such great results'. General Clinchant was placed in command.[127]

Bourbaki's suicide attempt failed. Deflected by his skull, the bullet was removed and he was out of danger within a week. On the night he shot himself a cease-fire came into force at Paris, but it would be three days before Clinchant heard of the armistice which, as we shall see, brought no end to the terrible ordeal of the Army of the East.

Launched too late, Bourbaki's disastrous eastern campaign had failed to relieve Belfort, where the hopes of the defenders, stirred by the sound of gunfire along the Lisaine, evaporated when the noise of battle receded. Nor had the campaign succeeded in striking a blow against German communications. Yet what was left unaccomplished by an army of 120,000 was spectacularly achieved in Lorraine by a column of fewer than 300 men on the night of 21–22 January.

The record of partisan troops during the war was chequered. Some independent troops served with distinction at Paris and with the Army of the Loire. Many of the 72,000 *francs-tireurs* who were enrolled (of whom 57,600 served outside Paris)[128] at least served to tie down tens of thousands of German troops in guarding rear areas, and inflicted over 1,000 casualties on them.[129] Others were utterly ineffectual and more of a scourge to French villagers than to the enemy. The Chasseurs des Vosges, composed largely of regular soldiers, proved the most effective of partisan groups, pulling off one of the most daring and skilful military feats of the war. Armed with explosives authorized by Gambetta over the reluctance of the military commander at Langres, the band stealthily covered 80 kilometres of occupied territory in three days in deep snow, moving through woods at night where possible and taking pains to conceal their tracks. Using German-speaking volunteers dressed in Landwehr uniforms during their approach, they surprised the German garrison at the village of Fontenoy-sur-Moselle, 9 kilometres east of Toul. Though wounded German soldiers managed to give the alarm to approaching trains, the Chasseurs dynamited the viaduct carrying the Paris-Strasbourg railway over the Moselle, sending a section of it crashing into the river. Evading capture, they returned across country having lost only one man, whilst in revenge the Germans pillaged and burned the blameless village of Fontenoy, killing two elderly civilians.[130]

This well-prepared and carefully reconnoitred operation cut the busiest stretch of railway used by the Germans for a fortnight. It came too late to affect the outcome of the war, and a day after the Germans had opened another line further north, but the raid did suggest what might have been achieved had the French adopted such tactics earlier in combination with larger operations. Acknowledging another lesson for future warfare, one underscored by the chaos of moving Bourbaki's army, on 28 January 1871 Gambetta signed a decree creating a commission to regulate military transportation by railway.[131] Next time, at least, France would be better prepared.

Chapter Nine

The Way Out of War

The Armistice

By the last week of January 1871 the armies of the French Republic had been comprehensively defeated. Taking advantage of his interior lines, Moltke had deftly parried every attempt to disrupt the siege of Paris or the supply lines of his armies. His task had been made easier by the lack of co-ordination between the various French forces.

On the day after the defeat at Saint-Quentin, the republican Defence Commissioner in the North, Dr Armand Testelin, wrote to Gambetta from Lille praising what he had done to save the honour of the country by resistance, but telling him frankly that the time had come for him to make a public pronouncement in favour of peace. Otherwise, Testelin warned, 'the mass of the nation will hold the Republic and you responsible for our material disasters, and will throw themselves at the feet of the first-comer who offers it peace. It is sad, but true.'[1] But Gambetta was not ready to yield. Two days later at Lille he gave one of his rousing speeches. He defended himself against the charges of dictatorship levelled against him in some quarters, and of putting the cause of the Republic before that of the country, protesting that he had never wanted this war which was being imposed upon France by German rapacity. Once again he strove to impart his own passion for continuing the struggle to the last extremity, arguing that if his countrymen could just hold on they could wear the enemy down. To yield meant to lose Alsace, and what government had the right to surrender French soil? The question for the country was 'to be, or not to be'.[2]

Yet it was difficult to see how a prostrated France could continue the unequal struggle, and in the wake of repeated military defeats discouragement was widespread. Though no republican zealot, General Chanzy was the only senior commander who urged continued resistance, and even his subordinates were less sanguine. Chanzy himself complained that 'when men fled the battlefield, instead of stigmatizing them and returning them to us, people hid them. When it came to raising more men, instead of encouraging those joining up people felt sorry for them and repeated, "They're leading you to the slaughter. You are betrayed!" Even the authorities themselves hid fugitives who returned to their communities.'[3] Though by no means universal, there were growing incidences of conscript units refusing to serve in a war that seemed irreparably lost.

German forces now occupied over a quarter of the country, and there was no further chance of loosening their grip. Of the besieged fortresses, only Belfort and Bitche still held out. Economic activity was severely disrupted. Within the occupied regions the inhabitants were under German administration, paid taxes and indemnities to German officials, and learned about the war largely through a mixture of wild rumour and the German-controlled press. They endured the wanton destruction incidental to the passage of armies, plus requisitioning, the billeting of enemy troops, sometimes forced labour and the taking of hostages; and, where occasional acts of resistance occurred, punitive shootings, burnings and fines. Village mayors fulfilled the unenviable role of having to satisfy the frequently exorbitant demands of imperious local commandants, mitigating them where they could in the face of draconian threats. All this, added to devastation in areas which had seen the most fighting and an outbreak of cattle-plague aggravated by wartime conditions, made for a winter of hardship and misery which were laying up a legacy of resentment against the occupier.

It was not only cattle that were sick, for in this desolate season infections were spreading throughout France. In the provincial armies smallpox, typhus and bronchial diseases were rife. (The Germans, who vaccinated their troops against smallpox, lost only 261 men to the disease during the war, while it claimed the lives of 23,470 unvaccinated French soldiers.) The French army medical service, the deficiencies of which had been so starkly exposed by the invasion of August 1870, was finally reorganized at Bordeaux in January 1871 under the supervision of Dr Charles Robin, but the problems it faced were daunting: at the end of the month 65,000 troops were in hospital.[4] Although the zeal of local communities caused an over-provision of hospital beds, there was at first no co-ordinated system for allocating them, with the result that wounded men were directed haphazardly and were repeatedly turned away from towns where the hospitals were already full. One of Robin's inspectors reported that:

> The poor wretches shunted thus from town to town made the most senseless and painful journeys, desperately chasing after the hospital bed that had been promised them, but which seemed to recede perpetually before them. How many times have I seen them, weary and dispirited, lying down in some lonely corner of a railway station and refusing to get back on the train to continue an apparently endless journey. Several died in this way for lack of treatment, not because they had been abandoned, but because they remained unnoticed and had been forgotten or lost amid the overcrowding in the stations caused by this ceaseless coming and going without method or order.[5]

It was sad testimony to the cruelties of a war in which France had been as far outclassed in the medical field as in strategy and tactics.

Meanwhile at Paris the Government of National Defence, whatever criticisms might be levelled against its conduct of the war, had held out so long as food stocks lasted. For all the fury of the German bombardment and the damage inflicted on the forts, the Parisian will to resist remained firm, but it was the prospect of starvation (bearing in mind that several days would be needed to bring more food into the capital) that forced Jules Favre to seek an armistice in the knowledge that there was no further hope of rescue from outside.

On the cold, foggy afternoon of 23 January, following a roundabout route to avoid observation, Favre's carriage drove to the ruined bridge at Sèvres. He crossed the Seine in a bullet-riddled skiff which, with one of his aides baling it out with a saucepan, stayed precariously afloat as it nosed its way through drift-ice. To the north, recently arrived German batteries were bombarding Saint-Denis, while the river reflected the glow of the burning town of Saint-Cloud. When Favre reached Bismarck's quarters at Versailles and announced that he wished to resume the negotiations broken off at Ferrières, the German Chancellor responded, 'You've come too late. We have entered negotiations with your Emperor.'[6]

In fact, Bismarck's continuing contacts with the imperial family had reached no conclusion. Although by December the Empress Eugénie had apparently accepted the necessity of a substantial cession of territory as the price of restoration, from his captivity at Wilhelmshöhe Napoleon III had written to warn her against associating the dynasty with what would be seen as a shameful peace.[7] Had Bismarck seriously sought to introduce 'this ferret into the Gallic hen-house'[8] as a means of dividing and weakening France he would doubtless have met strong opposition from Kaiser Wilhelm, the General Staff, German public opinion and the Tsar; but in any case, since he refused the Bonapartists better terms than the republicans, Napoleon declined the bait.

Bismarck was using the imperial threat to pressure Favre into negotiating a peace that would bind not only Paris but the government at Bordeaux, and Favre soon modified his initial stance of speaking only for the capital. Despite his previous assurances to Gambetta that if Paris surrendered the Delegation would be free to fight on, the Cabinet had authorized him to treat for France rather than just Paris. Bismarck proved amenable to Favre's proposal that free elections to a National Assembly would be a better basis for peace negotiations than any attempt to revive the Bonapartist Legislature under the protection of German bayonets, and the discussion then turned to the terms which Paris might receive. That evening, after an audience with Wilhelm, Bismarck came to dine with his staff seeming 'unusually pleased' and whistling a huntsman's call signifying that the stag had been killed. 'I think it is all over,' he told them.[9] Details of an armistice were hammered out in discussion with Favre over the next five days, and were sufficiently advanced for a cease-fire to be agreed on the 26th. After a final flurry of bombardment which killed four citizens and injured nine,[10] at midnight the long echo of the last shell faded away and 'Paris relapsed into silence and numbness.'[11]

Moltke was fully involved in the latter stages of the talks that led to the signing of the armistice convention on 28 January. France by comparison was disadvantaged not only by lack of information from outside Paris but by the absence of consistent senior military representation. The discredited Trochu's removal as Governor excused him from the duty. His boast that 'the Governor of Paris will not capitulate' appeared to Parisians in retrospect to have been sophistry calculated to evade personal responsibility. Ducrot's attempts to persuade him to attend the negotiations came to nothing.[12] Ducrot himself, whom Vinoy had quietly removed after Buzenval by abolishing his command, was hardly the man for diplomatic negotiations, and the Germans wanted to court-martial him for allegedly violating his parole.[13] Trochu ordered one of Bellemare's division commanders, General Beaufort d'Hautpoul, to accompany Favre. Portrayed in German testimony as a drunken boor, or in French accounts as an outraged patriot, the Marquis de Beaufort had experience in boundary negotiations following the Italian and Syrian campaigns, the latter of which he had commanded. He attended only under strong protest, and proved outspoken and refractory, challenging German demands with some success on points of detail. Whether because of threats from Bismarck, or because he embarrassed Favre, or at his own request, Beaufort was left behind next day and replaced with Vinoy's less argumentative chief of staff, General Horix de Valdan.[14]

The convention provided for a three weeks' armistice, until 19 February, to allow France to elect a National Assembly that would meet at Bordeaux to consider peace terms. Meanwhile the opposing armies in the provinces would keep 10 kilometres back from a defined demarcation line which, being based on German maps, actually yielded them some places (like Abbeville) still held by French troops. The German army would take possession of the Paris forts together with all their war material, and the defensive perimeter would be disarmed. The army defending Paris, comprising the regular army, the Garde Mobile and naval troops, would surrender their weapons and become prisoners of war. However, they would remain in the city, and only if peace had not been concluded at the expiry of the armistice would they be sent to already overflowing prisoner of war camps in Germany. The Paris garrison would be allowed to keep only 12,000 armed troops for the purpose of maintaining order, together with 3,500 gendarmes and firemen. In addition, France undertook to dissolve all units of *francs-tireurs* and to hand over all German prisoners of war in exchange for an equal number of French prisoners of the same rank.

The city of Paris would pay a war contribution of 200 million francs within a fortnight. Crucially, the Germans would facilitate immediate re-supply of the city.[15]

Bismarck had not pushed the French as hard as excited national opinion in Germany would have liked; the armistice convention did not include the word capitulation, the surrender of flags was not required and, for the moment at least, German forces would not enter Paris. Yet once the fighting had stopped it would be exceedingly hard for the French to restart it, and if they did the German advantage would be overwhelming. Whilst the Germans avoided an onerous and perhaps dangerous occupation of Paris, possession of the forts gave them the military keys to the city. From Bismarck's viewpoint, Germany had achieved her war aims, which it was now his object to secure through a peace signed with a legitimate government. He no longer needed to play the French parties off against each other. Shortly after Favre's departure another emissary arrived from Napoleon III. Bismarck wrote on his card 'too late!'[16]

According to Vinoy, Favre seemed puffed up with pride at having secured reluctant German agreement to the entire National Guard keeping its weapons, sharing the belief of his civilian Cabinet colleagues 'that the honour of the capital was safe, since those of its inhabitants who had taken part in its defence would not suffer the humiliation of disarmament'.[17] Yet Favre was fearful too that attempting to disarm the National Guard would be difficult and might well provoke a popular uprising,[18] as indeed it would on 18 March. However deep the causes of that uprising – the prologue to the Commune – its initial success was only made possible by the dramatic reversal of the balance of power in Paris brought about by the armistice terms. With the regular army reduced to one division, the National Guard had an enormous preponderance of armed force and could dominate the city at will.

At first, though, it appeared that Paris would accept the armistice tamely. There were a few isolated demonstrations. Officers of the National Guard who drew up resolutions never to surrender were told in insulting terms by General Clément Thomas that it was a pity they hadn't shown such resolution at Buzenval. Disgust at the appearance of quantities of hoarded food in the markets at the first news of armistice, before any new food supplies had arrived, provoked some incidents of pillage over succeeding days. But, though nursing 'a mute rage against destiny'[19] and against the government, most Parisians seemed resigned, relieved, and utterly exhausted now that their 132-day ordeal was over. Although there had been fewer than half a dozen suicides during the siege, a naval officer and a gunner at Fort Montrouge shot themselves rather than surrender. Overall, the siege had cost the Germans 13,286 men either killed, wounded or missing.[20] Ducrot estimated casualties in the defence forces at 28,450.[21]

The armistice terms were executed on 29 January. The French surrendered their forts together with 1,362 fortress guns, 602 field guns, 177,000 stands of arms including over 150,000 Chassepots, and great stores of ammunition.[22]

In view of what followed several weeks later, Favre was to ask pardon 'of God and man'[23] for leaving the National Guard its weapons. But another omission of his had more immediate and serious consequences for a French army. After he signed the armistice convention Favre hastened to send a wire to Gambetta announcing it and telling him to hold elections on 8 February. Yet astonishingly he failed to copy the convention to Gambetta or to mention two of its key military stipulations. The first was that, while the armistice became effective immediately at Paris, it did not come into force in the provinces until the 31st. Secondly, despite Beaufort having strongly challenged Moltke on the subject, Favre had accepted that the armistice should not extend to the three Departments of the Côte d'Or, Doubs and Jura; precisely the region in which Manteuffel was closing in on the Army of the East.

Agony of an Army

The German motive in wishing to defer an armistice on Manteuffel's front, supposedly while awaiting further information, was self-evidently to exploit their opportunity to capture or destroy the Army of the East. Favre, unwilling to yield to Bismarck's demands for the surrender of Belfort, agreed to the deferment. In the absence of confirmation, he was reluctant to accept what Bismarck told him about the defeat of Bourbaki's army, and nursed some lingering hope for its success.[24] Favre was anyway so intent on securing favourable armistice terms for Paris that he failed to press the question of the Army of the East. His self-contradictory post-war explanations gave the impression of a man trying unconvincingly to excuse an oversight that had consequences he failed to grasp.

Nevertheless, much as political opponents were to pillory Favre as solely responsible for the loss of the Army of the East, in reality it was doomed before news of the armistice arrived. Even before the army reached Besançon, officers were saying, 'We're heading for another Sedan.'[25] The parallels were ominous: just as MacMahon's army had been corralled against the Belgian border in late August, Bourbaki's was being herded up against the Swiss border by rapidly pursuing German columns, and both French forces underwent a change of command at a critical juncture. Freycinet hoped that the army might yet break out to the west, perhaps with the help of a hastily organized rescue force from Lyon, but General Clinchant judged that his only resort was to continue the retreat to Pontarlier begun by Bourbaki. There he expected to find food, and to occupy strategic passes that would give him a defensible perimeter. Leaving two divisions to reinforce the garrison of Besançon, his army marched towards Pontarlier on 27 and 28 January. Numbly, mechanically, men put one foot in front of another along roads which, despite the efforts of the engineers and local people to clear stretches, were quickly covered again in knee-deep snow. Frequently falling on treacherous roads, horses took on the appearance of phantoms as their sweat froze on them. Desperate to feed but unable to graze, they gnawed at tree bark, leather, wood, and even each other's manes. Peasants in the sparsely inhabited Jura hid their supplies of hay, which was particularly scarce because of the previous summer's drought. The army's passage became marked by hundreds of dead horses.

Gaunt and shivering with cold or fever, men too fell by the wayside in great numbers. 'At first a fifth of the army were stragglers,' said Clinchant, 'then a quarter, then a half, then more.'[26] Even when adequate food supplies were available, regular issues of rations became all but impossible in such circumstances. In Pontarlier, a small town of 6,000 people, there was simply not enough shelter for everyone. While their officers headed off to the hotels, men squeezed into any available building to find warmth, while those who could not huddled in the streets, building fires with whatever they could find.[27] 'Everything conspired to overwhelm this unfortunate army,' wrote Dr Henri Beaunis, 'not only cold, exhaustion, disease and discouragement but at times starvation too.'[28]

Out on the army's flanks reconnaissance was as poor as ever, and the first rumours of a German presence sufficed to persuade units that they could not reach the passes that they had been ordered to hold. On 26 January the town of Salins asked French artillery not to fire on the Germans for fear of provoking a bombardment. At Sombacourt on 29 January a German battalion, at a cost of two killed and five wounded, captured the best part of a French division, though French troops at Chaffois still showed fight. That evening Clinchant got news of the armistice. Following receipt of Favre's telegram, Freycinet told the general to cease hostilities immediately. The relief of the troops, who believed that their sufferings were over, was palpable. Some German commanders suspended hostilities for a few hours while awaiting instructions from their headquarters. Manteuffel soon ordered them to keep moving, and wrote to Clinchant on the 30th advising him that there was no armistice on their front. Even now Clinchant believed, as did Gambetta, that there must be some failure of communication on the German side, and he proposed a thirty-six hours' truce to Manteuffel until clarification came. Manteuffel refused, telling him that he could only discuss capitulation. Meanwhile, hostilities would continue, although Manteuffel allowed Clinchant to send a telegram to Bordeaux via German-controlled lines.

By this time, 31 January, Gambetta had finally received a copy of the armistice convention by courtesy of the Germans, for Friedrich Karl had wired the text to Chanzy. When Gambetta read its terms he became incandescent with rage, grabbing the nearest general by the throat and shouting, 'I can understand that a lawyer, stupefied by fear, might have committed such a stupid blunder and vile act, but Jules Favre had a general with him when he discussed the clauses of the convention with Bismarck. Let the blood of the Army of the East and the shame of defeat be upon his head.'[29] Gambetta could only authorize Clinchant to act in the best interests of his army.

Clinchant lost no time in doing so, for there was now no question of successful resistance. While his army had remained stationary the Germans had been bringing up troops in readiness for a concentric attack on Pontarlier and had blocked all escape routes. He learned that the key defensive positions he had ordered to be held had been abandoned by his troops, who had retired before the advancing Germans. One of his officers reported that the men showed 'complete apathy' and 'an all too evident refusal to fight'. When the officer ordered some men to fire at the nearest Germans, a few shells from a German gun in riposte were enough to start a stampede.[30] News of the false armistice had been a final blow to morale. The troops asked, 'why should we be fighting if our comrades in the other armies are not?'[31] Clinchant's only hope now was to avoid capitulation and imprisonment in Germany. He set his columns in motion for the Swiss frontier. In the early hours of the next morning, 1 February, he signed a convention with the commander of the Swiss observation corps, General Hans Herzog, for the passage of his army into the neutral territory of Switzerland on condition of surrendering its arms and equipment. French columns began crossing at the frontier village of Les Verrières and points further south.

Pontarlier was evacuated, but it was necessary to protect the army from German pursuit. A rearguard was formed of still reliable troops from 18 Corps and the Army Reserve. Supported by the fire of two forts, they held the pass at La Cluse all afternoon, inflicting 384 casualties on the Germans.[32] The French lost more heavily, and the Germans took over 1,600 prisoners and many wagons, but the bulk of the army meanwhile reached safety. Thus the Franco-German conflict, conjured in the heat of Paris the previous July, sputtered out in the darkness, fog and ice of winter high in the Jura Mountains.

All that day Swiss border guards watched a pitiful procession of 90,000 French troops crossing the frontier:

> A great many of them marched barefoot or with their feet wrapped in wretched rags. Their boots, made of spongy leather, badly tanned and mostly too tight, had not stood up to marches in snow and mud

and, not having been replaced, had soon let in water at every seam.
The soles were absent or in an awful state, so many of these poor
men had feet that were frostbitten or all bloody. Their uniforms were
in shreds, and as the troops had appropriated all the clothing that
they could find to replace what had worn out, they presented the
most varied appearance imaginable. Many of them still wore the
linen trousers issued at the start of the campaign and were shivering
pitifully.[33]

A continual hacking cough could be heard from the head of every column to its
tail. Hardly a man was not afflicted by it, and some 5,000 needed hospital
treatment.[34] A fifth of the men had no rifle to hand over.

The Swiss noted that while French cavalrymen treated their horses reasonably, the artillerymen and teamsters showed a revolting brutality. Some horses
had not been out of harness for weeks, and 'their bodies sometimes were
nothing but one disgusting sore'. Some could only be shot on the spot. The
pathetic spectacle of the tatterdemalion French army passing into Switzerland
was later strikingly commemorated in the cyclorama by the Swiss artist
Édouard Castres, who had accompanied the army as a Red Cross volunteer
(the 1881 painting, notable for its absence of heroic poses, is the only one of the
great cycloramas illustrating the war to have survived in one piece).[35] As one
Swiss officer reflected, 'the whole generation of men in Switzerland who
witnessed this dismal epilogue to a cruel war retains the imperishable and
tragic memory of it. Never in our fortunate country had we witnessed such a
disaster.'[36]

The French troops were dispersed across the country for internment and
subjected to Swiss military discipline. They were showered with charity and
kindness, and their generous treatment was warmly appreciated by the French.
Rested and restored, they were repatriated in the third week of March.[37]

Perhaps 10,000 French troops managed to avoid both internment and
capture, making their way to safety via snow-covered byways through pine
forests along the border. The Germans had captured 15,000 prisoners in the
last days of January.

On the same day that the Army of the East crossed into Switzerland, 1
February, Garibaldi evacuated Dijon to avoid the large German force that
Manteuffel had sent to deal with him. On 15 February the armistice was
formally extended to the three Departments excluded under the convention
signed at Versailles.[38] The Germans had been unable to take Belfort, but
insisted on its rendition. Only on 17 February, on the orders of his government, did Colonel Denfert-Rochereau march his 13,000 men out with their
arms and equipment and the honours of war after a siege of 103 days that had

cost him 4,745 casualties, besides 336 civilian deaths.[39] For the French, the steadfastness of the Belfort garrison had been the only beacon of pride in a disastrous campaign.

The Peace Preliminaries

The Paris Government's signature of an armistice put it at odds with Gambetta who, quite apart from the matter of the Army of the East, was livid at not having been consulted over an agreement that tied his hands and prevented him from continuing resistance. On 31 January he issued a circular to Prefects announcing that the armistice was only a breathing space that must be used to reinforce the army. His policy remained 'war to the knife; resistance until complete exhaustion'.[40] In a proclamation scathing of the Paris Government he urged the necessity of a 'truly national, republican' Assembly prepared to resume the war if the peace terms proved unacceptable.[41] To procure such a legislature another decree specified that no one who had held office or been an official candidate under the 'forever cursed' imperial regime would be eligible for election.[42] His wire communicating this to Favre was intercepted by Bismarck, who responded directly, warning Gambetta that his use of 'arbitrary oppression' to exclude his political opponents was a breach of the armistice terms, which required free elections.[43] Bismarck also wrote to Favre about the issue, but the Paris Government had already concluded that it must bring Gambetta under control.

Unabashed at a reproof from the unelected German Chancellor, Gambetta publicly denounced Bismarck's 'insolent pretension' to interfere in a French election.[44] But by 1 February Jules Simon had arrived on a mission not dissimilar to Gambetta's in October. Receiving a hostile reception, he told Gambetta in the name of the Cabinet to revoke his decree on ineligibility. Supported by the rest of the Delegation, Gambetta defied him, and left the meeting raging 'You are no republicans! You are no republicans!'[45]

For a few days there was a tense stand-off with the potential for open conflict. Simon resorted to subterfuge in his attempts to publish the Paris Government's decree ordering free elections, but Gambetta's supporters seized the newspapers that printed it and tore down posters. Finding his correspondence intercepted, Simon took precautions against being arrested. Nevertheless, he refused to be intimidated. Like Favre, he had not spent his political career denouncing the electoral manipulations of the Empire just to see them applied in reverse. At a tempestuous meeting he announced that the Paris Government had empowered him to overrule the Delegation, though prudently he did not disclose that he was also authorized to remove Gambetta in case of resistance. Still the Delegation would not yield, until on 5 February three more members of the Paris Government – Garnier-Pagès, Emmanuel Arago and Pelletan –

arrived at Bordeaux to support Simon's insistence that the authority of Paris be obeyed and the armistice terms honoured.[46]

If Gambetta maintained his open resistance to the government he could count upon the support of the radicals in the big southern cities, whose enthusiasm for continuing the war seemed to be in inverse proportion to their distance from its realities: notably in Marseille, Toulouse, Lyon, Saint-Étienne and Bordeaux itself, where on that day a boisterous demonstration called on him to lead a Committee of Public Safety. But Gambetta did not appear. He was now outnumbered in the Cabinet, and if his aim had been to force his colleagues to bow to his will he clearly had failed. Moreover, even he had finally to concede that military options were exhausted.[47] When told that the Army of the East had crossed into Switzerland, he put his head between his hands in grief, and none of his colleagues had the heart to speak a word.[48] Whether from political calculation that the odds were against him, or from the wish to dissociate himself from capitulation, or from a patriotic resolve to spare the country civil war – or all three – Gambetta resigned on 6 February.

This crisis passed, France went to the polls on 8 February. Gambetta was elected in nine Departments, and symbolically chose to sit for the Northern Alsace constituency. Alsace and Lorraine voted for republican candidates who favoured continuing the war, as did the south-eastern cities and Paris, where radical heroes such as Victor Hugo and Garibaldi headed the lists. But the rest of the country voted overwhelmingly for peace, turning to figures who could be trusted to work for a return to normality. Monarchist and conservative Deputies outnumbered republicans by more than two to one, while only thirty Bonapartists were elected, mostly from Corsica. Very few radicals won seats. Above all, the election was a landslide vote of confidence in Adolphe Thiers, who topped the lists in no less than twenty-six Departments, polling some 2 million votes. Thiers, a renowned historian of the Revolution and First Empire, offered the experience and wisdom of an elder statesman just when the country craved one. His patriotism was incontestable. In 1840 his government had commenced the fortifications that had protected Paris. He also had the aura of a prophet, having been a withering critic of Napoleon III's foreign policy, and in 1870 he had courageously opposed an ill-advised war. He regarded Gambetta as a 'raging madman' for continuing the war after it was obviously lost. The issue between the two men seemed simple. In the Army of the North Captain Patry was asked by the men of his company to explain the rival candidacies. Disclaiming any political expertise, he told them that Thiers 'stands for the conclusion of peace', while Gambetta was 'for continuation of the war. The next day when the votes were counted up I found that not a single Gambetta slip had been put into the ballot box.'[49]

The new National Assembly convened in the Grand Theatre at Bordeaux on 12 February. Its temper and its disposition to apportion blame for the disasters of the war on party political lines were manifested by the barracking it gave Garibaldi when he took his seat. He resigned, while, to general relief, the French authorities repatriated his men to Italy. Three weeks later, when Victor Hugo rose to defend Garibaldi as 'the only one of the generals who has fought for France who has not been beaten', he provoked such a furious uproar (led by General Ducrot, who had been elected in his home town of Nevers) that Hugo too resigned.[50] Such scenes were symptomatic of a bitter rift between Left and Right, and between Paris and rural France, that was fast becoming a chasm.

The Government of National Defence formally handed over its powers on 13 February. Pending agreement on the future form of government to be adopted, Thiers was elected Chief of the Executive Power of the French Republic. His Cabinet included four members of the former government – Simon, Picard, Le Flô and Favre, who stayed on as Foreign Minister. In an eloquent speech on 19 February Thiers announced that his programme was to rid the country of the enemy, to repatriate French prisoners of war and reconstitute a disciplined army, to restore order and economic life and repair all the material damage caused by the war.[51] Insisting on being given full powers to negotiate, he and Favre went to meet Bismarck at Versailles on 21 February to settle the terms on which peace would be made. An extension of the armistice for a few days was agreed for that purpose.

The negotiations were at times stormy, with Bismarck using the threat to resume hostilities as his trump card. If Thiers hoped that his election and negotiating skills might significantly soften German terms, he was quickly disillusioned. Yet both parties wanted a rapid liquidation of the conflict. Bismarck at first demanded from France the huge sum of 6 billion francs, but allowed himself to be beaten down to 5 billion. This indemnity was intended to cover Germany's entire war expenses and, as far as her military were concerned, to reduce their dependence on grants from the Reichstag. Bismarck arrived at the sum based upon what he thought the French could pay, but calculated too on weakening them and dampening their appetite for military adventure for some time to come. The French firmly rejected Bismarck's offer to have Bleichröder, his favoured Prussian banker, handle the payments on their behalf.

Germany's territorial demands were based on the green boundary line drawn on a map published by the General Staff in Berlin in September 1870; namely, Alsace and the German-speaking part of Lorraine plus the fortress city of Metz. Privately Bismarck had some misgivings about Metz. 'I do not like so many Frenchmen being in our house against their will,' he ruminated, and wondered about selling it back to the French for the price of building a new fortress a few miles further back: 'The military, however, will not be willing to let Metz slip, and perhaps they are right.'[52] He was unwilling to swim against the tide of royal, military and popular desire for the city that had been conquered at such cost, and he proved inflexible on the point in negotiations.[53] Over Belfort, however, he was prepared to barter when Thiers threatened to walk away from the table over the issue. After all, Belfort was French-speaking, and Moltke did not regard its retention as strategically vital. Bismarck offered Thiers the choice of accepting either a German victory parade through Paris or the annexation of Belfort. Without hesitation Thiers chose to keep Belfort. As part of the same bargain, Germany would annex the villages of Ste Marie-aux-Chênes and Vionville, west of Metz, where thousands of her dead in the battles of 16 and 18 August 1870 were interred.

It was agreed that upon ratification of the Peace Preliminaries, which were signed on 26 February, the Germans would evacuate Paris and the forts on the left bank, followed by all territory west of the Seine. German troops would remain in occupation of the Departments east of the Seine, evacuating them by stages as France paid successive instalments of the war indemnity over a period of three years. The French civil authorities would be responsible for collecting taxes within the occupied zone, where German troops would be maintained at French expense. Further negotiations would be held in Brussels to draw up a definitive peace treaty.[54]

In France and abroad Bismarck's terms were considered exceptionally harsh, although they did not include any claim on French colonies or limitation on her navy. Nor, apart from temporarily limiting the Paris garrison to 40,000 and a requirement to withdraw all other forces south of the Loire until the final peace was signed, was any limit set on the size of the French army. The terms imposed upon Prussia by France following her defeat in 1806 had been more draconian: as General Changarnier remarked in the Assembly, 'Today we are paying for the crimes of Napoleon I.'[55] Few Frenchmen had the honesty to admit, as did Viollet-le-Duc, that in the event of a French victory public opinion would have demanded the annexation of the Rhineland.[56]

Thiers returned to Bordeaux on 28 February to press for urgent ratification by the Assembly. A confidential report by Admiral Jauréguiberry confirmed France's military weakness, with only 222,000 infantry fit for combat, whereas on 1 March the German field army in France numbered 683,672.[57] To eloquent speeches from the Left opposing the peace, Thiers replied, 'Give us the means then. Otherwise spare us your words.'[58] An interjection from a Bonapartist Deputy that 'Napoleon III would never have signed a shameful treaty!' brought a furious reaction from the Assembly, which promptly passed a motion confirming the deposition of Napoleon III, declaring him 'responsible for the ruin, invasion and dismemberment of France'.[59] Finally, Thiers's

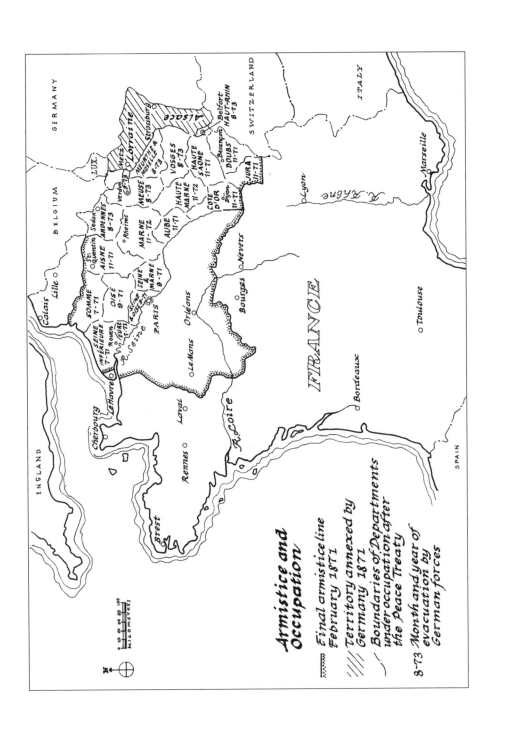

Armistice and
Occupation

~~~~~ Final armistice line
      February 1871

//// Territory annexed by
     Germany 1871

~~~ Boundaries of Departments
    under occupation after
    the Peace Treaty

8-73 Month and year of
     evacuation by
     German forces

arguments for the necessity of sacrifice carried the day and the Peace Pre-liminaries were ratified by 546 votes to 107, Gambetta and Chanzy being amongst those voting against.

At the end of the session Deputy Jules Grosjean read out a dignified protest on behalf of the annexed provinces, affirming their wish and their right to remain French:

> Handed over to foreign dominion in contempt of all justice and by an odious abuse of force, we ... declare null and void a pact which disposes of us without our consent ... Your brothers of Alsace and Lorraine, separated at this moment from the common family, will conserve a filial affection for France ... until the day when she returns to take her place.[60]

Then the Deputies from Alsace and Lorraine, Gambetta among them, filed out of the chamber amid a mournful silence 'like that which weighs upon a household where somebody has died'.[61] That night one of them, the respected Mayor Küss of Strasbourg, did die, and at his funeral Gambetta promised Alsatians that 'Force separates us, but for a time only.' France would have no other policy but the deliverance of her lost provinces, and republicans must unite 'in the patriotic thought of a revenge which will be the protest of right and justice against force and infamy'.[62]

Meanwhile, 30,000 German troops had begun their triumphal entry into Paris on the radiant morning of 1 March, accompanied by regimental bands. They kept within a defined area around the Arc de Triomphe, the Champs Élysées and the Place de la Concorde, where the artist Carpeaux had draped the statues representing French cities in black crape. Along the route many windows were shuttered, black flags flew and shops were closed. Vinoy had posted a cordon of French troops around the area to keep back 'a densely packed crowd of angry, truculent faces',[63] so preventing any incidents more serious than some catcalling. Bismarck himself appeared, and disarmed a menacing stare by asking the Frenchman for a light for his cigar.[64] The crowd found ways to vent its anger later, ransacking cafés that had opened to the Germans, beating up a British journalist, publicly stripping and beating women who had consorted with the invader, and ostentatiously 'disinfecting' areas where the conqueror had passed. To prevent them falling into German hands, the National Guard had removed cannon which they considered right-fully theirs to their strongholds in Montmartre and Belleville. Paris, filled with disbanded soldiers and other unemployed, and temporarily abandoned by many of its wealthier residents and the government, was in a state of revo-lutionary fermentation.

Favre rushed the ratified Peace Preliminaries to Bismarck at Versailles on 2 March. The surprised Germans were bound by their terms to evacuate Paris, which they did on 3 March, much to the chagrin of Kaiser Wilhelm, who had set great store by a victory parade but who got no further than reviewing his troops at Longchamp. Favre's coup in curtailing the occupation of the French capital was one of the few French successes of the last eight months, but it could not erase the sense of insult felt by Parisians.

Within days Bismarck had started back for Berlin followed, after a round of inspection visits, by the royal headquarters. The Franco-German War was effectively over, but the formalities of concluding it were to be complicated by the outbreak of a ferocious civil war in France.

The Reckoning
Urged on by the Assembly, Thiers was determined to assert the authority of the elected government of France over its unruly capital. He ordered the army, with insufficient troops, to remove the cannon claimed by the National Guard from Montmartre. The attempt, on the rainy dawn of Saturday 18 March, sparked a popular uprising. The troops were swamped by protesting crowds, and many soldiers fraternized and deserted. General Lecomte, who had vainly ordered his men to fire, and General Clément Thomas, who had resigned from command of the National Guard in February but was recognized in civilian clothes, were imprisoned by National Guards. That afternoon a furious mob, including some of Lecomte's own men, invaded the house where the generals were held and massacred them in its garden. Within hours the insurgents were in possession of Paris. Thiers fled the city in panic. Over the protest of civilian Cabinet ministers, Vinoy and Le Flô ordered their dangerously unsteady troops to evacuate the city entirely. The army withdrew south-westward without even holding the forts. Power within the city fell to the Central Committee of the National Guard. Efforts by the mayors and Parisian Deputies to broker a compromise between it and the National Assembly failed, while on 22 March conservative counter-demonstrators were shot down by National Guards in the Rue de la Paix near the Place Vendôme. Four days later Paris elected its own municipal government, the Commune, which was proclaimed on 28 March. By the beginning of April hostilities had begun between it and the government of the country, which had moved from Bordeaux to Versailles, so recently vacated by the Germans.

Much has been written about the origins of the Commune: of its character as the last great revolutionary event in the tradition of 1789; of the resurfacing of resentments harboured since the bloody repression of the Paris workers in the June Days of 1848; of the role of the International Working Men's Association in politicizing workers and in diffusing co-operative, decentralizing, socialist and other progressive ideas; of long-standing Parisian aspirations to democratic self-government; and of the disputed effects of Haussmann's rebuilding of the capital in the 1860s. The immediate prelude to insurrection lay in the series of provocations felt by Parisians in the weeks following the armistice. The military action of 18 March seemed to them to confirm that the Republic was in imminent peril from a monarchist coup by a reactionary government led by Thiers, the very man who had ushered in the Orléans monarchy after the 1830 Revolution and who was blamed by radicals for the shooting of workers in the Rue Transnonain in 1834. The appointment of General d'Aurelle de Paladines – reviled as a monarchist and defeatist – to command the Paris National Guard appeared to lend credence to such a plot. The new Assembly, not wanting to be at the mercy of the revolutionaries, had preferred to sit at a distance from the capital, a decision regarded in Paris as an affront. The new legislators had made plain their hostility to the fiercely egalitarian and anti-clerical capital, and by their economic measures seemed intent on ruining Parisian livelihoods. The ending of pay for the National Guard, on which so many families without other work depended, only strengthened its determination not to disband.

Yet the convulsion of the Commune remains inexplicable without the legacy of a disastrous war and the experience of the siege which, combined with the election results, heightened the Parisian sense of alienation from rural France. It was the war that gave Paris radicals the weapons and organization with which to defend their vision of the Republic. It was the war that led the insurgents to demonize government forces not merely as priest-ridden rustic reactionaries but as defeatists and capitulators who supposedly had done little or nothing to save the capital and whom they accused of having given in all too easily. For Parisians who had assumed in 1870 that France was invincible, treason and cowardice by generals and politicians could be the only explanations for the army having apparently fought the war like a man with one hand tied behind his back.

For both sides, the civil conflict represented a settling of scores for the alleged betrayals of the war. Anger at the injustices and sufferings of the siege, and sheer frustration at the failures that were popularly believed to have caused defeat were potent ingredients of the violence that erupted on 18 March. Crowds were heard shouting 'Down with Trochu!' and 'Down with the officers!'[65] That day saw lynch mobs in full cry after some of the political and officer class whom they held responsible. General Chanzy, who was changing trains in the capital, was arrested and narrowly escaped massacre by a crowd that mistook him for Ducrot.[66] Jules Ferry barely evaded his pursuers by jumping out of a window and onto a train pulling out of the Gare Montparnasse. His deputy was not so lucky. Gustave Chaudey, accused of having ordered the Breton Mobiles to fire on Sapia's men on 22 January, was among the hostages, including the Archbishop of Paris, shot by the revolutionaries in May. On the other side, following the first fighting in the western suburbs on 3 April, a captain of gendarmes who had just lost men to insurgent fire recognized their leader at an inn near Rueil, and cleft the skull of the eternal revolutionary Flourens with a sabre. Following the shooting of the two generals on 18 March Vinoy summarily executed Communard prisoners, setting a tone of brutal reprisal. The reluctance to use extreme violence exhibited by both the Government of National Defence and the revolutionaries during the siege was abandoned by both sides in the savage 'social war' of the Commune.

The insurrection weakened Thiers in his dealings with the Germans, for he had to depend on the release of French prisoners of war to build up an army at Versailles strong enough to retake the capital, something the terms of the Peace Preliminaries did not permit. The Germans were at first apprehensive that the Paris rebels would re-start the war, and briefly suspended both their evacuation of territory and the release of prisoners of war. Their fears were soon allayed. It had been one thing during the siege for Paris radicals to claim a monopoly on patriotism and to clamour for a torrential sortie against the national enemy. Once in power they became suddenly pragmatic and sent a message that their revolution was 'in no way aggressive towards the German armies'.[67] Knowing that they could not afford to take on two enemies, they were later willing to offer the Germans money in return for neutrality and weapons.[68] But the Germans remained spectators of the 'Franco-French War' from the forts north and east of Paris.

Actually Bismarck was impatient for Thiers to suppress the Commune, and lesser disturbances in several other cities, as soon as possible. For a government that could not rule its own capital might rapidly become uncreditworthy and unable to fulfil its treaty obligations. He soon came to an agreement to expedite the return of prisoners of war to swell the ranks of the army being formed at Versailles under Marshal MacMahon, the vanquished of Sedan, to suppress the Commune. The French also needed their troops home to quell a revolt in Algeria. In return for this co-operation Bismarck piled pressure on the French for further concessions, and his temper became frayed during April as talks between French and German negotiators at Brussels became bogged in detail and seemed to have stalled. The Germans accused the French of being dilatory in fulfilling their obligations and of wanting to renegotiate every clause of the Peace Preliminaries, while the French complained that the Germans were making ever more exacting and unreasonable demands at a time when they knew that the French Government was facing enormous difficulties.

Bismarck could not let this diplomatic impasse continue. He met Favre at Frankfurt-am-Main on 6 May to try to resolve outstanding issues. Next day he read out a formal ultimatum that unless France gave guarantees of fulfilling its obligations Germany would force her army back behind the Loire, deal with the Commune itself and extend its occupation as it saw fit. This was partly bluff, as he had no wish to extend Germany's commitment, and she too wanted her troops home. Conversely, Favre wanted to be rid of the Germans as soon as possible so that France could settle her own affairs. After four days of intense discussions a treaty ending the war was agreed and signed at the Swan Hotel in Frankfurt on 10 May.

The Treaty of Frankfurt modified the provisions of the Peace Preliminaries in only a few respects. The method of French payments to Germany, their due dates and rates of interest, were specified. In return for conceding a more generous zone of territory around Belfort, the Germans took an additional small strip of land in Lorraine, west of Thionville, where their reports indicated the presence of valuable iron ore deposits – a consideration dismissed by Thiers as unimportant. This was apparently the only instance in which German territorial demands were governed by economic rather than strategic motives. Inhabitants of the annexed provinces would have the right to opt for French nationality until October 1872, and to remove to France. To prevent any trade war between two nations which had been good customers since their 1862 commercial treaty, France and Germany agreed to set tariffs on each other's products on a 'most favoured nation' basis. Otherwise both sides dropped some of their more extravagant demands for compensation. Secondary administrative and commercial issues arising from the boundary change were resolved through subsequent conventions.[69]

Following ratification of the treaty by the Reichstag and the French Assembly, Bismarck and Favre met for the last time at Frankfurt, where the formal exchange took place on 21 May. Bismarck ventured the hope that good relations could now be restored. Favre responded that 'the conditions of peace you have dictated to us weigh against that. We shall conform to them scrupulously. We can promise nothing more.'[70]

Once the peace treaty had been signed Bismarck facilitated the operations of the French army against Paris, and the return of prisoners of war was speeded up. The stage was thus set for the last, most horrific act of France's 'Terrible Year', in which the capital itself became a battlefield. Government troops had already taken the forts south-west of Paris. After a protracted siege of the western suburbs, during which their artillery did much damage, they entered Paris through an unguarded south-western gate on 21 May. Over the following week they methodically retook the city from west to east, being welcomed as liberators by wealthier citizens in the western districts as the red flag gave way to the tricolour. Many National Guardsmen whose support for the Commune had been lukewarm or motivated only by the need for pay soon made themselves scarce once it became apparent that defeat was inevitable. The leadership of the Commune, formed of competing committees, seemed to awake to its mortal danger too late. Previous attempts by its two successive 'War Delegates', Cluseret and Rossel, to impose discipline and a co-ordinated strategy had led to their dismissal and condemnation by committees deeply mistrustful of anything that smacked of militarism or dictatorship. With the army successfully turning Communard positions, the revolutionaries fell back to defend their home districts in eastern Paris, sometimes setting fires to cover their retreat. Meanwhile, those Parisians who had remained in the city took shelter in their apartments or cellars until the fighting had passed by their neighbourhood.

To the hard core of National Guards who resisted them from behind street barricades, government troops showed no mercy. Those taken with arms in their hands, particularly those over 40 or under 20 who must therefore be volunteers, anyone – male or female – whose blackened hands indicated that they had fired a gun or set a fire, the revolutionary leaders (or anyone unfortunate enough to resemble them physically), deserters from the army or navy, anyone with a foreign accent or deemed to be a criminal – often judged on appearance – was either shot on the spot or sent before a drumhead tribunal which dispensed summary justice, sometimes on the flimsiest evidence or mere suspicion. 'Some died bravely enough,' wrote an army surgeon who witnessed one street execution, 'but most wept and wailed. They clutched at the clothing of the soldiers assigned to execute them, who were thus sometimes obliged to shoot them point blank and finish them off on the ground.'[71]

The scale of the slaughter can only partly be explained by the fury of government troops called upon to risk their lives against those whom they regarded as rebels, traitors and criminals. They were conducting a deliberate purge ordered by their commanders, incited by the Right-wing press and unrestrained by the government. Certain generals, including conspicuously Vinoy and the capriciously cruel Marquis de Gallifet, took their opportunity for a merciless settling of accounts with the 'Reds', whom they regarded as 'scum' responsible for the subversion and indiscipline that had brought France to defeat, and whom they blamed for fomenting revolution and civil war in the face of the enemy. In the streets of a city that had claims to be the heart of western civilization the generals applied the brutal methods which European armies normally reserved for non-whites. Columns of thousands of prisoners of all ages were marched away under guard, showered with insults by crowds enraged by the fires that threatened to engulf the city. For days the city streets reverberated periodically to the sinister roll of rifle and *mitrailleuse* volleys as the capital's parks, prisons and barracks became execution yards where captives awaited their turn to face firing squads in batches.

The Communards in their turn slaughtered about 100 hostages, including notably policemen and clergy. They also deliberately burned many of the great public buildings of central Paris, symbols of a political and social order they detested. 'Better Moscow than Sedan' said their War Delegate, Charles Delescluze, invoking the Russian example in 1812.[72] The most fanatical revolutionaries seemed determined to fulfil their frequent wartime boast to bury themselves in the ruins of the city rather than surrender.[73] Such acts only reinforced the government propaganda image of the insurgents as criminals and savages beyond the pale of civilization. Yet civilization seemed to be in abeyance as government troops, assisted by the police, extinguished the Commune amid apocalyptic scenes of fire, smoke and blood. The last fighting of 'Bloody Week' took place in eastern Paris on 28 May, marking the end of an era of Parisian revolutions, of an epoch in the life of the capital, and the beginning of a cult of the Commune that was to inspire the political Left around the world for a century.

In the two months' campaign against the Commune the army lost 877 killed, 6,454 wounded and 183 missing.[74] The losses of the Communards in the fighting and subsequent massacres were never conclusively established, though for the latter the figure of 17,000 is commonly quoted.[75] Harsh repression followed this paroxysm of violence, fuelled by a flood of denunciations by those who had suffered under the Commune, or who were seeking revenge or to buy their own immunity. In this 'tricolour terror' 43,500 people were arrested, of whom 36,000 were charged and 10,000 convicted. Of these, 23 were executed; 4,500, including Henri Rochefort, were deported to the penal colonies of New Caledonia, and the rest imprisoned, 251 with hard labour.[76] Many prominent Communards nevertheless managed to flee abroad.

Every French government since Waterloo had lived under the threat of violent overthrow by the Paris mob, while the rest of France had become accustomed to having changes of government dictated by telegraph from the capital. Republican leaders had advocated arming their Parisian supporters in the last weeks of Napoleon III's regime. Seizing power on 4 September 1870, as the Government of National Defence they gave out thousands of weapons in response to popular demand, without thereby gaining any significant military advantage against the besieging Germans. Instead, they found themselves menaced by the most radical elements of the hugely inflated National Guard they had created, which under the terms of the armistice became the dominant force in the dangerously disaffected capital. Under Thiers a legally elected government opted to meet this challenge to its authority head-on, rebuffing pleas for conciliation from radicals in the southern cities. With the over-whelming support or at least acquiescence of the possessing classes and the provinces, it brutally and effectively eliminated the threat from the revolutionary Left for decades to come. This reaffirmation of the sovereignty and power of the French state in the wake of defeat was not the least of the unforeseen consequences of a foreign war launched by Napoleon III in the hope of uniting France behind him.

Conclusion

Europe Takes Stock

German victory in 1871 transformed the European balance of power, but Germany was not the sole beneficiary. Once the Peace Preliminaries were signed Wilhelm publicly thanked Tsar Alexander II: 'Prussia will never forget that it has You to thank that the war did not take on more extensive dimensions.'[1] Russia thus received credit for restraining Austria and Denmark from joining in a war of revenge, leaving Germany free to defeat an isolated France. Alexander could also delight in a major diplomatic triumph. By deft timing and without firing a shot, Russia had overturned the limitations on her Black Sea fleet imposed by Britain and France following her defeat in the Crimean War. Her action was regularized by a treaty signed in London in March. Not only was she back in the front rank of the Great Powers with German gratitude, but France was now in a situation where she needed to court Russian friendship.

Italy too had gained by the war without participating. She had taken Rome from the Papacy, which Napoleon III's defeat had left without a temporal defender, thus capping the process of national unification begun with Napoleon's help in 1859.

The effect of the war on the other two neutral Great Powers was more ambivalent. Austria–Hungary, like Italy, had avoided being dragged into France's defeat. Having passed up the opportunity for revenge against Prussia, she was on a path towards an accommodation with the new Germany as her best protection against Russia.

In Britain critics of the Gladstone government had denounced its alleged passivity, though often without specifying any practical alternative. Public sympathy had generally swung towards the French underdog in the latter stages of the war, and generous British relief efforts helped to feed Paris in the days following the armistice. Antagonism between the British and German press had been fuelled by minor incidents during hostilities. For instance, Bismarck's menaces against Luxembourg in December 1870[2] increased mistrust of his intentions and cynical methods and added to disquiet at Germany's growing strength and her conduct as a belligerent. Suspicions of Prussian collusion over the Black Sea clauses deepened this unease, and portents of future Anglo–German rivalry were already visible. Bismarck himself suggested that the English 'are out of humour because we have fought great battles here, and won them by ourselves. They grudge the little, shabby Prussian his rise in the world. They look upon us as a people who are only here to make war for them, and for pay.'[3]

Whilst it was acknowledged in Britain that France must lose some territory as a consequence of her defeat, the annexation of Alsace and Lorraine without their inhabitants' consent was viewed by many as a potential source of trouble. Lord Salisbury feared that this 'outrage' would be 'a constant memorial of humiliation' which no Frenchman could forget, and doomed Europe to 'a future of chronic war'.[4] Historically, most states had achieved unity by force of arms and had conquered neighbouring territory, but Bismarck's annexations seemed a brutal atavism in a more liberal age accustomed by Napoleon III to plebiscites which acknowledged the principle of consent.

Disraeli famously summed up the meaning of German victory in a Commons speech of 9 February 1871:

> The war represents the German Revolution, a greater political event than the French Revolution of last century ... You have a new world, ... new and unknown ... dangers with which to cope ... The balance of power has been entirely destroyed, and the country which suffers most, and feels the effects of the great change most, is England.'[5]

A week later another Member of Parliament spoke of the unification of Germany under a military despotism as 'a great peril to Europe'.[6] Public anxiety that a militarily weak Britain might suffer the same fate as France found expression in an enormously successful pamphlet published that spring entitled *The Battle of Dorking*, which envisaged a successful German invasion followed by the defeat of the British army.[7]

Yet Britain, like Russia, had long accepted that some measure of German unification had been both inevitable and desirable as a counterweight to France. After all, the achievement of unification had removed one dangerous source of conflict. There were hopes that once the Crown Prince succeeded to the throne a largely Protestant and industrious Germany, with so many fine achievements to her credit in the fields of industry, science, medicine and the arts, might follow a more liberal path. Whatever anxieties there might be for the future, undoubtedly a victory for Napoleon III would have alarmed Britain more and might sooner or later have embroiled her in a new trial of strength with an over-mighty Napoleonic state. Such a prospect, wrote the diplomat Sir Robert Morier, ought to make 'anyone in his senses' incapable of wishing the result of the war to have been other than it was.[8]

German Victory

German troops returning from the war were greeted with jubilation and thanksgiving, culminating in a great victory parade in Berlin led by the Kaiser on 16 June 1871. In the wake of victory Moltke was made a Field Marshal and Bismarck a prince, and both were richly rewarded for their achievements, which had made Wilhelm I an emperor and one of the most successful Prussian kings ever. When Bismarck had come to power less than nine years previously Prussia had been the least of the European Great Powers, and Germany had seemed irretrievably fragmented. Now it was united and the foremost military power on the continent.

The campaign waged by German forces ranks among the most successful in European history. Certainly it had had its anxious and trying passages, particularly since Sedan. Occasionally French movements had mystified and surprised the German high command. Guerrilla warfare had been an exasperating nuisance, and the war had dragged on much longer than anyone at Versailles had expected or wanted. But German strategic dominance had never been seriously upset, every French attempt to relieve Paris had been defeated and the enemy had been forced to sue for peace. If Moltke had not been as omniscient and infallible as his admirers later claimed, his judgement had proved equal to every challenge. Imperfect intelligence caused the Germans to miss or fail to exploit some opportunities, but relatively few. Undeniably superior numbers, achieved by the rapid and efficient mobilization and concentration of an army greatly expanded by trained reservists, had given the Germans a crucial advantage up to October 1870. But in most of the later campaigns of the war they actually fought at a numerical disadvantage, French representations to the contrary notwithstanding. Unity of command, superiority in artillery, superior generalship, discipline, training, organization, and skilful use of reserves at threatened points had made the crucial difference in every theatre.

During the war Moltke had reflected, 'the question of which is preferable, a trained army or a militia, will be solved in action. If the French succeed in throwing us out of France, all the Powers will introduce a militia system, and if we remain the victors, then every State will imitate us with universal service in a standing army.'[9] So it proved, and Germany's spectacular success in 1870 inspired military reform by other powers, making it less probable that she could ever again achieve the same startling and decisive superiority.

During the war the German states had mobilized 1,494,412 men, of whom 1,143,355 served in France.[10] The campaign had cost the lives of 40,881 German servicemen, of whom nearly 70 per cent – 28,282 men – had died by enemy action. Of the remainder, 12,253 died from disease, 316 in accidents and 30 by suicide. Additionally, 12,869 men were listed as missing, and 88,543 had been wounded, bringing total German casualties to over 140,000: approximately 10 per cent of all men who took part in the campaign. In all, 295,644 sick and wounded German troops had been treated in field hospitals during the war.[11] However gruelling the months of campaigning after Sedan had been, they were far less deadly than the first month of combat up to 2 September, during which the French imperial army had inflicted about 17,000 of the deaths and 52,000 of the wounds detailed above. Lower German casualties in the 'republican' phase of the war can be accounted for partly by a strategy that was deliberately economical of German lives, but more by the insufficient training of France's improvised levies.

Whilst German losses were significant, German leaders and a majority of the public accepted them as a proportionate price to pay for such an historic triumph and for the attainment of national unity. War as an instrument of future policy was rendered far from unthinkable. The conquest of Alsace and Lorraine provided a strong rampart against future French aggression, and neither the formidable challenges of the Germanization of the new provinces nor the alarm felt by some German manufacturers at the prospect of strong internal competition from their industries dampened euphoria over what Germans had been taught to regard as the righting of a historic wrong.

Crown Prince Friedrich Wilhelm yielded to none in his enthusiasm for what he termed the 'restoration' of the German Empire, but his was amongst the few Liberal consciences privately critical of 'the insolent, brutal "Junker"' and his policy of iron and blood that had triumphed in the wars against Denmark, Austria and France in the space of seven years. On New Year's Eve 1870 he had reflected, 'Bismarck has made us great and powerful, but he has robbed us of our friends, the sympathies of the world, and – our conscience.'[12] Not only had the war finally exploded the Liberal and Romantic dream that a Europe organized into nation-states would inaugurate an era of universal peace and fraternity, it had ushered in instead one of heightened nationalism, large and costly standing armies, heavy armaments and a pervasive fear of war. The growing militarization of Europe was especially marked in Imperial Germany, where the army, and particularly the General Staff, enjoyed a unique authority and respect in a society that regarded the triumph of 1870–71 as one not merely of superior organization and intelligent leadership, but as a manifestation of divine favour. As pseudo-Darwinian ideas became popular, victory in battle was also seen as a proof of racial superiority. With the passage of time, too, popular memory of the war focused on the lightning campaign that had led to the stunning victory of Sedan. The frustrations of the following months and the possibility of what might have happened had France had a reliable ally were less dwelt upon, feeding a popular assumption that future wars would be as short and decisive as Bismarck's three.

It is legitimate to see in the military, political and cultural legacy of the war of 1870–71 some of the first seeds of the next great conflict, but that is by no means to assert that its outcome determined the future course of events, let alone that the war of 1914 was somehow a necessary and inevitable consequence of Germany's earlier victory. The Crown Prince's son, the future Kaiser Wilhelm II, was aged 13 when he attended the victory parade in Berlin in June 1871. Nobody could then foresee that in his reign Germany's new 'Second Empire' would disappear in circumstances curiously reminiscent of Napoleon III's. Beset by tensions between authoritarianism and democracy, fearing encirclement (for which, unlike France, she had mainly herself to blame), urged on by generals and politicians convinced that they must seize a disappearing opportunity to strike the enemy, and beguiled by intoxicating legends of past military glory, Germany in July 1914, like France in July 1870, gambled on a foreign war. It too met with disastrous defeat which brought down the imperial dynasty, leaving a Republic to call upon the army to suppress a rebellion by the extreme Left. Forced in 1918 to restore Alsace and Lorraine and to sign a humiliating peace in the same Hall of Mirrors at Versailles where Wilhelm I had been acclaimed Kaiser in 1871, Germany, like France after her defeat, was left nursing a grudge, unable to accept either the loss of her borderlands or her permanent relegation.

After the cataclysm of the world wars it seemed that German unity had proved to be a failed experiment with utterly disastrous consequences. For decades her division seemed likely to be perpetual. Yet nationhood is a persistent idea, and Germany was peacefully reunited in 1990 under the black, red and gold flag of the Liberals and democrats of 1848. German nationhood survives: but gone is the reactionary warrior-state founded by Wilhelm I, Bismarck and Moltke in 1871, and with it the three props that they considered to be both the foundation of their achievement and its justification – the monarchy, much of the old Prussia, and the originally Prussian army which Germany's neighbours learned to fear as one of the most formidable instruments of conquest ever unleashed.

French Defeat

As the defeated and invaded nation in 1870–71 France suffered more severely than her enemy by every measure. After conscientous enquiry, in 1874 Dr Chenu of the French 'Red Cross' calculated French military deaths from all causes during the war (excluding the campaign against the Commune and the Algerian revolt) as 138,871, including 2,331 naval personnel: greater than French losses in the Crimean and Italian wars combined and over three times the official German total. He put the number of men wounded by enemy fire at 143,066 and the number treated for sickness or frostbite at 328,000, plus a further 11,421 hospitalized for sore feet on the march.[13] Subsequent pains-taking work at the War Ministry modified some of his findings in detail – for instance reducing his figure of 2,881 dead officers by over 500 as more of the 'missing' were accounted for.[14] But since in the chaos of retreat some units never did file returns, and since the official history of the war remained un-completed in 1914, Chenu's findings were never superseded by any author-itative official total.

Another graphic measure of the debacle is the total of 383,841 French troops captured by the German army during the war, not including the 250,000 who laid down their arms at Paris and the 90,000 who crossed into Switzerland at the end of the war.[15]

Civilian losses are harder still to calculate, for the hundreds killed by enemy shells or in reprisal were only part of the story. We have seen that mortality through disease in the besieged cities was greatly increased by wartime con-ditions: by 2,000 in Strasbourg and over 40,000 in Paris. Similarly, for 1870 Metz recorded over 2,300 deaths in excess of the peacetime average.[16] Yet even these figures may be an underestimate. In the case of Paris, by extending the calculation of mortality rates to include the weeks immediately before and after the siege, that is from 4 September 1870 to 18 March 1871, the excess of deaths over the pre-war figure rises to 52,303, and for a year after the siege the number of stillbirths remained high and the conception rate depressed.[17] Increased mortality in the smaller besieged towns and the countryside un-doubtedly added thousands more to the toll of the war. Taking military and civilian deaths together, it is reasonable to estimate that the war may have cost France the lives of perhaps 200,000 of her citizens, not counting either the Commune or the Algerian revolt.

France suffered population loss in another way. The annexation of Alsace and Lorraine deprived her of nearly 15,000 square kilometres of territory and some 1.6 million inhabitants. A significant minority of these – 128,000, or 8.5 per cent of the population – removed to France in 1871–72, followed by thousands more in the ensuing decades.[18] The emigrants were mostly French-speaking town dwellers who could afford to leave: some transferred their businesses to France or sold up and started again. Thousands were young men anxious to avoid conscription into the German army. The diaspora took many emigrants only as far as eastern France or Luxembourg, but others to Paris, Algeria or across the Atlantic. They were not always welcomed with open arms, but they made a significant contribution to French economic and intellectual life, and helped keep alive the spirit of revenge. However, their departure was welcome to the German authorities in their efforts to Germanize the annexed territories and to encourage German migration to them.

The financial cost of the war has been calculated at between 9 billion and 16 billion francs, or ten times the French annual budget in 1870. The cost included not only fighting the war (2.25 billion), but the war indemnities, the interest on them, and the cost of maintaining German troops during the occupation (totalling 5.7 billion), plus damage to property (0.56 billion), the cost of requisitions and taxes levied by the Germans, the servicing of government debt and pensions for the wounded.[19] All this posed a heavy budgetary burden for a decade, but France proved far more resilient than Bismarck expected. A highly successful series of government loans raised by public subscription enabled her to pay the Germans off ahead of schedule and to liberate her territory. The last German troops evacuated France in September 1873, so closing a humiliating chapter in her history.

The shame of defeat haunted France for a generation, and was effaced really only by victory in 1918. Placing the blame for the manifold failures in its conduct inspired a flood of books and pamphlets aimed at vindicating the many reputations tarnished by defeat and envenomed party politics. The Left blamed the Right for starting the war and for Sedan. The Right blamed the Left for having opposed the army budget before the war, for encouraging revolution, for the conduct of the war after Sedan, or even for carrying it on at all. Devout Catholics saw defeat as retribution for Napoleon III's failure to defend the Papacy and as expiation for the nation's sins. To republicans defeat was the fatal consequence of a corrupt despotism ushered in by Napoleon's coup d'état. The politicians blamed the generals, the generals blamed the politicians, officers blamed their men, and vice versa. However, if in the wake of the war Frenchmen could not agree about the responsibilities for defeat nor upon their future form of government, there was general acceptance of the necessity for military reform.

The efforts of the Delegation in raising and equipping armies had been prodigious. Between September 1870 and the end of January 1871 it had created a dozen new army corps, numbered 15 to 26, to fight the war outside Paris. To the 548,000 men nominally with the colours on 1 October 1870 it had added over 400,000 by the end of the war. Deducting 50,000 men stationed in Algeria, provincial France could in theory muster 900,000 troops in January 1871. In reality, however, nearly half of these, 418,000, never got near the enemy, still being crowded into their depots and training camps when hostilities ended. Of some 482,000 men who did serve with the provincial armies, 136,000 were field battalions of the National Guard, of very little military value.[20]

These masses of men had for the most part been no match for their enemy – 'inexperienced lads snatched away from their homes, poorly clothed and shod … hungry for much of the time … shivering with cold in tents that let in the biting wind ... their poor hands numbed by frost and split with bloody chil-blains'.[21] Most had done their best, but the lesson was clear: 'You cannot improvise a great war.'[22] At the armistice talks Bismarck had upbraided Favre for trying to fight on with armies of raw conscripts, insisting that 'If all that were necessary to make a soldier was to give a citizen a rifle, it would be a giant swindle for governments to spend so much of their wealth on forming and maintaining standing armies.'[23] The cherished belief, widely shared by repub-licans, that the patriotic citizen in arms was militarily the equal of the trained soldier had been shattered by the war. Its last gasp came during the dying convulsions of the Commune, when Charles Delescluze rallied the insurgents by proclaiming that a worker with a rifle in his hands had no fear of the clever manoeuvres of strategists: 'Enough of militarism, no more braided and gilded staff officers. Make way for The People, for the fighters in shirtsleeves!'[24] Three days later, climbing a barricade in a gesture of despair, Delescluze was shot dead by Versailles troops – a symbolic end to the myths surrounding the invincibility of the revolutionary *levée en masse*. On the eve of the Great War the socialist Jean Jaurès was still advocating a militia system, although as a cousin of one of Chanzy's corps commanders he should perhaps have known better. But few who had lived through the searing ordeal of 1870–71, Gambetta included, were left in any doubt that the national defence was too important to be entrusted to anyone but adequately trained, disciplined and equipped soldiers.[25]

In 1871 General Chanzy introduced a Bill abolishing the politically dangerous and militarily unreliable National Guard. That summer also saw the creation of an embryonic General Staff, albeit one firmly subordinated to the War Ministry. In 1872 began a crucial reform of the conscription law which yielded a larger army supported by trained reserves and a territorial army. Payment for substitutes was abolished and, although various exemptions remained, France moved closer to the principle of universal military service. There followed measures to match the army's peacetime organization to its war footing (1873), to reorganize its command structures and to improve training for officers and NCOs. Infantry and artillery weapons were improved and, since the war seemed to have proved the value of fortifications, funds were found for building fortresses along the new eastern frontier, the work being directed by General Séré de Rivières.

The Germans were alarmed at this military revival, and among the French officer corps a strong desire for a war of revenge had been hatched in German prisoner of war camps. Nevertheless, French policy remained primarily defen-sive, as was shown during the crises of 1875 and 1887. Gambetta was popularly (if erroneously) credited with saying of revenge 'Let us think of it always, speak of it never.'[26] In reality, as a wag remarked, France practised just the opposite policy.[27] Whilst France never renounced hope of recovering her 'lost provinces', she was not prepared to start a war for them, and popular interest in the subject was flagging by the end of the century as a new generation came to the fore. In 1914 it was Germany that attacked France following a crisis triggered not in Alsace but in the Balkans. The war of 1870–71 had nevertheless ensured that France remained unreconciled, well-armed and apprehensive of an attack by her powerful and menacing neighbour, and that the recovery of Alsace and Lorraine would be a war aim if hostilities with Germany did arise. The legacy of 1871 also played its part in shaping French demands at the peace settlement of 1919, helping to perpetuate the Franco-German feud for another generation.

In 1914 the French Government showed that it had learned from the errors of the Government of National Defence. Defying criticism, it removed to Bordeaux at the approach of the German armies. Paris was partially evacuated while French armies fought outside it. It was the wisdom of dearly bought experience. However, the government of 1914 was much more strongly established than its predecessor, and could leave the capital without the risk of losing power. The future Marshal Foch retrospectively criticized Gambetta for 'tying the fate of the nation to that of the capital', making the relief of Paris the object of his strategy instead of taking time to regroup and train before launching a co-ordinated counter-offensive.[28] The Delegation had come to grief in trying to relieve Paris and Belfort as surely as the imperial government had courted disaster in trying to relieve Metz. Charles de Gaulle, writing in 1938, agreed that in theory it would have been better for Gambetta's armies to wait out the terrible winter of 1870–71 and to have attacked the Germans in the spring, but the strangulation of Paris meant that 'We didn't have the time!'[29]

Only with the passage of years and some republican myth-making did Gambetta become an honoured symbol of national resistance to all Frenchmen. At the polls in February 1871 the French people had firmly ruled out resistance to the bitter end and a guerrilla war that risked reducing France to a wasteland. In the years after the war Gambetta was reviled by the Right as 'the organizer of defeat' and blamed for the failures of the National Defence. The ambition of the 'Dictator' was also mistrusted by many within his own party, and although he remained the guiding spirit of the republican and democratic cause he held power only briefly in 1881. He died prematurely in 1882 following an accident with a firearm.

Yet an increasing number of conservatives came to appreciate what he had stood for in upholding French self-respect. The bluff General Beaufort d'Hautpoul exclaimed in 1873, 'People attack Gambetta a great deal. Well, he had faith, and I'm grateful for it. Patriotism is not enough. You need faith!'[30] Gambetta had incarnated the patriotic spirit at a time when, as one of his generals put it, 'the country was invaded, ravaged, trampled underfoot, our

towns held to ransom, our villages burned, our peasants executed; we therefore
had to fight and battle to the end, and if we could not win, at least to save the
ancient honour of France'.[31] Former enemies paid guarded tribute. Field
Marshal von Hindenburg rejected the common German insistence that the
French should have given up after Sedan, seeing in their continued resistance
'not only a proof of ideal patriotic spirit, but of far-seeing statesmanship as
well. I firmly believe ... that if France had abandoned her resistance at that
moment she would have surrendered the greatest part of her national heritage,
and with it her prospects of a brighter future.'[32] Analyzing Gambetta's errors
as commander-in-chief, Baron von der Goltz nevertheless acknowledged his
qualities and hoped that if Germany ever suffered a Sedan she would find
a man capable of igniting the same spirit of resistance.[33] In the hour of victory
in 1918 Clemenceau invoked his name, and his heart was reinterred in the
Panthéon in 1920. During the occupation of 1940–44 the Germans had
statues of him melted down to aid their war effort, while Vichy propagandists
denigrated his memory. Today Gambetta has many streets in France named
after him and inspires frequent biographies, while Favre, Trochu and Ducrot
are all but forgotten. As Jules Ferry said of the Government of National
Defence, 'This country doesn't like losers, and we had the misfortune to be
beaten.'[34]

What Marshal Bazaine ruefully called 'that accursed war of 1870'[35] has
passed into the dust and shadows of history. Yet in its day and generation it left
a livid emotional scar on France. As in Germany, it gave a potent boost to the
spirit of nationalism and to the very consciousness of nationality, profoundly
altering each nation's image of itself and of the other. Patriotic literature
and illustrations assiduously nourished an ethos of heroic sacrifice which was
inculcated in the classroom, in barracks, and through commemorations of the
dead. The dedication of numerous monuments to those killed in the national
defence – typically obelisks or a statue of a soldier advancing against the enemy
or expiring in the arms of an angel – helped to keep remembrance alive and to
prepare the next generation to defend the country.[36] A quarter of a century
after the event one French critic complained that the real war was in danger of
becoming lost in a legend as pernicious in its own way as that of the Revolutionary Wars which had seduced the generation of 1870. The welter of
parades and patriotic speeches, the desire to decorate everyone who had taken
part, and a literature that celebrated French feats of arms in which everyone
exhibited the purest heroism, had become a kind of escapism or collective
denial of the bitter reality of utter defeat.[37]

Yet behind the patriotic fustian of public commemoration, behind the
bloodless euphemisms and evasions of the formal histories written for the
instruction of officers, lay more troubled personal responses to a calamitous

war. Men who had imbibed the Napoleonic legend since childhood felt the burden of individual and collective failure. Thus, although cynics attributed General Ducrot's refusal of decorations for the campaign to a reluctance to accept honours from a Republic which he hoped to overthrow, there is little reason to doubt the sincerity of the explanation he gave privately of his feelings as a defeated soldier: 'I have made it an absolute rule not to accept any honour, so heavily does the double capitulation of Sedan and Paris weigh upon me ... These emblems that recall the glories and virtues of our fathers make such a ludicrous contrast with the shame and miseries of our own epoch, that I am loath to wear them.'[38]

Amongst a younger generation Alphonse Daudet, whose story 'The Last French Lesson' helped nurture the spirit of revenge, nevertheless rejected any sentimentality about his war service. Finding his dusty and crumpled National Guard kepi at the back of a wardrobe, he was at first tempted to wax nostalgic about his nights of guard duty on the Paris ramparts, but recoiled as he conjured up inglorious memories of the siege and the Commune: 'kepi of revolt and indiscipline, kepi of laziness, of drunkenness, of the clubs, of talking drivel, kepi of civil war ... Into the bin with you!'[39]

More vehemently still, Guy de Maupassant combined hatred of the invader and of Prussian militarism with angry rejection of the barbarity and waste of war. In a tone increasingly affected by anti-militarist writers towards the end of the century, he deplored the loss of so many young men, lovingly raised to manhood by their parents, who might have made a useful contribution to civilization instead of being butchered on the battlefield like animals.[40] Seizing on a phrase of Moltke's that war was divinely ordered and fostered great and noble sentiments in men: honour, self-abnegation, virtue, courage, 'and in a word prevents them from falling into the most hideous materialism', Maupassant vented his disgust at what he had witnessed in 1870:

> I have seen war. I have seen men revert to brutes, maddened and killing for pleasure, or through terror, bravado and ostentation. At a time when right existed no longer, when the law was a dead letter, when all notion of fair play had disappeared, I saw innocent people encountered along the road shot because their fear made them suspects. I saw dogs chained at their master's door killed by men trying out new revolvers, and cows lying in fields riddled with bullets for no reason – for the sake of shooting, 'for a laugh'. That's what you call not falling into the most hideous materialism.[41]

The artist Gustave Doré evoked the horror of the conflict in his haunting picture *The Enigma* (1871), showing a hilltop littered with dead soldiers and civilians overlooking a ruined city in a plain from which dark pillars of smoke rise, while a winged female figure (perhaps France, or Paris or History) vainly interrogates a sphinx.

Nor did popular art depicting the war always arouse nationalist sentiments. Following the great success of their cyclorama painting of the Battle of Champigny, the artists Édouard Detaille and Alphonse de Neuville created another illustrating the Battle of Rezonville, outside Metz, fought on 16 August 1870. Its opening in Paris in 1887 attracted crowds who marvelled at its realism. Pondering the sinister evening light illuminating a battlefield littered with dead and wounded, an elderly woman 'for whom, no doubt, this episode of the war stirred some deep sorrow', voiced the timeless question of the bereaved. Her eyes full of tears, she asked simply, 'After seeing all these horrors, how can men still make war?'[42]

Appendix

Chronology

Date	Political & Diplomatic	Military
1870		
2 July	News reaches Paris of the Hohenzollern candidature to the Spanish throne, initiating a diplomatic crisis.	
6	Duc de Gramont, French Foreign Minister, delivers a bellicose speech in the Chamber.	
12	Hohenzollern candidature withdrawn. French demand that it should never be renewed.	
13	Publication of Prussia's refusal in the Ems telegram.	
14	Imperial Council decides on war.	Mobilization of French reserves.
15	Chamber of Deputies votes war credits 245 to 10.	King Wilhelm orders Prussian mobilization.
16		Bavaria and Baden mobilize.
17	French formal declaration of war (delivered in Berlin on 19th).	Württemberg mobilizes. Mobilization of French Garde Mobile begins. France authorizes voluntary enlistments for the duration of the war.
19		Formation of temporary regiments from 4th (depot) battalions begins in France.
20		French army contingent for 1870 set at 140,000 and its call-up date is advanced from 1 July to 1 January 1871.
26		French army contingent of 1869 mobilized. Customs officers and, later, forest-wardens assigned to military service.

Date	Political & Diplomatic	Military
28	Napoleon III leaves for front. Empress becomes Regent.	
1 August	French troops recalled from Rome.	
2		Minor French success at Saarbrücken.
4		German invasion begins. French defeat at Wissembourg.
6		French defeats in frontier battles of Spicheren and Frœschwiller.
8	Republican disturbances at Le Creusot and Marseille.	
9	Demonstrations in Paris. Fall of Ollivier Ministry. Prussia signs treaty with Britain guaranteeing Belgian neutrality during hostilities.	
10	New Ministry under Palikao. Further measures to increase manpower follow, including conscription of single men (bachelors and widowers without children) aged 25–35, and expansion of 1870 contingent to include all fit men becoming 21 that year.	Phalsbourg bombarded.
11	France signs treaty with Britain guaranteeing Belgian neutrality during hostilities.	Strasbourg invested.
12	Paris National Guard increased to 60 battalions of 1,500 men each. National Guard re-established throughout France.	Bazaine given command of the army at Metz.
13	Republican disturbances at Lyon.	
14	Abortive insurrection by Blanqui's followers at La Villette (Paris). Bismarck appoints a German Military Governor of Alsace.	Battle of Borny (east of Metz). Shelling of Strasbourg begins.
16	Napoleon III leaves army around Metz for Châlons.	Battle of Rezonville-Mars-la-Tour (west of Metz).
17	Châlons conference. Trochu appointed Military Governor of Paris.	New army in formation at Châlons.
18		Battle of Gravelotte-St Privat (west of Metz).

Date	Political & Diplomatic	Military
19		Bazaine withdraws to Metz. French bombard Kehl. Toul invested.
20		Blockade of Metz begins.
21	Authority of German Military Governor of Alsace extended to occupied Lorraine.	
23		Army of Châlons under MacMahon marches to relieve Bazaine.
24		Bitche bombarded. Verdun besieged.
26		'Day of Dupes': French sortie from Metz aborted.
30		Army of Châlons suffers defeat at Beaumont (Ardennes).
31		Battle of Noisseville-Servigny (east of Metz).
1 September		Battle of Sedan: Army of Châlons encircled and defeated. MacMahon wounded. Bazaine withdraws into Metz.
2		Army of Châlons capitulates: Napoleon III goes into captivity. Vinoy retreats from Mézières.
3	News of disaster of Sedan reaches Paris.	German armies prepare to advance on Paris.
4	Republic proclaimed at Lyon and Marseille. Revolution in Paris. Government of National Defence formed. Empress flees to England.	Montmédy bombarded.
5		German GHQ at Rheims.
6	Favre's circular declares that France will not yield an inch of her territory. Gambetta decrees expansion of Paris National Guard.	
9	Paris Government decrees national elections for 16 October. Paris National Guard given 1.50 francs per day.	Germans enter Laon: citadel explodes. Vinoy's retreat to Paris completed.
11	Government decides to send Crémieux to Tours.	
12	Thiers leaves for London.	

Date	Political & Diplomatic	Military
13	Trochu reviews troops in Paris. Crémieux reaches Tours.	
14		Soissons bombarded.
15	First 'Red Poster' in Paris.	Germans begin encirclement of Paris.
16	Fixed prices for beef and mutton introduced in Paris. Paris Government brings forward national elections to 2 October.	
17	Glais-Bizoin and Fourichon join Delegation of Tours. Bazaine in correspondence with enemy.	
19	Favre begins armistice talks with Bismarck.	French rout at Châtillon. Siege of Paris begins.
20	Régnier reaches German GHQ. Failure of armistice talks at Ferrières. Italian troops enter Rome.	
22	Paris Government fixes bread prices.	
23	Paris Government postpones national elections until further notice. Régnier arrives at Metz. Thiers reaches Vienna. First manned balloon flight of siege leaves Paris.	French recover Villejuif plateau (south of Paris). Toul capitulates.
24	Régnier and Bourbaki leave Metz.	
26	Thiers at St Petersburg.	
27	Germans sever telegraph between Paris and Tours.	
28	Bourbaki meets Empress at Chislehurst. Insurrection at Lyons. Paris Government begins slaughtering 500 cattle and 4,000 sheep per day to meet public need.	Germans capture Strasbourg.
29	Delegation conscripts single men aged 21–40 to form National Guard battalions for field service. Paris Government requisitions all corn, wheat and flour.	
30		French offensive towards Chevilly (south of Paris) repulsed.

Date	Political & Diplomatic	Military
1 October	Delegation decrees elections for 16th.	Recruits of French class of 1870 enter military service.
2		Fourichon's decree on courts martial.
3	Fourichon resigns as War Minister. Formation of Ligue du Midi.	
5	Flourens leads demonstration at Hôtel de Ville.	German GHQ moves to Versailles.
6		Battle of La Bourgonce.
7	Gambetta leaves Paris by balloon. Garibaldi lands at Marseille. Paris Government fixes price of horsemeat.	Neuf-Brisach besieged.
8	Further demonstrations at Hôtel de Ville.	Germans destroy village of Ablis. German raiders repelled from Saint-Quentin.
9	Gambetta reaches Tours. Thiers leaves St Petersburg.	
10	Gambetta takes over War Ministry at Tours. Paris *arrondissements* authorized to introduce meat rationing.	Battle of Artenay.
11	Thiers returns to Vienna. Freycinet appointed Gambetta's deputy.	First Battle of Orléans: Germans capture city. Sélestat invested.
13	Thiers in Florence.	Delegation's decree on promotions. French offensive at Bagneux (south-west of Paris) repulsed. Palace of St Cloud destroyed.
14	Boyer with Bismarck at Versailles.	Delegation's decrees forming Auxiliary Army and Local Defence Committees.
15		Soissons capitulates.
16	Paris Government calls on National Guards to volunteer for field service.	
17	Boyer returns to Metz.	
18	Gambetta at Besançon.	Germans capture and destroy Châteaudun.
19	Paris Government requisitions all cereals.	

Date	Political & Diplomatic	Military
21		French offensive at La Malmaison (west of Paris) repulsed. Chartres surrenders.
22	Boyer meets Empress at Chislehurst.	
23	Paris Government decrees abolition of Imperial Guard.	
24	Morgan & Co purchase bonds issued by Delegation.	Sélestat capitulates.
26	Mayor of Paris orders gas consumption for lighting to be reduced by half from 1 November.	
27	Offices of *Le Combat* sacked for reporting negotiations at Metz.	Capitulation of Metz.
28		French capture of Le Bourget (north of Paris).
29	Russia denounces Black Sea Clauses of the Treaty of Paris (1856).	Bazaine's army marches out of Metz into captivity.
30	Thiers returns to Paris. Gambetta proclaims Bazaine's 'treason'.	First Battle of Le Bourget. French defend Dijon.
31	Insurrection in Paris: government held hostage in Hôtel de Ville.	Germans enter Dijon.
1 November	Government rescued. Further insurrectionary activity in eastern Paris. Thiers begins armistice talks with Bismarck at Versailles.	
2	Delegation conscripts all married men aged between 21 and 40.	German II Army (Friedrich Karl) begins its march from the Moselle to the Loire.
3	Referendum in Paris gives the government a mandate. Attempted insurrection at Lyon.	Belfort invested.
5	Thiers returns to Paris to report on armistice talks. Government rejects German terms. Municipal elections in Paris.	
6		Reorganisation of Army of Paris announced.
7	Moderate republicans recover control in Marseille.	Manteuffel's I Army begins its northward advance.

Date	Political & Diplomatic	Military
8	Paris National Guard ordered to form battalions for field service. Paris Government requisitions all horned livestock (including milch cows) and sheep.	Verdun capitulates.
9		French victory at Coulmiers: Germans evacuate Orléans.
10		Neuf-Brisach capitulates.
15	Baden and Hesse sign treaties of accession to North German Confederation.	La Fère invested.
16		Mecklenburg begins advance south-west towards Le Mans.
19		Trochu abandons plans for sortie to west. Ricciotti Garibaldi captures Châtillon-sur-Seine. French Army of the East arrives by rail at Gien to reinforce Army of the Loire as 20 Corps.
20	Ferry notifies Parisians that gas supplies to private premises will cease from 30 November.	
23	Bavaria signs treaty of accession to North German Confederation.	Mecklenburg turns away from Le Mans.
25	Württemberg signs treaty of accession to North German Confederation.	Thionville capitulates. Delegation establishes eleven training camps.
26		Garibaldi repulsed from Dijon.
27		Battle of Amiens. La Fère capitulates. Ducrot's Second Army moves from west to south-east of Paris.
28	Ducrot's 'dead or victorious' proclamation. Award of 0.75 francs per day to wives of National Guardsmen.	Battle of Beaune-la-Rolande.
29	Census of all horses, donkeys and mules in Paris.	Crossing of the Marne postponed because of failure to lay bridges. Diversionary attacks proceed.
30		Marne offensive: Battle of Champigny (first day). Amiens capitulates.

Date	Political & Diplomatic	Military
1 December		Germans reinforce Marne peninsula. French victory at Villepion. German I Army enters Normandy. Garibaldi repulses attack on Autun.
2		Battle of Champigny (second day). Battle of Loigny-Poupry.
3		Ducrot withdraws from Marne peninsula. German offensive at Orléans. Bombardment of Belfort begins. Faidherbe takes command in north.
4		Germans recapture Orléans.
5	Moltke informs Trochu of capture of Orléans.	Germans enter Rouen.
6	D'Aurelle removed from command.	
7–10		Battle of Beaugency.
8	Delegation evacuates Tours for Bordeaux.	
9	Reichstag approves accession treaties 195 to 32.	Raid on Ham. Germans reach Dieppe.
10	Reichstag votes constitutional changes necessary to form German Empire.	
11	Paris bakers forbidden to sell flour.	Chanzy retreats to Vendôme.
12	Paris Government announces that bread will not be rationed.	Phalsbourg capitulates.
14		Montmédy capitulates.
14–15	Paris Government requisitions all privately owned horses, donkeys and mules.	Engagements at Vendôme.
16		Chanzy retreats from Vendôme. Germans temporarily evacuate Amiens.
17	Bombardment of Paris agreed at German GHQ.	
18	Wilhelm I agrees to accept imperial crown.	Battle of Nuits-St Georges (Burgundy).
19		Chanzy reaches Le Mans. Orders given for Bourbaki's eastward offensive.

Date	Political & Diplomatic	Military
20	Disturbances at Lyon.	
21		Second Battle of Le Bourget.
22		Bourbaki's eastward advance by rail begins.
23		Battle of La Hallue.
24		Faidherbe withdraws towards Arras.
25	Gambetta abolishes Departmental Councils elected under the Empire, few of which had been under republican control.	
26		French troops pull back from Le Bourget sector.
27		Germans begin bombardment of Mont Avron (south-east of Paris). Péronne besieged. Werder evacuates Dijon.
28	Ligue du Midi dissolved.	French evacuate Mont Avron.
31		Engagement at Vendôme.
1871		
1 January	German Empire comes into formal existence.	Mézières capitulates.
2		Faidherbe advances to relieve Péronne.
3		Battle of Bapaume.
4		German II Army begins advance on Le Mans.
5		Bombardment of Paris begins. Rocroy capitulates.
6	Second 'Red Poster' in Paris. Trochu proclaims 'the Governor of Paris will not capitulate'.	
9		French victory at Villersexel. Péronne capitulates.
11		Moltke creates South Army.
11–12		Battle of Le Mans: Chanzy retreats.
13		Engagement at Arcey.
14		Manteuffel begins advance against Bourbaki's army.

Date	Political & Diplomatic	Military
15–17		Battle of the Lisaine.
16		Faidherbe begins advance on Saint-Quentin.
17	London Conference on Black Sea question begins.	Chanzy's army regroups around Laval.
18	Wilhelm I proclaimed German Emperor in Hall of Mirrors at Versailles.	Army of Paris concentrates for a sortie south-westwards. Germans attack Faidherbe's columns west of Saint-Quentin. Bourbaki begins withdrawal to Besançon.
19	Bread rationing begins in Paris.	Battle of Buzenval (west of Paris): French repulsed. Battle of Saint-Quentin: Army of the North defeated.
20	Wilhelm rules that Bismarck will lead armistice negotiations.	
21		German bombardment of Paris extended to Saint-Denis and north-western forts. Fontenoy raid destroys rail bridge over Moselle.
21–23		Garibaldi defends Dijon from German assaults.
22	Insurrection in Paris. Demonstrators at Hôtel de Ville dispersed by rifle fire. Clubs closed down.	Vinoy replaces Trochu in command of Army of Paris.
23	Armistice talks between Favre and Bismarck begin at Versailles.	
25		Longwy capitulates.
26	Cease-fire at Paris.	Army of the East begins retreat from Besançon to Pontarlier. Bourbaki attempts suicide.
28	Armistice signed at Versailles.	
29		Armistice implemented. Germans occupy Paris forts. Army of the East attacked at Sombacourt and Chaffois near Pontarlier.
31	Gambetta decrees that Bonapartists are ineligible for election.	Clinchant learns that armistice does not apply to the Army of the East.

Date	Political & Diplomatic	Military
1 February	Jules Simon at Bordeaux.	Convention of Les Verrières. Army of the East crosses Swiss frontier: rearguard fighting at La Cluse. Garibaldi evacuates Dijon.
6	Gambetta resigns.	
8	National elections produce large majority for peace.	
13	Government of National Defence relinquishes its powers to the Assembly.	
15	Armistice extended to three excluded eastern Departments. Federation of Paris National Guard formed.	
17	Thiers elected Chief of Executive Power.	French evacuate Belfort.
21	Thiers and Favre at Versailles for peace negotiations with Bismarck.	
26	Peace Preliminaries signed.	National Guard remove cannon to Paris strongholds.
1 March	National Assembly ratifies Peace Preliminaries 546 to 107 and confirms deposition of Napoleon III.	German military parade in Paris.
3		Germans evacuate Paris.
10	National Assembly votes to move from Bordeaux to Versailles.	
13	London Conference closes. France signs treaty conceding Russian naval rights in the Black Sea.	
18	Insurrection in Paris. Massacre of Generals Lecomte and Clément Thomas. Government forces withdraw from capital.	Army attempts to remove cannon from Montmartre and other points.
22	National Guard fires on counter-revolutionary demonstrators in Rue de la Paix.	
26	Municipal elections in Paris.	
27		Fortress of Bitche evacuated by the French garrison under Commandant Teyssier, who had held it for the entire duration of the war.

Date	Political & Diplomatic	Military
28	Paris Commune proclaimed. Negotiations for final peace treaty between France and Germany begin at Brussels.	
2 April		Government troops attack Courbevoie.
3–4		Commune forces attack west of Paris but are repulsed. Flourens killed.
6	Commune passes decree on hostages.	
11		Army of Versailles begins operations west of Paris.
3 May	Communard prisoners massacred at Moulin-Saquet.	
6	Talks between Favre and Bismarck begin at Frankfurt.	
9		Army of Versailles takes Fort d'Issy.
10	Treaty of Frankfurt signed.	
16	Communards demolish Vendôme column.	
21	Exchange of ratified treaty documents at Frankfurt.	Army of Versailles enters Paris.
21–28	'Bloody Week': fires in central Paris; Communards kill hostages; Army suppresses the Commune, killing thousands.	Army recovers control of Paris.
16 June		Victory parade in Berlin.
27	First French government loan to pay war indemnity: it is a huge success and massively oversubscribed.	
29		Thiers reviews 120,000 French troops at Longchamp.
25 August	National Guard abolished.	
12 October	Convention with Germany advances evacuation schedule against early payment.	
1872		
14 May	Bazaine under house arrest.	

Date	Political & Diplomatic	Military
29 June	Second convention with Germany to speed evacuation of occupied Departments in return for early payment.	
15 July	Second successful government loan launched.	
27	French army reform: new conscription law.	
1873		
15 March	Further convention with Germany advances final evacuation against early payment of outstanding instalments.	
24 May	Thiers resigns. MacMahon elected President of the Republic.	
16 September	Last German troops evacuate France.	
10 December	Bazaine condemned by court martial.	

Notes

Chapter 1

1. La Gorce, vol. 7, p. 408.
2. Favre, vol. 1, p. 77.
3. [France] Assemblée Nationale, *Enquête ... Rapport Daru*, pp. 26–8.
4. Trochu, vol. 1, p. 199; Favre, vol. 1, p. 80.
5. Lehautcourt, *Siège de Paris* (cited hereafter as *SP*), vol. 1, p. 143 fn., citing Gambetta's secretary, Antonin Proust.
6. Favre, vol. 1, p. 378.
7. Favre, vol. 1, p. 97.
8. Sarcey, p. 29.
9. *Journal Officiel*, 6 September 1870, Heylli, *Journal*, vol. 1, p. 56.
10. [France] Assemblée Nationale, *Enquête ... Dépositions des témoins*, (cited hereafter as *Dépositions*), vol. 1, pp. 547–8 (Gambetta).
11. [France] Assemblée Nationale, *Enquête ... Procès verbaux des délibérations du gouvernement de la Défense nationale*, (cited hereafter as *Procès verbaux*), p. 17 (night session of 11 September 1870).
12. *Dépositions*, vol. 1, p. 283 (Trochu).
13. Jacqmin, p. 145. On the retreat see Vinoy, *Siège de Paris*, pp. 60–101, and Yriarte, *La Retraite de Mézières*.
14. Bagenski, quoted in Lehautcourt, *SP*, vol. 1, p. 65 fn.; Verdy, p. 149.
15. German General Staff (cited hereafter as GGS), vol. 3, p. 17: Rousset, *Histoire Générale* (cited hereafter as *HG*), vol. 3, pp. 19–22.
16. Wilhelm I to Queen Augusta, 15 July 1870, quoted by Hans Fenske, 'Die Deutsche und der Krieg von 1870/71', in Levillain & Riemenschneider, p. 171.
17. Schneider, vol. 2, pp. 231–2.
18. Quoted in Lehautcourt, *SP*, vol. 1, p. 151 fn.
19. Bagenski, quoted in Lehautcourt, *SP*, vol. 1, p. 91.
20. Hindenburg, p. 44.
21. Details in Sarrepont, *Histoire*, pp. 188–204; see also Richard, pp. 167–8.
22. Larchey, pp. 38–9.
23. Rials, p. 92.
24. Goncourt, vol. 2, p. 284.
25. Sarcey, p. 49; Claretie, *Paris assiégé*, p. 27.
26. Favre, vol. 1, p. 49.
27. Ducrot, *La Défense de Paris*, (cited hereafter as *DP*), vol. 1, pp. 1–3; Sarcey, p. 44.
28. Trochu, vol. 1, p. 223.
29. For the circumstances see J. Ducrot; and Faverot de Kerbrech, pp. 95–114.
30. Trochu to Ducrot, 18 September 1870, in Ducrot, *DP*, vol. 1, pp. 20–22; Trochu, vol. 1, pp. 279–80.

31. Sarazin, p. 168.
32. Labouchère, p. 33; Y.K., pp. 7–12; Viollet-le-Duc, pp. 16–17.
33. GGS, vol. 3, Appendix LXI.
34. *Journal Officiel*, 19 September 1870, Heylli, *Journal*, vol. 1, p. 182.
35. Moltke, *The Franco-German War*, p. 127.
36. Favre, vol. 1, pp. 383–6.
37. Sorel, vol. 1, pp. 206–7; Busch, *Bismarck in the Franco-German War*, vol. 2, pp. 138–40.
38. Millman, p. 210.
39. Sorel, vol. 1, pp. 339–40.
40. Allinson, p. 131, entry for 23 September 1870.
41. Favre, vol. 1, p. 161.
42. Favre, vol. 1, p. 163.
43. Favre, vol. 1, p. 165.
44. Verdy, p. 150, entry for 8 September 1870.
45. Blumenthal, p. 130.
46. Favre, vol. 1, pp. 175, 180.
47. Circular of 22 September 1870, Favre, vol. 1, p. 419.

Chapter 2

1. GGS, vol. 2, pp. 437, 446.
2. Signouret, p. 324.
3. Uhrich, p. 6.
4. M.Z., p. 15.
5. Brice & Bottet, p. 405; Beaunis, pp. 44–8.
6. Fischbach, p. 120.
7. GGS, vol. 5, Appendix CLXXXV, pp. 98–100.
8. Flach, pp. 1–2, 95.
9. Nouzille, p. 91; GGS, vol. 3, p. 93.
10. Flach, p. 4 and Appendix 1.
11. Moltke, *The Franco-German War*, p. 133.
12. Sarazin, p. 319.
13. Allinson, p. 138.
14. L'Hullier, *Histoire de l'Alsace*, p. 86.
15. Rousset, *HG*, vol. 4, pp. 3–5.
16. Gambetta to Favre, 26 November 1870, Favre, vol. 2, p. 118; and see Glais-Bizoin, p. 48.
17. Source: Revue d'histoire, *Guerre de 1870–71: La Défense nationale en province: mesures générales d'organisation*, p. 125.
18. Thoumas, *Paris, Tours, Bordeaux*, pp. 83–4.
19. *The Times*, 15 October 1870, p. 9.
20. Bury, *Gambetta and the National Defence*, pp. 299–300.
21. Favre, vol. 1, p. 261.
22. Dupont, pp. 81–4.
23. Proclamation aux citoyens des départements, Tours, 9 October 1870, Reinach, *Dépêches*, vol. 1, pp. 44–5.
24. GGS, vol. 3, p. 150; Genevois, *Les Coups de Main*, pp. 47–61; Busch, *Bismarck in the Franco-German War*, vol. 1, p. 234.
25. Thoumas, *Paris, Tours, Bordeaux*, p. 64.
26. Martin des Pallières, p. 57.

27. Lehautcourt, *Campagne de la Loire: Coulmiers, Orléans*, p. 41; GGS, vol. 3, Appendix LXXI, p. 20.
28. Moltke, *The Franco-German War*, p. 148.
29. Boucher, *Combat d'Orléans*, pp. 60, 67–8; Helvig, vol. 1, p. 153.
30. GGS, vol. 3, pp. 162–3 and Appendix, LXXI, pp. 20–1.
31. Freycinet, pp. 369–438.
32. Legens, pp. 45–50.
33. Lehautcourt, *Campagne de la Loire: Coulmiers, Orléans*, p. 15; Montarlot, pp. 54–6.
34. Isambert, pp. 33, 103–7.
35. GGS, vol. 3, p. 166.
36. Montarlot, pp. 75–6.
37. Isambert, p. 85.
38. Montarlot, p. 83.
39. GGS, vol. 3, p. 166 and Appendix LXXI, p. 22; Isambert, pp. 78–84; Lehautcourt, *Campagne de la Loire: Coulmiers, Orléans*, p. 78.
40. Isambert, pp. 143–6.
41. GGS, vol. 3, Appendix LXXXIII, p. 67; Dumas, p. 58.
42. Cambriels to War Minister, 15 December 1870, Rousset, *HG*, vol. 5, p. 271 fn.
43. Aube, pp. 6–7.
44. Dumas, p. 81 fn.
45. Georg Cardinal von Widdern, 'The Guerrilla Warfare in the Districts in Rear of the German Armies', in Maurice, pp. 542–66. See also Pierre Bertin, 'La Guérilla sur les communications allemandes dans l'est de la France', *Revue historique de l'Armée*, 1971 (No. 1, Spécial: Guerre de 1870–1871), pp. 187–202.

Chapter 3

1. Patry, *La guerre telle qu'elle est*, p. 116.
2. Bazaine, *L'Armée du Rhin*, p. 83.
3. Chandler, p. 214; see also Rousset, *HG*, vol. 2, p. 474 fn.
4. Bazaine, *L'Armée du Rhin*, pp. 82–93.
5. Bazaine, *L'Armée du Rhin*, pp. 106, 215–16; GGS, vol. 2, Appendix LVIII, p. 117.
6. Bazaine, *L'Armée du Rhin*, p. 120.
7. Report of Lieutenant Dieskau to Friedrich Karl, quoted in Baumont, *Échiquier*, p. 174.
8. Fay, pp. 226, 234–5.
9. Coffinières to Bazaine, 5 October 1870, in Bazaine *L'Armée du Rhin*, p. 138.
10. Bazaine *L'Armée du Rhin*, pp. 136, 215–16; GGS, vol. 3, Appendix LXXVII, p. 50.
11. Bazaine *L'Armée du Rhin*, pp. 114–15, 233–40.
12. Rousset, *HG*, vol. 2, p. 439.
13. GGS, vol. 3, pp. 176 fn., 179; vol. 5, p. 221.
14. Régnier, p. 33.
15. Baumont, *Échiquier*, p. 176.
16. *L'Indépendant rémois*, 11 September 1870, quoted in Séré de Rivières, p. 52.
17. Régnier, p. 26.
18. Bazaine, *L'Armée du Rhin*, pp. 176–8. On Boyer's library loans see testimony of Colonel Humbert, *Procès Bazaine*, p. 628; and on the Mainz precedent Frossard's testimony, ibid., p. 637.
19. Boyer's testimony, *Procès Bazaine*, p. 619.
20. Boyer's testimony, *Procès Bazaine*, pp. 612–16; and *Dépositions*, vol. 4, pp. 248, 257 (Boyer).
21. Letter in Hohenzollern Archive quoted in Ruby & Regnault, pp. 249–50.

22. Text in Ruby & Regnault, p. 251.
23. Baumont, *L'Échiquier de Metz*, pp. 284–5; Busch, *Bismarck in the Franco-German War*, vol. 2, pp. 329–30.
24. King Wilhelm to Empress Eugénie, 26 October 1870, in Ruby & Regnault, pp. 255–6.
25. Coffinières de Nordeck, p. 66.
26. *Procès Bazaine*, p. 782; Bazaine, *Épisodes*, pp. 229–32.
27. Bazaine, *L'Armée du Rhin*, pp. 190–1.
28. Jarras, p. 328.
29. Jarras, p. 256.
30. Fay, p. 284, entry for 19 October 1870.
31. Quesnoy, pp. 181–2.
32. Montaudon, vol. 2, pp. 185–7, 191, 198–9.
33. Patry, *La guerre telle qu'elle est*, p. 210. See also Lecaillon, *Les Français et la guerre de 1870*, pp. 134–5, 143–4.
34. Coffinières de Nordeck, pp. 57–64; Baumont, *Bazaine*, p. 234.
35. Note of Commandant Pardon, Prost, p. 252.
36. Ruby & Regnault, p. 286.
37. Bazaine, *L'Armée du Rhin*, p. 207.
38. Andlau, pp. 388–9, 414.
39. Busch, *Bismarck in the Franco-German War*, vol. 1, p. 267.
40. GGS, vol. 3, p. 201; Lehautcourt, *HG*, vol. 7, pp. 490 fn., 499.
41. Patry, *La guerre telle qu'elle est*, p. 216.
42. Andlau, p. 410.
43. Deligny, p. 73.
44. Reinach, *Dépêches*, vol. 1, pp. 48–9.
45. Montaudon, vol. 2, pp. 175, 185, 202.
46. Ruby & Regnault is an eloquently argued defence of Bazaine; see also Lecaillon, *Les Français et la guerre de 1870*, pp. 121–44.
47. Rousset, *HG*, vol. 1, pp. 261–5.
48. The formula of Article 209 of the Code of Military Justice. Full verdict of 10 December 1873 in *Procès Bazaine*, p. 799.
49. Bazaine, *Épisodes*, p. 92; Patry, *La guerre telle qu'elle est*, p. 167.
50. Bazaine to his brother, October 1887, quoted in Baumont, *Bazaine*, p. 357.

Chapter 4

1. 36 per cent according to Serman, *La Commune*, p. 31.
2. *Journal Officiel*, 5 September 1870, Heylli, *Journal*, vol. 1, p. 43.
3. Heylli, *Journal*, vol. 1, pp. 55, 58 (decrees of 6 & 10 September 1870); vol. 2, p. 531 (decree of 28 November 1870). On the organization and armament of the National Guard see also Ducrot, *DP*, vol. 1, pp. 96–108.
4. Dumont, p. 322; [France] Assemblée Nationale, *Enquête ... Rapport Chaper*, pp. 80–86; *Procès verbaux*, p. 62 (session of 6 November); *Dépositions*, vol. 1, p. 392 (Ferry); Favre, vol. 1, pp. 299–300; Garnier, pp. 39–40, entry for 19 October.
5. Sarazin, p. 180.
6. Manifesto for *La Patrie en danger*, quoted in Bourgin, p. 86.
7. Rougerie, *Paris libre*, p. 36.
8. Rougerie, *Paris libre*, p. 37.
9. Larchey, p. 78.
10. Favre, vol. 1, p. 292.

11. Sarrepont, *Histoire*, p. 52.
12. Sarrepont, *Histoire*, p. 52.
13. Adapted from figures in [France] Assemblée Nationale ... *Rapport Chaper*, p. 41 and table, Pièce justicative No. III, p. 14; also Lehautcourt, *SP*, vol. 1, p. 112 and fn.
14. GGS, vol. 3, Appendix LXXVI. Note though that Blume, pp. 36–7, puts total German strength in front of Paris on 21 October at 202,030 infantry and 33,794 cavalry.
15. Trochu, vol. 1, pp. 223–6.
16. Larchey, p. 67 (29 September 1870); Sarrepont, *Histoire*, pp. 133–8.
17. Moltke, *Letters*, vol. 2, pp. 51–2.
18. Trochu, vol. 1, p. 273.
19. Ballue, p. 64.
20. Sarcey, pp. 129–30.
21. Favre, vol. 1, pp. 311–13.
22. Trochu's version in *Œuvres*, vol. 1, pp. 337–63; Bellemare's in Ozou de Verrie, pp. 42–52.
23. Lehautcourt, *SP*, vol. 2, p. 25; GGS, vol. 3, Appendix LXXI, p. 31.
24. Forbes, vol. 2, pp. 57–68; Ozou de Verrie, p. 40.
25. Palmer, p. 248, quoting A. Buchanan to Lord Granville, 16 November 1870, FO 65/805/466.
26. Text in Sorel, vol. 1, p. 409.
27. Report of Ambassador Schweinitz, quoted in Baumont, *L'Échiquier de Metz*, pp. 254–5.
28. Proclamation of 31 October, [France] Assemblée Nationale, *Enquête ... Rapport Daru*, p. 174.
29. Hérisson, p. 189.
30. Hérisson, pp. 190–2.
31. Larchey, p. 38.
32. Trochu, vol. 1, p. 381.
33. Blanqui's account from *La Patrie en danger*, Heylli, *Journal*, vol. 2, pp. 598–602.
34. Simon, p. 352.
35. Simon, p. 348.
36. *Dépositions*, vol. 2, p. 40 (Cresson).
37. Larchey, p. 132.
38. Trochu, *Ordre du jour aux gardes nationales de la Seine*, 1 November 1870, Heylli, *Journal*, vol. 2, p. 289.
39. Sorel, vol. 2, p. 77.
40. Thiers, pp. 96, 101; and see *Dépositions*, vol. 1, pp. 24–7 (Thiers).
41. Thiers's despatch from Tours, 9 November 1870, reprinted in Favre, vol. 2, pp. 29–40, p. 38.
42. Ducrot, *DP*, vol. 2, pp. 74–5.
43. Ducrot, *DP*, vol. 2, p. 76.
44. Favre, vol. 2, p. 26.
45. Busch, *Bismarck in the Franco-German War*, vol. 1, p. 290.
46. Sorel, vol. 2, p. 92.
47. Ducrot, *DP*, vol. 1, p. 320; vol. 2, p. 108.
48. Vinoy, *Siège de Paris*, p. 246.
49. Trochu, vol. 1, p. 325.
50. Favre, vol. 2, pp. 101–2.
51. Larchey, p. 139; Favre, vol. 2, p. 102.
52. Garnier, pp. 75–6, entry for 17 November; Ballue, pp. 136–7.
53. Sarcey, pp. 167–71.

54. Sarcey, p. 176; Larchey, p. 106, entry for 23 October; Goncourt, vol. 2, p. 305, entry for 6 October; Paradis, pp. 102–3, 107, 259, 277, entries for 30 September, 2 October, 7 & 16 December; Dumont, pp. 337–8; Garnier, pp. 75, 106, entries for 17 November, 20 December; [France] Assemblée Nationale, *Enquête ... Rapport Daru*, p. 292; *Procès verbaux*, p. 77 (19 November 1870).
55. Sarrepont, *Histoire*, pp. 253–4; Heylli, *Journal*, vol. 2, pp. 259, 421–2, 479, 496–7 (decrees of 26 October, 16 and 20 November and notice of 23 November).
56. Goncourt, vol. 2, p. 323, entry for 28 October.
57. Debuchy, *Les Ballons*, p. 403.
58. Trochu, vol. 1, pp. 407–8.

Chapter 5

1. Freycinet, p. 72.
2. Martin des Pallières, pp. 44–50.
3. Delorme, *Journal*, pp. 98–100, 103–12.
4. Freycinet, p. 82.
5. D'Aurelle, pp. 55–6.
6. Freycinet–Gambetta correspondence, 4 November 1870, in Freycinet, pp. 86–9.
7. D'Aurelle, p. 102; Chanzy, p. 27.
8. Bitteau, pp. 159–60.
9. Helvig, vol. 1, p. 210; Lehautcourt, *Campagne de la Loire: Coulmiers et Orléans*, pp. 152–3.
10. D'Aurelle, pp. 133–4.
11. D'Aurelle, p. 146.
12. Blume, p. 81.
13. Helvig, vol. 1, pp. 223–30, 239–40, 245.
14. Mauni, pp. 81–7 (French edition).
15. Jacqmin, pp. 167–9.
16. D'Aurelle to Freycinet, 20 November 1870, D'Aurelle, pp. 187–8.
17. Boucher, *Bataille de Loigny*, p. 12.
18. Martin des Pallières to d'Aurelle, 1 December 1870, Martin des Pallières, p. 165; Crouzat, p. 54; Aube, pp. 7, 19.
19. Gambetta's proclamation to the Army of the Loire, 12 November 1870, in Reinach, *Dépêches*, vol. 1, p. 52.
20. D'Aurelle, pp. 181, 189–91.
21. Freycinet to d'Aurelle, 23 November 1870; Freycinet, pp. 122–3.
22. Freycinet, p. 114.
23. D'Aurelle to Freycinet, 23 November 1870, d'Aurelle, pp. 204–7.
24. Goltz, p. 49.
25. Aube, p. 14.
26. Crouzat, p. 52.
27. Beaunis, p. 93.
28. Freycinet, pp. 129–31.
29. Freycinet, p. 133.
30. Debuchy, *Les Ballons*, pp. 224–38.
31. D'Aurelle, pp. 275–6; Chanzy, pp. 61–7.
32. Érard, p. 64.
33. GGS, vol. 3, p. 329 and Appendix XCIII, p. 112.
34. Freycinet to d'Aurelle, 5.30 p.m., 1 December 1870, d'Aurelle, pp. 289–90.
35. Order of the Day, 1 December 1870, d'Aurelle, p. 292.

36. General von Colomb, 1 December 1870, quoted in Lehautcourt, *Campagne de la Loire: Coulmiers et Orléans*, p. 298 fn.
37. Chanzy, p. 72.
38. Commemorated in Charles Castellani's painting *La bataille de Loigny* in the Musée de l'Armée. Charette's report of 10 January 1871 in Boucher, *Bataille de Loigny*, pp. 104–6.
39. Commandant de Fouchier to General von Kotwitz, quoted in Boucher, *Bataille de Loigny*, p. 81.
40. GGS, vol. 3, Appendix XCIII, p. 113.
41. D'Aurelle, pp. 318–20.
42. D'Aurelle, pp. 297–8; and similarly Aube, p. 18.

Chapter 6

1. Sarcey, p. 209; Trochu, vol. 1, pp. 429–30; Lehautcourt, *SP*, vol. 2, pp. 166–71.
2. Chalvet-Nastrac, p. 12.
3. Ducrot, *DP*, vol. 2, pp. 154–7.
4. Hérisson, p. 244; Trochu, vol. 1, pp. 430–2; 'Une phrase célèbre', *Le Figaro*, 1 December 1892, p. 1; letter of General Boissonnet, 'Les mots historiques', *Le Figaro*, 19 December 1892, p. 2.
5. Faverot de Kerbrech, p. 174.
6. Sarazin, p. 205.
7. Ballue, p. 72; and see Paradis, p. 243, entry for 29 November; Garnier, p. 82, entry for 28 November.
8. Lehautcourt, *SP*, vol. 2, p. 219; La Roncière-Le Noury, p. 186.
9. Trochu, vol. 1, p. 434.
10. GGS, vol. 3, pp. 369–70.
11. Sarazin, p. 209.
12. Claretie, *Paris assiégé*, p. 119.
13. Hérisson, p. 246.
14. Sarazin, p. 214.
15. Ducrot, *DP*, vol. 2, pp. 295–6.
16. Trochu, vol. 1, p. 448.
17. Sarazin, p. 217.
18. Ducrot, *DP*, vol. 3, p. 63.
19. Heylli, *Journal*, vol. 3, p. 35.
20. Trochu, vol. 1, pp. 463–5; Sarazin, pp. 225–6; Labouchère, p. 226; Richard, pp. 187–8.
21. Favre, vol. 2, p. 142. For Parisian opinion during the offensive see Heylli, *Journal*, vol. 2, pp. 706–9 and vol. 3, pp. 523–5; Paradis, pp. 241–55; and Lecaillon, *Le Siège de Paris*, pp. 137–57.
22. Rampal, pp. 12–13.
23. Goncourt, vol. 2, p. 350.
24. Dr Sarazin, quoted in Faverot de Kerbrech, p. 195.
25. Le Fort, vol. 2, p. 377.
26. Faverot de Kerbrech, pp. 202–4; *Le Gaulois*, pp. 301–2, 7 December 1870.
27. Sarazin, pp. 235–6; and see the account by Dardenne de la Grangerie, Secretary of the Press Ambulance Association, in *Le Gaulois*, 8 December 1870.
28. Ducrot, *DP*, vol. 3, pp. 68–103. A German source put the French dead at 2,316 – Blume, p. 108.
29. On Hoff see the article by Louis-Lande; Claretie, *Histoire de la Révolution*, p. 402 fn.; and Roblin, pp. 57, 271.

30. Busch, *Bismarck in the Franco-German War*, vol. 2, p. 46.
31. D'Aurelle, pp. 334–5.
32. Freycinet to d'Aurelle, 10.50 p.m., 3 December, and 5.00 a.m., 4 December 1870, d'Aurelle, pp. 337–41.
33. D'Aurelle to Freycinet, 8.00 a.m., 4 December 1870, d'Aurelle, pp. 341–3.
34. D'Aurelle, p. 344.
35. Martin des Pallières, p. 218.
36. Ryan, p. 264.
37. GGS, vol. 3, Appendix XCIII, p. 16; Lehautcourt, *Campagne de la Loire: Coulmiers et Orléans*, p. 378.
38. Faidherbe, pp. 14, 87.
39. Daussy, p. 32.
40. Lehautcourt, *Campagne du Nord*, p. 34.
41. GGS, vol. 4, Appendix CII, p. 12.
42. GGS, vol. 4, Appendix XCIX, p. 12; Faidherbe, p. 29.
43. Rolin, pp. 207–17.
44. Freycinet to Prefect Desseaux, 10.30 p.m., 2 December 1870, Le Roy, p. 115.
45. Le Roy, pp. 139–41.
46. Rolin, pp. 257–8. Guy de Maupassant made the experience of this retreat the background to his story *L'Horrible*.
47. Rolin, pp. 268–9.
48. Text of Moltke's letter in Trochu, vol. 1, pp. 467–8; on peace feelers at the outpost line see Sarazin, p. 229.

Chapter 7

1. Labouchère, p. 188; Sarazin, pp. 232–3.
2. Trochu, vol. 1, pp. 471–2.
3. *Dépositions*, vol. 3, p. 96 (Ducrot).
4. Proclamation of 7 December 1870, Heylli, *Journal*, vol. 3, p. 42; Cabinet discussion of 6 December in *Procès verbaux*, pp. 87–90.
5. Ducrot, *DP*, vol. 3, pp. 112–36.
6. Trochu, vol. 1, p. 476.
7. Sarrepont, *Histoire*, pp. 221–33; Larchey, p. 87.
8. Simon, pp. 388–91, offers an unconvincing defence of the policy.
9. Heylli, *Journal*, vol. 3, pp. 81–2.
10. Evans, p. 497.
11. Sarcey, p. 173.
12. Sarrepont, *Histoire*, pp. 237–9.
13. See Sheppard, pp. 303–9, for week-on-week increases in food prices.
14. Larchey, pp. 205–6; Serman, *La Commune*, p. 149.
15. Duveau, p. 118.
16. *Le Gaulois*, p. 376, 30 December 1870; Larchey, p. 210.
17. Larchey, pp. 206, 222.
18. Sarcey, p. 254; and compare Favre, vol. 2, pp. 178–9.
19. Ducrot, *DP*, vol. 3, p. 117.
20. *Procès verbaux*, 5 December 1870, p. 86 (Simon); 10 & 12 December, pp. 91–2 (Favre).
21. Trochu, vol. 1, p. 481.
22. Trochu, vol. 1, pp. 345–6, 485.
23. Ducrot, *DP*, vol. 3, p. 162.

24. Lehautcourt, *SP*, vol. 3, Annexe 1; GGS, vol. 4, Appendix CXVII, pp. 87–8.
25. Viollet-le-Duc, p. 39.
26. Favre, vol. 2, p. 195.
27. *Journal Officiel*, 23 December 1870, Heylli, vol. 3, p. 179.
28. Rousset, *HG*, vol. 3, p. 339.
29. Ducrot, *DP*, vol. 3, p. 191.
30. Trochu, vol. 1, p. 487.
31. Favre, vol. 2, p. 197.
32. Hérisson, p. 266; Sarazin, p. 245; Ballue, p. 106.
33. Robinet de Cléry, p. 178.
34. Gambetta to Freycinet, 2.35 p.m. and 8.56 p.m., 12 December 1870, Reinach, *Dépêches*, vol. 1, pp. 267, 270.
35. Moltke, *The Franco-German War*, p. 236.
36. Érard, p. 102.
37. GGS, vol. 4, Appendix CVI, p. 33; Rousset, *HG*, vol. 4, p. 272.
38. Helvig, vol. 1, p. 313; Delorme, *Journal*, pp. 251–2; Érard, p. 113.
39. Delorme, *Journal*, pp. 229–30, 246–50.
40. Érard, pp. 112–22.
41. Quoted in Rousset, *HG*, vol. 4, pp. 311–12; and see Goltz, p. 190.
42. Molis, p. 90.
43. Moltke to Werder, 8 December 1870, GGS, vol. 4, Appendix CXII, p. 71.
44. GGS, vol. 4, p. 103 and Appendix CXIII, p. 72; Lehautcourt, *Campagne de l'Est: Nuits, Villersexel*, pp. 79–80.
45. Gambetta to Favre, 26 November and 11 December 1870, Favre, vol. 2, pp. 122–3, 176; Lehautcourt, *Campagne de l'Est: Nuits, Villersexel*, pp. 60, 131–3.
46. Freycinet, pp. 218–24.
47. Order of the day, 5 December 1870, Faidherbe, p. 85.
48. Revue d'histoire, *Guerre de 1870–71: Armée du Nord*, (cited hereafter as *Guerre: Armée du Nord*), vol. 2, pp. 36–8 & *documents annexés*, pp. 19–21; Genevoix, *Les coups de main*, pp. 97–109; and for an eyewitness account Patry, *La guerre telle qu'elle est*, pp. 276–87.
49. Daussy, p. 96.
50. GGS, vol. 4, p. 26.
51. Wartensleben, *Operations of the First Army*, p. 152.
52. Wartensleben, *Operations of the First Army*, pp. 165–6; *Guerre: Armée du Nord*, vol. 2, p. 128.
53. Allinson, p. 176, entry for 1 November.
54. Allinson, p. 224, entry for 16 December.
55. Allinson, p. 212, entry for 3 December.
56. For details see Pflanze, vol. 1, pp. 480–90.
57. Allinson, p. 224, entries for 15 & 16 December.
58. Sorel, vol. 2, pp. 91–132, 146–59.
59. *Bismarck's Letters to his Wife from the Seat of War*, pp. 56 (12 September), 76–7 (28–29 October), 85 (16 November), 87 (22 November).
60. Busch, *Bismarck in the Franco-German War*, vol. 1, pp. 196, 234, 242–3, 278, 333, vol. 2, pp. 19, 24, 30–1, 41, 42, 156, 224, 231.
61. GGS, vol. 3, p. 136, vol. 4, pp. 128–9.
62. Blumenthal, p. 197, and similarly pp. 158, 163, 165, 174, 178, 207.
63. Bronsart, pp. 249 (23 December), 281 (7 January) and 310 (25 January).
64. Blumenthal, pp. 240–1; Busch, *Bismarck in the Franco-German War*, vol. 1, p. 237.
65. Blumenthal, p. 177.

66. Allinson, pp. 165, 168, 175, 202–3, 221; Blumenthal, pp. 226, 229.
67. Sarrepont, *Le Bombardement*, pp. 73–8; Sarcey, pp. 303–4.

Chapter 8

1. Sarcey, p. 294; Paradis, pp. 299–300, entry for 29 December; Garnier, pp. 114–15, entries for 28 & 29 December 1870.
2. Ducrot, *DP*, vol. 3, pp. 253–71.
3. Ducrot, *DP*, vol. 3, p. 271.
4. Trochu, vol. 1, p. 459.
5. Ducrot, *DP*, vol. 4, pp. 33–6; Trochu, vol. 1, pp. 521–4.
6. Trochu, vol. 1, pp. 519–20; Heylli, *Journal*, vol. 3, p. 264.
7. Hérisson, pp. 175–9; Trochu, vol. 1, pp. 507–10.
8. Labouchère, p. 355.
9. Lehautcourt, *SP*, vol. 3, p. 219.
10. Ducrot, *DP*, vol. 3, pp. 203, 261, 265.
11. Ponchalon, p. 208; Sarazin, pp. 269–72; Dumont, pp. 332–3.
12. Viollet-le-Duc, p. xxxi.
13. Sarrepont, *Histoire*, pp. 155–7.
14. Larchey, pp. 206, 227, 231 (24 December 1870, 4 & 6 January 1871); Paradis, pp. 282, 290, 295–8, entries for 20, 25, & 28–9 December 1870; Sarrepont, *Histoire*, pp. 255–61.
15. Sarazin, p. 272.
16. GGS, vol. 5, Appendix CLXXXV, p. 100.
17. GGS, vol. 4, Appendix CLV, p. 222.
18. Correspondence in GGS, vol. 4, Appendix CXLVIII, p. 205 and Trochu, vol. 1, pp. 510–12.
19. Bismarck to Kern, Minister of the Swiss Confederation, 17 January 1871, in *Le Gaulois*, pp. 422–3.
20. Ducrot, *DP*, vol. 3, p. 282, vol. 4, pp. 412–3.
21. *Le Gaulois*, p. 45; Sarrepont, *Le Bombardement*, pp. 235–40.
22. *Le Gaulois*, pp. 397–8; Sarcey, pp. 304–6.
23. Sarrepont, *Le Bombardement*, pp. 223, 225–7, 277–81.
24. Sarrepont, *Le Bombardement*, pp. 169–71, 181, 261–3.
25. Lehautcourt, *SP*, vol. 3, annexe 10, p. 398; Sarrepont, *Le Bombardement*, pp. 181, 283–302; and on variations between sources see Rials, p. 135 & fn.
26. *Le Gaulois*, pp. 402–3, 405; Larchey, pp. 233–4; Sarcey, p. 308.
27. Sarazin, p. 267.
28. Sueur, pp. 28, 51; Morillon, p. 194; Brice & Bottet, p. 400.
29. Morillon, p. 192; Rials, pp. 201–2.
30. Pflanze, vol. 1, p. 497.
31. Bismarck to Johanna, 21 January 1871, *Bismarck's Letters to his Wife from the Seat of War*, p. 111.
32. Verdy, p. 244.
33. Letter of 2 February 1871, quoted in Gall, vol. 1, p. 372.
34. See Bartmann, pp. 332–69.
35. Busch, *Bismarck: Some Secret Pages of His History*, vol. 1, p. 255.
36. Allinson, p. 253.
37. Allinson, p. 258.
38. On the Bismarck-Moltke feud see Bronsart, pp. 303–4, 309–11 (22 & 25 January); and on its significance Craig, pp. 204–16; Ritter, vol. 1, pp. 219–27; and Stig Förster, 'The

Prussian Triangle of Leadership in the Face of a People's War' in Förster & Nagler, pp. 115–40.

39. Text in Heylli, *Journal*, vol. 3, pp. 505–8.
40. See reports of Clément Thomas dated 6 & 14 December 1870 in Ducrot, *DP*, vol. 2, pp. 420–4.
41. Favre, vol. 2, pp. 316–17.
42. Gambetta to Trochu, 23 & 24 December 1870, Gambetta to Favre 31 December 1870, in Reinach, *Dépêches*, vol. 1, pp. 189–212.
43. Ducrot, *DP*, vol. 3, p. 294; *Procès verbaux*, p. 125 (session of 17 January 1871).
44. *Dépositions*, vol. 2, p. 284 (Schmitz).
45. Hérisson, p. 270.
46. Sarcey, p. 319.
47. *Le Français*, 20 January 1871.
48. Trochu, vol. 1, p. 528; Lehautcourt, *SP*, vol. 3, p. 252 fn.
49. Faverot de Kerbrech, pp. 253–5.
50. GGS, vol. 4, p. 385 and Appendix CLV, p. 219; Lehautcourt, *SP*, vol. 3, p. 289 and Annexe 12.
51. Ducrot, *DP*, vol. 4, pp. 67–191; Sarazin, pp. 288–9.
52. Rouquette, p. 7; and see Duportal, pp. 52–3, 76–7.
53. Trochu, vol. 1, p. 536; and see Ballue, pp. 120, 128–9, 136–7; Vinoy, *Siège de Paris*, pp. 411–12, 414; Garnier, pp. 141, 148, entries for 18 & 21 January 1871; and for the postwar controversy involving Ducrot see Heylli, *Journal*, vol. 3, pp. 629–39.
54. *Le Gaulois*, p. 435.
55. On Regnault see Clayson, pp. 234–72 and Milner, pp. 123, 212–13.
56. Sarcey, pp. 321–2.
57. Maury, p. 34; and see Garnier, pp. 153–4, entry for 22 January 1871.
58. Favre, vol. 2, p. 342.
59. Favre, vol. 2, pp. 334, 360, 362–3.
60. Claretie, *Paris assiégé*, p. 188.
61. *Dépositions*, vol. 2, pp. 225–6 (Legge) and p. 233 (Vabre). For an assessment of the evidence see Rials, pp. 175–8.
62. Favre, vol. 2, p. 358.
63. Favre, vol. 2, p. 346; Reinach, *Dépêches*, vol. 1, pp. 222–9.
64. Chanzy to Gambetta, 23 & 30 December 1870, 2 & 6 January 1871; Gambetta to Chanzy, 27 December 1870, 5 January 1871; Freycinet to Chanzy, 7 January 1871, in Chanzy, pp. 251–72.
65. GGS, vol. 4, Appendix CXXI, p. 96.
66. Érard, pp. 154–5.
67. General Orders Nos. 208 & 209, 9 & 10 January 1871, in Chanzy, pp. 313–16, 328–32.
68. Gougeard, pp. 50–1.
69. Gougeard, p. xviii.
70. Gambetta to Freycinet, 10.45 a.m., 18 December 1870, in [France] Assemblée Nationale, *Enquête parlementaire ... Rapport par A. de la Borderie: Le Camp de Conlie et l'Armée de Bretagne*, p. 233, No. 54.
71. Chanzy, p. 350.
72. Mauni, pp. 187, 189 (French edition), letters of 15 & 16 January 1871.
73. GGS, vol. 4, p. 210 and Appendix CXXII; Lehautcourt, *Campagne de la Loire: Josnes, Vendôme, Le Mans*, pp. 288, 290.
74. Daussy, pp. 170–4.

75. *Guerre: Armée du Nord*, vol. 3, pp. 6–7, 11–13.
76. Gensoul, p. 67.
77. Rappe, p. 135.
78. Patry, *La guerre telle qu'elle est*, pp. 345–6.
79. Rappe, p. 155; Patry, *La guerre telle qu'elle est*, p. 353.
80. Faidherbe, p. 47.
81. Wartensleben, *Operations of the First Army*, p. 198 fn.; Faidherbe, p. 48; *Guerre: Armée du Nord*, vol. 3, p. 68.
82. Patry, *La guerre telle qu'elle est*, pp. 364–5.
83. GGS, vol. 4, Appendix CXXVII, p. 126; Faidherbe, p. 61.
84. GGS, vol. 4, p. 264 and Appendix CXXVI, p. 123: *Guerre: Armée du Nord*, vol. 4, pp. 46–7.
85. Patry, *La guerre telle qu'elle est*, pp. 376–9.
86. Gensoul, p. 103.
87. *Guerre: Armée du Nord*, vol. 4, p. 148; GGS, vol. 4, p. 276 and Appendix CXXVII, p. 127.
88. Freycinet to Gambetta, 12.45 p.m., 14 December, 1870, [France] Assemblée Nationale, *Enquête ... Rapport Rainneville*, p. 489.
89. Freycinet to Gambetta, 10.57 a.m., 24 December 1870, [France] Assemblée Nationale, *Enquête ... vol. 2, Expédition de l'Est*, (cited hereafter as *Rapport Perrot*), p. 535, No. 589.
90. Bourbaki to Fourichon, 25 October 1870, *Dépositions*, vol. 3, p. 367 (Bourbaki) and p. 383 (Leperche).
91. *Rapport Perrot*, pp. 86–7; Grenest, *L'Armée de l'Est*, pp. 959–60; Genevois, *Les Premières Campagnes dans l'Est*, pp. 345–6 fn.
92. Chanzy, p. 270.
93. Moltke to Werder, 6.00 p.m., 30 December 1870, *Guerre: Étude sur la campagne du Général Bourbaki dans l'est*, vol. 1, p. 369.
94. Freycinet to de Serres, 10.10 p.m., 1 January, 1871, *Rapport Perrot*, p. 604, No. 5376.
95. Grenest, *L'Armée de l'Est*, p. 596.
96. Secrétan, pp. 106–7.
97. Intendant Général Friant, quoted in Secrétan p. 93 fn.
98. Secrétan, p. 107.
99. Beauquier, p. 122.
100. Secrétan, p. 118.
101. GGS, vol. 4, Appendix CXLI, p. 182; *Guerre: Étude sur la campagne du Général Bourbaki dans l'est*, vol. 2, p. 500.
102. Bitteau, pp. 311–12.
103. Circular from Interior and War Ministries to Prefects, 11.30 p.m., 9 January 1871, *Rapport Perrot*, p. 654, No. 7252a.
104. Spelled Lizaine on modern maps.
105. GGS, vol. 4, p. 358.
106. GGS, vol. 4, Appendix CXL, p. 176.
107. Thoumas, *Paris, Tours, Bordeaux*, p. 227; and see Beaunis, pp. 185–6.
108. Beaunis, p. 188.
109. GGS, vol. 4, Appendix CXLI, p. 186; *Dépositions*, vol. 3, p. 396 (Leperche).
110. Allinson, p. 210.
111. Wartensleben, *Operations of the South Army*, p. 125 (returns for 21 January 1871).
112. Bourbaki's conversation with chef d'escadron d'artillerie Bruyère, 17 January 1871, *Dépositions*, vol. 3, p. 478 (Billot).
113. Wartensleben, *Operations of the South Army*, p. 30 fn.
114. Colonel Lobbia, quoted in *Rapport Perrot*, p. 317.

115. Bordone to Freycinet, 8.30 a.m. and 10.35 a.m., 16 January, and 9.45 p.m., 17 January 1871, *Rapport Perrot*, pp. 683, 685, 689, Nos. 7912, 7972, 746.
116. GGS, vol. 5, Appendix CLXXI, p. 42. On instances of German atrocities during the fighting around Dijon see Theyras, pp. 580–2; Lehautcourt, *Campagne de l'Est: Héricourt, La Cluse*, pp. 132, 139 fn. 1, and Molis, pp. 190–1, 196.
117. Freycinet to Gambetta, 10.45 a.m., 24 January 1871, *Rapport Perrot*, p. 743, No. 7278.
118. Freycinet to Bourbaki, 9.40 a.m., 24 January 1871, *Rapport Perrot*, pp. 741–2, No. 7269.
119. Freycinet to Bourbaki, 2.30 p.m. and 4.55 p.m., 25 January 1871, Freycinet, pp. 264–6. Possibly Freycinet hoped that Pontailler, west of Besançon, was intended.
120. Bourbaki to Freycinet, 8.30 p.m., 24 January 1871, *Dépositions*, vol. 3, p. 375.
121. Bourbaki to Freycinet, 9.00 p.m., 24 January, and 0.45 a.m., 25 January 1871, *Dépositions*, vol. 3, pp. 375–6.
122. Déroulède, p. 219.
123. Beauquier, p. 158.
124. Bourbaki's report to the War Minister, 3 March 1871, *Rapport Perrot*, pp. 196–7; Eichthal, pp. 320, 321, 335.
125. *Dépositions*, vol. 3, p. 479 (Billot).
126. Leperche's diary narrating the circumstances is reproduced in Eichthal, pp. 336–54.
127. Gambetta to Bourbaki, 5.56 p.m., 26 January 1871, *Rapport Perrot*, p. 767, No. 7561.
128. *Guerre: Mesures d'organisation depuis le début de la guerre*, p. 57; *Guerre: La Défense nationale en province: mesures générales d'organisation*, vol. 1, p. 553 fn.
129. GGS, vol. 5, Appendix CLXXIV.
130. Grenest, *L'Armée de l'Est*, pp. 874–94; Genevois, *Les coups de main*, pp. 111–41.
131. *Guerre: La Défense nationale en province: mesures générales d'organisation*, vol. 1, pp. 42–3; text in Jacqmin, pp. 19–20.

Chapter 9

1. Testelin to Gambetta, 20 January 1871, Reinach, *Dépêches*, vol. 2, p. 530.
2. Reinach, *Dépêches*, vol. 1, pp. 72–6.
3. *Dépostions*, vol. 3, p. 216 (Chanzy).
4. *Guerre: La Défense nationale en province: mesures générales d'organisation*, vol. 1, p. 553 fn.
5. Gallard, pp. 343–4; and similarly Beauquier, pp. 159–60.
6. Favre, vol. 2, p. 382.
7. Napoléon III to Eugénie, 21 December 1870, quoted in Baumont, *L'Échiquier de Metz*, pp. 337–8; and see generally pp. 331–45 on Bismarck's contacts with the Bonapartes in the winter of 1870–71.
8. Bismarck to Manteuffel, 20 February 1871, quoted in Baumont, *L'Échiquier de Metz*, p. 344.
9. Busch, *Bismarck in the Franco-German War*, vol. 2, p. 239.
10. Larchey, p. 271.
11. Sarazin, p. 303; and see Favre, vol. 2, p. 405.
12. Ducrot, *DP*, vol. 4, pp. 267–9.
13. See Ducrot, *DP*, vol. 4, pp. 242–4, 450–6. The Germans eventually decided not to pursue the matter – see Faverot, pp. 271–81.
14. On the Beaufort episode see Busch, *Bismarck in the Franco-German War*, vol. 2, pp. 261–2, 264–5; Allinson, p. 285; Hérisson, pp. 305–7; and Guillemin, *La Capitulation*, pp. 320–5. Beaufort's and Valdan's testimonies are in *Dépositions*, vol. 3, pp. 163–85.
15. Text of the convention in GGS, vol. 4, Appendix CLVI, pp. 227–32.
16. Baumont, *L'Échiquier de Metz*, p. 341.

17. Vinoy, *L'Armistice et la Commune*, pp. 102–3.
18. Favre, vol. 2, pp. 374–5, 398; Sorel, vol. 2, pp. 168–9, 173–4; Hérisson, pp. 294–5.
19. Sarcey, p. 333. For reactions to the armistice in the capital see also Paradis, pp. 359–75; Garnier, pp. 156–64; Lecaillon, *Le Siège de Paris*, pp. 227–40.
20. Based on cumulative totals of returns for III & IV Armies in GGS, vol. 3, Appendix LXXI, pp. 24, 32; Appendix XCVII, p. 175, and vol. 4, Appendix CXVII, p. 90 and Appendix CLV, p. 225.
21. Ducrot, *DP*, vol. 4, pp. 392, 397. Note though that Vinoy, *L'Armistice et la Commune*, p. 107, states that 32,000 men wounded by the enemy were still in hospital on 1 March.
22. GGS, vol. 4, p. 390; Sarrepont, *Histoire*, pp. 436–7.
23. In the National Assembly on 21 March 1871; see Guillemin, *L'Avènement de M. Thiers*, p. 189.
24. Favre, vol. 2, pp. 401–3; Busch, *Bismarck in the Franco-German War*, vol. 2, pp. 336–7; Sorel, vol. 2, pp. 169, 179; *Dépositions*, vol. 3, p. 179 (Valdan). Verdy, p. 249, claimed that the exclusion had been made at the request of the French negotiators, but the account of Lieutenant Calvel, who was present at the negotiations as Beaufort's aide, makes clear that the deferment was at the initiative of Moltke and Bismarck. See *Dépositions*, vol. 3, p. 173.
25. Beaunis, p. 197.
26. *Dépositions*, vol. 3, p. 313 (Clinchant).
27. Beauquier, pp. 187–8.
28. Beaunis, p. 201.
29. Thoumas, *Paris, Tours, Bordeaux*, p. 219.
30. *Dépositions*, vol. 3, pp. 336–7 (Rapport Clamorgan).
31. *Dépositions*, vol. 3, p. 309 (Clinchant).
32. GGS, vol. 5, p. 73.
33. Davall, p. 42.
34. Davall, pp. 44, 83; *Dépositions*, vol. 3, p. 344.
35. See Meyer & Horat and Finck & Ganz. The restored painting is housed in Lucerne.
36. Secrétan, p. 557.
37. For details, besides the official report of Davall, see Ortholan, *L'Armée de l'Est*, pp. 77–102; and Meyer & Horat, pp. 65–107.
38. Text of the protocol, signed by Bismarck and Favre, in GGS, vol. 5, Appendix CLXX, pp. 39–40.
39. GGS, vol. 5, p. 102.
40. *Circulaire aux préfets et sous-préfets*, 0.35 a.m., 31 January 1871, Reinach, *Dépêches*, vol. 1, p. 407.
41. *Proclamation aux Français*, 31 January, 1871, Reinach, *Dépêches*, vol. 1, pp. 55–8.
42. *Décret relatif aux élections du 8 février*, 31 January 1871, Reinach, *Dépêches*, vol. 2, pp. 124–5.
43. Bismarck to Gambetta, 2 February 1871, Favre, vol. 3, p. 24.
44. *Intérieur aux préfets – Circulaire*, 10.30 p.m., 2 February 1871, Reinach, *Dépêches*, vol. 1, pp. 411–12.
45. *Dépositions*, vol. 4, p. 552 (Silvy).
46. *Dépositions*, vol. 1, pp. 505–8 (Simon).
47. Thoumas, *Paris, Tours, Bordeaux*, pp. 224–5.
48. Glais-Bizoin, p. 204.
49. Patry, *La guerre telle qu'elle est*, p. 390.
50. Hugo, pp. 248–51.
51. Favre, vol. 3, pp. 81–7.
52. Busch, *Bismarck in the Franco-German War*, vol. 2, p. 341.

53. Allinson, p. 316.
54. Text of the Peace Preliminaries in GGS, vol. 5, Appendix CLXXIX, pp. 74–9. On the negotiations see Thiers, pp. 109–27; Favre, vol. 3, pp. 89–120.
55. Favre, vol. 3, p. 139.
56. Viollet-le-Duc, p. xi.
57. Chanzy, p. 444; Claretie, *Histoire*, pp. 566–7; GGS, vol. 5, Appendix CLXXX, pp. 80–1.
58. Claretie, *Histoire*, p. 575.
59. See Welschinger, vol. 2, pp. 162–7, which includes a facsimile of the draft motion.
60. Grosjean, pp. 247–8.
61. Rousset, *L'Armistice*, p. 101.
62. *La Gironde*, 4 March 1871, reprinted in Reinach, *Discours*, vol. 2, p. 14.
63. Forbes, vol. 2, p. 457. See also Russell, pp. 573–6, and Yriarte, *Les Prussiens à Paris*, pp. 55–111.
64. Busch, *Bismarck in the Franco-German War*, vol. 2, p. 346.
65. Flamarion, pp. 131–2.
66. Chuquet, *Le Général Chanzy*, p. 207.
67. Paschal Grousset to commander of German III Corps, 27 March 1871, Sorel, vol. 2, p. 268.
68. Mitchell, *The German Influence*, p. 18.
69. Text of the Treaty in GGS, vol. 5, Appendix CLXXXII, pp. 86–93. On the negotiations see Favre, vol. 3, pp. 352–76, and Giesberg, p. 127 ff.
70. Favre, vol. 3, p. 433.
71. Flamarion, p. 169.
72. Words attributed in Claretie, *Histoire*, p. 681.
73. On the extent of the fires and the evidence concerning their origins see Rials, pp. 482–509.
74. Serman, *La Commune*, p. 512.
75. Lissagaray, p. 393. For a cautionary note see Tombs, *The War Against Paris*, pp. 190–1 and Rials, p. 271 fn.; and for a recent discussion Milza, *La Commune*, pp. 467–74.
76. Rougerie, *Paris libre*, p. 257.

Conclusion

1. Quoted in Mosse, p. 355.
2. See Sorel, vol. 2, pp. 119–20.
3. Busch, *Bismarck in the Franco-German War*, vol. 2, p. 253.
4. *The Quarterly Review*, (London), vol. 129, October 1870, pp. 547–8, 556.
5. Hansard, *Parliamentary Debates*, Third Series, vol. 204, cols. 81–2.
6. Sir Robert Peel, 17 February 1871, Hansard, *Parliamentary Debates*, Third Series, vol. 204, cols. 404–5.
7. See Bibliography under Chesney; and for the stir caused by the pamphlet Raymond, pp. 403–4 and Briggs.
8. Morier to Lady Derby, 5 January 1871, quoted in Mosse, pp. 357–8.
9. Quoted in Howard, p. 299.
10. GGS, vol. 5, Appendix CLXXXIX, p. 105.
11. GGS, vol. 5, pp. 223, 229–30, and Appendix CXCIII, pp. 109–10.
12. Allinson, p. 241.
13. Chenu, vol. 1, p. xxvi; and for analysis of French medical performance Delorme, *Traité*, vol. 1, pp. 338–62, 371, vol. 2, pp. 972–80.
14. Martinien, vol. 1, p. 138, vol. 2, p. 228, and supplements and errata pp. 229–34.
15. GGS, vol. 5, p. 247.
16. Prost, p. 136 fn. This figure included 354 refugees in the town.

17. Sueur, pp. 28, 51, 74.
18. Poidevin & Bariéty, p. 103.
19. Roth, *La Guerre de 70*, pp. 512–22.
20. *Guerre: La Défense nationale en province: mesures générales d'organisation*, pp. 124–8. These figures exclude 88,000 men raised in the Departments but not mustered into national service at the end of the war.
21. Bitteau, p. 272.
22. Sarazin, p. 322.
23. Favre, vol. 2, p. 383.
24. Proclamation of 22 May 1871, Rougerie, *Paris libre*, p. 251.
25. See Gerd Krumeich, 'The Myth of Gambetta and the "People's War" in Germany and France, 1871–1914' in Förster & Nagler, pp. 641–55.
26. A paraphrase of words used by him in a speech at Saint-Quentin on 16 November 1871: see Bury, *Gambetta and the Making of the Third Republic*, p. 68.
27. Becker & Audoin-Rouzeau, p. 155.
28. Foch, pp. 16–17.
29. De Gaulle, p. 185.
30. *Dépositions*, vol. 3, p. 167.
31. Crouzat, p. 41.
32. Hindenburg, p. 42.
33. Goltz, p. 358.
34. Dépositions, vol. 1, p. 421.
35. Bazaine to his brother, December 1887, quoted in Baumont, *Bazaine*, p. 334.
36. See Annette Becker, 'War Memorials: a Legacy of Total War?' in Förster & Nagler, pp. 657–80.
37. Gabriel Syveton, *Revue Bleue: Revue politique et littéraire*, 11 December 1897, p. 791. On commemoration of the war and its legacy see Roth, *La Guerre de 70*, pp. 605–726.
38. Ducrot to General Du Barail, 26 & 27 March 1874, Chalvet-Nastrac, pp. 204–5; Du Barail, vol. 3, p. 474.
39. Daudet, 'The Last French Lesson' and 'Mon képi' in *Contes du Lundi*.
40. Maupassant, *Sur l'eau* (English edition), pp. 30–4.
41. Maupassant, 'La Guerre', *Gil Blas*, 11 December 1883. Digeon remains the classic study of the war's influence on French writers.
42. G.V., 'Le Panorama de la Bataille de Rezonville', *Le Moniteur Universel*, 31 March 1887, p. 466. For modern illustrations of the surviving fragments of the cyclorama see Robichon, pp. 46–9.

Bibliography

Square brackets around the author's name indicate that the work was published anonymously.

About, Edmond, *Alsace, 1871–1872*, 4th ed., Paris, 1874.

Achard, Amédée, *Récits d'un soldat*, Paris, 1947.

Allinson, A.R. (trans. and ed.), *The War Diary of the Emperor Frederick III*, London 1927.

Ambert, Joachim, *Gaulois et Germains: récits militaires*, 4 vols., Paris, 1883–85.

———, *Les Frères des Écoles Chrétiennes*, Paris, 1878.

Amson, Daniel, *Adolphe Crémieux: l'oublié de la gloire*, Paris, 1988.

[Andlau, Comte Joseph d'], *Metz: Campagne et Négociations*, Paris, 1872.

Antonmattei, Pierre, *Gambetta, héraut de la République*, Paris, 1999.

Arsac, Joanni d', *Les Frères des Écoles Chrétiennes pendant la Guerre de 1870–1871*, Paris, 1872.

Astruc, Pierre, 'La guerre de 1870–1871 et la médecine', *Le Progrès Médical*, Paris, 1960, pp. 219–26, 236–46, 256–9, 275–81, 295–300.

Aube, Théophile, 'Le Vingtième Corps de l'Armée de la Loire', *Revue des Deux Mondes*, Paris, 1 July 1871, pp. 5–25.

Audoin-Rouzeau, Stéphane, *1870: La France dans la Guerre*, Paris, 1989.

Aurelle de Paladines, Louis Jean-Baptiste d', *La Première Armée de la Loire*, Paris, 1872.

Autin, Jean, *L'Impératrice Eugénie: ou l'empire d'une femme*, Paris, 1990.

Baconin, Jérôme, *Mémoire en images: Paris 1870–1871, L'Année terrible*, Saint-Cyr, 2007.

Badsey, Stephen, *The Franco-Prussian War* (Osprey Essential Histories), Oxford, 2003.

Baldick, Robert, *The Siege of Paris*, London, 1964.

Ballue, Arthur, *Les Zouaves à Paris pendant le siège (Souvenirs d'un zouave)*, Paris, 1872.

Barjaud, Yves, *La Garde nationale mobile (1868–1872)*, Aire-sur-l'Adour, 1970.

Barral, Pierre, *Léon Gambetta: Tribun et stratège de la République (1838–1882)*, Toulouse, 2008.

Barry, Quintin, *The Franco-Prussian War*, 2 vols., Solihull, 2007.

Baumont, Maurice, *Bazaine: les secrets d'un maréchal (1811–1888)*, Paris, 1978.

———, *L'Échiquier de Metz: Empire ou République 1870*, Paris, 1971.

Bazaine, François Achille, *Épisodes de la guerre de 1870 et le blocus de Metz*, Madrid, 1883.

———, *L'Armée du Rhin*, 2nd ed., Paris, 1872.

———, *Procès Bazaine. Seul compte rendu sténographique in extenso des séances du 1er Conseil de Guerre de la 1re Division Militaire ayant siégé à Versailles (Trianon) du 6 octobre au 10 décembre 1873*, Paris, 1873.

Beaunis, Henri, *Impressions de campagne (1870–1871)*, Paris, 1887.

Beauquier, Charles, *Les dernières campagnes dans l'Est*, Paris, 1873.

Becker, Jean-Jacques & Audoin-Rouzeau, Stéphane, *La France, La Nation, La Guerre 1850–1920*, Paris, 1995.

Bertin, Pierre, *1870–1871: Désillusions dans l'Est*, Besançon, 2007.

Binoche, Jacques, *Histoire des relations franco-allemandes de 1789 à nos jours*, Paris, 1996.

Bismarck, Otto von, *Bismarck the Man and the Statesman: Being the Reflections and Reminiscences of Otto Prince von Bismarck* (trans. A.J. Butler), 2 vols., London, 1898.

————, *Bismarck's Letters to his Wife from the Seat of War, 1870–1871*, (translated by Armin Harder, with an introduction by Walter Littlefield), New York, 1903.

Bitteau, J., *Strasbourg – L'Armée de la Loire – L'Armée de l'Est: souvenirs d'un télégraphiste*, Épinal, 1898.

Blume, Wilhelm, *Die Operationen der deutschen Heere von der Schlacht bei Sedan bis zum Ende des Krieges*, Berlin, 1872.

Blumenthal, Karl Konstantin Albrecht Leonhard von, *Journals of Field-Marshal Count von Blumenthal for 1866 and 1870–71*, London, 1903.

Bodenhorst, G., *Le Siège de Strasbourg en 1870*, Paris & Antwerp, 1876.

Bois, Maurice, *Sur la Loire: batailles et combats*, Paris, 1888.

Boissier, Pierre, *Histoire du Comité International de la Croix-Rouge: du Solférino à Tsoushima*, Paris, 1963.

Bordone, Joseph, *Garibaldi et l'Armée des Vosges*, Paris, 1871.

Boucher, Auguste, *Bataille de Loigny, avec les combats de Villepion et de Poupry*, 2nd ed., Orléans, 1872.

————, *Combat d'Orléans, 11 octobre 1870*, 3rd ed., Orléans, 1871.

————, *Récits de l'invasion. Journal d'un bourgeois d'Orléans pendant l'occupation prussienne*, Orléans, 1871.

[Bourgeois de Paris]. *See* Paradis.

Bourgin, Georges, *La Guerre de 1870–1871 et la Commune*, Paris, 1947.

Bournand, François, *Le Clergé pendant la Guerre de 1870–1871*, Paris, 1891.

Brice, Léon Raoul Marie & Bottet, Maurice, *Le Corps de Santé Militaire en France, 1708–1882*, Paris, 1907.

Briggs, Asa, ed., *The Battle of Dorking Controversy: A Collection of Pamphlets*, London, 1972.

Broglie, Gabriel de, *MacMahon*, Paris, 2000.

Bronsart von Schellendorf, Paul, *Geheimes Kriegstagebuch, 1870–1871*, Bonn, 1954.

Brunet-Moret, Jean, *Le Général Trochu 1815–1896*, Paris, 1955.

Bucholz, Arden, *Moltke and the German Wars, 1864–1871*, New York, 2001.

Bury, J.P.T. & Tombs, R.P., *Thiers 1797–1877: A Political Life*, London, 1986.

Bury, J.P.T., *Gambetta and the National Defence: A Republican Dictatorship in France*, London, 1936.

————, *Gambetta and the Making of the Third Republic*, London, 1973.

Busch, Moritz, *Bismarck in the Franco-German War 1870–1871*, 2 vols., London, 1879.

————, *Bismarck: Some Secret Pages From His History*, 3 vols., London, 1898.

Camô, Charles, *2me Armée de la Loire. Colonne mobile de Tours . . . Combats du 7 décembre 1870. Bataille de Josnes*, Paris, 1888.

Carr, William, *A History of Germany 1815–1990* (4th edition), London, 1990.

————, *The Origins of the Wars of German Unification*, Harlow, 1991.

Challener, Richard D, *The French Theory of the Nation in Arms 1866–1939*, New York, 1965.

Chalvet-Nastrac, Henry Charles F.M.D. de, *Les Projets de restauration monarchique et le Général Ducrot, député et commandant du 8 Corps d'armée, d'après ses mémoires et sa correspondance*, Paris, 1909.

Chanal, Michel, *La Guerre de 70*, Paris, 1972.

Chandler, David, *The Military Maxims of Napoleon*, London, 1987.

Chanzy, Alfred, *La Deuxième Armée de la Loire*, 10th ed., Paris, 1894.

Chenu, Jean-Charles, Dr, *Aperçu historique, statistique et clinique sur le Service des Ambulances et des Hôpitaux de la Société Française de Secours aux Bléssés des Armées de Terre et de Mer pendant La Guerre de 1870–1871*, 2 vols., Paris, 1874.

Chesnais, Jean-Claude, *Les Morts violentes en France depuis 1826: comparaisons internationales*, Paris, 1976.

[Chesney, George Tomkyns], *The Battle of Dorking: Reminiscences of a Volunteer*, Edinburgh & London, May 1871.

Chevalier, Casimir, *Tours capitale: La Délégation gouvernementale et l'occupation prussienne, 1870–1871*, Tours, 1896.

Christiansen, Rupert, *Paris Babylon: The Story of the Paris Commune*, New York, 1996.

Chuquet, Arthur, *La Guerre 1870–71*, Paris, 1895.

————, *Le Général Chanzy, 1823–1883*, Paris, 1884.

Cilleuls, J. des, *Le Service de Santé Militaire de ses origines à nos jours*, Paris, 1961.

Claretie, Jules, *Histoire de la Révolution de 1870–71*, Paris, 1872.

————, *Paris assiégé: journal 1870–1871*, reprint, Paris, 1992.

Clayson, Hollis, *Paris in Despair: Art and Everyday Life under Siege (1870–71)*, Chicago, 2002.

Cochin, Augustin, 'Le Service de Santé des Armées avant et pendant le Siège de Paris', *Revue des Deux Mondes*, Paris, 1 November 1870, pp. 58–80.

Coffinières de Nordeck, Grégoire Gaspard Félix, *Capitulation de Metz: réponse du Général Coffinières de Nordeck à ses détracteurs*, 2nd ed., Brussels, 1871.

Comité d'Histoire du Service de Santé, *Histoire de la Médecine aux Armées*, 3 vols., Paris-Limoges, 1984.

Comité des Ambulances de la Presse, *Les Ambulances de la Presse ... pendant le Siège et sous la Commune 1870–1871*, Paris, 1872.

Contamine, Henry, *La Revanche 1871–1914*, Paris, 1957.

Coursier, Alain, *Faidherbe, du Sénégal à l'Armée du Nord*, Paris, 1989.

Craig, Gordon A., *The Politics of the Prussian Army 1640–1945*, 2nd ed., New York, 1964.

Crane, Edward A. (M.D.), *The Memoirs of Dr. Thomas W. Evans: Recollections of the Second French Empire*, 2 vols., London, 1905.

Crouzat, Joseph Constant, 'Le 20e corps à l'Armée de la Loire', *Journal des sciences militaires des armées de terre et de mer*, Paris, 1873, pp. 41–56.

Daily News, *The Daily News Correspondence of the War Between Germany and France 1870–1*, London, 1871.

Dalsème, Achille J., *Paris pendant le siège et les soixante-cinq jours de la Commune*, Paris, 1871.

Dansette, Adrien, *Du 2 décembre au 4 septembre*, Paris, 1972.

Daudet, Alphonse, *Contes du lundi*, Paris, 1873.

Daussy, H., *La Ligne de la Somme pendant la Campagne 1870–1871*, Paris, 1875.

Davall, E., *Les Troupes françaises internées en Suisse à la fin de la guerre franco-allemande en 1871: Rapport rédigé par ordre du Département Militaire Fédéral ...*, Berne, 1873.

Debuchy, Victor, *La Vie à Paris pendant le Siège 1870–1871*, Paris, 1999.

————, *Les Ballons du Siège de Paris*, Paris, 1973.

Decaux, Alain, *Blanqui l'insurgé*, Paris, 1976.

Deligny, Édouard Jean Étienne, *1870: Armée de Metz*, 3rd ed., Paris, 1871.

Delorme, Amédée, *Journal d'un sous-officier, 1870*, Paris, 1891.

Delorme, Edmond, *Traité de chirurgie de guerre*, 2 vols., Paris, 1888.

Delpérier, Louis, *La Garde impériale de Napoléon III*, Nantes, 2000.

Déroulède, Paul, *70–71: Nouvelles feuilles de route*, 23rd ed., Paris, 1907.

Deschaumes, Edmond, *L'Armée du Nord (1870–1871): Campagne du Général Faidherbe*, Paris, 1895.

————, *Journal d'un Lycéen de 14 ans pendant le Siège de Paris (1870–1871)*, Paris, 1893.

————, *La Retraite infernale: Armée de la Loire (1870–1871)*, Paris, 1891.

Desmarest, Jacques, *La Défense Nationale 1870–1871*, Paris, 1949.

Digeon, Claude, *La crise allemande de la pensée française*, Paris, 1959.

Du Barail, François Charles, *Mes Souvenirs*, 3 vols., Paris, 1894–96.

Du Camp, Maxime, *La Croix Rouge de France: Société de Secours aux Blessés Militaires de Terre et de Mer*, Paris, 1889.

————, *Souvenirs d'un demi-siècle*, 2 vols., Paris, 1949.

Ducrot, Auguste, *La Défense de Paris (1870–1871)*, 4 vols., Paris, 1875–78.

————, *La Vie militaire du Général Ducrot d'après sa correspondance (1839–1871). Publiée par ses enfants*, 2 vols., Paris, 1895.

Ducrot, Joseph, *L'Évasion du Général Ducrot: 11 septembre 1870*, Fécamp, 1913.

Dumas, J.-B., *La Guerre sur les communications allemandes en 1870*, Paris, 1891.

Dumont, Albert, 'Les mobilisés aux avant-postes', *Revue des Deux Mondes*, Paris, 15 January 1871, pp. 321–45.

Dunant, Henry, *Mémoires* (ed. Bernard Gagnebin), Lausanne, 1971.

Dupont, Léonce, *Tours et Bordeaux: Souvenirs de la République à outrance*, Paris, 1877.

Duportal, Armand, *Procès du Général Ducrot contre l'Émancipation: comte-rendu complet des débats*, Paris, 1872.

Dupuy, Aimé, *1870–1871: La Guerre, La Commune et la Presse*, Paris, 1959.

Dutrait-Crozon, Henri [pseudonym of Colonels Larpent & Delebecque], *Gambetta et la Défense Nationale 1870–1871*, Paris, 1934.

Duveau, Georges, *Le Siège de Paris, septembre 1870 – janvier 1871*, Paris, 1939.

Edgar-Bonnet, George, *Ferdinand de Lesseps: après Suez – Le pionnier de Panama*, Paris, 1959.

Edwards, Stewart, *The Paris Commune 1871*, London, 1971.

[Eichthal, Louis d'], *Le Général Bourbaki. Par un de ses anciens officiers d'ordonnance*, Paris, 1885.

Engels, Friedrich, *Notes on the War: Sixty Articles reprinted from the Pall Mall Gazette*, Vienna, 1923.

Érard, Denis, *Souvenirs d'un Mobile de la Sarthe, 33e Régiment, Armée de la Loire (16e corps)*, 3rd ed., Le Mans, 1911.

Evans, Thomas W., *History of the American Ambulance Established in Paris During the Siege of 1870–71*, London, 1873.

Faidherbe, Louis, *Campagne de l'Armée du Nord en 1870–1871*, Paris, 1871.

Faverot de Kerbrech, F.N.G.N., *Mes Souvenirs: La Guerre contre l'Allemagne (1870–1871)*, Paris, 1905.

Favre, Jules, *Gouvernement de la Défense Nationale*, 3 vols., Paris, 1871–75.

Fay, Charles, *Journal d'un Officier de l'Armée du Rhin*, 5th ed., Paris, 1889.

Félix, Gabrielle, *Le Général Ducrot*, Tours, 1896.

Feuchtwanger, Edgar, *Bismarck*, London, 2002.

Finck, Heinz Dieter & Ganz, Michael T., *Le Panorama Bourbaki*, Besançon, 2002.

Fischbach, Gustave, *Le Siège et le bombardement de Strasbourg*, Strasbourg, 1871.

Flach, Jacques, *Strasbourg après le bombardement, 2 octobre 1870 – 30 septembre 1872*, Strasbourg, 1873.

Flamarion, Dr A., *Le Livret du docteur: souvenirs de la campagne contre l'Allemagne et contre la Commune de Paris, 1870–1871*, Paris, 1872.

Foch, Ferdinand, *De la conduite de la guerre*, 3rd ed., Paris, 1915.

Forbes, Archibald, *My Experiences of the War Between France and Germany*, 2 vols., London, 1871.

Förster, Stig & Nagler, Jörg, *On the Road to Total War: The American Civil War and the German Wars of Unification, 1861–1871*, Cambridge, 1997.

[France], *Annuaire de la marine et des colonies*, Paris, 1870.

————, *Annuaire militaire de L'Empire français pour l'année 1870*, Paris, January 1870.

————, Assemblée Nationale, *Enquête parlementaire sur les actes du Gouvernement de la Défense Nationale*, 18 vols., Versailles, 1872–75.

————, État-major. *See* Revue d'histoire.

Freycinet, Charles de, *La Guerre en province pendant le Siège de Paris, 1870–1871*, 14th ed., Paris, 1894.

Furet, François, *La Révolution*, 2 vols., Paris, 1988.

Fustel de Coulanges, N.D., *L'Alsace est-elle allemande ou française? Réponse à M. Mommsen, professeur à Berlin*, Paris, 27 October 1870.

Gaillard, Jeanne, *Communes de province, Commune de Paris 1870–1871*, Paris, 1971.

Gall, Lothar, *Bismarck: The White Revolutionary*, 2 vols., London, 1986.

Gallard, T, 'Malades et blessés de l'Armée de la Loire: services médicaux supplémentaires créés pendant la guerre: rapport au Ministre', *L'Union Médicale de la Province*, 3rd Series, June–July 1871, pp. 337–44.

Gambetta, Léon Michel. *See* Reinach.

Garnier, Francis, *Le siège de Paris: journal d'un officier de marine*, 7th ed., Paris, 1887.

Gaulle, Charles de, *La France et son armée*, Paris, 1938.

Genevois, Henri, *Les coups de main pendant la guerre*, Paris, 1896.

————, *Les dernières cartouches (janvier 1871)*, Paris, 1893.

————, *Les Premières Campagnes dans l'Est (Cambriels, Garibaldi, Cremer)*, Paris, 1909.

————, *Les Responsabilités de La Défense Nationale 1870–71*, Paris, 1904.

Gensoul, Louis, *Un Bataillon de Mobiles pendant la Guerre de 1870–1871: Souvenirs de l'Armée du Nord*, Paris, 1914.

Georges-Roux, François, *La Guerre de 1870*, Paris, 1966.

German General Staff, *The Franco-German War, 1870–71* (Authorised translation by F.C.H. Clarke), 5 vols., London, 1874–84, reprint, Nashville, 1995.

Giesberg, Robert I., *The Treaty of Frankfort: A Study in Diplomatic History, September 1870–September 1873*, Philadelphia, 1966.

Giovanangeli, Bernard, ed., *1870: Les soldats et leurs batailles*, Paris, 2006.

Girard, Louis, *La Garde Nationale 1814–1871*, Paris, 1964.

————, *Nouvelle Histoire de Paris: La Deuxième République et Le Second Empire 1848–1870*, Paris, 1981.

Glais-Bizoin, Alexandre, *Dictature de cinq mois: Mémoires pour servir à l'histoire du Gouvernement de la Défense Nationale et de la Délégation de Tours et de Bordeaux*, 2nd ed., Paris, 1873.

Goldschmidt, Dr D., *Autour de Strasbourg assiégé*, Strasbourg, 1912.

Goltz, Wilhelm Leopold Colmar von der, *Gambetta et ses armées*, 4th ed., Paris, 1877.

Goncourt, Edmond & Jules de, *Journal: mémoires de la vie littéraire*, vol. 2, 1866–1886, Paris, 1989.

Gougeard, Auguste, *Deuxième Armée de la Loire: Division de l'Armée de Bretagne*, Paris, 1871.

Grenest [pseudonym of Eugène Désiré Edouard Sergent], *L'Armée de la Loire: Relation anecdotique de la Campagne de 1870–1871*, Paris, 1893.

————, *L'Armée de l'Est: Relation anecdotique de la Campagne de 1870–1871*, Paris, 1895.

————, *Les Armées du Nord et de Normandie: Relation anecdotique de la Campagne de 1870–1871*, Paris, 1897.

Grosjean, Eric, *Belfort: la sentinelle de la liberté 1870–1871*, Colmar, 1970.

Guedalla, Philip, *The Two Marshals: Bazaine & Pétain*, London, 1943.

Guérin, André, *La Folle Guerre de 1870*, Paris, 1970.

Guériot, Paul, *La Capitivité de Napoléon III en Allemagne (septembre 1870–mars 1871)*, Paris, 1926.

Guillemin, Henri, *Cette curieuse guerre de 70: Thiers-Trochu-Bazaine*, Paris, 1956.

————, *L'Héroïque défense de Paris 1870–1871*, Paris, 1959.

————, *La Capitulation (1871)*, Paris, 1960.

————, *L'Avènement de M.Thiers et réflexions sur la Commune*, Paris, 1971.

Guiral, Pierre, *Adolphe Thiers*, Paris, 1986.

Guivarc'h, Marcel, *1870–1871. Chirurgie et Médicine pendant la Guerre et la Commune: un tournant scientifique et humanitaire*, Paris, 2006.

Haffner, Sebastian, *The Rise and Fall of Prussia*, London, 1980.

Hahnke, W. von, *Opérations de la III Armée*, Paris, 1874.

Hale, Lonsdale, *The 'People's War' in France 1870–1871*, London, 1904.

Halévy, Ludovic, *Récits de la Guerre: l'invasion 1870–1871*, Paris, 1892.

[Hanneken, Hermann von], *La Campagne de Metz par un Général Prussien*, Brussels, 1871.

Hazareesingh, Sudhir, *Intellectual Founders of the Republic: Five Studies in Nineteenth Century French Republican Political Thought*, Oxford, 2001.

Helvig, Hugo, *Operations of the I Bavarian Army Corps*, 2 vols., London, 1874.

Hérisson, Maurice d'Irisson, Comte d', *Journal of a Staff Officer in Paris during the events of 1870 and 1871*, London, 1885.

Heylli, Georges d', ed., *Journal du Siège de Paris: décrets, proclamations, circulaires, rapports, notes, renseignements, documents divers officiels et autres*, 3 vols., Paris, 1871–74.

————, *Le Moniteur prussien de Versailles*, 2 vols., Paris, 1871.

Hindenburg, Paul von, *Out of My Life*, translated by F.A. Holt, London, 1920.

Horne, Alistair, *The Fall of Paris: The Siege and the Commune 1870–71*, London, 1965.

————, *The Terrible Year: The Paris Commune, 1871*, London, 1971.

Howard, Michael, *The Franco-Prussian War: The German Invasion of France, 1870–1871*, London, 1961.

Hughes, Daniel J., ed., *Moltke on the Art of War: Selected Writings*, Novato, 1993.

Hugo, Victor, *L'Année terrible* (ed. Yves Gohin), Paris, 1985.

Humbert, Jacques, *Bazaine et le drame de Metz*, Paris, 1929.

Hutchinson, John F., *Champions of Charity: War and the Rise of the Red Cross*, Boulder, 1996.

Isambard, Gustave, *La Défense de Châteaudun, 18 octobre 1870*, Paris, 1886.

Jacqmin, F., *Les Chemins de Fer pendant La Guerre de 1870–1871*, Paris, 1872.

Jarras, Hugues Louis, *Souvenirs du Général Jarras, Chef d'État-Major de l'Armée du Rhin (1870)*, Paris, 1892.

Joly, Bertrand, 'La France et la revanche (1870–1914)', *Revue d'Histoire Moderne et Contemporaine*, 1999, vol. 46 (2), pp. 325–47.

Kanter, Sanford, 'Exposing the Myth of the Franco-Prussian War', *War & Society*, vol. 4, No. 1 (May, 1986), pp. 13–30.

Klein, Jean-Pierre, 'La vie quotidienne et la lutte à outrance à Strasbourg pendant le siège de 1870', *Revue Historique de l'Armée*, 1973, No. 1, pp. 171–83.

[Labouchère, Henry], *Diary of a Besieged Resident in Paris*, London, 1871.

La Gorce, Pierre de, *Histoire du Second Empire*, 7 vols., Paris, 1912–14.

Lambert, André, *Jules Favre: Le Siège de Paris*, Paris, 1965.

Larchey, Lorédan, *Mémorial illustré des deux sièges de Paris*, Paris, 1872.

La Roncière-Le Noury, C.A.C. de, *La Marine au siège de Paris*, 2nd ed., Paris, 1872.

Lavisse, Ernest, 'L'Invasion dans les Départments du Nord', *Revue des Deux Mondes*, Paris, 1 September 1871, pp. 46–79.

Lecaillon, Jean-François, *La Commune de Paris racontée par les Parisiens*, Paris, 2009.

————, *Le Siège de Paris en 1870: récits et témoins*, Paris, 2005.

————, *Les Français et la guerre de 1870*, Paris, 2004.

Le Fort, Léon, *Oeuvres*, Paris, 3 vols., 1895–97.

Le Gaulois, *Le Journal du Siège de Paris, publié par Le Gaulois*, Paris, 1871.

Legens, Jean-Louis et al., 'La Guerre Franco-Allemande 1870–1871: L'armement français', *Gazette des armes*, hors-série no. 11, Paris, 2001.

Le Goff, Jean Yves, *Le Général Adolphe Le Flô: promoteur de l'alliance Franco-Russe*, Lesneven, 1993.

Le Guillou, Louis, *La Campagne d'été de 1870*, Paris, 1938.

Lehautcourt, Pierre [pseudonym of B. Palat], *Bibliothèque de bibliographies critiques: La Guerre de 1870–1871*, Paris, 1906.

————, *Campagne de la Loire en 1870–1871*, 2 vols., Paris, 1893–95.

————, *Campagne de l'Est en 1870–1871*, 2 vols., Paris, 1896.

————, *Campagne du Nord*, Paris, 1897.

————, *Guerre de 1870–1871: Aperçu et Commentaires*, 2 vols., Paris, 1910.

————, *Histoire de la Guerre de 1870–1871*, 7 vols., Paris, 1900–08.

————, *Siège de Paris*, 3 vols., Paris, 1898.

Le Potier, Rear Admiral, 'Les Marins de L'Amiral Exelmans au Siège de Strasbourg en 1870', *Revue Historique de l'Armée*, 1971, No. 1, pp. 135–46.

Lerman, Katherine Anne, *Bismarck*, London, 2004.

Le Roy, Albert, *Le Havre et la Seine-Inférieure pendant la guerre de 1870–1871*, Le Havre, 1877.

Leroy-Beaulieu, Paul, 'La Guerre en province', *Revue des Deux Mondes*, Paris, 1871, pp. 145–77.

Levillain, Philippe & Riemenschneider, Rainer, *La Guerre de 1870/71 et ses conséquences*, Bonn, 1990.

L'Hospice, Michel, *La Guerre de 70 et la Commune en 1000 Images*, Paris, 1965.

L'Huillier, Fernand, *Histoire de l'Alsace*, Paris, 1955.

————, ed., *L'Alsace en 1870–1871*, Strasbourg, 1971.

Lissagaray, Prosper, *History of the Commune of 1871* (translated by Eleanor Marx Aveling), London, 1886, reprinted, New York, 1967.

Livet, Georges & Rapp, Francis, (eds), *Histoire de Strasbourg des origines à nos jours*, 4 vols., Strasbourg, 1980–82.

Louis-Lande, L., 'Le Sergent Hoff: Épisode du Siège de Paris', *Revue des Deux Mondes*, Paris, January 1873, pp. 66–94.

Lucas-Championnière, Just, 'Souvenirs de campagne, et notes médicales prises à la cinquième ambulance internationale pendant la guerre de 1870–1871', *Journal de Médecine et de Chirurgie Pratiques*, vol. 42, 3rd Series, Paris, 1871, pp. 102–10, 152–61, 199–203, 247–52.

Mallet, D., *La bataille du Mans*, Le Mans, 1873.

Martin des Pallières, Charles, *Campagne de 1870–1871: Orléans*, Paris, 1872.

Martinien, Aristide, *Guerre de 1870–1871: État nominatif par affaires et par corps des officiers tués ou blessés*, 2 vols., Paris, 1902–06.

Marx, Karl and Engels, Friedrich, *Writings on the Paris Commune*, ed. Hal Draper, New York, 1971.

[Mauni, Roger de], *Mémoires sur l'armée de Chanzy: journal du bataillon des gardes mobiles de Mortain (Manche), 24 août – 26 mars 1871*, Paris & Brussels, 1871. (Translated as *Eight Months on Duty: Diary of a Young Officer in Chanzy's Army* (ed. C.J. Vaughan), London, 1872: reprint edited by David Clarke published as Mauni, Roger de, *The Franco-Prussian War*, London, 1971.)

Maupassant, Guy de, *Boule de suif et autres histoires de guerre*, (ed. Antonia Fonyi), Paris, 1991.

————, *Sur l'eau*, Paris, 1888. (Translated by Douglas Parmee as *Afloat*, New York, 2008.)

Maurice, J.F., ed., *The Franco-German War 1870–71 by Generals and Other Officers who took part in the Campaign*, London, 1900. (Translated from Julius von Pflugk-Harttung ed., *Krieg und Sieg 1870–71*, Berlin, 1895.)

Maury, Émile, *Mes Souvenirs sur les événements des années 1870–1871*, (ed. Alain Dalotel), Paris, 1999.

Mayeur, Jean-Marie, *Léon Gambetta: La Patrie et la République*, Paris, 2008.

Mazade, Charles de, *La Guerre de France (1870–1871)*, 2 vols., Paris, 1875.

McAllister, William B., 'Fighting Reformers: The Debate over the Reorganization of the French Military Medical Service, 1870–1889', *Essays in History* (University of Virginia), vol. 35, 1993, pp. 93–109.

Medlicott, W.N., *Bismarck and Modern Germany*, London, 1965.

Mercier, Jacques & Dominique, *4 septembre 1870: Napoléon III quitte la scène*, Paris, 1967.

Meyer, André & Horat, Heinz, *Les Bourbakis en Suisse*, Lucerne, 1983.

Millman, Richard, *British Foreign Policy and the Coming of the Franco-Prussian War*, Oxford, 1965.

Milner, John, *Art, War and Revolution in France 1870–1871*, Yale, 2000.

Milza, Pierre, '*L'année terrible*': vol. 1, *La guerre franco-prussienne, septembre 1870 – mars 1871*, vol. 2, *La Commune, mars–juin 1871*, Paris, 2009.

Mitchell, Allan, *Bismarck and the French Nation 1848–1890*, New York, 1971.

————, *The German Influence in France after 1870: The Formation of the French Republic*, Chapel Hill, 1979.

————, *Victors and Vanquished: The German Influence on Army and Church in France after 1870*, Chapel Hill, 1984.

Mohrt, Michel, *Les Intellectuels devant la défaite, 1870*, Paris, 1943.

Molis, Robert, *Les Francs-Tireurs et Les Garibaldi: Soldats de la République. 1870–1871 en Bourgogne*, Paris, 1995.

Moltke, Helmuth von, *Letters of Field Marshal Count Helmuth von Moltke to His Mother and His Brothers*, (translated by Clara Bell and Henry W. Fisher), 2 vols., London, 1891.

————, *Correspondance militaire du maréchal de Moltke: Guerre de 1870–71*, 2 vols., Paris, 1899–1901.

————, *The Franco-German War of 1870–71* (Introduction by Michael Howard), London, 1992.

Monod, Gabriel, *Allemands et Français. Souvenirs de Campagne: Metz – Sedan – La Loire*, Paris, 1872.

Montarlot, Paul, *Journal de l'Invasion: Châteaudun*, Châteaudun, 1871.

Montaudon, Jean-Baptiste Alexandre, *Souvenirs militaires*, 2 vols., Paris, 1898–1900.

Morillon, A., *L'Approvisionnement de Paris en temps de guerre: souvenirs et prévisions*, Paris, 1888.

Mosse, Werner E., *The European Powers and the German Question 1848–1871*, Cambridge, 1958.

M. Z., *Strasbourg: Sa Description, ses fortifications, son role militaire avant la Guerre de 1870*, Paris, 1873.

Napoleon III, 'Lettres à l'Impératrice Eugénie (1870–1871)', *Revue des Deux Mondes*, Paris, 1 September 1930, pp. 5–30.

Noël, Bernard, *Dictionnaire de la Commune*, Paris, 1971.

Nouzille, Jean, 'Le dernier siège de Strasbourg (11 août–28 septembre 1870)', *Revue Historique des Armées*, 1981, No. 3, pp. 77–95.

Ollier, Edmund, *Cassell's History of the War between France and Germany, 1870–1871*, 2 vols., London, 1899.

Ortholan, Henri, *L'Armée de la Loire 1870–1871*, Paris, 2005.

————, *L'Armée de l'Est 1870–1871*, Paris, 2009.

Ozou de Verrie, Auguste, *Les trois journées du Bourget: la mort du Commandant Baroche*, Paris, 1871.

Palat, B., *Bazaine et nos désastres en 1870*, 2 vols., Paris, 1913.

————, *Bibliographie générale de la Guerre de 1870–1871*, Paris, 1896.

————, *La Stratégie de Moltke en 1870*, Paris, 1907.

Palikao, Général Cousin de Montauban, Comte de, *Un Ministère de la Guerre de vingt-quatre jours du 10 août au 4 septembre 1870*, 2nd ed., Paris, 1871.

Palmer, Alan, *The Crimean War*, New York, 1987.

Paradis, Jacques-Henry, *Journal du siège de Paris*, (ed. Alain Fillion), Paris, 2008. (Original edition 'par un bourgeois de Paris' published anonymously in 1872.)

Patry, Léonce, *Étude d'ensemble de la guerre franco-allemande de 1870–1871*, Soissons, 1876.

————,'Le Général Ducrot d'après sa correspondance', *Revue Bleue: revue politique et littéraire*, 20 July 1895, pp. 79–84.

————, 'Le Général Trochu et la Défense Nationale', *Revue Bleue: revue politique et littéraire*, 24 October 1896, pp. 514–6.

————, *La guerre telle qu'elle est*, Paris, 1897. (English translation: *The Reality of War*, London, 2001.)

Perrod, Pierre Antoine, *Jules Favre: Avocat de la liberté*, Lyon, 1988.

Pflanze, Otto, *Bismarck and the Development of Germany*, 3 vols., Princeton, 1990.

Piedagnel, Alexandre, *Les Ambulances de Paris pendant le Siège (1870–1871)*, 2nd ed., Paris, 1871.

Piton, Frédéric, *Siège de Strasbourg: journal d'un assiégé*, Paris, 1900.

Plamenatz, John, *The Revolutionary Movement in France 1815–71*, London, 1952.

Poidevin, Raymond & Bariéty, Jacques, *Les relations franco-allemandes, 1815–1975*, Paris, 1977.

Ponchalon, Henri de, *Souvenirs de guerre, 1870–1871 et l'alliance franco-russe*, Paris, 1897.

Porch, Douglas, *The March to the Marne: The French Army 1871–1914*, Cambridge, 1981.

Price, Roger, *The French Second Empire: An Anatomy of Political Power*, Cambridge, 2001.

Prost, Auguste, *Le Blocus de Metz en 1870*, Nogent-le-Rotrou, 1898.

Quesnoy, Ferdinand, *Campagne de 1870: Armée du Rhin*, Paris, 1872.

Ralston, David B., *The Army of the Republic: The Place of the Military in the Political Evolution of France, 1871–1914*, Cambridge, Mass., 1962.

Rampal, Benjamin, *Souvenirs du Siège de Paris*, Marseilles, 1871.

Rappe, Axel, *Campagne de l'Armée française du Nord en 1870–71*, Paris, 1884.

Raymond, Dora Neill, *British Policy and Opinion during the Franco-Prussian War*, New York, 1921.

Reclus, Maurice, *Jules Favre 1809–1880: Essai de biographie historique et morale*, Paris, 1912.

Regnier, Edmond Victor, *What is Your name? N. or M. 'A Strange Story' Revealed*, London, 1870.

Reinach, Joseph, *Dépêches, circulaires, décrets, proclamations et discours de Léon Gambetta (4 septembre 1870–6 février 1871)*, 2 vols., Paris, 1886–91.

————, *Discours et plaidoyers politiques de M. Gambetta*, vol. 2, 19 février 1871–24 juillet 1872, Paris, 1881.

Rémond, René, *La Droite en France de la première restauration à la Ve République*, 2 vols., 3rd ed., Paris, 1968.

Renouvin, Pierre, *Histoire des relations internationales*, vol. 5, *Le XIX Siècle: 1. De 1815 à 1871*, Paris, 1954.

Reshef, Ouriel, *Guerre, mythes et caricature: au berceau d'une mentalité française*, Paris, 1984.

[Réunion d'habitants et d'anciens officiers], *Strasbourg: journal des mois d'août et septembre 1870 – Siège et bombardement avec correspondances, pièces officielles, documents français et étrangers: réponse au conseil d'enquête*, Paris, 1874.

Reuss, Rodolphe, *Histoire de Strasbourg depuis ses origines jusqu'à nos jours*, Paris, 1922.

————, *Le Siège de Strasbourg en 1870: conférence ... et chronique strasbourgeoise juillet-août 1870* (textes inédits publiés par Jean Rott etc.), Strasbourg, 1971.

Revue d'histoire, *La Guerre de 1870–71*, rédigé à la Section historique de l'État-major de l'Armée, 48 vols., Paris, 1901–13.

Rials, Stéphane, *Nouvelle Histoire de Paris: De Trochu à Thiers 1870–1873*, Paris, 1985.

Richard, Jules, *L'Armée et la guerre*, Paris, 1896.

Richardson, Joanna, *Paris under Siege: A Journal of the events of 1870–1871 kept by contemporaries*, London, 1982.

Rieux, J. & Hassendorfer, J., *Histoire du Service de Santé Militaire et du Val-de-Grâce*, Paris, 1951.

Ritter, Gerhard, *The Sword and the Scepter: The Problem of Militarism in Germany*, 4 vols., Miami, 1969–73.

Roberts, J.M., 'The Paris Commune from the Right', *English Historical Review*, Supplement 6, 1982.

Robichon, François, *Édouard Detaille: un siècle de gloire militaire*, Paris, 2007.

Robinet de Cléry, Gabriel Adrien, *Les Avant-postes pendant le siège de Paris*, Paris, 1887.

Roblin, Jean, *Et Ducrot passa La Marne ... 30 novembre 1870: les combats du siège de Paris en Val-de-Marne racontés par des témoins*, La Mée-sur-Seine, 1987.

Rocolle, P., 'Anatomie d'une mobilisation', *Revue historique des armées*, 1979, pp. 34–69.

Rolin, Louis Paul, *La Guerre dans l'Ouest*, Paris, 1874.

Rolland, Jules, *Portraits militaires: Le Général Ducrot*, Paris, 1871.

Rossel, Louis, *Les derniers jours de Metz*, France & Belgium, 1871.

Roth, François, *La Guerre de 70*, Paris, 1990.

————, *La Lorraine dans la Guerre de 1870*, Nancy, 1984.

Rougerie, Jacques, *La Commune de 1871*, Paris, 1988.

————, *Paris insurgé: La Commune de 1871*, Paris, 1995.

————, *Paris libre 1871*, Paris, 1971.

Rouquette, Jules, *Célébrités contemporaines: Ducrot*, Paris, 1872.

Rousset, Léonce, *L'Armistice de 1871*, Paris, 1927.

————, *La seconde campagne de France: Histoire Générale de la Guerre Franco-Allemande (1870–71)*, 6 vols., Paris, 1896.

Ruby, Edmond & Regnault, Jean, *Bazaine: Coupable ou victime?* Paris, 1960.

Rundle, Henry, *With the Red Cross in the Franco-German War, A.D. 1870–1*, London, 1911.

Russell, William Howard, *My Diary during the Last Great War*, London, 1874.

Ryan, Charles E., *With an Ambulance during the Franco-German War, 1870–1871*, London, 1896.

Saint-Genest [pseudonym of A. M. Durand de Bucheron], *La Politique d'un soldat*, Paris, 1872.

Sarazin, Charles, *Récits sur la dernière guerre franco-allemande*, Paris, 1887.

Sarcey, Francisque, *Le Siège de Paris: impressions et souvenirs*, Paris, 1871.

Sarrepont, Major H. de [pseudonym of Eugène Hennebert], *Histoire de la Défense de Paris en 1870–1871*, Paris, 1872.

————, *Le Bombardement de Paris par les Prussiens en janvier 1871*, Paris, 1872.

Schneider, Louis, *Aus dem Leben Kaiser Wilhelms, 1849–1873*, 3 vols., Berlin, 1888.

Secrétan, Édouard, *L'Armée de l'Est: 20 décembre 1870–1 février 1871*, 2nd ed., Neuchatel, 1894.

Seignobos, Charles, *Le Déclin de L'Empire et l'établissement de la 3e République (1859–1875)*, Paris, 1921 (vol. 7 of E. Lavisse, *Histoire de France Contemporaine*).

Séré de Rivières, Raymond Adolphe, *Procès du Maréchal Bazaine: Rapport Complet*, Paris, 1874.

Serman, William & Bertaud, J.-P., *Nouvelle Histoire Militaire de la France 1789–1919*, Paris, 1998.

Serman, William, *La Commune de Paris*, Paris, 1986.

Serreau, René, *L'Armée de la Loire*, Orléans, 1970.

Service Historique de l'Armée, *Revue Historique de l'Armée, Numéro 1, 1971 (Spécial): Guerre de 1870–1871*, Paris, 1971. See also *Revue d'Histoire*.

Shafer, David A., *The Paris Commune*, Basingstoke, 2005.

Shann, Stephen & Delperier, Louis, *French Army 1870–71: Franco-Prussian War 2: Republican Troops*, London, 1991.

Sheppard, Nathan, *Shut Up In Paris*, London, 1871.

Showalter, Dennis, *The Wars of German Unification*, London, 2004.

Sieur, Inspecteur Général C., 'Histoire des Tribulations du Corps de Santé Militaire depuis sa création jusqu'à nos jours', *Bulletin de la Société Française d'Histoire de la Médecine*, vol. XXII, Paris, 1928, pp. 92–163. (Translated as 'Tribulations of the Medical Corps of the French Army From its Origins to Our Own Time', *The Military Surgeon*, vol. 64, pp. 843–56, vol. 65, pp. 210–28, Washington, 1929.)

Signouret, P. Raymond, *Souvenirs du bombardement et de la capitulation de Strasbourg – Récit critique de ce qui est passé dans cette ville du 15 juillet au 28 septembre 1870*, Bayonne, 1872.

Silverman, Dan P., *Reluctant Union: Alsace-Lorraine and Imperial Germany 1871–1918*, University Park, Pennsylvania, 1972.

Simon, Jules, *Souvenirs du 4 septembre: Origine et chute du Second Empire; Le Gouvernement de la Défense Nationale*, Édition illustrée, Paris, [n.d.].

Sirinelli, Jean-François, ed., *Histoire des droites en France*, 3 vols., Paris, 1992.

Sorel, Albert, *Histoire diplomatique de la Guerre Franco-Allemande*, 2 vols., Paris, 1875.

Steenackers, F.F. & Le Goff, F., *Histoire du Gouvernement de la Défense Nationale en province, 4 septembre–8 février 1871*, 2 vols., Paris, 1884.

Steinbach, Matthias, *Abgrund Metz*, Munich, 2002.

Stone, David, *'First Reich': Inside the German Army during the War with France, 1870–71*, London, 2002.

Stoneman, Mark R., 'The Bavarian Army and French Civilians in the War of 1870–1871: A Cultural Interpretation', *War in History*, 2001 (vol. 8, No. 3), pp. 271–93.

Sueur, Henri, *Étude sur la Mortalité à Paris pendant le Siège*, Paris, 1872.

Swain, Valentine A.J., 'Franco-Prussian War 1870–1871: Voluntary Aid for the Wounded and Sick', *British Medical Journal*, 29 August 1970, 3, pp. 511–14.

Sylvestre de Sacy, Jacques, *Le Maréchal de MacMahon, Duc de Magenta (1808–1893)*, Paris, 1960.

Taithe, Bertrand, *Citizenship & Wars: France in Turmoil 1870–1871*, London, 2001.

————, *Defeated Flesh: Welfare, Warfare and the Making of Modern France*, Manchester, 1999.

The Times, *The Campaign of 1870–1, Republished from 'The Times'*, London, 1871.
Theyras, G., *Garibaldi en France: Dôle, Autun, Dijon*, Autun, 1888.
Thiers, Louis Adolphe, *Notes et Souvenirs de M. Thiers 1870–1873*, Paris, 1904.
Thiriaux, L., *La Garde Nationale Mobile de 1870*, Brussels, 1909.
Thomas, Edith, *The Women Incendiaries*, London, 1967.
Thoumas, Charles Antoine, *Les Transformations de l'Armée française*, 2 vols., Paris, 1887.
————, *Souvenirs de la Guerre de 1870–71: Paris, Tours, Bordeaux*, Paris, 1892.
Tombs, Robert, *The Paris Commune 1871*, Harlow, 1999.
————, *The War Against Paris*, Cambridge, 1981.
Tranquille, P., 'Général Ducrot (1817–1882)', *Les Contemporains*, No. 222, Paris, 10 January 1897.
Trochu, Louis Jules, *Oeuvres posthumes*, 2 vols., Tours, 1896.
Uhrich, Jean J.A., *Documents relatifs au Siège de Strasbourg*, Paris, 1872.
Vallès, Jules, *L'Insurgé* (ed. E. Carassus), Paris, 1970.
Vapereau, G., *Dictionnaire Universel des Contemporains*, 4th ed., Paris, 1870; 5th ed., 1880.
Verdy du Vernois, Julius von, *With the Royal Headquarters in 1870–71*, London, 1897.
Véron, Eugène, *La Troisième Invasion*, 2 vols., Paris, 1876–7.
Vinoy, Joseph, *L'Armistice et la Commune: opérations de l'Armée de Paris et de l'Armée de Réserve*, Paris, 1872.
————, *Siège de Paris: opérations du 13 Corps et de la Troisième Armée*, Paris, 1872.
Viollet-le-Duc, E.E., *Mémoire sur la défense de Paris, septembre 1870 – janvier 1871*, Paris, 1871.
Vizetelly, Ernest Alfred, *My Days of Adventure: The Fall of France 1870–71*, London, 1914.
Wahl, Alfred & Richez, Jean-Claude, *L'Alsace entre France et Allemagne 1850–1950*, Paris, 1994.
Wartensleben, Herrmann von, *Operations of the First Army under General von Manteuffel* (trans. C.H. von Wright), London, 1873.
————, *Operations of the South Army in January & February 1871* (trans. C.H. von Wright), London, 1872.
Wawro, Geoffrey, *The Franco-Prussian War: The German Conquest of France in 1870–1871*, Cambridge, 2003.
————, *Warfare and Society in Europe, 1792–1814*, London, 2000.
Welschinger, Henri, *La Guerre de 1870: causes et responsabilités*, 2 vols., Paris, 1910.
Williams, Roger L., *Henri Rochefort, Prince of the Gutter Press*, New York, 1966.
————, *Manners and Murders in the World of Louis-Napoleon*, Seattle, 1975.
————, *The French Revolution of 1870–1871*, New York, 1969.
Willing, Paul, *L'Armée de Napoleon III (2): L'expédition du Mexique, la Guerre Franco-Allemande 1870–1871*, Arcueil, 1984.
Y.K., *Le Combat de Châtillon et l'investissement de Paris au sud par le Ve corps prussien et le IIe corps bavarois*, Paris, 1893.
Yriarte, Charles, *La Retraite de Mézières effectué par le 13e Corps d'Armée aux ordres du Général Vinoy*, Paris, 1871.
————, *Les Prussiens à Paris et le 18 mars*, Paris, 1871.

Index